AF478492

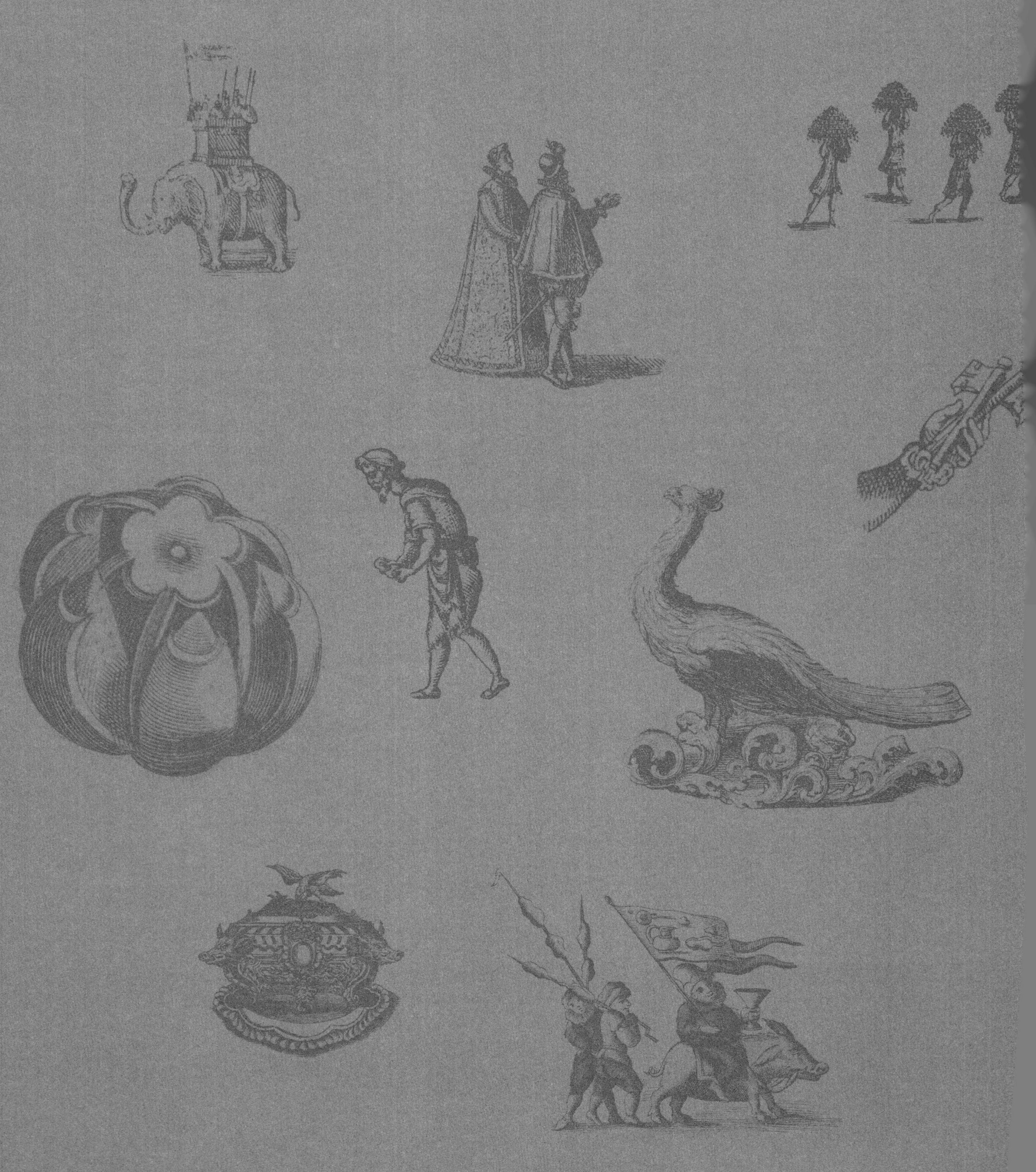

THE EDIBLE MONUMENT

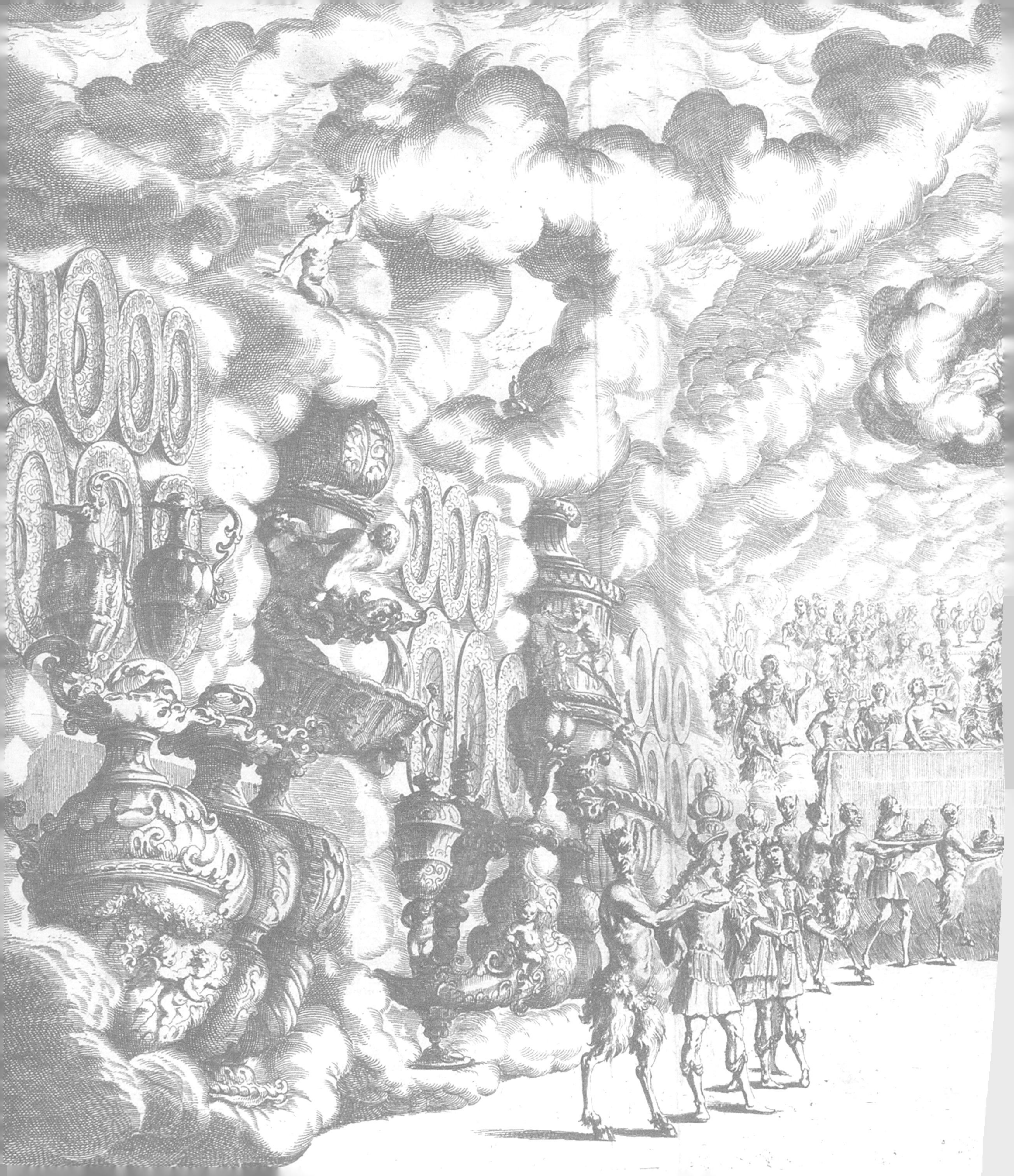

THE EDIBLE MONUMENT

THE ART OF FOOD FOR FESTIVALS

EDITED BY MARCIA REED

THE GETTY RESEARCH INSTITUTE

The Getty Research Institute Publications Program

Thomas W. Gaehtgens, *Director, Getty Research Institute*

Gail Feigenbaum, *Associate Director*

© 2015 J. Paul Getty Trust

Published by the Getty Research Institute, Los Angeles

Getty Publications

1200 Getty Center Drive, Suite 500

Los Angeles, California 90049-1682

www.getty.edu/publications

Lauren Edson, *Manuscript Editor*

Catherine Lorenz, *Designer*

Amita Molloy, *Production Coordinator*

Distributed in the United States and Canada by the University of Chicago Press

Distributed outside the United States and Canada by Yale University Press, London

Printed in China

Type composed in Odile and Naive

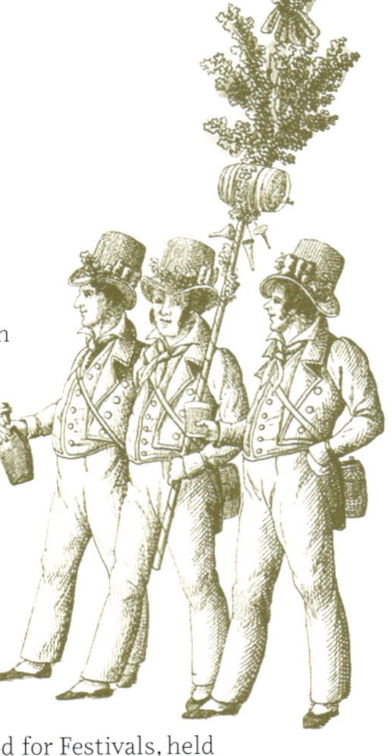

Library of Congress Cataloging-in-Publication Data

The edible monument : the art of food for festivals / edited by Marcia Reed.

    pages cm

  «This volume accompanies the exhibition The Edible Monument: The Art of Food for Festivals, held at the Getty Research Institute from 13 October 2015 to 13 March 2016.»—ECIP data view.

  Includes bibliographical references and index.

  ISBN 978-1-60606-454-2

  1. Food—Social aspects—History—Exhibitions. 2. Table setting and decoration—History—Exhibitions. 3. Food in art—Exhibitions. I. Reed, Marcia, 1945- editor. II. Getty Research Institute, host institution, issuing body.

  GT2860.E35 2015

  394.1′2—dc23

               2015013114

Front cover: Abraham Bosse, The pastry shop (detail), 17th century, published by Jacobus Allard. See p. 173, fig. 14.

Frontispiece: Mathäus Küsel, after Lodovico Ottavio Burnacini, *The Banquet of the Gods* (detail), 1668. See p. 35, fig. 6.

This volume accompanies the exhibition *The Edible Monument: The Art of Food for Festivals*, held at the Getty Research Institute from 13 October 2015 to 13 March 2016.

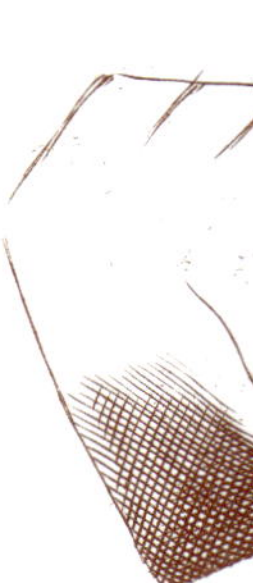

CONTENTS

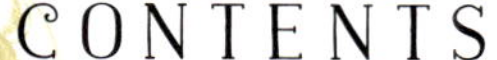

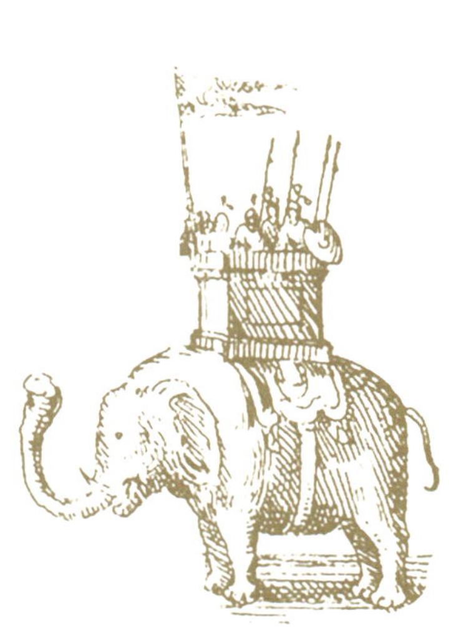

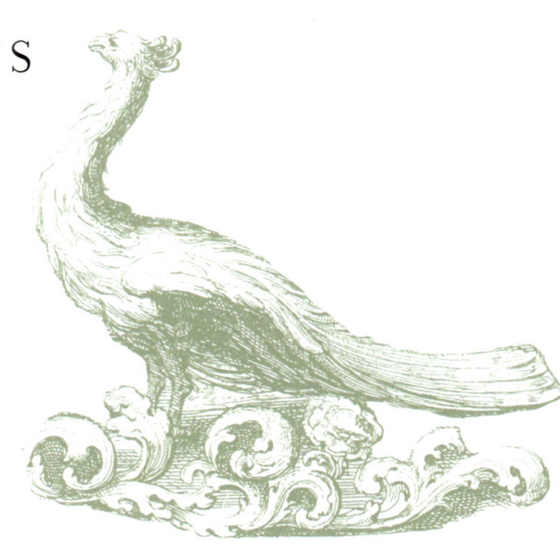

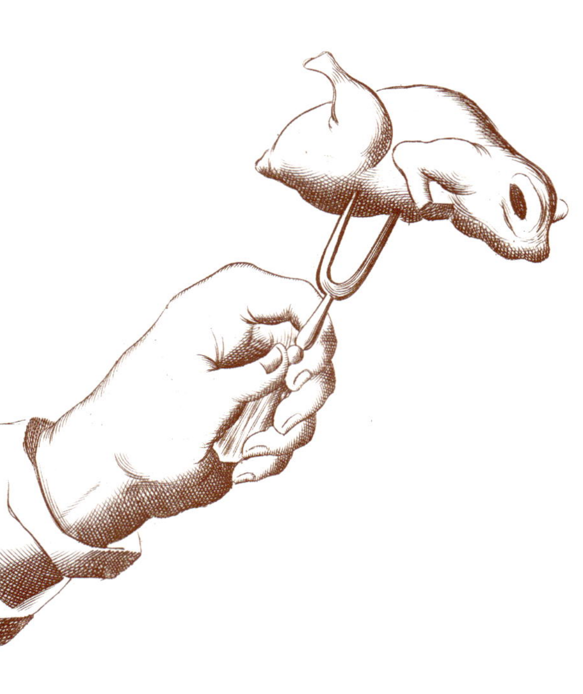

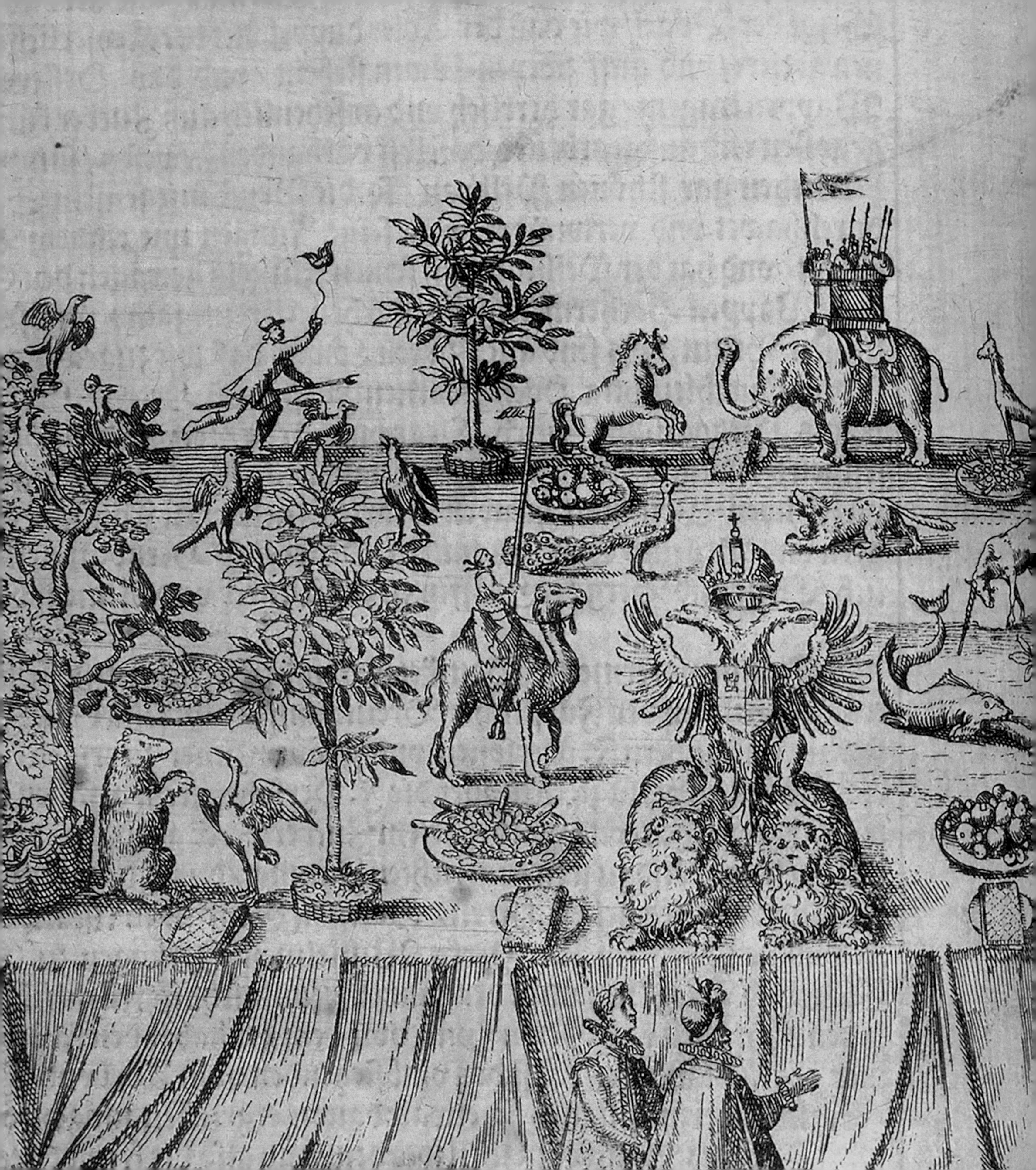

ACKNOWLEDGMENTS

These days we are accustomed to lavishly illustrated cookbooks that make the food look really good. But the story of this project begins in times before photography, with images of food that did not look very good at all. More than twenty years ago, at the Getty Research Institute (GRI), I was processing a very large collection of rare books and prints on the ephemeral arts of festivals. A historic area of collecting that goes back centuries, the documentation of fireworks, feasts, elaborate garden settings, costumes, dance, and theater pieces seemed like a promising area for the GRI because the works survive only through their description and illustration. As I examined the collection, I was completely stumped but also fascinated by prints of eighteenth-century Neapolitan festivals that showed architectural monuments with strange bumps on them. The clue was in their name, "Cuccagna"; these bumps were pieces of cheese, bread, and sausages tacked onto the structures. Stories of the Land of Cockaigne (in Italian, Cuccagna), where no one ever goes hungry or works too hard, started me down the path that led to *The Edible Monument: The Art of Food for Festivals,* the GRI exhibition mounted in 2000.

The importance of ceremonial banquets and elite feasts is well known and published in historical and cultural studies. Culinary historians have researched the significance of different foods and their presentations, the creation of menus, and proper serving protocols. What was challenging and fun was to combine these interests with bibliographic analysis, which revealed that these festival publications had long but highly diverse histories. During the early modern era, there were illustrative prints and a developing literature of how-to books by expert practitioners, which are the incipient mode of contemporary cookbooks and celebrity chefs. The history of food service is really still in progress, as evidenced by the current trend of food trucks filled with edible offerings on the roads of US cities today.

I have had the good fortune to meet many enthusiastic participants in the world of food as well as a growing number of ardent researchers who are pushing the

Attributed to Frans Hogenberg (Netherlandish, ca. 1539–90). Sugar banquet for the wedding of John William, Duke of Jülich-Cleves-Berg, and Jakobea of Baden (detail). See p. 31, fig. 4.

boundaries of this lively and inherently appealing (not to mention, mouthwatering) field. It was a privilege to be invited to the Oxford Symposium on Food and Cookery in 1998, where I met many captivating specialists—culinary historians, food writers, chefs, and academics—who come together annually to discuss a specific topic. Food historian Ivan Day and I gave papers in the same session at Oxford; for the 2000 exhibition, I invited him to remount the sugar-paste centerpiece that he had created for Fairfax House, York, England, after Menon's mirror tableau showing Circe turning men into pigs. Some Valley girls admired his re-creation; the more knowledgeable ones were overheard correcting their friends' first impressions: "That is so not a wedding cake!" I was amazed at the unexpected popularity of this small exhibition and was sorry that I hadn't had the time to write a catalog. People kept telling me they wanted to buy the book, and there wasn't one.

Therefore I appreciate the opportunity for a do-over. The 2015 exhibition is far larger, providing the context for food in festivals. We have collected many more books, prints, and manuscripts in the last fifteen years. The exhibition features a number of loans from Anne Willan and Mark Cherniavsky's superb gastronomy collection, which combines her expertise as a culinary authority, writer, and teacher at La Varenne in Paris with Mark's superb bibliophilic instincts and his dedicated and discerning practice as a collector. I appreciate their sophisticated advice and informed comments, as well as their friendly and supportive enthusiasm.

I am very grateful to have a position at the Getty that allows me to do what I love: to collect and then to tell the stories revealed by the old books, manuscripts, and prints. Thank you to our director, Thomas Gaehtgens, and his wife, Barbara, art historians who are both rare book and print lovers. It is a wonderful gift to have a director who spurs us to acquire interesting works for the special collections and then encourages us to pursue the pleasures of researching, exhibiting, and publishing them. My erudite colleagues reliably notice important details, and they graciously share their knowledge. I am grateful to the GRI curators, especially David Brafman and Louis Marchesano, and many other colleagues for their insights into the festival books and prints, and to a cascade of research assistants who contributed to this project for almost fifteen years, including Paul Arenson, Julia Grimes, Melissa Lo, and Courtney Wilder, but especially Rhiannon Knol, whose efforts have been invaluable. Thanks go to GRI associate director and head of publications Gail Feigenbaum and editor Lauren Edson for their engaged interest and kind, enthusiastic support and to Catherine Lorenz and Amita Molloy for producing such a beautiful book. Over the years, I have profited from my discussions with Barbara K. Wheaton, honorary curator of the culinary collection at Schlesinger Library, Radcliffe Institute, Harvard University; many memorable visits in New York City with my dear departed friends and noted festival collectors Paul and Marianne Gourary, some of whose books and prints are now in the GRI special collections; discussions on festivals with Elizabeth Roth, formerly of the Spencer Collection in the New York Public Library, whose archive on her unpublished book on festivals is at the GRI; and my time with Dan Strehl and Romaine Ahlstrom, who introduced me to the rich culinary collections at the Los Angeles Public Library.

Finally, a big thank-you to my family: my husband, Mike Morrison, and son, Reed Morrison, for patiently allowing me to take time to read and write. My grandson, Jens, reminds me of the child's perspective: food is fun! It is my good fortune to have a daughter-in-law, Yuko Oda Morrison, who is an excellent cook. Thank you for all the delicious meals that have sustained our ties with family and friends! When there's no more food, the party's over!

—Marcia Reed

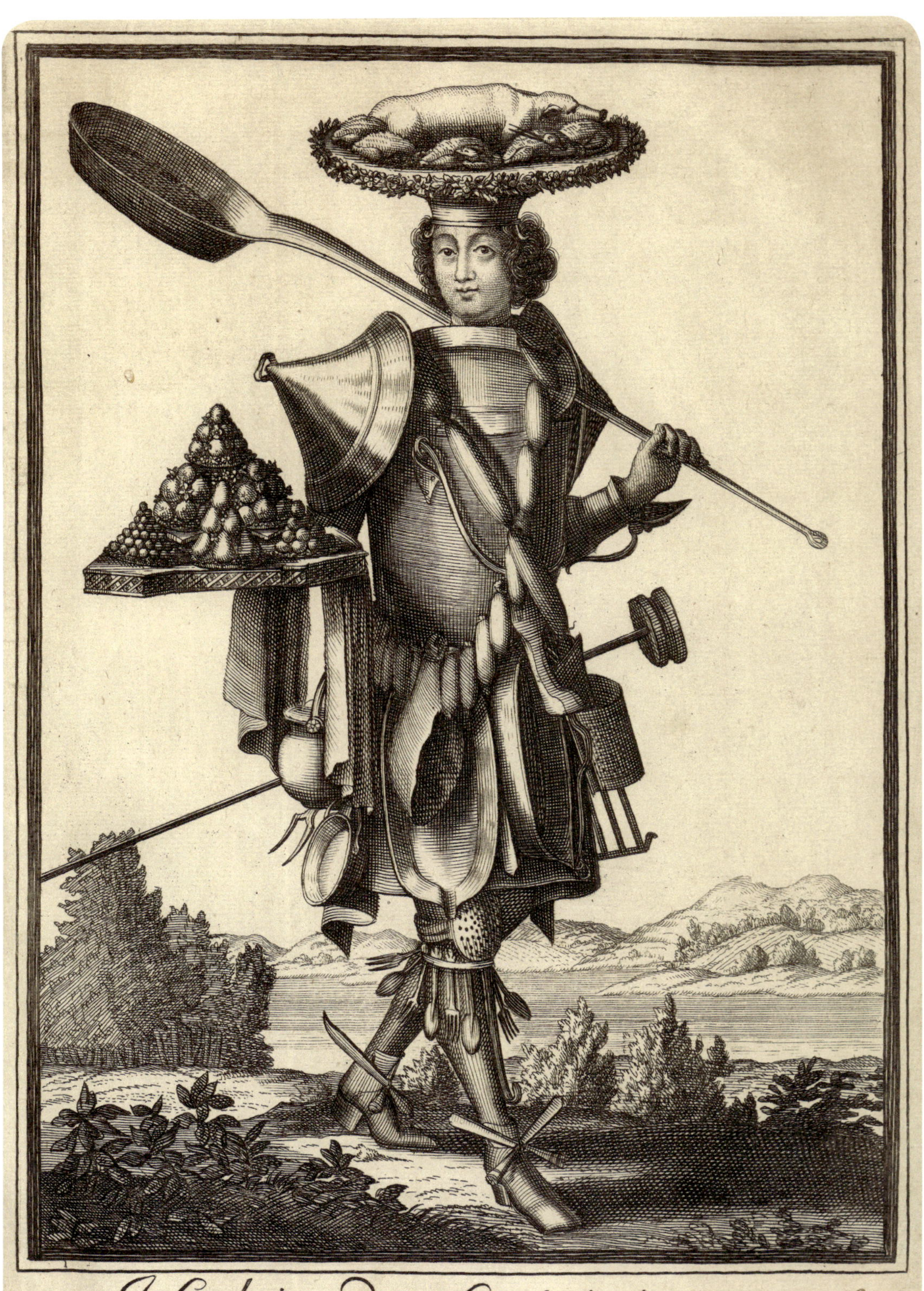

Habit de Cuisinier.

18

FOOD, MEMORY, AND TASTE

MARCIA REED

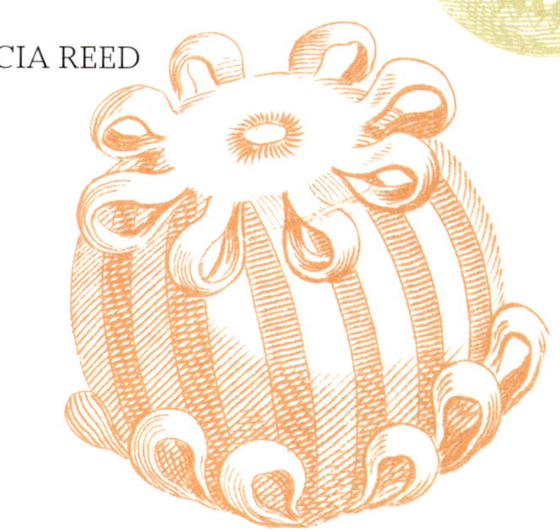

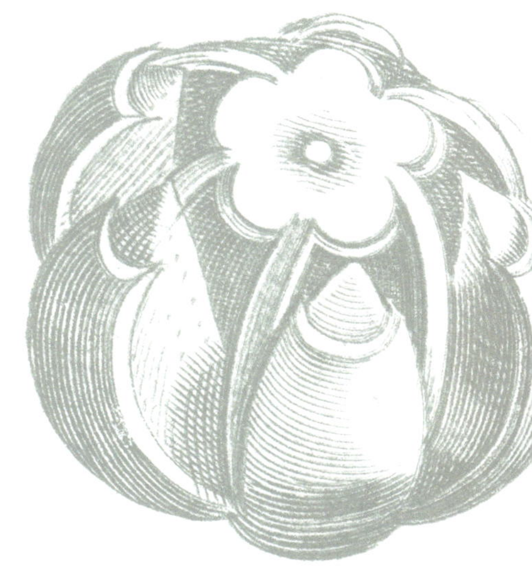

FESTIVE CELEBRATIONS

In the early modern era, festivals were parties staged on a grand scale for very special occasions, such as royal birthdays and marriages, coronations, funerals, military triumphs, and diplomatic visits. Events related to notable persons were not the only reasons for festivals; from the fifteenth century until today, they also celebrated recurring religious and traditional holidays. For European court society, these spectacles were opportunities to present lavish banquets and extraordinary entertainment, including music, dance, and theatrical productions. The artists who designed the ephemeral decorations for the feasts collaborated with colleagues in emerging professions, such as the cook or chef (fig. 1), the master carver, and the pastry chef.

While festivals were meant to be enjoyable and fun, they had serious purposes. Both formal ceremonies and spontaneous celebrations connected communities, bridging high and low culture and creating shared memories and histories. Harking back to ancient Roman triumphs, Renaissance and baroque festivals ranged from aggressive political statements to expansive displays of civic resources. The layering of history and interwoven traditions only became more complicated as festivals progressed through time.

In our own time, the Macy's Thanksgiving Day parade in New York City commemorates the early American settlers' turkey feast with hot-air balloons and marching bands (fig. 2). Now choreographed for viewing on television, with the parade route passing by the sponsor's department store on Herald Square. The Macy's parade began in 1924. Many of the department store's employees were first-generation immigrants. With its signature floats—called "falloons" (balloon floats) and "balloonicles" (balloon vehicles)—cartoon characters, and fairy-tale figures, the Thanksgiving Day parade was purposely intended to be an American celebration that approached the grand scale of the European festivals the store's employees had

FIG. 1.

Nicolas I de Larmessin (French, 1632–94).

Costume of the Cook, etching and engraving, 27.9 × 20.3 cm (11 × 8 in.). Los Angeles, Collection of Anne Willan and Mark Cherniavsky.

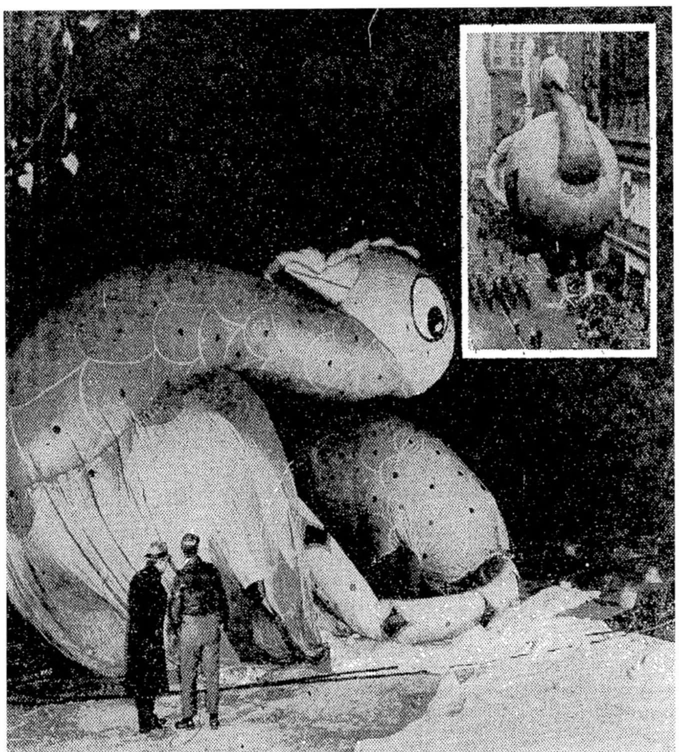

grown up with.[1] In the twenty-first century, families still gather to watch the parade on their flat-screen TVs, and then they sit down to traditional turkey dinners.

EDIBLE MEMORIES

Food has always been essential to festivals. Thoughts of the holidays bring memories of special dishes and elaborate menus. To celebrate with food, to be fed and catered to, satisfied and sated, is to feel special and honored. We see the linked meanings in various languages: feast, festival, *festa, fête.* Festive times give people permission to be extravagant, to imagine a paradise on earth where there is everything we ever wanted to eat and drink.

In the early modern era, feasts were carefully prepared meals with extraordinary dishes that required substantial amounts of imagination, labor, and time. Vast sums of money were spent on food and drink. Artistically designed courses and settings presented exotic edibles on special plates and étagères. Fruits and candies were made into monuments and sculptures, displaying a wealth of food to be admired, desired, and consumed—or destroyed and thrown away.

Edibles not only ornamented significant celebrations, providing attractive and enjoyable sensory features, they also delineated social status. Specific foods were served only to notables; by design, they were unavailable to others. The order of

service, arrangement of tables, and even the location of the festivities—whether inside the castle or outside in the palace gardens, in the city streets and neighborhoods or on the central plazas—established and underlined social boundaries. Royal banquets took place in a guarded palace hall where only a few guests, or just the king, dined. Others watched, and most waited, either in view of the table or outside, hungrily hoping for leftovers. The scene of the fourth day of the 1674 court festival at Versailles does not show any guests eating; rather, they are watching the king and his court, as armed guards hold viewers back (fig. 3).

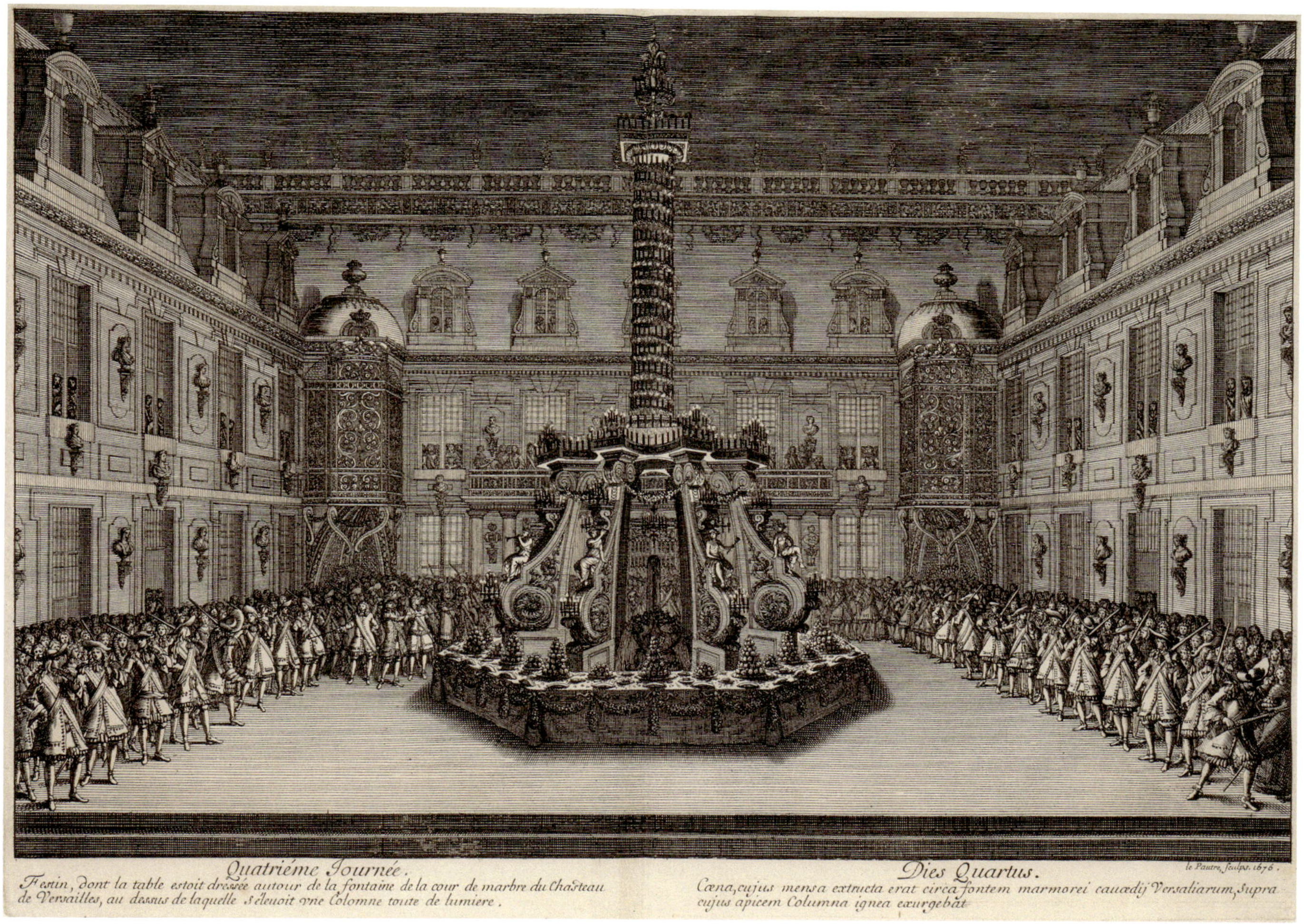

Decorative food had its own protocols of serving and decorum in order to maximize the impressive artistry and display. Renaissance and baroque paintings depict the showy (but not so tasty) peacock or swan—nature's own colorful avian centerpiece—gutted, reconstructed, painted, and stuffed (fig. 4). Such paintings maximize the tactile qualities and material luxury of the foodstuffs on display, stressing their sensuous attractions. Edible artworks were frequently made of expensive ingredients,

FIG. 3.

Jean Le Pautre (French, 1618-82).

Fourth Day, etching and engraving, 29.4 × 41.9 cm (11½ × 16½ in.). From André Félibien, *Les divertissemens de Versailles donnez par le roy a toute sa cour au retour de la conqueste de la Franche-Comté en l'année M.DC.LXXIV* (Paris: Imprimerie royale, 1676), after p. 18. Los Angeles, Getty Research Institute.

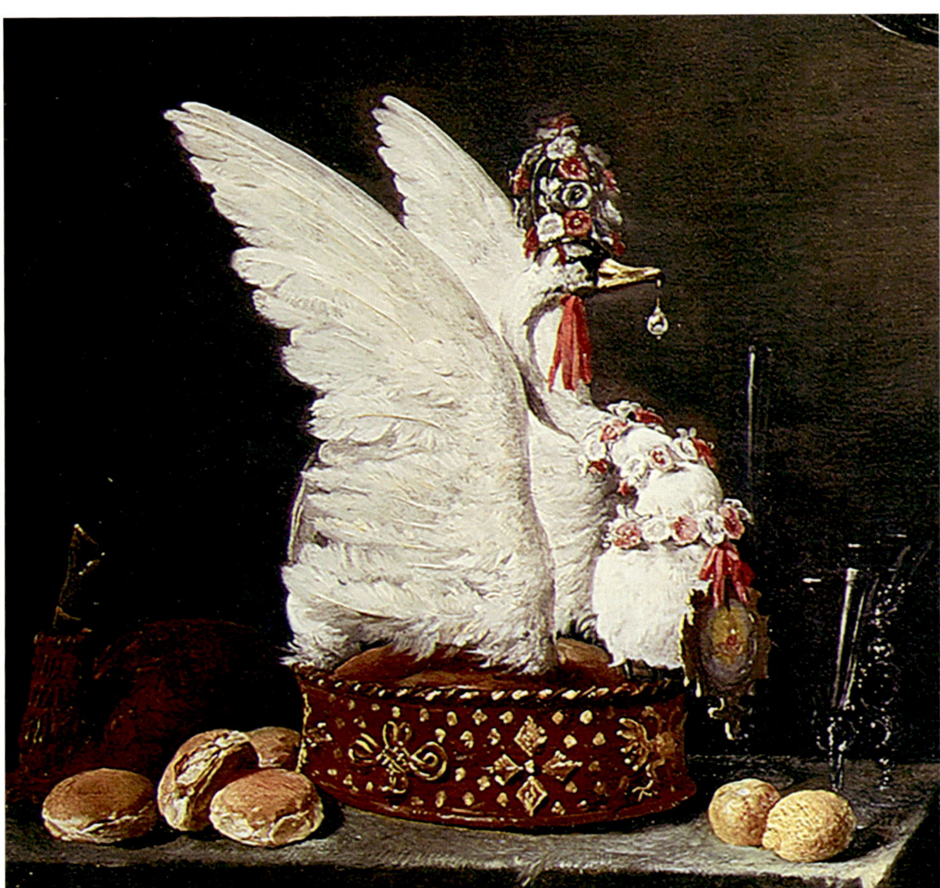

FIG. 4.

**David Teniers the Younger
(Dutch, 1610-90).**

Kitchen Scene (detail), Antwerp, 1644,
oil on copper, 77.8 × 75 cm
(30⅗ × 29½ in.).
The Hague, Mauritshuis.

such as pure white sugar or rare fruits out of season. Foods were transformed into extraordinary objects that appealed to an array of senses. Most intriguingly, edible monuments, though often constructed from natural products, were made not to be consumed but rather to surprise and entertain, much like the famous and impossibly inedible pastry and poultry combination of the children's rhyme line "Four and twenty blackbirds baked in a pie." Defying categories of art history and museum collections, edible art formed a conundrum: it was created for the magic moment and not meant to endure or be collected. These exquisite creations were the exact opposite of that cliché of aesthetic appreciation, timeless beauty.

Turning the tables on court banquets staged as theater for the less privileged, it was the elite who watched the spectacles of street festivals, looking down from palace balconies at the parades and processions and the festival floats and monuments, which had been erected only to be torn down. From this lofty perspective, the throngs of hungry people ravaging the temporary art and architecture were, in the most basic sense, entertaining as they ate (see Reed, "Feasting in the Streets," figs. 18, 19). An enormous *Cuccagna* was built in the central city plaza in Naples for the festival given by Charles, the king of the Two Sicilies (later, Charles III, king of Spain), to celebrate the birth of his firstborn son, Philip, in 1747. The court watched from palace balconies as the people wrecked the temporary structure and helped themselves to the bread, cheeses, and meats. They either ate on the spot or carried off all that was edible. Prints show the beautiful, ideal versions of these types of monuments but almost never the postpillage ruins.

In the eighteenth century, artists created graphic images of elaborate monuments decorated with food, notably for the Cuccagna in Naples and the Chinea in Rome; these finely engraved images became collectible souvenirs of the temporary artworks.[2] Similarly, the floats and costumes of vintners' processions in Switzerland were depicted on scrolls, capturing the entire lengths of the parades in panoramas. Suites of single prints showed the decorated wagons in Carnival parades in Germany.

CEREMONIES AND RITUALS OF FOOD

Sex perpetuates our species, but eating is essential to life. Therefore, food has an inescapable and powerful draw. We eat and drink, or we simply cease to exist. Preparing food is possibly the most human activity, but unlike other animals, we do not simply kill or gather, grab and go. For most, eating is never just about the food. The ways in which we eat are well-crafted, age-old rituals that are different for every culture. Emblematic edibles and significant meals are deeply embedded in festival programs. Selections of food and rituals of eating and service are themselves symbols of power and evidence of social control. Food choices are always revealing, and their preparation and service vary greatly across time and cultures.

The act of eating involves an array of senses. As we see, touch, taste, and smell our food and drink, we assess and experience what we eat. Rituals and habits of eating are comforting, whether they are reenactments of celebrations or ceremonies or part of a daily routine. (How well do you do without your morning coffee?) Certain foods evoke thoughts of past times and significant places and events, making meals memorable and meaningful for the future. Planning holiday meals always raises the questions of which dishes are obligatory—in order to bring back memories or create new ones.

Food can also elicit humor and surprise. All too often, the specter of disaster hovers when food is prepared and presented. Today, a beautifully decorated cake is expected at formal occasions, such as weddings, birthdays, and anniversaries. As such, many families have stories about cake mishaps: the cake was dropped as it was delivered; it was crooked; it capsized or crumbled inauspiciously. In earlier times, professional carvers played an important role in the theatrical presentations of food. Holding roasted meats and poultry aloft, master carvers provided tableside entertainment at grand banquets (see Willan, "Behind the Scenes," fig. 2). Beautifully

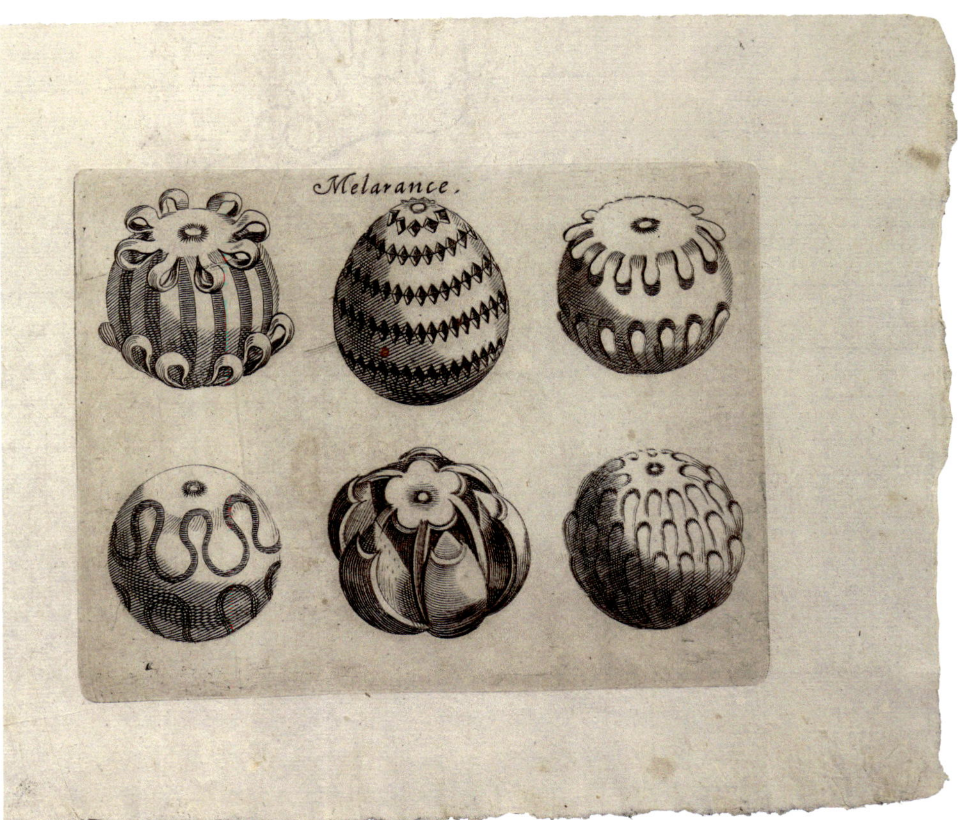

sculpted fruits and vegetables, again the work of carvers, were displayed with pyramids of smaller fruits (fig. 5).

Throughout history, important events and memorable moments have been commemorated with food. To celebrate victories, triumphal processions finished with a feast. In contemporary society, as part of a fall ritual, football fans stage elaborate meals on tailgates in stadium parking lots before watching their team in "combat."

All religions and cultures have defining rituals and traditions centered on signal foods as well as prohibitions and practices of fasting. In conceptual and visceral ways, food serves to identify certain groups—be it ethnic or religious. Sausages, for example, make us of think of German and Italian menus, the latter with pasta. In both daily habits and special ceremonies of eating, food works to satisfy. It serves as a pretext to bring people together to bond over a shared experience as they engage in extended and meaningful social rituals. Internally and externally, it makes us feel full and hence, good.

TASTE

The experience of food combines sensual, motor, and intellectual faculties. The essential sense that is responsible for the pleasurable part of eating, the sense of taste, is a dynamic of ocular, oral, and haptic enjoyment. We eat not only with our mouths

FIG. 5.

Oranges.

Engraving, 10.1 × 13.5 cm (4 × 5½ in.).

From Mattio Molinari, *Il trinciante* (Padua: Per Liuio Pasquati, 1636), pl. 32.

Los Angeles, Getty Research Institute.

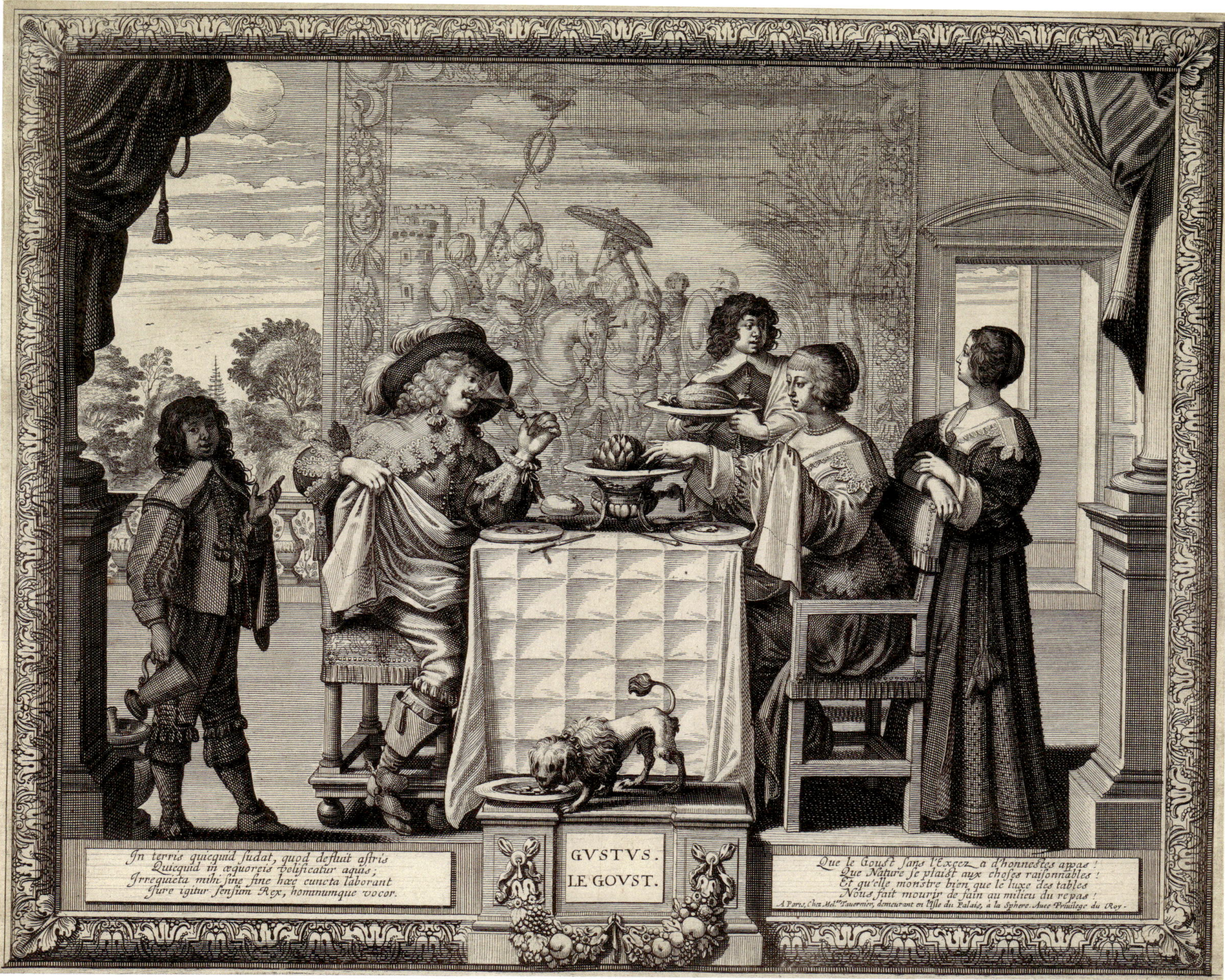

FIG. 6.

Abraham Bosse (French, 1602–76).

Taste, etching, 22.3 × 29.2 cm
(8¾ × 11½ in.).
From *Les cinq sens* (Paris: Chez
Melor, 1635), a suite of 5 etchings.
Los Angeles, Collection of Anne
Willan and Mark Cherniavsky.

but also with our eyes, nose, and hands. Taste triggers immediate reactions, including judgments about quality and feelings of appreciation that are grounded in social training and knowledge (fig. 6). In his mid-eighteenth-century article for the *Encyclopédie,* Chevalier Louis de Jaucourt writes: "Taste [*gout*] in general is the motivation of a sensory organ which enjoys its object and which senses all that is good. This is why Taste concerns all types of sensations: one has a taste for music and painting, at the same time as stews [*ragouts*] when the sensory organ savors, so to speak, these objects."[3] Jaucourt nicely captures how taste compels us to seek out good things. In the process, he makes a pun: *ragout,* the word for "stew" (itself an artful food mash-up), echoes *gout,* the word for "taste" or the "act of discrimination."

In a second article on taste, as applied to the arts, Voltaire writes about how sight alone is insufficient for comprehending the beauty of a work; rather, the observer must fully sense the art in order to understand it in a discerning way. He draws a parallel from intellectual taste for art to sensual taste. Just as a gourmet will immediately recognize the mixing of two liqueurs, the connoisseur will in the blink of an eye recognize a mixture of two styles.[4] Thus, taste is an important factor in all areas of the arts, from painting to fashion, interior decoration to pastry. The search for savors and pleasures can be sensual and thoughtful; it can become elevated through the appreciation of art and music, while also being propelled by physical appetites that desire favorite foods and comforting dishes.

The senses come together in an appreciation of all types of edible offerings, on the table and in the street. Diverse sensory qualities combine memory and physical activity. The oral pleasures of a favorite dish include chewing, swallowing, and digestion. The philosophy of taste brings up questions of subjectivity (what one person likes) and the universal (what a person *should* enjoy and comprehend). Combined with the act of eating, taste is an experience of anticipation, appreciation, and, finally, consumption; it transcends hunger but is always definitively physiological. Eating epitomizes experience and judgment. When we do not like something—not only food—we say it is in "bad taste" or is "tasteless."

MAKING THE MONUMENT:
RECORDING FESTIVALS IN BOOKS AND PRINTS

"The edible monument" is an intentional oxymoron that seeks to describe the complex and diverse roles that food has played in festivals. Food is material and substantial; and yet, by nature, both festivals and foodstuffs are ephemeral. Prepared dishes spoil; fruits and vegetables rot. Festivals have dates, schedules, and programs, but then the party is over. Food's seasonal appearance and its rarity as an exotic product from distant places are employed not only to express luxury but also to signal special elements of the occasion. Echoing the large stuffed birds in earlier European feasts, the turkey is an essential food at Thanksgiving. Americans still look forward to it and eat more turkey on Thanksgiving than any other holiday.[5]

Edible elements were intricately woven into festival programs. Chosen and prepared to be appropriate to the architecture, landscape, or interior settings, displays of food were enhanced by candles, torches, fireworks, or water features—all made to be admired and commented upon by eminent guests, the invited audience, and, on occasion, the crowd of onlookers. Serving vessels and tableware made of silver and porcelain portrayed animals, vegetables, and other natural ingredients. Obviously inedible, they were displayed as opulent decorative complements (or possibly as replications or echoes of the actual edibles), staged as art on the table, and presented as extravagant entertainment for the banquet guests.

The ways in which works on paper—publications and prints—told stories of the art of food and portrayed the edible monuments are the subjects of this book. Paper was an important material for the production of festivals. It was used to create festival monuments, which were frequently constructed out of papier-mâché or cardboard. Paper also preserved the designs and recipes and illustrated the dishes and table settings, covers, serving arrangements, and working designs. Festival publications described the monuments and disseminated images of them. Printed descriptions of celebrations and parties describe how food was staged and served in theatrical ways— as a kind of performance, sometimes exploding, sometimes intended to be torn apart or demolished, like a piñata, spilling food and prizes for the crowd. For artworks, this impending destruction and planned obsolescence could seem to be a disconcerting fate, yet it was routinely part of an overarching festival program. Unlike paintings and sculptures, which were collected by private collectors and museums, the ephemeral art of festivals can be known only from contemporary images and descriptive texts. As documents of the events, books and prints are significant as the single nonephemeral elements. These works on paper were vital to festivals, reviving memories of past occasions and heralding and recording new ones. More than simply surrogate experiences, festival books and prints were designed to be communication devices.

Information concerning the art of food for festivals comes from a wide variety of documentary sources. Official records and publications on the festival were an important component of the program. When these accounts were printed—as they were increasingly after 1500—they were intended to disseminate information and to circulate beyond the immediate site, publicizing the politically correct account of the festival. Some prints were made to be collected as souvenirs; others, such as handouts or broadsides, were meant to be discarded. Publications were produced in small editions with a wide variety of formats. Festival books themselves commenced as small, neatly printed volumes; these were modest pamphlets and libretti that served as programs, listing the sequence of events, important and honored participants, and others in attendance. The broadsides—among the rarest survivals—and suites of prints showed the elaborate decorations, staged events, and pageant wagons. Toward the end of the seventeenth century, some of the grandest illustrated folios appeared, which mirrored the lavish festival designs in their production values. Designed to be both records and gifts, these publications convey far more than the art of the festival. They are key to understanding the overarching political statements and cultural aspirations of festivals. Like the ceremonies, the books and prints are freighted with heraldry and symbols that require complex interpretations. Festivals should never be seen as merely fancy, frivolous parties.

Moving beyond the historic volumes and prints on festivals, official archives record the preparations in terms of goods and costs, with lists of supplies, inventories, and invoices. The accounts highlight the significance of specific household or palace papers, many of which include instructions and recipes. Initially, the documents were handwritten and kept by the chief stewards, cooks, and carving masters, among others. With the professionalization of their positions, these key figures began to publish more detailed information, which reveals the importance of their work. By the end of the seventeenth century, they were no longer just anonymous house managers or cooks. Their names are noted in the most important festival books, with praise for their work on the programs; there were even caricatures of them (fig. 7; see fig. 1).

By recording menus and ingredients, table settings, and plate and decorative table arrangements, these impresarios created handbooks that give a behind-the-scenes story of festivals, feasts, and their larger social contexts. Like the festival books but more portable, these published manuals were made to travel. In the sixteenth century— surprisingly early—they proliferated and then reappeared in later editions and translations. Service protocols were copied. Table settings were borrowed; menus and recipes circulated widely in Europe's developing culinary culture.

Ancestors of cookbooks, early recipe books and books of secrets are also key sources.[6] Books of secrets were filled with information on all kinds of substances and techniques, including medical treatments, pharmaceuticals, and alchemical formulas. As late as the mid-eighteenth century, such concoctions of herbs, medical compounds, and confections were sold in groceries and drugstores. Possibly made for good customers, a popular print showing a "medicinal monument" preserves the elaborate window display of Gaetano de Luca's pharmacy in Rome (fig. 8). A three-tier banquette topped by a shelf of drug jars frames the table of herbs and other sundries, which the proprietor organized to celebrate the Jubilee Year of 1750 on June 30. Portraits of the Greek physicians Galen and Andromacus (the latter was the inventor of

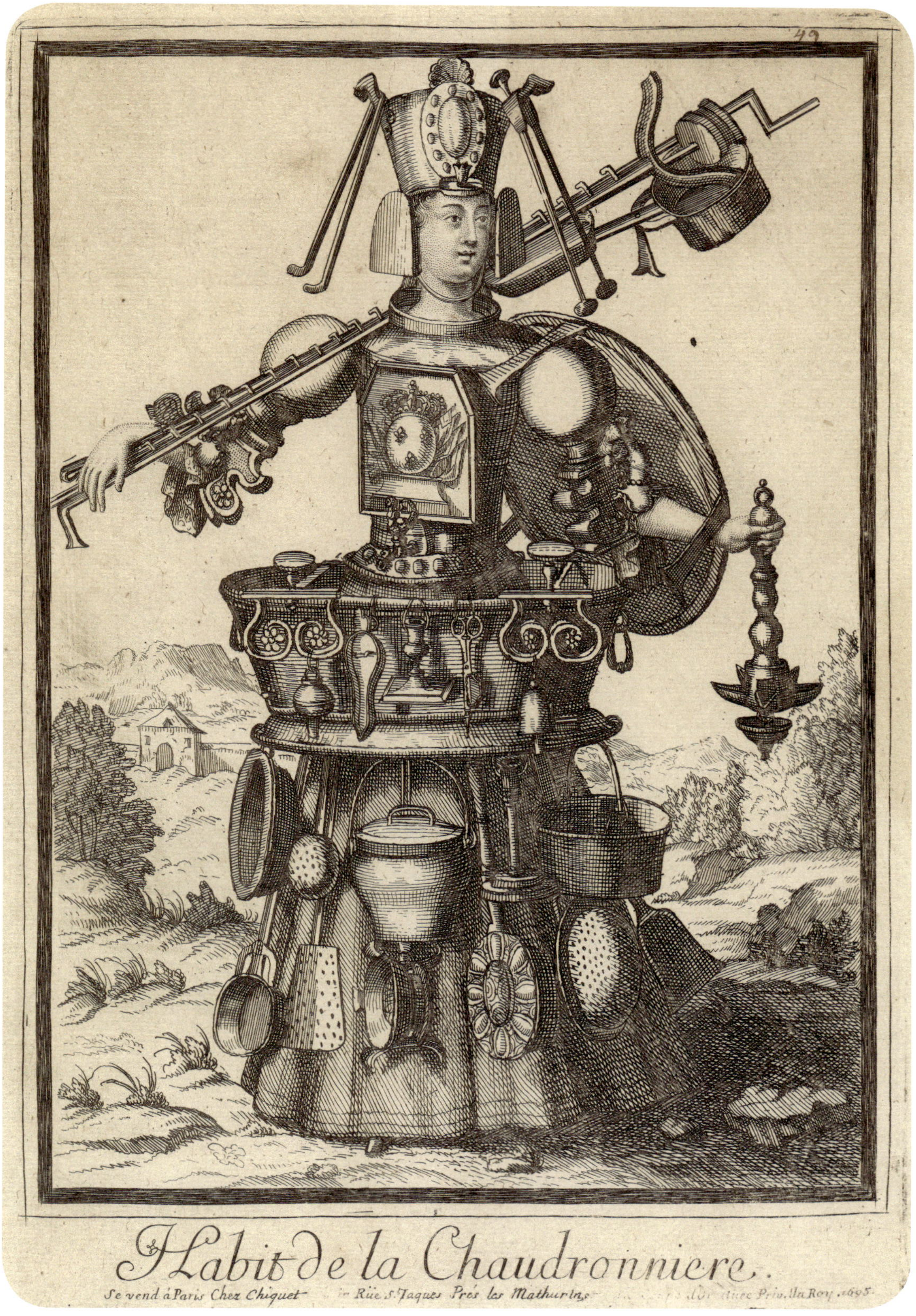

FIG. 7.
**Nicolas I de Larmessin
(French, 1632–94).**
Costume of the Boilermaker,
etching and engraving,
27.9 × 20.3 cm (11 × 8 in.).
Los Angeles, Collection of Anne
Willan and Mark Cherniavsky.

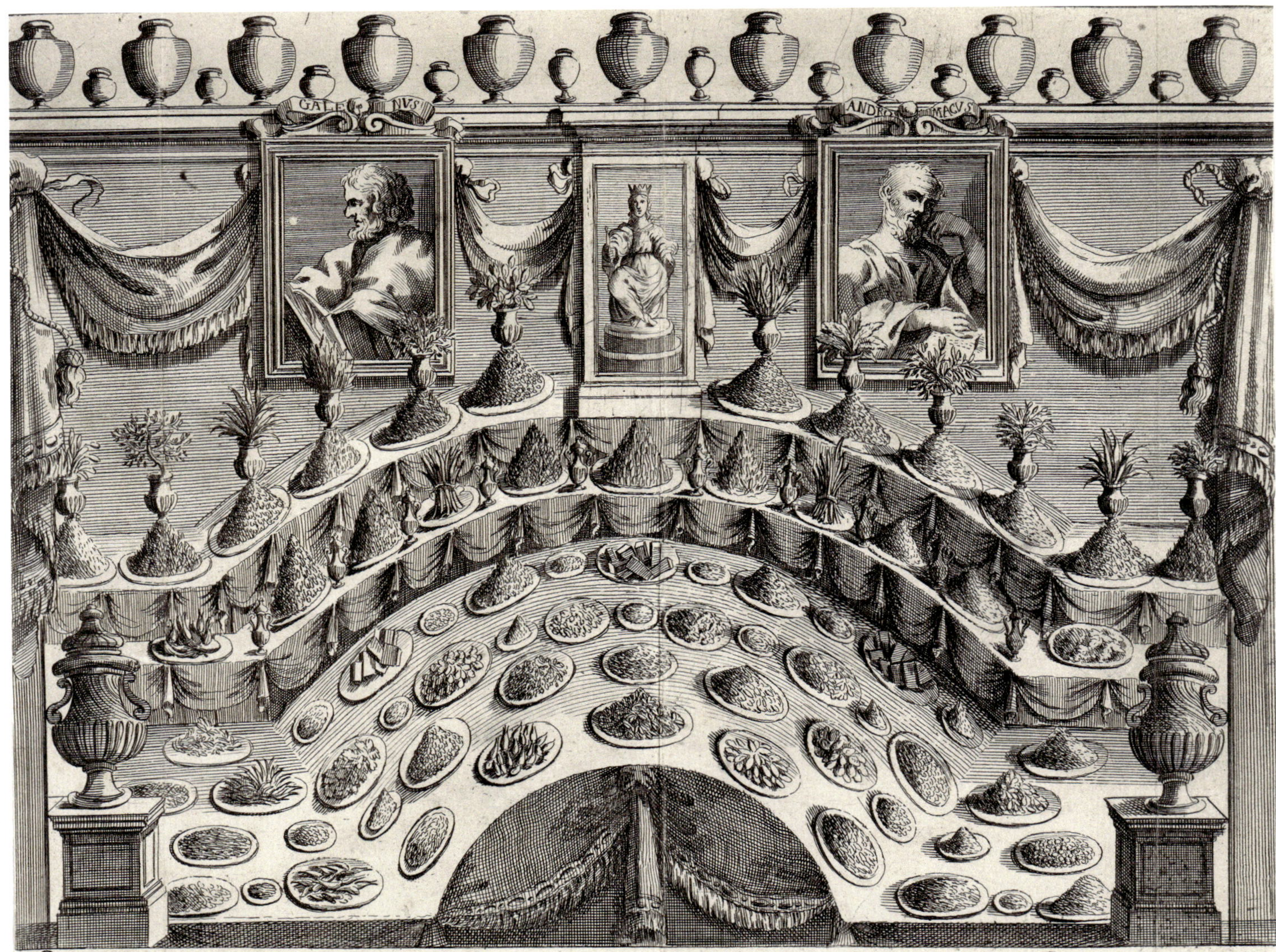

GALENVS
ANDROMACVS
Son.º Aparato di Theriaca, e Mitridato fatto da Gaetano de Luca nella sua Spet.ª della Reggina, posta in Roma al Paradiso, li 30. Giugno Anno del Giubileo 1750.

the famous medicine and antidote theriaca) are shown in the print with medicinals such as mithridate, another remedy for poisoning.

Like late-medieval books of secrets, the first cookbooks were nearly always anonymous. Even when there was an author's name, little is known about him.[7] There was considerable borrowing, which we might call plagiarism today: although recipes were repeated verbatim, new versions almost never credited their sources. Increasingly, the manuals and how-to books corresponded to the growing specialization of professions, such as the chief steward (called the *scalco* in Italy and the *maître d'hôtel* in France) or even the gardeners, as their expertise became discrete applied sciences that developed from general natural history. Herbals, horticulture, and incipient botany combined with books of secrets. Directed toward uses in the kitchen, oral and manuscript recipes became printed cookbooks. Knowledge of methods and materials, such as sugar, metals, and porcelain, informed the development of culinary preparation as well as tableware. Texts and illustrations describe and provide visual records of the edibles and table designs, moving from three-dimensional depictions drawn directly from nature to lifelike representations in porcelain and silver. Two-dimensional works on paper—book illustrations and prints—communicate the food and the art, as well as table settings and arrangements. The prints integrate these festival details into vertical elevations of the tables, credenzas, or buffets. Others show table settings and covers in symmetrical organizations closely related to formal garden plans.

Like modern cookbooks in which we write and file additional recipes, these early printed works became personal handbooks and vade mecums. They were books to use, tear apart, and copy; they were certainly not intended for libraries or bibliophilic collections. The publication of cookbooks—a meld of household manuals, books of secrets, and natural history books—accelerated in the seventeenth century and coincided with the production of elaborate festival books and prints, which disseminated elite tastes in both art and food. The famed chef François Pierre de la Varenne's *Le cuisinier françois* (The French cook), the foundational publications on French cuisine, was issued almost each year between 1651 and 1715; other works such as *Le pastissier françois* (1653; The French pastry cook) and *L'escole parfaite des officiers de bouche* (1662; The ideal school for household officers) were translated into English in subsequent decades. Like Parisian fashion plates that circulated styles in fabric and clothing to other European cities, cookbooks and serving manuals gave detailed instructions on how to prepare an elegant presentation in the most sophisticated manner ordained by the French court. Such publications were quintessentially made to travel, frequently excerpted, and translated. They circulated favorite recipes, stylish serving presentations, and even gossip about court affairs. Who was this year's favorite chef and what foods did he feature?

RECORDING FESTIVALS IN BOOKS AND PRINTS

Philosophers, critics, and commentators published theoretical books on festivals that often tied the events to ancient or religious contexts. At the same time, natural history and the developing sciences of botany and chemistry provided information, history, and advice on ingredients, which then led to discussions on the significance of food, matters of taste, and related properties of the senses employed to appreciate both food and festivals. All these parallel printed sources developed and proliferated in the early modern era. Did the same people read and use them? No. But they provide a broader picture of the social and cultural aspects of festivals, as well as diverse perspectives on their preparation and execution. These books expand our often limited view to a comprehension of the ambitious nature of festivals and the deft employment of complex presentations of food to impress and assert authority. The big question is: Do the festival books and prints describe what the planners and political figures wanted to happen—the insiders' point of view—even if weather or other failures altered the vision? Or do the descriptions detail the festival in a journalistic way, from the point of view of the spectator? The less formal, more revealing reports are often found in travelers' diaries and published accounts. And truth to tell, it is a losing battle to obtain a faithful and complete description of a festival. Like pageant wagons in a parade or fireworks exploding against the night sky, festival events are quintessentially fleeting moments made to be witnessed, relished, and consumed. Books and prints are the best evidence we have.

As a pendant to *The Edible Monument: The Art of Food for Festivals* exhibition, this volume focuses on a selection of these varied works, among which are beautifully illustrated folios produced as genteel but serious political propaganda as well as popular prints created as broadsides and flyers for city walls. This catalog features the different kinds of publications that together provide a broad picture of the role that food played in festivals, from significant formal publications such as illustrated books, single prints, and libretti, to recipe books, books of secrets, tradesmen's manuals, and guides to carving meats, fruits, and vegetables and to setting tables and organizing food service.

Festival books reveal how foodstuffs were carefully woven into the implicit protocols and highly important order and form of festival programs. Prints illustrate spectacular displays of food, the choreography of the meal, and its dénouement. Often produced as part of a series of festival images, these prints echo and complement the processions, theater, dance, architecture, and water- and fireworks. Although there are substantial numbers of publications on festivals, the study of artistic food made for display and service at festivals does not have similar heft. Individual celebrations have been analyzed—some are legendary, such as those of the Este court in Ferrara and the banquets created for the Medici in Florence and Queen Christina of Sweden in Rome—but an overview of the range of publications does not exist. This book seeks to present new and different perspectives on food as art, bringing food more prominently into the context of festivals. Essays by diverse experts from the overlapping fields of art history, the history of books and prints, culinary history, and decorative arts present different voices and complementary interpretations of the art of food created for festivals.

Rather than a comprehensive catalog of the literature, this volume is an in-depth sampling of the documentary sources that circulated from the sixteenth to the early nineteenth century. It is not intended to be a general history of festivals or feasting but rather a selected account that draws on the art and history in the Getty Research Institute's special collections. The aim is to show how the art of food was a complex endeavor that brought together practical and theoretical knowledge. The books and prints were created for a competitive world of political alliances and social traditions in the principal cities and courts of Europe. Like Munich, New Orleans, Pasadena, and Rio de Janeiro in the twenty-first century, certain cities—Bologna, Rome, Versailles, and Vienna—were known for their extravagant celebrations. This volume focuses on some of the signal festivals and the unique and fascinating books and prints by which we know them.

NOTES

1. Robert M. Grippo and Christopher Hoskins, *Macy's Thanksgiving Day Parade* (Charleston, SC: Arcadia, 2004), 11.

2. Based on the mythical Land of Cockaigne (in Italian, Cuccagna), where no one went hungry, this Italian festival was known for its monuments made of food. The Chinea was the tribute paid by the king of Naples to the pope. From about 1550 to 1776, temporary monuments were placed all over Rome on 29 June, the feast day of Saints Peter and Paul. See Reed, "Feasting in the Streets," this volume.

3. Denis Diderot and Jean-Baptiste le Rond d'Alembert, eds., *Encyclopédie; ou, Dictionnaire raisonné des sciences, des arts, et des métiers*…(Paris: Chez Briasson, 1757) 7:758. Translation mine.

4. Diderot and d'Alembert, *Encyclopédie,* 761.

5. According to the National Turkey Foundation, "In 2013, more than 240 million turkeys were raised. More than 200 million were consumed in the United States. We estimate that 46 million of those turkeys were eaten at Thanksgiving, 22 million at Christmas and 19 million at Easter." "Turkey History and Trivia," National Turkey Foundation, http://www.eatturkey.com/why -turkey/history.

6. See William Eamon, *Science and the Secrets of Nature: Books of Secrets in Mediaeval and Early Modern Culture* (Princeton, N.J.: Princeton University Press, 1993).

7. On early cookbooks and their authors, see Gilly Lehmann, "The Cook as Artist," in Harlan Walker, ed., *Food in the Arts: Proceedings of the Oxford Symposium on Food and Cookery, 1998* (Devon, UK: Prospect, 1999), 125-26.

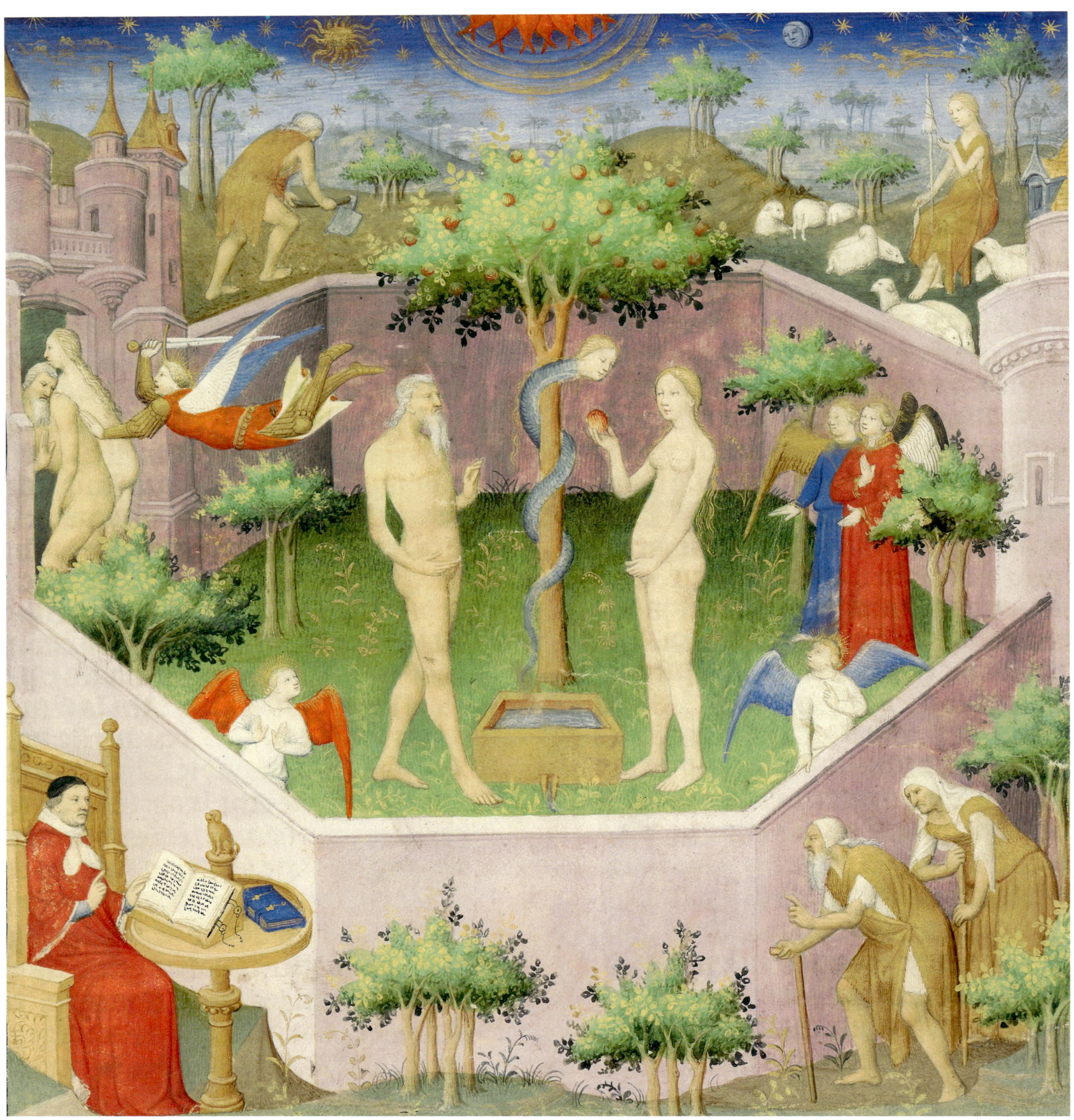

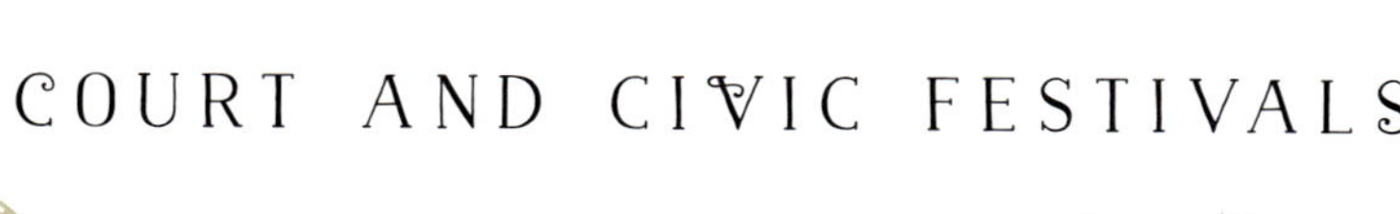

COURT AND CIVIC FESTIVALS

MARCIA REED

EDIBLES IN PARADISE

From miraculous appearances to devilish temptations, food is at the center of many famous stories. The book of Genesis starts with the creation of the natural world and potential edibles and continues on to the unfortunate tale of Adam and Eve's fall from grace in the Garden of Eden. The introduction of sin and evil is instigated by an act of eating. Adam and Eve's desire for the forbidden fruit (later designated as the apple) demonstrates humankind's apparently irrepressible attraction to food.

Such narratives of a past paradise present visions of heaven on earth. Illuminated manuscripts from the Middle Ages and the Renaissance depict the Garden of Eden as a beautiful and fertile domain (fig. 1). Popular woodcut or engraved broadsides from these periods illustrate a fantastic land called Cockaigne, where boundless delicious foods and drinks are available for the taking (see Reed, "Feasting in the Streets," fig. 13). Its denizens are happy, satisfied, and, significantly, well fed.

The Bible highlights how food is used for celebrations and ceremonies and how it appears as wondrous apparitions. New Testament parables tell about the astonishing materialization of food to feed multitudes. Miracles make it possible to feed the Ten Thousand, to provide drink for guests at the Wedding at Cana, and for manna to rain down like snowballs in the desert. Food is employed as a marvelous gift that circumvents hunger and famine and prevents a social disaster. In the Bible, the miracle of food evokes the supernatural presence and recalls a divine intervention. Recognition of this generous gesture fuels the celebratory feast. The shared acceptance and eating of the food foreshadows the sacrament of Communion, depicted in the best-known and significant banquet scene in European religious art: the Last Supper. Strangely, though characteristically for this period, it is not food that is on display but rather those at the ceremonial gathering around the table (fig. 2).

Depictions of food in scenes of medieval and Renaissance feasts are remarkably

FIG. 1.

Boucicaut Master and workshop (French illuminator, fl. ca. 1390–1430).

Adam and Eve in the Garden of Eden (detail), ca. 1413–15, tempera colors, gold leaf, gold paint, and ink on parchment bound between pasteboard covered with brown calfskin, leaf: 42 × 29.6 cm (16⁹⁄₁₆ × 11⅝ in.). From Giovanni Boccaccio, *Des cas des nobles hommes et femmes,* trans. Laurent de Premierfait, Paris, ca. 1415, Ms. 63, fol. 268. Los Angeles, J. Paul Getty Museum.

restrained. Although the table itself serves as the principal object or the stage for religious narratives in Simon Bening's *The Last Supper,* only a small number of dishes are shown on the table, effectively diminishing the importance of the food and table decorations. Food is implied or taken for granted in this symbolic shared meal. The focus is on the depicted figures—Jesus, his disciples, and the guests— rather than on the food, which is represented as simplified shapes—fishes or a roast—along with drinking vessels and plates. From this same period, the archetypal

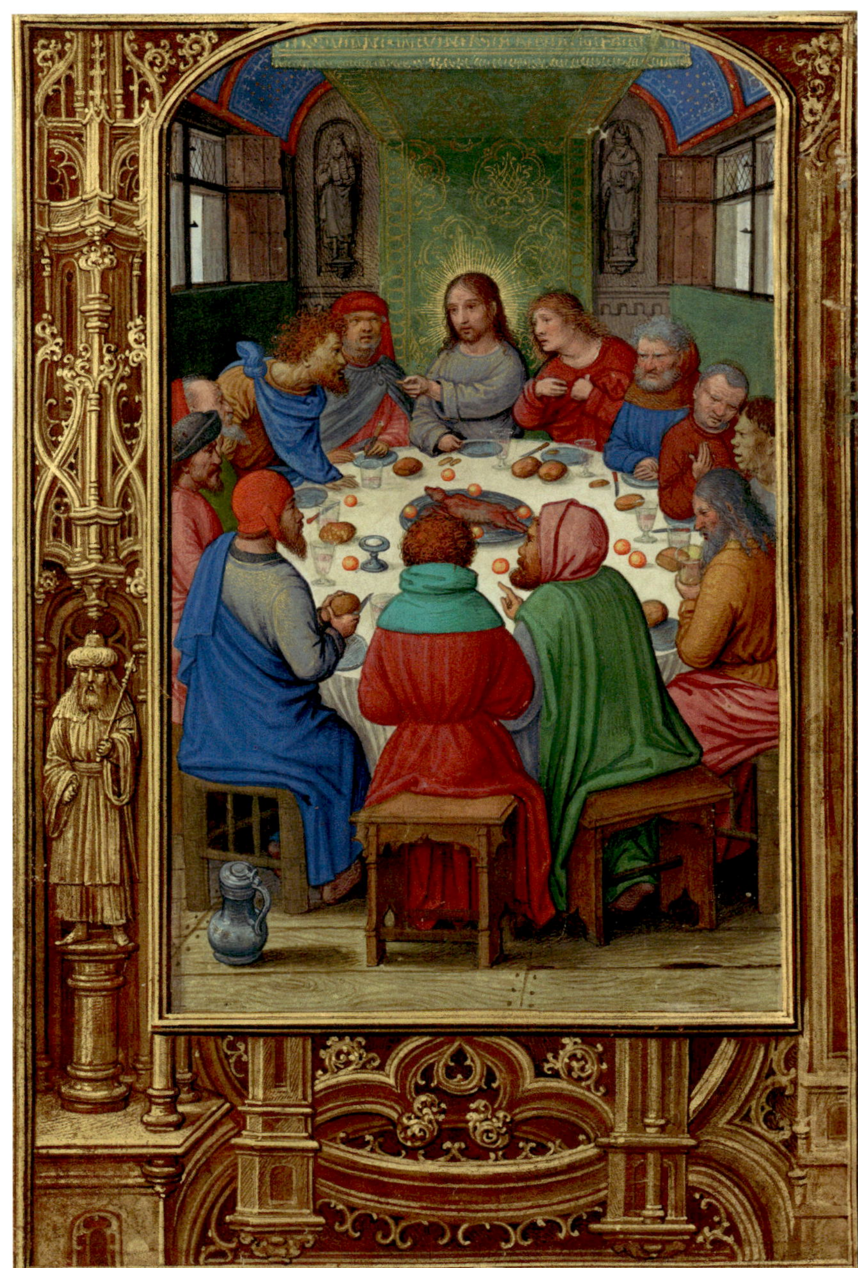

FIG. 2.

Simon Bening (Flemish illumina- tor, ca. 1483-1561).

The Last Supper, tempera colors, gold paint, and gold leaf on parchment, leaf: 16.8 × 11.4 cm (6⅝ × 4½ in.).

From *Prayer book of Cardinal Albrecht of Brandenburg,* ca. 1525- 30, Ms. Ludwig IX 19, fol. 83v. Los Angeles, J. Paul Getty Museum.

antithetical banquet scene to *The Last Supper* is the shocking illustration of John the Baptist's head served on a platter at the request of Herodias's daughter, Salome. Table service that substitutes the decapitated head of a revered religious figure for a customary dish, such as a boar's head, only emphasizes how barbaric the rulers were at the time of Christ.

Court feasts and civic banquets reached back to religious traditions and historic antiquity, reviving and embodying familiar narratives woven from well-loved themes. The habit of preparing food by following time-honored recipes was a reassuring ritual that renewed court protocols and reinforced social values. The essence of festive parties and meals, which were designed to be grand and spectacular, could be found in their repetitions and referential details. The purpose of the celebrations was to effectively indicate the ruler's connections to historic and mythical heroes such as Hercules, defining the honored guests' virtues in terms of attractive mythological narratives. The folkloric customs, traditional foods and drinks, parades, theatrical events, and mythological figures represented in the decorations not only amused participants but also reminded them of their cultural origins and the fundamental meanings of rituals, effectively grounding these seemingly carefree and frivolous times of entertainment and commemoration.

The etched title page of the festival book published for the wedding of John William, Duke of Jülich-Cleves-Berg, and Jakobea of Baden on 16 June 1585 in Düsseldorf is a mélange of heraldry, mythology, and religious narratives bearing on the theme of marriage (fig. 3). The images bring together scenes of the gods Jupiter, Juno, Neptune, and Amphitrite standing on plinths above Pluto and Proserpina and vignettes of biblical scenes, including the birth of Eve in Genesis 2, Rebecca at the well (the story leading up to the marriage of Rebecca and Isaac) in Genesis 24, and the Wedding at Cana in John 2 (shown in the center). The wedding festival events were dominated by tournaments; however, two etched double-page plates show the banquet hall with servants carrying covered dishes to guests seated at the long table, a buffet with drinks, and guests dancing. The seventh print depicts the finale, a sugar banquet: a large cloth-covered table is filled with sugar sculptures of a castle, animals, birds, fishes, heraldic and emblematic devices, potted orange trees, and dishes of fruits and other edibles (fig. 4). Scale is important. Diminutive guests admire the towering table on which the sculptures are displayed in the large hall of the Düsseldorf castle. The poem below the picture describes a pelican feeding its young by opening its own heart, an emblem of charity meant to inform the marriage. After the festival was over, guests broke the table sculptures into pieces, demolishing the art on the table, and then took pieces away as souvenirs.

FIG. 3.

Attributed to Frans Hogenberg (Netherlandish, ca. 1539–90).

Frontispiece with coats of arms, engraving, 24.2 × 16.2 cm (9½ × 6¾ in.). From Theodor Graminaeus, *Beschreibung derer fürstlicher güligscher &c. Hochzeit* (Cologne: Graminaeus, 1587), pl. 1. Los Angeles, Getty Research Institute.

FIG. 4.

Attributed to Frans Hogenberg (Netherlandish, ca. 1539–90).

Sugar banquet for the wedding of John William, Duke of Jülich-Cleves-Berg, and Jakobea of Baden, etching, 21 × 26 cm (8¼ × 10¼ in.). From Theodor Graminaeus, *Beschreibung derer fürstlicher güligscher &c. Hochzeit* (Cologne: Graminaeus, 1587), pl. 7. Los Angeles, Getty Research Institute.

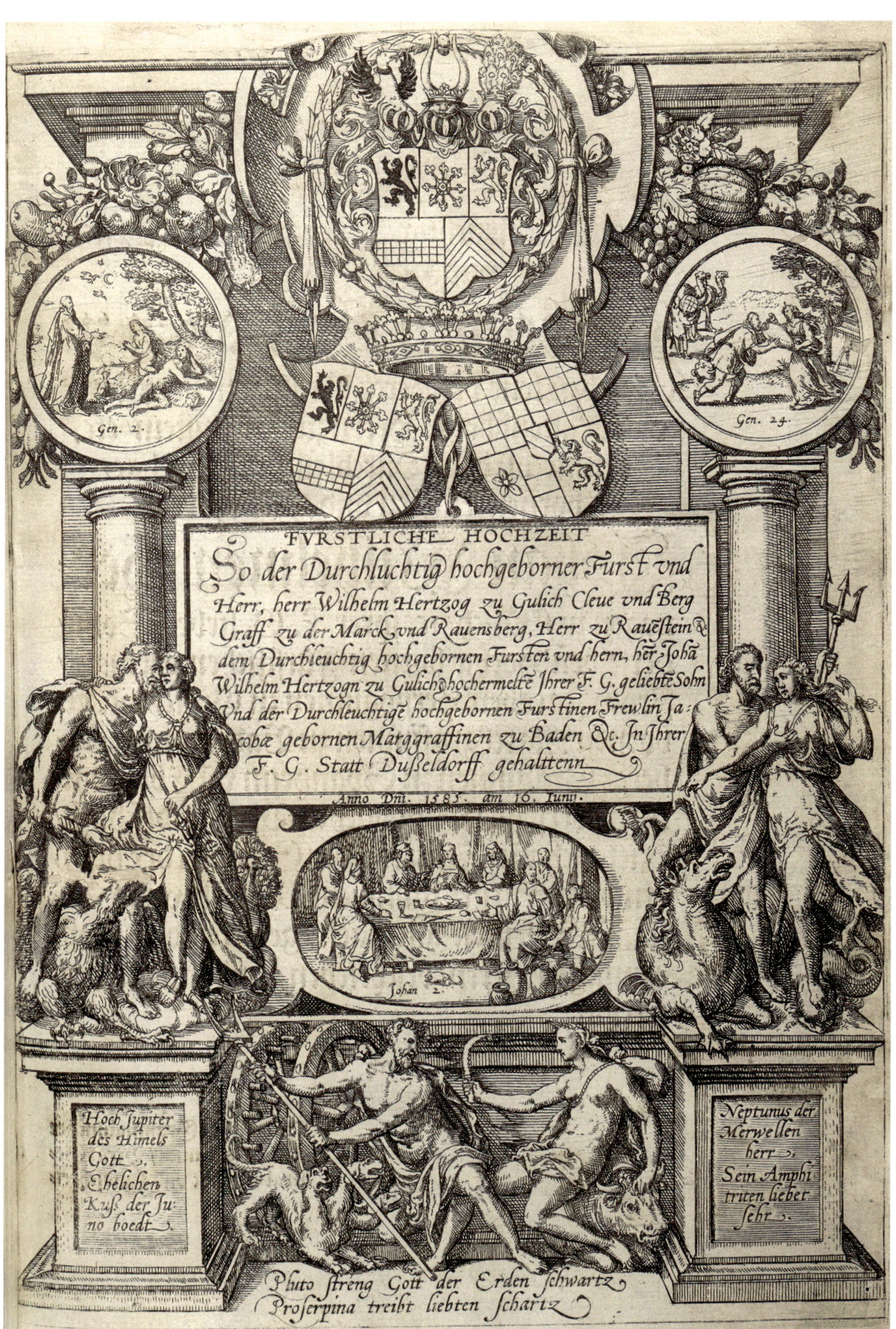

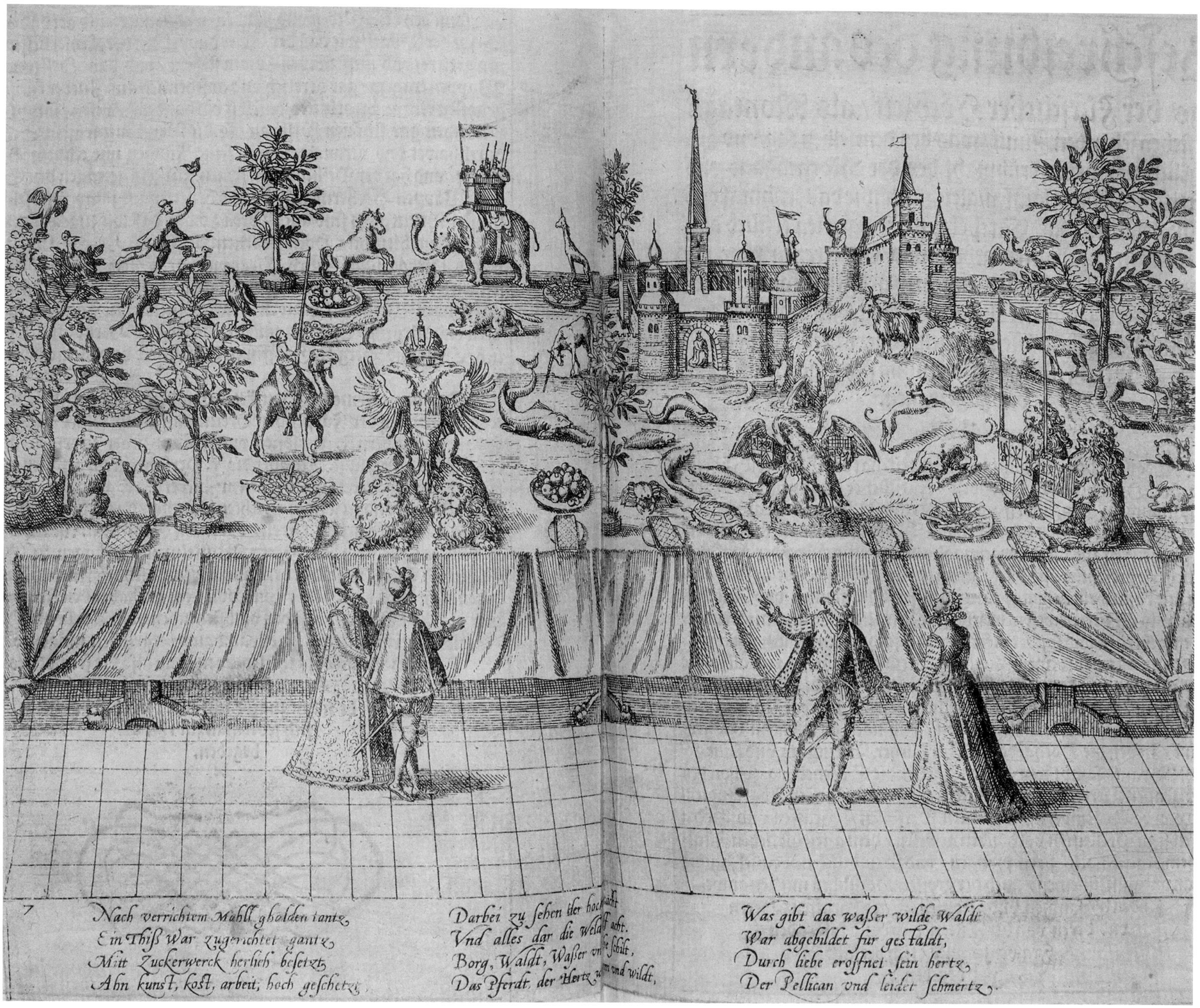

7
Nach verrichtem Mahll gholden tantz,
Ein Thiß war zugerichtet gantz,
Mitt Zuckerwerck herlich besetzt,
Ahn kunst, kost, arbeit, hoch geschetzt.

Darbei zu sehen tier hoch acht.
Vnd alles dar die Welt acht.
Borg, Waldt, Waßer vnd schilt,
Das Pferdt, der Hertz vnd wildt,

Was gibt das waßer wilde Waldt
War abgebildet fur gestaldt,
Durch liebe eroffnet sein hertz,
Der Pellican vnd leidet schmertz.

ON EARTH AS IT IS IN HEAVEN

Mythic feasts described in classical sources served as inspiration and often provided narratives for the grand banquets that took place in courts of the sixteenth and seventeenth centuries. Although the foods prepared for these opulent tables are not shown in great detail in the visual arts, a number of classical texts memorialize ancient banquets. Just as biblical stories were important sources for paintings, such as the Venetian painter Paolo Veronese's *Wedding at Cana* (1562), themes from ancient myths were canonized in art, music, and festivals of the early modern period. As seen in representations of "Banquets of the Gods" as well as the popular Cuccagna street festival, these motifs depict past idyllic times with evocative images of paradise.[1]

In the *Iliad,* Homer describes Zeus presiding over a Banquet of the Gods celebrating the marriage of Peleus and Thetis, future parents of Achilles.[2] Hovering in the clouds above is Eris, goddess of discord, who was not invited to the wedding banquet. She brings a golden apple from the Garden of the Hesperides, where the apples of immortality grow. The apple is intended as the prize for the fairest. Zeus is asked to judge between Aphrodite, Athena, and Hera; however, he defers the decision to the mortal, Paris. Paris chooses Aphrodite; she promises him Helen of Troy. Thus, the stage is set for the Trojan War and the destruction of the city. In this quick résumé, we can gather that there is an inevitable downside to feasts and celebrations. While the Banquet of the Gods could seem to be a purely positive occasion, Homer's narrative shows how the gods are motivated by human passions and destructive appetites. The ancient narrative of the Banquet of the Gods introduces a parallel epic: the ongoing social and political history of disharmony, war, and ruin. Likewise, festival banquets often ended with pillage of the food and table decorations; street monuments were designed to be demolished.

The ultimate price to pay for feasting comes the morning after, as guests return to the realities of life. If the paintings are to be believed, even gods drink and eat too much—some even have hangovers. Ovid's *Fasti* tells of the bacchanals, seasonal feasts held by Bacchus, the god of wine. The gods gather to celebrate, drinking and engaging in lascivious behavior.[3] The presence of Priapus, satyrs, and nymphs contributes to an over-the-top tone, just as party behavior often departs from everyday decorum, veering toward the unacceptable.

Following Homer, feasts were often associated with wedding celebrations. Apuleius's *Metamorphoses* (Book VI, 24) describes the banquet staged for Cupid and Psyche's marriage, with all the gods in attendance. Vulcan has cooked dinner; the Graces sprinkle balsam; Apollo sings and plays his lyre. To commemorate a significant event, important guests are present to engage in the festivities and give their blessings. Food is served and consumed in an elegant setting, often out of doors. There is music, and sometimes other entertainment is presented, enhancing and echoing the theme of the artistically designed celebrations. Many of the essential elements for festivals were defined by the precedents for the divine banquet.

Looking back to classical paradigms, Renaissance artists borrowed themes from Banquets of the Gods or from biblical feasts such as the Wedding at Cana. Combined with feasting, the nuptial theme and its staging were important elements that provided complementary content for festival celebrations. Giovanni Bellini's *Feast of the Gods* (1514) was the first of six painted bacchanals conceived by the Italian scholar Mario Equicola for Duke Alfonso d'Este's study, the Camerino d'Albastro, in Ferrara.[4] Bellini's painting is reminiscent of Raphael's fresco of 1517, *Wedding Banquet of Cupid and Psyche* (with its considerable amounts of nudity and suggestive leaning, indicating overheated passions), in the Loggia di Psiche at the Villa Farnesina in Rome, and, more specifically, of Giulio Romano's identically titled fresco painted a decade later (1526-28) at the Palazzo del Te in Mantua. The latter is a portrait of paradise that shows wealth, abundance, and celebrations in an outdoor setting. There is a banquet-style display of silver and gold urns and platters framed by a topiary trellis, exotic animals (a camel and elephant behind the gods), and a donkey frolicking with Bacchus. Yet the focus was on the spectacle and the participants. There was scarce information in the paintings about what foods were on the table. Up to that point in time, there were no traditional models for the representation of food.

THE MYTHIC MEAL AS THEATER:
THE GOLDEN APPLE IN HAPSBURG VIENNA

The composer Antonio Cesti's epic opera *Il pomo d'oro* (1668; The golden apple) was composed for the wedding of the Holy Roman Emperor Leopold I and Margaret Theresa, the Spanish infanta. The event took place in Vienna in 1666 and was commemorated with an extensive calendar of festivities. Celebrations in Vienna, several of which were published with large prints, included mock tournaments, processions, horse ballets, and fireworks. The wedding was envisioned on a world stage: one of the principal theatrical events was a battle of the elements between air and water. Floating on clouds, the fabulous chariots designed by the architect Carlo Pasetti as theater pieces could also have been used for table sculpture or silverware for a banquet setting (fig. 5). Festival processions, which included carousels (equestrian parades and tournaments), presented choreography that echoed the table service, paralleling similar practices of the French court at this time.

A foldout etching by Lodovico Burnacini in the printed libretto for *Il pomo d'oro* illustrates the scene of the Banquet of the Gods as it takes place on stage (fig. 6). The feast is at the palace of Jupiter amid an arched enclosure of clouds framed by an

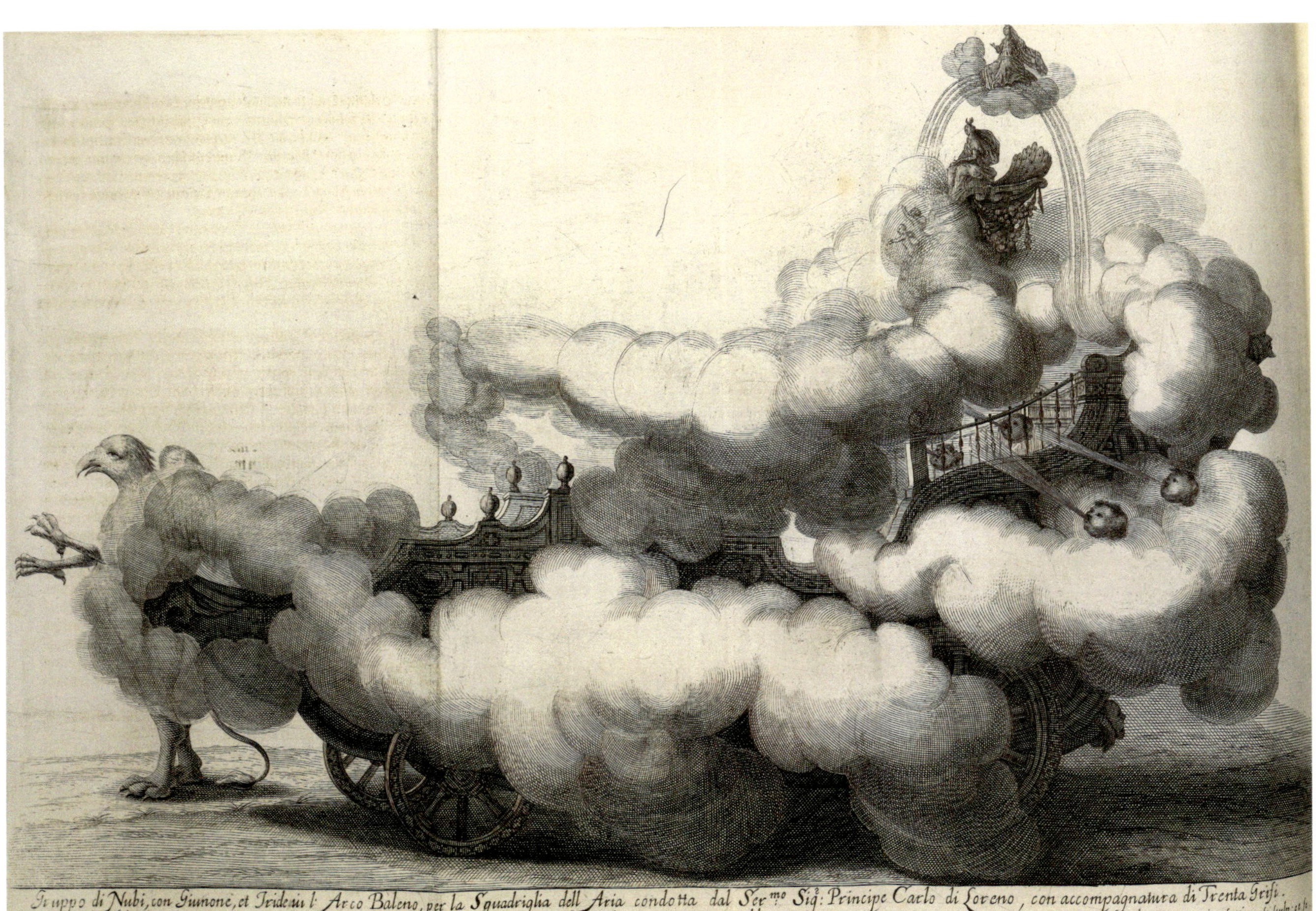

impressive display of silver plates and urns, as if this were an earthly dining space in a capacious hall decorated for the wedding dinner. The waitstaff are lively satyrs, who take their positions as if in a corps de ballet. These hooved, scantily dressed attendants proffer platters of pastry pies filled with large baked birds and roasts topped with trophies and birds' heads, in the manner of seventeenth-century grand dinners. Their platters are raised in a respectful gesture to the most eminent guests, who are seated facing the audience. A pleated cloth covers the central table. Several guests (a woman and a cupid) raise shallow glasses with delicate stems. Hebe, Ganymede, and a chorus of demigods serve the principal gods. Hovering in a cloud above the banquet, Discord, the sinister uninvited guest, hurls a golden apple down, casting a pall over the party. Thus, select elements of the Banquet of the Gods are seen as a court feast in an early opera performance. Mythic themes loosely borrowed from antiquity were recast into theater pieces and festival designs by artists, writers, and composers, whose works appeared in an international milieu of festival celebrations in seventeenth- and eighteenth-century Europe.

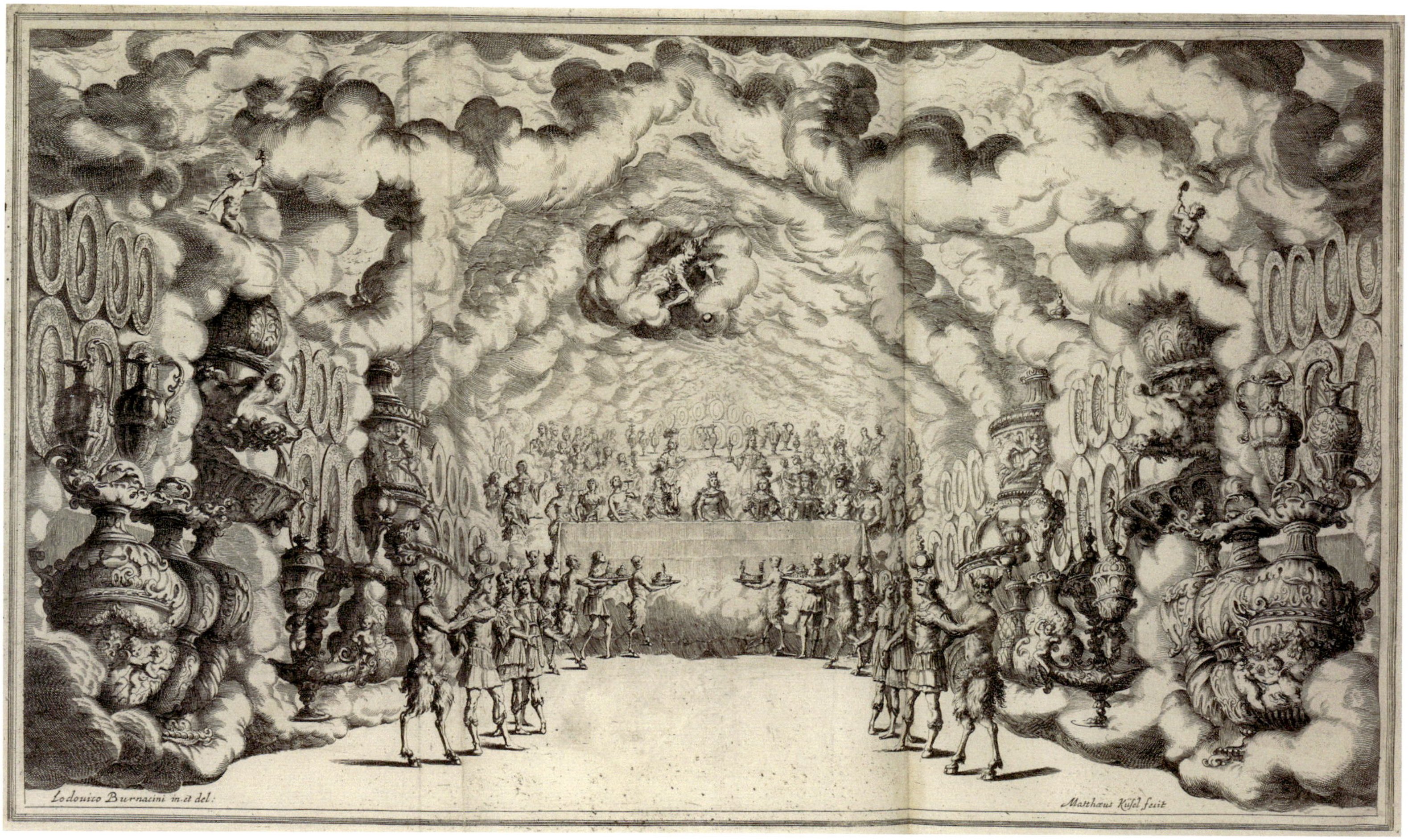

FIG. 6.

Mathäus Küsel (German, 1629–81), after Lodovico Ottavio Burnacini (Italian, 1636–1707).

The Banquet of the Gods, etching, 25.6 × 43 cm (10 × 17 in.). From Antonio Cesti, *Il pomo d'oro: Festa teatrale rappresentata in Vienna, per l'avgvstissime nozze delle Sacre Cesaree Reali Maesta di Leopoldo, e Margherita* (Vienna: Appresso Matteo Cosmerovio, 1668), pl. 3. Los Angeles, Getty Research Institute.

DIVINE VISTAS DECORATED WITH FOOD:
THE BANQUET OF THE GODS

Weddings were significant opportunities for feasts; so too were royal births, especially those of male heirs to the throne. In the late seventeenth century, the court of Louis XIV established the gold standard for festivals and for the books and prints about them, all of which were based on elaborated myths and cosmic metaphors that characterized the king and promoted his accomplishments. On the occasion of the birth in 1682 of Louis, the duc de Bourgogne and so-called petit dauphin of France, the writer and French academician Charles Perrault composed a narrative of a Banquet of the Gods in Parnassus.[5] It was written for Madame de Tallemant and begins with Perrault drafting the tale, having summoned the muse Polyhymnia. He imagines himself surrounded by other notables associated with the contemporary French theater—the playwright Molière and the actress Marie Champmeslé. Perrault describes how the gods, dressed in bejeweled garments and surrounded by the fruits of nature, are assembled for a meal.

> The tables are inconceivably lavish. Flora is sowing flowers; in her wake are many nymphs who carry filled baskets to decorate the large vases on the shelves of the buffet in a way that was as rich and astonishing as could be imagined. Bacchus has placed his satyrs and sylvans around the buffet under the lead of Silenus, who serves drinks to Hebe and Ganymede, especially the wine of Burgundy featured at this festival, and which the gods wish to drink in preference to all other wines, even [the divine] nectar.[6]

Perrault's vision is a parallel of two spheres of being, the sacred and the profane. Jupiter, the master of heaven and earth, arrives, and all the gods wait while he takes his place. The nymphs of the agricultural goddess Ceres carry great baskets of breads; for dessert, they serve biscuits and marzipan. Diana's nymphs bring their catch from hunting; and Vulcan, the god of fire, cooks. Pomona and her nymphs provide the most beautiful fruits in the world. During this time, there is discussion of the gardens cultivated at Versailles. Among the dishes served to the gods is ambrosia—not the ordinary variety but the version that each god liked best. What Mars is served smells strongly of garlic; the ambrosia brought to Venus has an odor of ambergris and orange blossoms. All the gods seem to dine and drink in a perfect manner, and none of them disdain such innocent (perhaps worldly) activities. Hebe and Ganymede happily mingle with the sylphs and satyrs at the table, drinking to the immortals. At the end of the meal, a concert of all kinds of instruments, both serious and majestic, is most agreeable to the assembled guests. Following a second, equally pleasant concert, Jupiter speaks the following words:

You know, immortal troupe
The happy news
Which makes our entire country rejoice
And which fulfills the happiness of Louis
Let us celebrate the fortunate birth
Of heroes whom Heaven bestows this day on France.[7]

Noting that it seems like a dream, Perrault elegantly summarizes the mythic themes of the pageantry that took place for various occasions at Versailles, on the palace grounds and in the gardens, for the court of Louis XIV.

THE ROLE OF BOOKS

Most books and prints about festivals were published to coincide with the events they accompanied, or they appeared shortly after the festival. With the exceptions of the festival books published for the wedding of Louis XIV and the infanta of Spain in 1660, and like the Grand Carousel in 1662, the most notable Versailles *fête* books were published after the celebrations.[8] The memoirs detailed a time of great brilliance in the French court and were part of Louis's collection, the *Cabinet du roi*. The folios in these magnificent illustrated books were paper monuments that packaged and gave permanence to ephemeral events for the delectation of future readers and viewers. In the description of a 1581 wedding ballet, the composer Balthazar de Beaujoyeulx deftly envisions the festival book as a box that holds confections of sugar offered by the king, playing the role of a confectioner. The text of *Le balet comique de la royne* (The comedic ballet of the queen)—the ballet of Circe performed by Louise of Lorraine and eleven court ladies for the wedding of Anne, duc de Joyeuse, and Marguerite de Vaudemont—Beaujoyeulx writes that it is the responsibility of the king to provide a taste of nectar and ambrosia to the people in order to satisfy their appetites. "Thus this refreshment of the spirit which you have found pleasant and which needs nothing but the country of your obedience, the sugar confection of your good graces, seasoned by your consent and preserved in the enclosure of this small monument: May it be possible for all the other nations to be able to taste the nectar and ambrosia of which you are full and of which you have satisfied the appetites of your people."[9]

Echoing contemporary French architectural designs, Jean Marot's prints of Louis's royal entry into Paris in 1660 following his wedding to the infanta of Spain portray the festival architecture in detail.[10] The texts describe the emblematic heraldry and symbols with equal attention, foreshadowing court historian and academician André Félibien's lively characterizations of subsequent festival programs. The prints hardly illustrate the festival celebrating the royal marriage; instead, they present the temporary architecture, sculptures, and monuments erected for the occasion. Not until the large folios on the Grand Carousel of 1662 or the Versailles festivals of 1664, 1668, and 1674 do the publications portray the grandeur of the costumes, the intertwining of royal virtues, heraldry, and the excitement of the celebrations, all of which are conveyed through astonishing panoramic images of the settings. In the earlier festival books, there is an evident difficulty and awkward feel to the integrations of text and image.

Les plaisirs de L'isle enchantée

Félibien's coyly modest motto was "Bene facere et vera dicere" (Do well and tell the truth). In fact, his texts further the embellishments of courtly life and speech, as seen in his description for the very grand scheme of the festival at Versailles in 1664. Félibien's text for the series of plates titled *Les plaisirs de L'isle enchantée* (The pleasures of the Enchanted Island) appeared almost ten years after the events took place.[11] Beginning on the seventh of May, the festival went on for about a week, with each day completely programmed from morning to night. Félibien notes that the festival, in both its pastoral setting and its presentations, brought art together with nature, rendering nature more perfect.[12] His point is illustrated by an emblem, titled *Naturam superabat* (Nature superceded), in the *Tapisseries du roi* (Tapestries of the king) volume of the *Cabinet du roi;* the emblem depicts a mountain constructed above a stage with machinery beneath.[13]

Grand banquets (*collations*) and less elaborate suppers (*soupers*) in gardens and grottoes are important parts of the overarching festival program credited to Carlo Vigarani of Modena. Serving the French king until 1690, Vigarani was an Italian scenographer who held the position of *intendant des machines et menus-plaisirs du roi* (supervisor of the king's entertainment and banquets). He collaborated with Paul de Beauvilliers, duc de Saint Aignan, the *premier gentilhomme de la chambre* (first gentleman of the chamber),[14] who focused on the ballets as well as the theater pieces. During this time period, the administrator and steward were still operating behind the scenes; there is no credit in the book for the people who conceived and managed the mounting of the elaborate feasts. Yet these positions are featured prominently in Félibien's texts for the festivals of 1668 and 1674, and the events are shown in three plates out of a total of nine for *Les plaisirs de L'isle enchantée.* On the title page of the latter, the performance and table settings with food are described as "collation ornée de machines." *Machine,* the term for "table pieces," is borrowed from stage design, where it describes theater sets and designs for street processions. *Machine* was also used, in both French and Italian (*macchina*), to refer to the tableaux erected along festival routes, elaborate festival carriages, and the designs for the Italian festival of

Cuccagna. At Versailles, the machines were elaborate sculptures and settings of food designed in complimentary ways as part of the overarching plan for the food service and display during meals (see Bremer-David, "Of Cauliflower and Crayfish," fig. 4).

All initial text pages of the three Versailles festival accounts are introduced by the engraver François Chaveau's playful chapter heads, which show putti engaged in the various activities planned for the festival (fig. 7). In a chapter head for *Les plaisirs de L'isle enchantée,* fireworks explode in the background. One putto carries a large platter of food over his head; a boy samples food from the banquet table as putti dance around it; others play a cello and dance with a tambourine. The chapter head serves as an "amuse-bouche" for the images and descriptions to come. With a large initial *L* ornamented with flowers, the text begins with an appropriate and obligatory nod to Louis XIV. Each festival in the *Cabinet du roi* series makes use of similar floriated initial *L*'s. More than just a beautifully designed page, the first leaf reveals the thoughtful coordination of all aspects of the festival, including the publications that came years later. The books serve to memorialize the events, craft the king's image, and write French history.

The prints depicting L'isle enchantée ceremonies were commissioned from Israël Silvestre, who held the title of *dessinateur et graveur du roi* (king's draftsman and engraver). Silvestre's skills as a vedutist were put to good use; he depicted the festival processions, theater productions, fireworks, and feasts as if they were on stage, all framed by architectural elements. The suite starts with an oblong vista that bears a

FIG. 7.

**François Chaveau
(French, 1613–76).**

Engraved chapter head, 7.2 × 15 cm (2⅞ × 6 in.). From André Félibien, *Les plaisirs de L'isle enchantée…* (Paris: Imprimerie royale, 1674), 3. Los Angeles, Getty Research Institute.

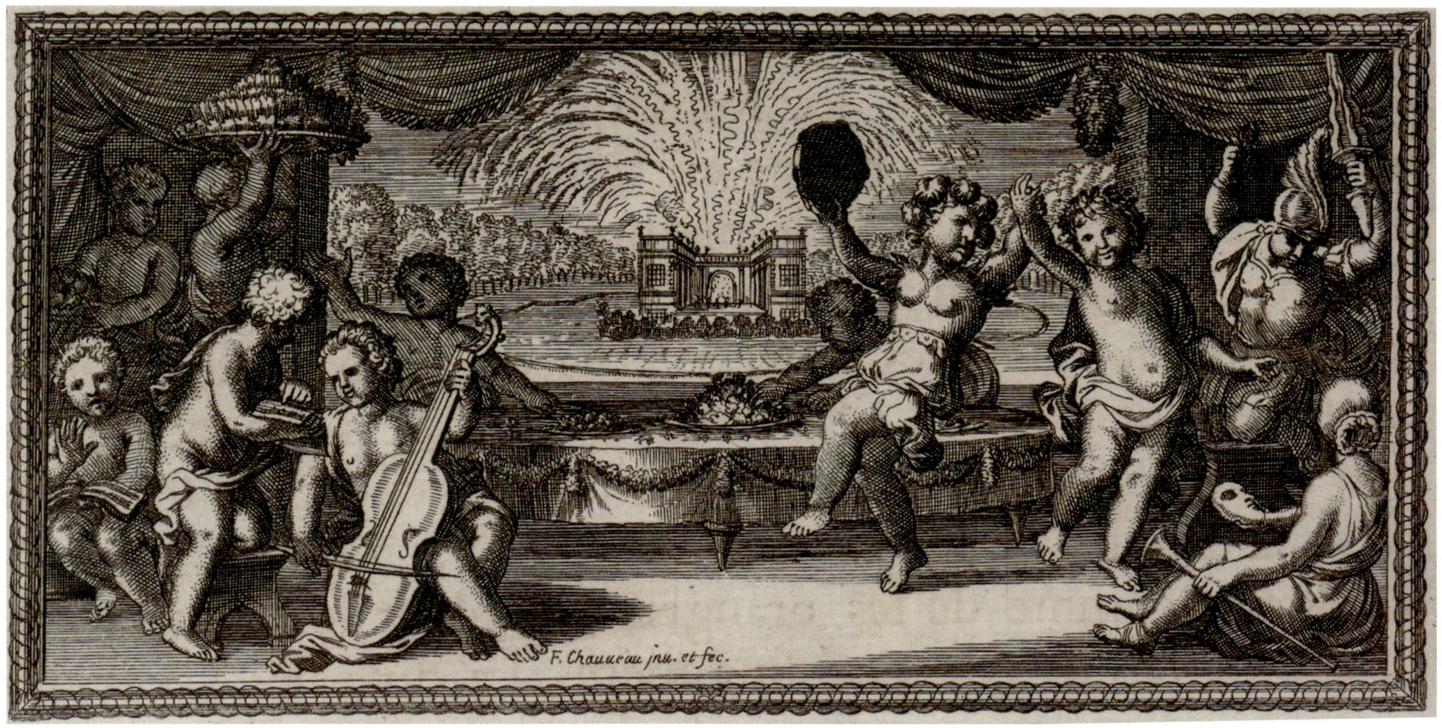

different version of the title, framed by heraldic escutcheons amid flower garlands, and then beautifully depicts the sequence of events.[15] Louis's court is in the garden. The ceremonies begin with the *course de bague*—richly dressed nobles competing on horseback to spear a ring in a display of beauty and might. That night, the first magnificent meal is preceded by a concert. The feast is introduced theatrically by members of the court who personify the Four Seasons: Madame du Parc, as Spring, rides on a Spanish horse (representing Europe); Sieur du Parc, as Summer, rides an elephant covered with rich fabric (Africa); Sieur de Thorilliére, as Autumn, rides a camel (Asia); and Sieur Béjard, as Winter, rides a bear (America). The exotic animals, possibly denizens of the menagerie at Versailles, serve to remind viewers that the whole world was in attendance. Although Félibien's text does not provide a specific list of dishes that were prepared for this banquet, the animals highlighted the diverse elements of the menu, including spices, sugar, and botanicals from all four corners of the world.

The choreographed procession of the Four Seasons continues for the dinner service; forty-eight servers, costumed as the seasons, carry great platters and bowls above their heads (figs. 8, 9). According to the caption for the print of the *première journée* (first day), these were foods and gifts made by the gods and the Four Seasons to be served to the king and queen, together with the princesses and ladies at their two tables.[16] Personifying spring, the first twelve servers are covered with flowers and bear, like gardeners, baskets painted green and silver and decorated with a great number of porcelain pieces; the baskets are so filled with sweets and other seasonal delicacies that the men are bent by the task. Representing summer, twelve harvesters wear farm clothes (but very nice ones) and hold basins of grains the color of the sunrise. For autumn, there are twelve vintners covered with grape leaves and grapes bringing baskets made of dead leaves, fruits, and autumnal delicacies. For winter, twelve old men, seemingly frozen, march slowly and feebly, carrying platters of ice and perfectly made snow.

In brief recitations, the Seasons speak to the queen, who is seated at a large crescent-shaped table decorated with flowers. Beginning with Spring, notably the month of this festival, the Seasons speak of their offerings to the banquet, echoing the service of the food: from the flowers to the harvest and the grapes, and finally the ices and snow of winter. Félibien concludes that the sumptuousness of this meal surpassed, as much in its abundance as in the delicacies that were served, all that was possible to write about it. The beautiful presentations appealed to all the senses; at nighttime there were an infinite number of chandeliers painted silver and green, each with twenty-four candles and two hundred torches in white wax, held by persons wearing masks.[17] Staged before an audience, this unimaginably rich garden banquet featuring the rich abundance of nature concluded the first day of the festival.

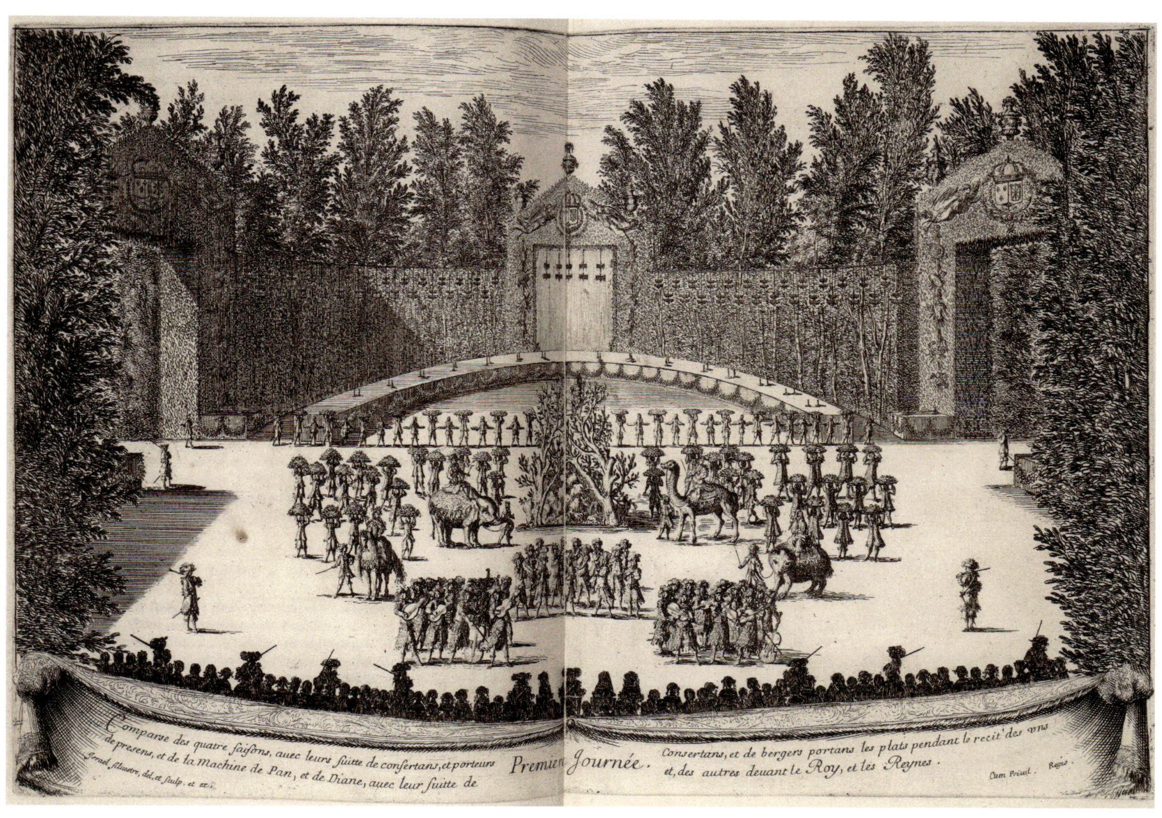

Comparse des quatre saisons, auec leurs suitte de consertans, et porteurs de presens, et de la Machine de Pan, et de Diane, auec leur suitte de consertans, et de bergers portans les plats pendant le recit des vns et des autres deuant le Roy, et les Reynes.   *Premiere Journée.*

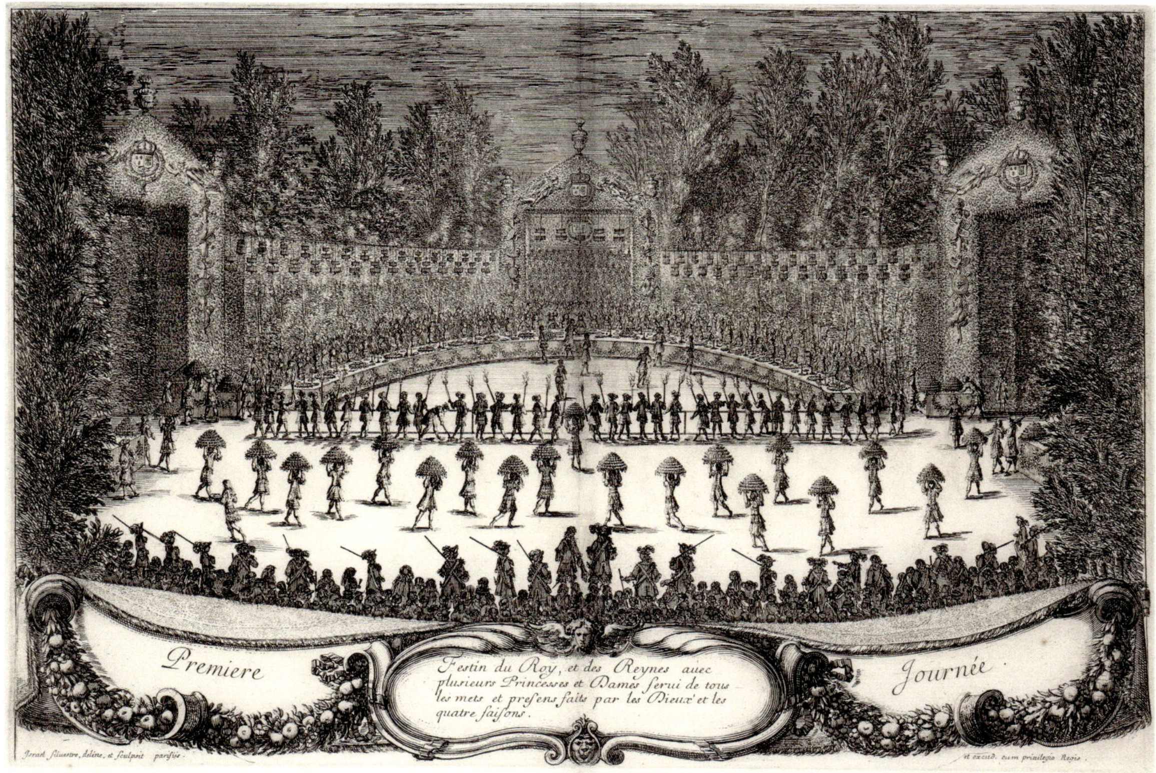

Premiere — Festin du Roy, et des Reynes auec plusieurs Princesses et Dames serui de tous les mets et presens faits par les Dieux et les quatre saisons. — *Journée.*

Relation de la feste de Versailles

Félibien's *Relation de la feste de Versailles* (1679; Account of the festival of Versailles) is the second festival book included in the *Cabinet du roi* compilation. The text states that the king had been absorbed by the business of the realm during Carnival and wished to show his beneficence to the citizens. Celebrating Louis's military conquests and the recent Treaty of Aix-la-Chapelle, the festival, held on 18 July 1668, sought to demonstrate balance in the king's administration by returning to the gardens at Versailles and providing entertainment and beauty for his subjects, rather than just a small selection of guests from his court. Making the most of the garden setting for this festival, the program included several grand banquets and suppers, a comedy by Jean-Baptist Lully, a ball, and spectacular fireworks. This time, the volume credits Bernardin Gigault de Bellefonds, the marshal of France and the king's *maître d'hotel* (household manager or steward), for the banquets, suppers, and all details regarding the table service.[18] Water was the special feature for this festival; fountains filled with sculptures of dragons and dolphins spewed bubbling jets.

As the guests walked through the labyrinths, taking five different paths, they found themselves in a leafy pentagonal enclosure where the paths came together. The gardeners had enclosed the space with greenery, bending and binding branches to make a kind of natural architecture. Jean Le Pautre's print *Collation donnée dans le petit parc de Versailles* (Banquet given in the little park at Versailles) depicts the central fountain with a grassy base (fig. 10). Five tables were set as buffets and offered all manner of things to compose a magnificent *collation.* Each table had a different food theme: a mountain with caverns in which guests saw all types of frozen meats; a palace facade constructed of marzipan and sugar paste; pyramids coated in cuttlefish confections; and one with innumerable vases full of liqueurs. The last display was made of caramels. The spaces were all decorated with garlands and flowers; green moss made a natural carpet. There were great vases of orange trees with candied fruit, accompanied by other kinds of fruit trees, also with candied fruit. In place of chairs, guests found "couches de melons" (possibly seats made of dense beds of melon or squash leaves), which seemed as if gods had created them to decorate the space.

The five paths leading to the garden enclosure formed a star. Out along the paths were twenty-six arcades of cypress trees, with grassy seats supporting vases planted with fruit-filled trees: the first path had only Portuguese orange trees; the second, white and red cherries mixed together; the third was lined with apricots and peaches; the fourth, Dutch currants; and the fifth, all kinds of pears. At the ends of the paths were leafy niches with sculptures, pilasters, and more vases of flowers. Flowers spelled out the king's initials amid the garlands and festoons.

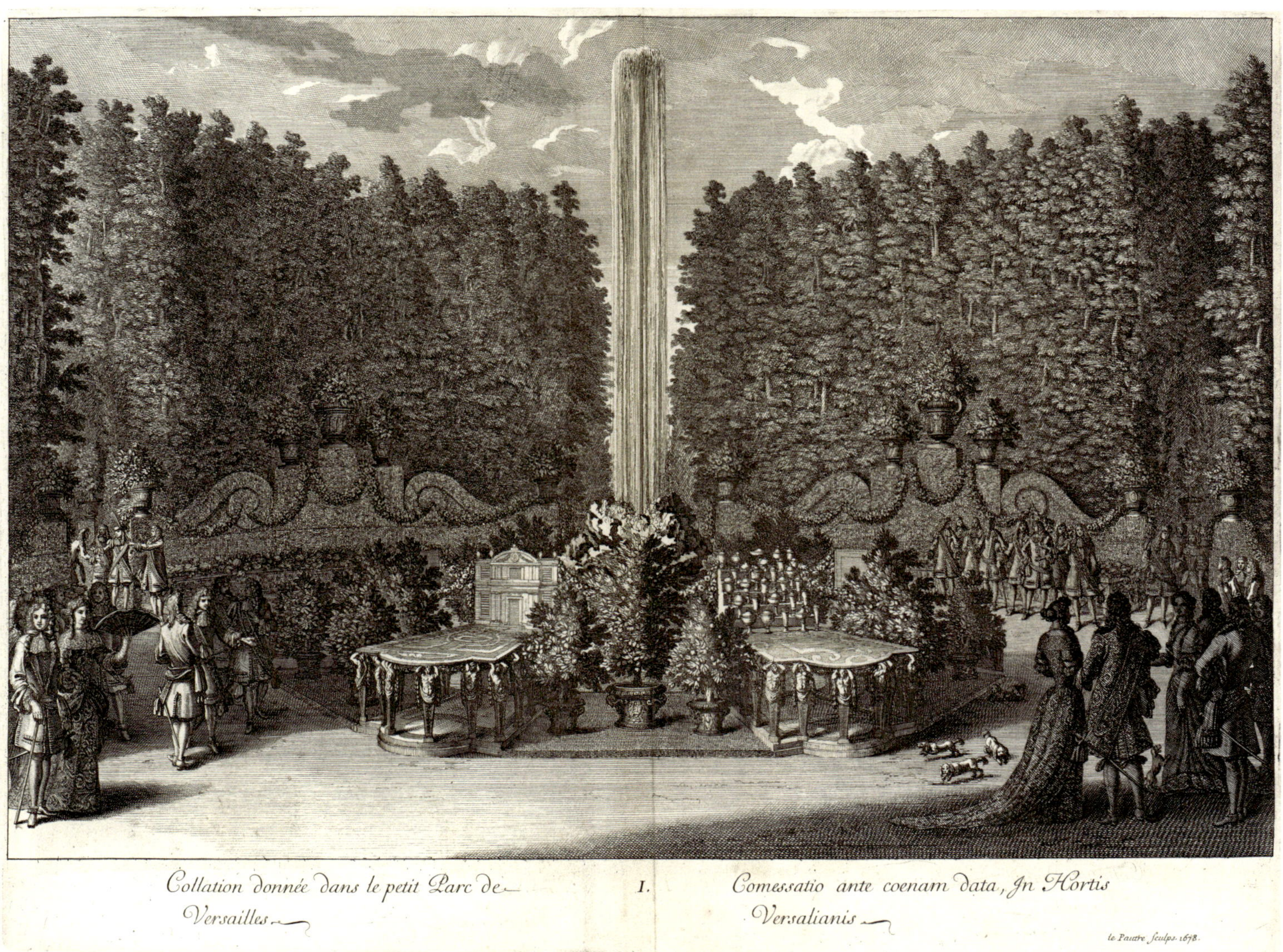

The final event of the night served two purposes: amusement and destruction. After the king and his court had finished their meals, the guests left the tables to be pillaged by the people who had been watching them dine. This activity served as entertainment for the court as they watched the tumult and confusion of the people as they demolished the marzipan castles and the mountains made of candies. The spectacle—enacted by the people—was often the finale of court banquets. It does much to explain how all the food was consumed and the theatrical presentations were broken down. The festival's decadence can be seen to presage the events of the revolution in the next century.

Following the conclusion of the banquet, the king and the court proceeded to the outdoor theater, which was decorated in honor of the festival with his coat of arms

FIG. 10.

Jean Le Pautre (French, 1618-82).

Banquet Given in the Little Park at Versailles, etching, 30.5 × 42.9 cm (12 × 16⅞ in.).

From André Félibien, *Relation de la feste de Versailles du 18. juillet mil six cens soixante-huit* (Paris: Imprimerie royale, 1679), pl. 1. Los Angeles, Getty Research Institute.

and figures representing peace and victory. Terms displayed satyrs who held baskets of fruit on their heads; jets of water came from fountains along a canal. The party then came upon a magnificent collation of Portuguese oranges, with thirty-six baskets stacked as a pyramid and many kinds of fruit at the base, continuing the theme of nature at the service of the king. The marshal de Bellefond and his men served, while Monsieur de Launay of the Menus-plaisirs du roi handed out libretti on the subjects of the comedy and the ballet. Members of the court acted out the pastoral piece by Lully, printed in full in the *Relation de la feste de Versailles.*[19] Their names and roles appear in the margins of the printed text.

After the comedy, the group repaired to another leaf-covered structure, this one octagonal with fountains, shown in Le Pautre's engraving of the *Festin donnée dans le petit parc de Versailles* (fig. 11). At the center is an eight-sided table set with sixty-four covers; a giant rock is set in the middle and Pegasus is rising, as the waters spill downward onto stones and shells. Rivulets of falling water are enameled with gold and azure, filling crystal cups. Apollo sits below, with the nine Muses and divinities. Félibien explains that no matter from which side one views the machine, there are different effects created by the light and water as they reflect the silver figures and the various colors of the stones and crystals.

Not surprisingly, the lavish displays at Versailles were not so much about the food and beverages as the extravagance and the art, except for those on the outside who waited for the signal to pillage, so they could satisfy their hunger and take away what they could gather. For the court, these edible monuments were about the materiality of food, displaying its perishable delicacies and desirable sensual beauties amid complementary special effects of scent, sound, light, and color. Candles twinkling ethereally were reflected in mirrors, silverware, colored stonework, and crystals. Gushing grottoes and torrents from fountains spewed streams on artistic rockeries with pearls and shells. As Félibien notes, the festivals at Versailles were intended to be a sensory barrage. The designs were meant to be astonishing not only to those in attendance but also to others who heard and read about them, so that they would long to be there and wish to give similar parties. Putting the French court on a world stage, the festivals were given substantial coverage in publications such as the *Mercure galant.* Félibien writes: "During such a charming entertainment, their majesties and all the court enjoyed the diversion of the ball, in view of the beautiful objects and the sound of the water which agreeably interrupted the sound of the instruments. Other spectacles were to come which no one would have imagined and which would astonish the entire world."[20]

As a finale, fireworks exploded over pools of water. Exactly when guests were leaving the ball, at a moment when everything seemed to be well ordered and

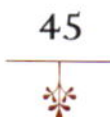

completely under control, the grounds of the chateau appeared to be on fire. Félibien describes how guests were taken by surprise, both in a startling or frightening way— as if there had been an attack or disaster—and in a way that gave pleasure and admiration. Recalling the military victories of the king, the fireworks displays provoked an agreeable disorder. Not knowing what to do, everyone withdrew or hid, sheltering in the shrubbery or throwing themselves on the ground.[21]

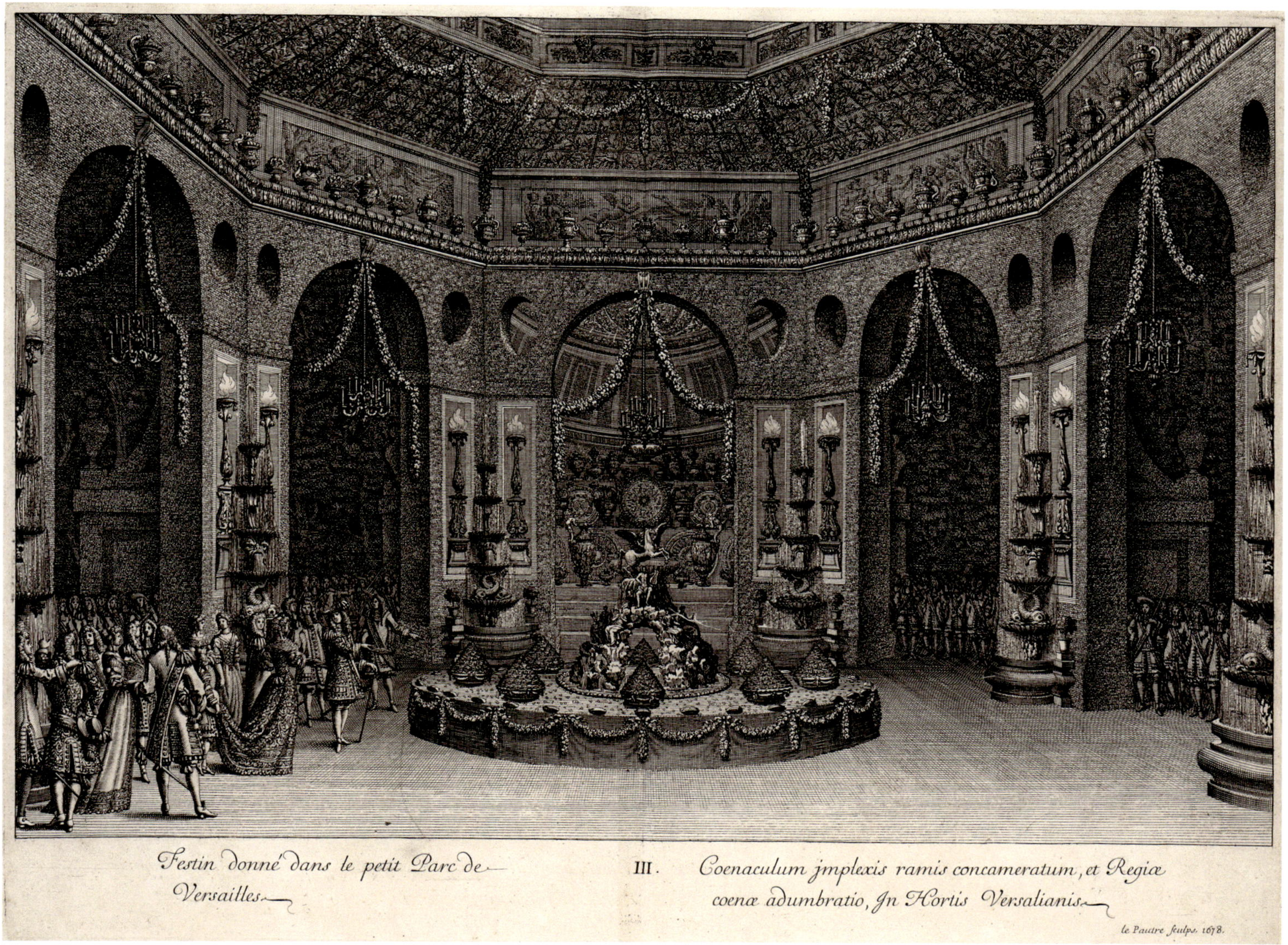

Yet this still was not the end of the spectacle. Another massive explosion of fireworks engulfed the sky, engraving the heavens with the initials of the king, the double *L*, shimmering overhead in the sky, leaving no doubt about the theme and subject of the celebrations. Now the party was officially over. Their majesties left with the court on the rue Saint Germain, while the dauphin remained at the chateau.

FIG. 11.

Jean Le Pautre (French, 1618–82).

Banquet Given in the Little Park at Versailles, 1678, etching and engraving, 30.5 × 42.9 cm (12 × 16⅞ in.). From André Félibien, *Relation de la feste de Versailles du 18. juillet mil six cens soixante-huit* (Paris: Imprimerie royale, 1679), pl. 3. Los Angeles, Getty Research Institute.

In all ways, this festival was the most memorable, surpassing all others. Félibien notes the extraordinary effort by which such a large number of events were prepared and presented in such a short space of time: the comedy, the ball, and the banquet; the diverse decorations with which they were embellished; the quantities of lights and waterworks created; and the sumptuous meals with inconceivably diverse quantities of meats. In the end, the astonishing amount of components and workers who made these spectacles possible elicited great admiration from the royal subjects. But who was the focus of the festival? Of course, it was the king who commanded great armies and effected swift conquests, triumphing over his enemies. In a similar way, the king had the power to assemble with similar efficacy the composers and musicians, the dancers, and all sorts of beautiful things.

In his laudatory summation, Félibien recalls Louis's antique precursors: "As a Roman captain said in earlier times, there is no less a great man who knows how to give an excellent celebration for his friends, as one who directs an army which is fearful to his enemies."[22] Félibien concludes that in the mounting of the festival, one can observe that in all his actions, the king demonstrated an equal and unique grandeur, in war and in peace. Thus, we see the importance and meaning of such a well-orchestrated and integrated festival program.

Les divertissemens

The third Versailles festival book in the *Cabinet du roi* compilation, *Les divertissemens* (1676; The entertainments), celebrated the "reduction" of the Spanish Franche-Comté upon the king's return from the Franco-Dutch War in 1674. In his prefatory comments, Félibien notes how the king's festivals were notable for their promptness. They appeared effortlessly, and almost miraculously, without the court's awareness of the people or the work involved.[23] Almost every day featured a collation with thousands of embellishments: fruits and pastries, flowers, festoons, and orange trees.[24] Liquid refreshments included crystal carafes and porcelains filled with liqueurs. The fourth day featured a spectacular buffet table in the garden with a marble fountain and illuminated column (see Reed, "Food, Memory, and Taste," fig. 3). This monumental outdoor table sculpture was a culmination. With the almost obligatory orange trees, seasonal fruits, pastries, and sweets, it was a collation of such grandeur and magnificence that it was truly royal.[25]

Moments of malfunction, such as the littered garden grounds after the fireworks, are not shown. The scene following the party is almost never described, though it is occasionally hinted at. Later, documentation of these realities would become the role of photography and twenty-first-century contemporary artists. The goal of Félibien and Perrault was to capture the king's world in its ideal form. How could the ruined

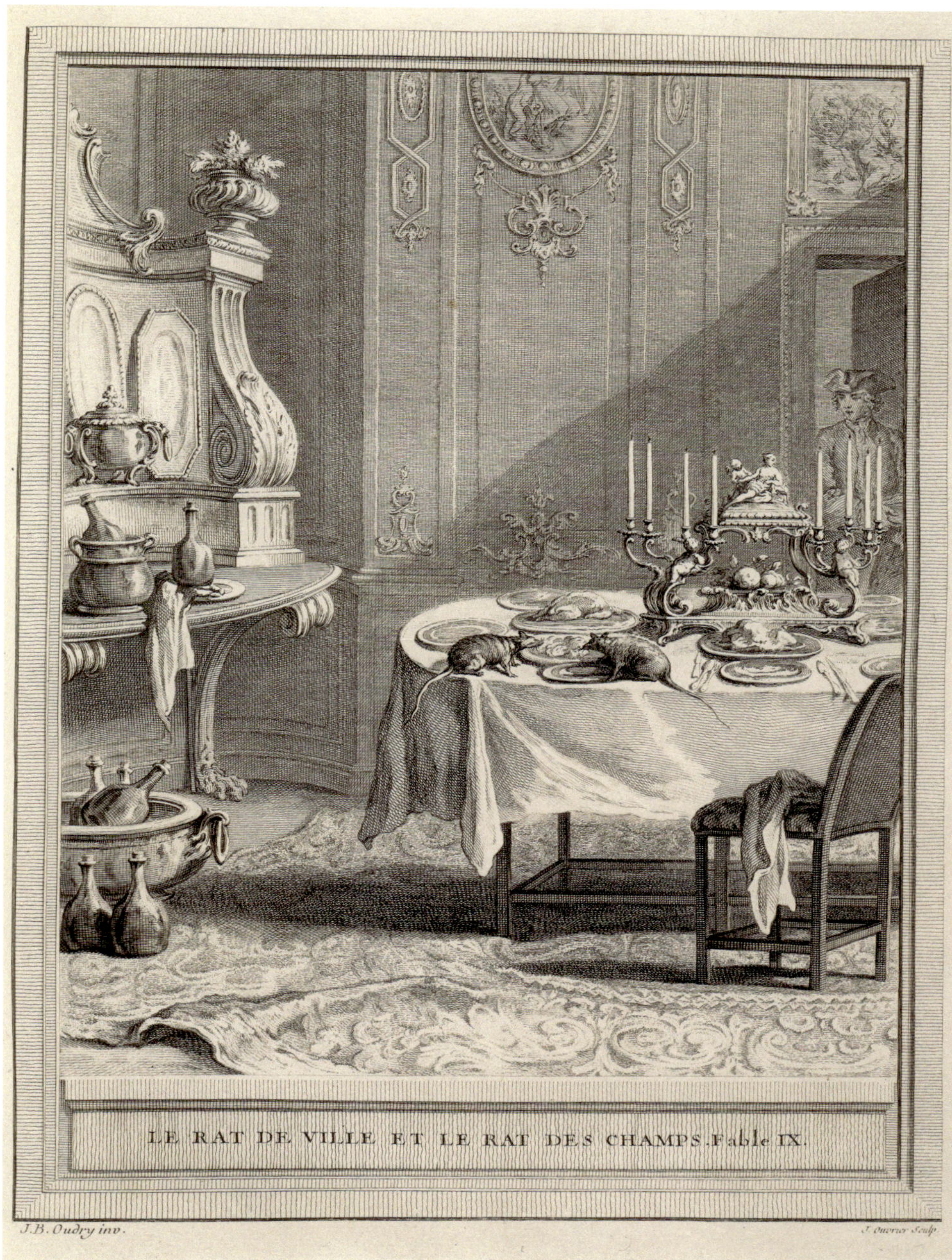

FIG. 12.

Jean Ouvrier (French, 1725–84), after Jean-Baptiste Oudry (French, 1686–1755).

The City Rat and the Country Rat, Fable IX, etching, 30.8 × 22.8 cm (12⅛ × 9 in.). From Jean de La Fontaine, *Fables choisies, mises en vers* (Paris: Desaint & Saillant, 1755–59), 1:18. Los Angeles, Getty Research Institute.

scene of a former garden of paradise be described? Who cleared the table after the Banquet of the Gods? What happened to the decaying, messy scene that needed to be cleaned up *tout de suite?* The closest we come to postprandial reportage is Jean-Baptiste Oudry's print published in *Fables choisies, mises en vers* (Selected fables written in verse), which illustrates the fable of the city rat and the country rat, who come to feast on the party leftovers. An ortolan remains on a table with a *surtout-de-table* as a centerpiece; a buffet with drinks and a display of plates faces the table (fig. 12).

HISTORIES ON PAPER

Like the festivals themselves, the illustrated *fête* books from the time of Louis XIV were planned down to the smallest details. A talented team was brought together to produce the books and prints, including the artists Israël Silvestre, Jean Le Pautre, and François Chaveau, as well as the writers Félibien and Perrault. Possessed of both literary and historical skills, they were well trained, on task, and on message for their roles. Félibien was the author of a multivolume biographical set on French artists, paralleling Giorgio Vasari's *Lives of the Artists* from a century before, and among numerous titles, he also wrote guides to Versailles, describing the gardens and grottoes.[26] Perrault was a member of the Académie française. He adapted Aesop's fables into the new genre of fairy tales and wrote the text for the first of Louis XIV's impressive series of illustrated festival books, *Festiva ad capita* (Festive figures; or, The Carousel), in 1662.

The artists brought complementary artistic skills, designing views that were dramatic, theatrical, and spacious—showing the conceptual breadth of the realm—and embellishing their designs with elegant decorative details. The texts and images are perfectly in sync and highly illustrative. In truth, this was easier to do when books were published after the events. The illustrations show what is described in a lifelike narrative, incorporating details on the persons involved and the food, demonstrating that they are not simply decorative but plausible and documentary. This is the value of the verisimilitude of Félibien's masterfully crafted texts, which fulfill their intention to illuminate the world of Louis XIV. They provide its decorum, describing all facets, particularly how things should operate in a world controlled by the king. As an integral part of the festival program, the deluxe publications contributed substantial added value, not only promoting the accomplishments of the king but also providing exemplars that could be emulated by other socially and politically ambitious rulers.

The books and prints were themselves extraordinary works, setting a new model for such publications. This is unsurprising because seventeenth-century French printmakers and publishers were considered to be the best in the world.[27] Designing the most lavish and heavily illustrated festival publications to date, they produced images and extended descriptions that were intended to travel. Far surpassing the Italian and German editions, the French festival books and prints were created as gifts and collectibles. They were made to be admired and, like the contemporary (seventeenth-century) French fashion plates, intended to disseminate French style and taste. The festival descriptions were published in the visionary series of the *Cabinet du roi,* a collection of printed works of the highest quality that exemplified French culture. These volumes circulated descriptions and images of French festival celebrations among European courts, traveling as far as the emperor of China, where the French missionaries included volumes among their many gifts to the Asian court. Among all the volumes in the *Cabinet du roi,* these publications prefigure the successes of the *Encyclopédie* in the next century. Like this far more extensive magnum opus, which encompasses the knowledge and culture of eighteenth-century France, the festival books and prints successfully enact the culture and social practices of the court of Louis XIV at the highest level. Even today, the publications are admired and much sought by bibliophiles and print collectors.

Designed to preserve the ensemble of the festival, the books and prints feature some of the most extravagant edible monuments and entertainment. Together, they provide the context of the entire festival program, which included theater pieces, garden amusements with water- and fireworks, mock tournaments, and costume parades, interspersed with elegantly designed banquets and informal buffets set out in the gardens and the labyrinths of the vast palace grounds at Versailles. Architecture and gardens in the prints frame and contain the banquets and suppers, showing them as beautiful vistas, and eminent guests populate the bejeweled world of French court culture. The banquet tables and food pieces themselves appear as theater. Service is choreographed—like a ballet, a carousel for food, or a parade. Displayed in leafy outdoor grottoes, the food sculptures and monuments are shown as wonders in a cabinet of curiosity. They are there to be admired and experienced by a variety of the senses. Significantly, the texts identify the king, the most favored guests, the chief stewards, and the event entrepreneurs, as well as the court, local audiences, and waitstaff. More than documentation of the table settings and covers, table sculptures, room arrangements, and buffet stagings, the illustrations and prints comprehend the entirety of the event designs in sweeping panoramic views that successfully show their grandeur. Candles and torches lighting night banquets are shown reflected by silver and mirrors; surprising pyramids of edibles in Versailles loom amid garden grottoes; explosions of fireworks rain down over the fountains.

There were many grand court festivals in this early modern era and considerable numbers of publications about them, yet these works cleverly seek to present and hence to preserve the ambitious nature of the festivities, conveying both their ephemerality and immediacy. Illustrations of all these events were made for beautiful, large-scale picture books that describe the circumstances of the celebration. Festival accounts characteristically contain prints that are inconveniently folded some eight times to fit into quarto-size volumes. Versailles festival books were responsible for a new innovation: illustrations as double-page spreads, made for easy viewing, bound with the texts. When bound properly, the illustrations are not ganged together in the front or back of the book but rather placed amid the accompanying texts to serve as an ongoing guide. This arrangement assists with composing a continuous narrative of the entire program.

Festival prints can be surprisingly schematic, showing the choreographic systems or the artistic designs but not the actual festival staging or events in progress. Created by the principal French printmakers of the time, the Versailles prints present signal festival events as artistic compositions, like theater scenes on a paper stage. Shown at different times of the day, and with various audiences, the prints capture the events and art at selected thrilling moments, conveying extreme sensations and strong emotions, such as anticipation when picturesque platters of food are being served; amazement when nobility arrive in costumes, parading on similarly dressed horses and riding exotic animals from the menagerie; and astonishment when the fireworks explode like giant shooting stars. As frames for the wondrous visions of the king and his court, the prints also show the gawking crowds. These images give the viewer a way back into history.

What was missing from the French *fête* books was color. Félibien describes the vivid hues of the settings: the greenery in the garden grottoes, the pearly sheen (nacre) of the shells, the orange trees with blossoms and fruit, the azure blue of the ceramics (the complementary color to orange), and the glittering gold and silver wares on display. The books and prints are almost never colored. While they were beautifully ornamented and illustrated, the black and white of the letterpress and engravings pales beside another parallel area of contemporary graphic production, fashion plates.

Another perspective concerning the pursuit of pleasure at Versailles, this time an insider's view, is provided by Antoine Trouvain's suite of six prints, *Appartements ou amusements de la famille royale à Versailles* (1694-98; Apartments or amusements of the royal family at Versailles). A student of the eminent court engraver Gérard Edelinck, Trouvain is known for his engraved portraits and especially sumptuous fashion plates, which circulated current Parisian modes of dress styles. The apartment scenes show daily life at Versailles, particularly the evening pastimes (*jours d'appartement*), such as card games, concerts, and dances. The sixth apartment scene depicts a group of fashionably dressed men posed stiffly to show their extravagant outfits (fig. 13). They stand in front of a tiered buffet, which displays valuable golden platters above fruit and sugar pyramids, while a servant pours drinks. The elaborately set table corresponds perfectly to the guests' decorous appearance. The hand-colored prints show that impressive displays of refreshments and tableware were well integrated into the established and expected practices of dressing up and courtly demeanor, revealing how both food and fashion were significant elements of the codified social graces at Versailles.

Trouvain's print does not show the exact contents of the buffet, but such details were described in the *Mercure galant:* In December 1697, in the Salle de Venus at Versailles, tables lit by silver torches and many kinds of ornamental candles were

presented together with flowers and pyramids of cooked fruit, lemons and oranges, pastries and cakes of all types. The buffet was available for about four hours during the entertainment, so that guests could help themselves.

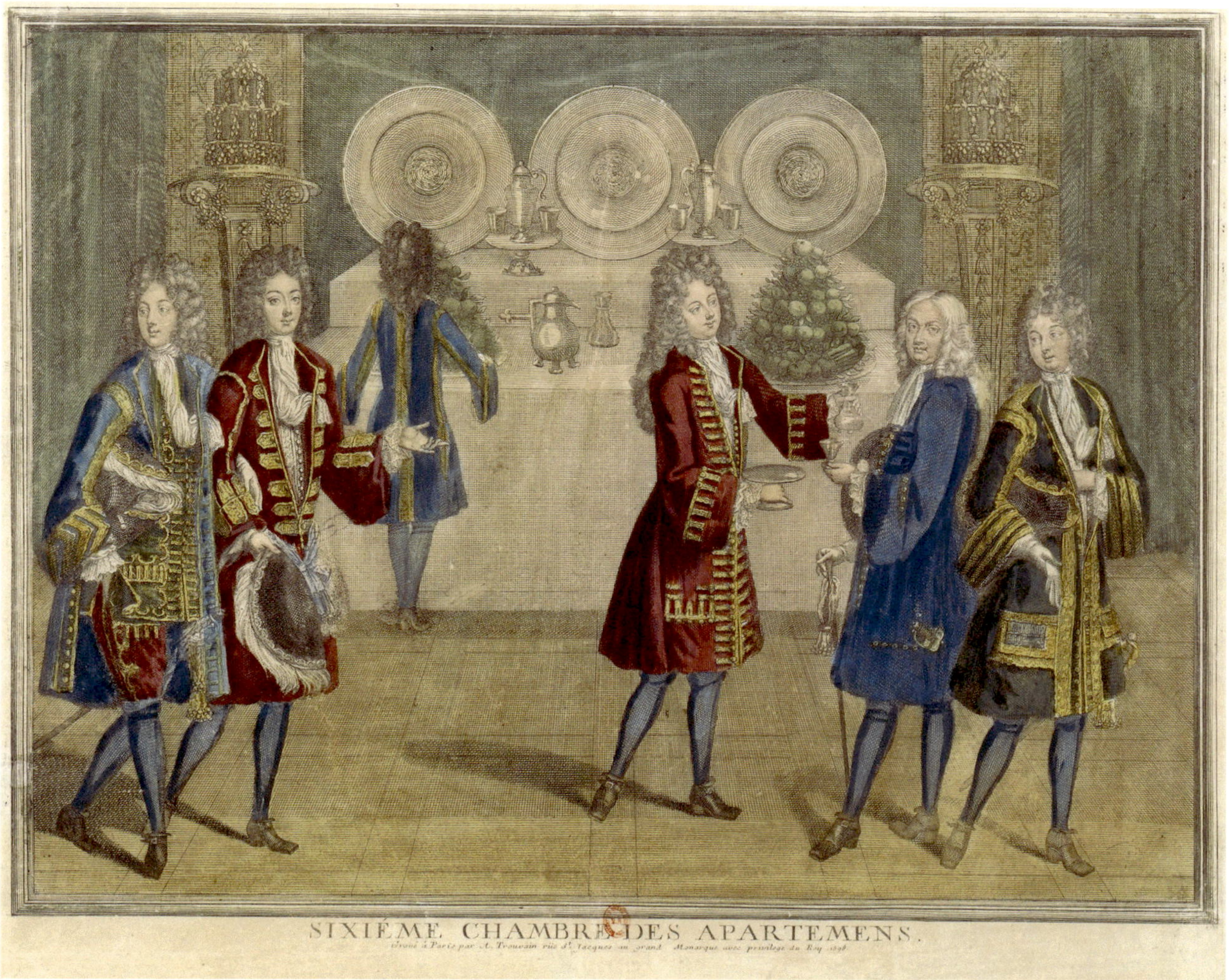

In the Salle des buffets, a considerable amount of art framed the offerings of sustenance. There were bas-reliefs depicting abundance and suitably embellished by festoons, paintings by Ludovico Carracci (*Aeneas Carrying His Father*)[28] and Guido Reni (*The Flight into Egypt*), a portrait of the king on horseback, Paolo Veronese's *Betsabée* (Bathsheba), porphyry busts, chandeliers on gold and blue pedestals, and a silver hanging chandelier in the middle. Three large buffets were set at the sides of the room. The middle one, below a large silver shell, held hot drinks: coffee and chocolate. The two other buffets offered liqueurs, sorbets, and water flavored by many kinds of fruits; and there was the excellent wine. The writer notes that all this was done with considerable order and propriety.[29]

FIG. 13.

Antoine Trouvain
(French, ca. 1653–1708).

The Sixth Chamber of the Apartments, 1698, engraving and etching, 35 × 43.5 cm (13¾ × 17⅛ in.). Paris, Bibliothèque nationale de France.

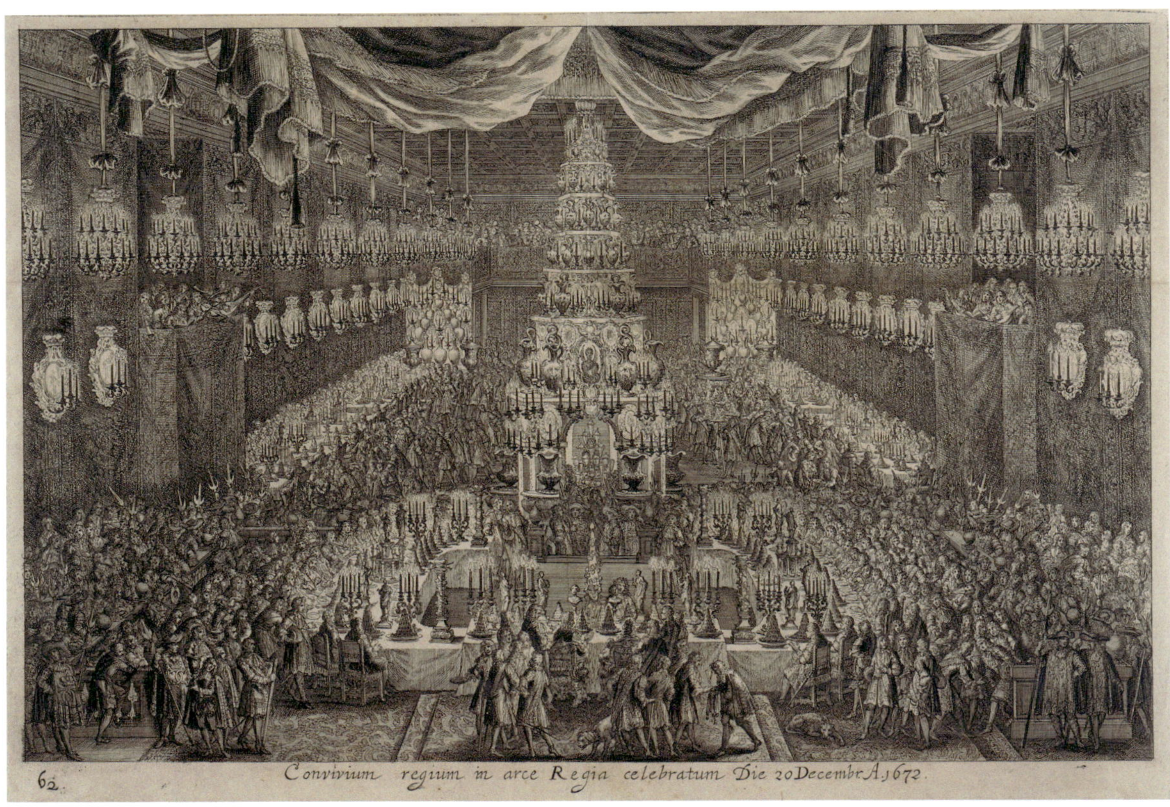

Convivium regium in arce Regia celebratum Die 20 Decembr A 1672.

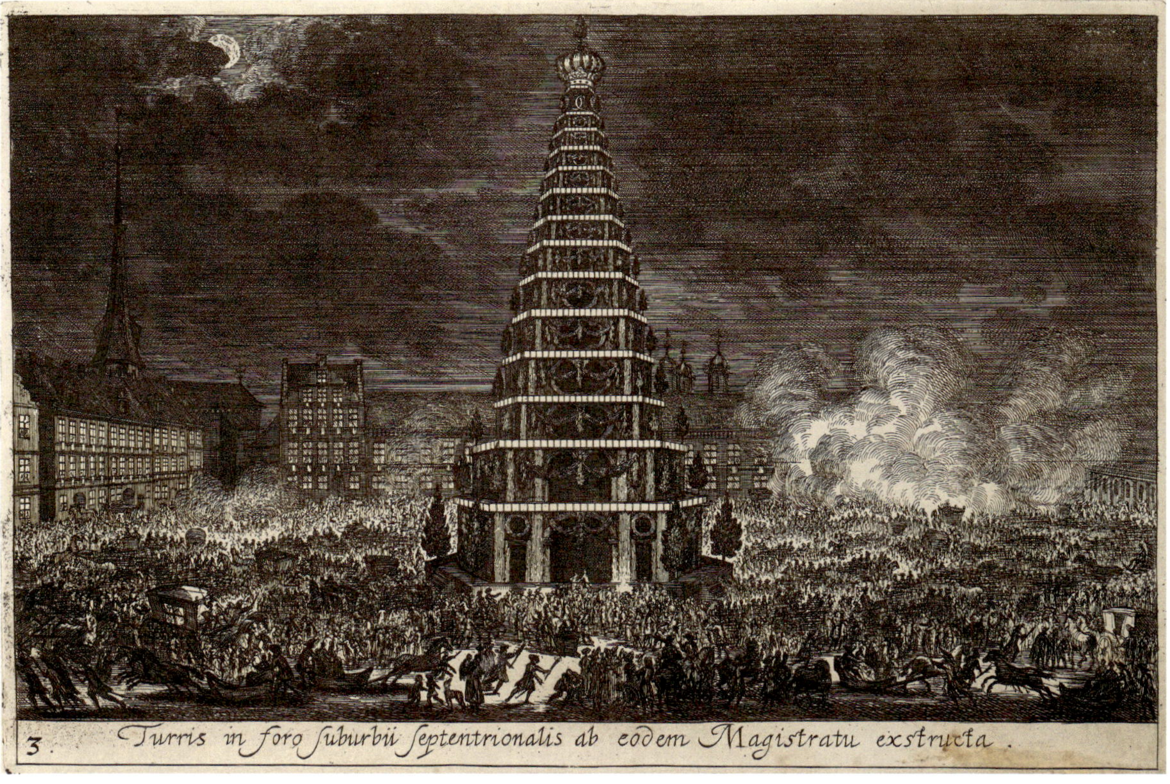

Turris in foro suburbii septentrionalis ab eodem Magistratu exstructa.

Presenting theatrical views, the French prints were elegantly populated by participants and onlookers. A more crowded, possibly truer view from this same period appears in the account of the festival given for the coronation of Charles XI of Sweden in 1672. Published more than a decade after the celebration, *Das grosse Carrosel und prächtige Ring-Rännen* (1685; The grand carousel and superb ring race) echoes the first great festival of Louis XIV, the Grand Carousel of 1662 at the Palais des Tuileries. The Swedish volume trumps the French publication, *Festiva ad capita,* with its lavish number of illustrations, totaling sixty-three etchings, including many plates of costumed riders, well-dressed horses, and the pressing crowds who came to see the festival. As the finale, the grandest illustration is the foldout scene of the banquet, which took place in a large hall with balconies, after the procession through Stockholm. Surrounded by hundreds of partygoers, the print shows the *Schau-Essen,* a towering candle-illuminated table piece mounted in the center of a vast throng of guests and servers (fig. 14). It ascends to the ceiling with eight tiers of urns and candelabra, repeating the design of an illuminated tower erected in a suburban city square, shown earlier in the book (fig. 15). "Beautiful and noble" table sculptures, architectural pieces, and pyramids of sweets at a reduced scale adorn the smaller tables, repeating the design of the decorative pyramids of food with candelabra at the head table, as more food is served from the rear of the hall.[30]

WHEN IN ROME

During the seventeenth and eighteenth centuries, Rome was a primary venue for festivals, many of which were organized there by foreigners, in an effort to stage celebrations at the ancient center of culture and to pay homage to the Catholic Church. At the end of the seventeenth century, Romans had festivals to celebrate the return to health of the French king Louis XIV following surgery. An especially lavish event was held in front of the church of Trinità dei Monti, with fireworks bursting above the church towers. Vicenzo Coronelli, the royal cosmographer in Venice in 1687, published images of this festival in *Roma festeggiante nel Monte Pincio* (Roman celebrations at Monte Pincio). The large print for this celebration of Louis's recovery, *Réjouissances publiques…* (Public rejoicing), features the Garden of the Hesperides, land of the golden apples. Cedar trees filled with transparent illuminated oranges line the ascent from the streets up to the French church portal. Cedar and orange trees were also staples of Versailles festivals; their strong fragrances and flavors, which were often combined with white sugar to make conserves, were treats for the senses.[31] As signature festival fruits, oranges were emblematic. In *Courses de testes et de bague* (Tournament games), the French edition of *Festiva ad capita,* Perrault describes the heraldic symbol of the Marquis de Ragny, noting that orange trees have the most beautiful blossoms and fruits, not to mention leaves. Concerning the similar heraldry

FIG. 14.

Georg Christoph Eimmart the Younger (Swedish, 1638–1705), after David Klöcker Ehrenstrahl (Swedish, 1628–98).

Royal Banquet Celebrating the Coronation …, etching, 31.8 × 49.4 cm (12½ × 19½ in.). From *Das grosse Carrosel…* (Stockholm: Joh. G. Eberdt, 1685), pl. 62. Los Angeles, Getty Research Institute.

FIG. 15.

Georg Christoph Eimmart the Younger (Swedish, 1638–1705), after David Klöcker Ehrenstrahl (Swedish, 1628–98).

Tower Erected in a City Square Celebrating the Coronation, etching, 31.8 × 49.4 cm (12½ × 19½ in.). From *Das grosse Carrosel…* (Stockholm: Joh. G. Eberdt, 1685), pl. 3. Los Angeles, Getty Research Institute.

of the Count de Sery, he writes that flowers of the tree are the assurance of the fruit they will bear.[32] If real, the oranges could have been eaten as well. Like the festivals at Versailles, the Roman event held for Louis XIV conjured a sensory assault to astonish and satiate both the guests who were present and those who viewed the large-format prints. Echoing the Versailles festival books, *Roma festeggiante nel Monte Pincio* has design elements that integrate festival themes—for example, the opening pages have a leafy, historiated, large initial *L* in the dedication by Coronelli to the French king. However, the large prints of the ephemeral festival arts are folded within the volume, with the bulky images inserted into the text awkwardly. By comparison, they demonstrate the elegant and thoughtful design of the French festival volumes.

The History of the Coronation of James II

Although quantities of books were printed in London, the English never had a fine-tuned industry for publishing festivals. Compared with continental examples, English festival books are disappointing, lacking graceful designs and presentations that would have enhanced and memorialized their subjects. Such publications seem to be most concerned with documenting events and writing history, rather than achieving an artistic elegance that would itself represent the festival in an impressive way. With the exception of the one particular work by John Michael Wright, to be discussed below, the English vision for festival books, including prints of banquets, was certainly not on the scale of the French, whose books successfully illustrate the sophisticated sensibilities of French culture as displayed in ephemeral performances or artworks.

Sad to say, English festival books, including prints of banquets, simply do not convey a suitably artistic grand view. The lofty title of Francis Sandford's publication for the coronation of James II in London in April 1685 makes special note of the banquet and the accompanying illustrations: *The History of the Coronation of…James II … and of his royal consort Queen Mary…with an Exact Account of the Several Preparations in Order Thereunto, Their Majesties Most Splendid Processions, and Their Royal and Magnificent Feast in Westminster-Hall* (1687). The ceremonies themselves are shown with stiff formality. These depictions were relatively easy to produce because, by this time, there were visual models and elaborate rituals and ceremonies, still enacted today, for coronations, weddings, and funerals. Hence, standard images of banquets show the king and queen at the head table, with long tables of guests seated beneath paintings or tapestries. Sewers stand behind them. Servants, dishes for bones, and dogs milling around and beneath the tables efficiently clear the tables. Seen from above, table settings are shown as a circular pattern of the covers (place settings for guests) and food placements. Like formal garden designs, these images were borrowed from the serving manuals that had begun to proliferate and circulate among chefs and stewards (fig. 16).

FIG. 16.

Samuel Moore

(English, fl. 1680–1720).

A Prospect of the Inside of West-minster Hall, Shewing How the King and Queen with the Nobility and Others Did Sit at Dinner on the Day of the Coronation, 23 April 1685…, engraving, 42.3 × 50 cm (16¾ × 19¾ in.).

From Francis Sandford, *The History of the Coronation of…James II… and of His Royal Consort Queen Mary…* (London: In the Savoy, printed by T. Newcomb, 1687). Los Angeles, Getty Research Institute.

Chapter 8, "The Royal Feast," close to the end of the book, describes "Their Majesties Table." The banquet was furnished by the king's master cook, Patrick Lamb, whose own cookbook, *Royal Cookery; or, The Compleat Court-Cook,* appeared in 1710. Lamb not only provides recipes but also documents the table arrangements for specific meals (fig. 17). The text for Sandford's coronation book lists the guests at each table (noting how many and indicating what their status deserved) and the dishes they were served. "The Catalogue" of the dishes takes six full pages, divided into three sections: "Their Majesties Table at the Upper End"; "Peers and Peeresses (Upper End of the First Table on the West Side)"; and "Archbishops, Bishops, Barons of the Cinque-Ports, Judges, etc. (Upper End of the First Table on the East Side)." The list is a riveting array of the 1,445 dishes, including pistachio cream, anchovies,

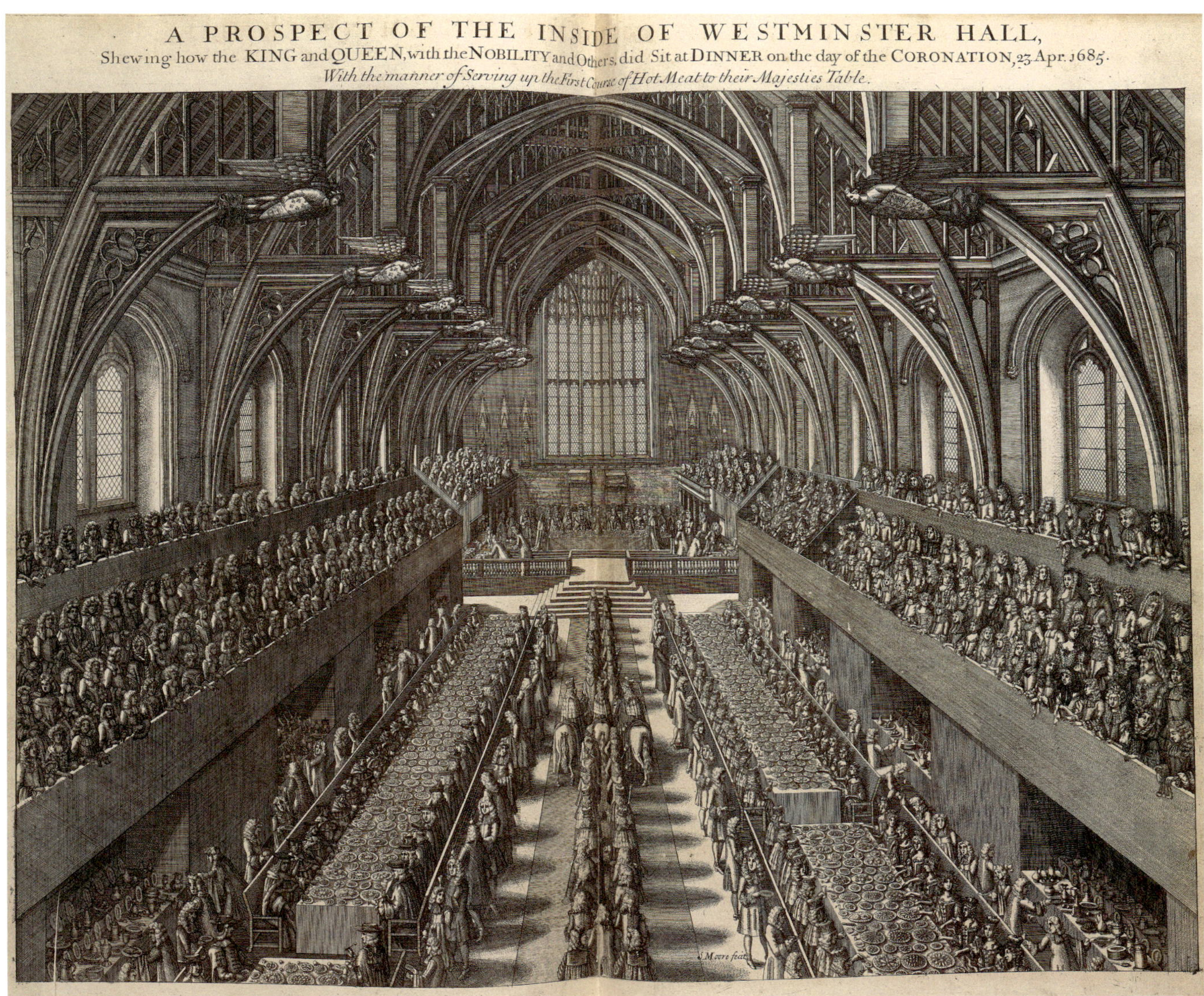

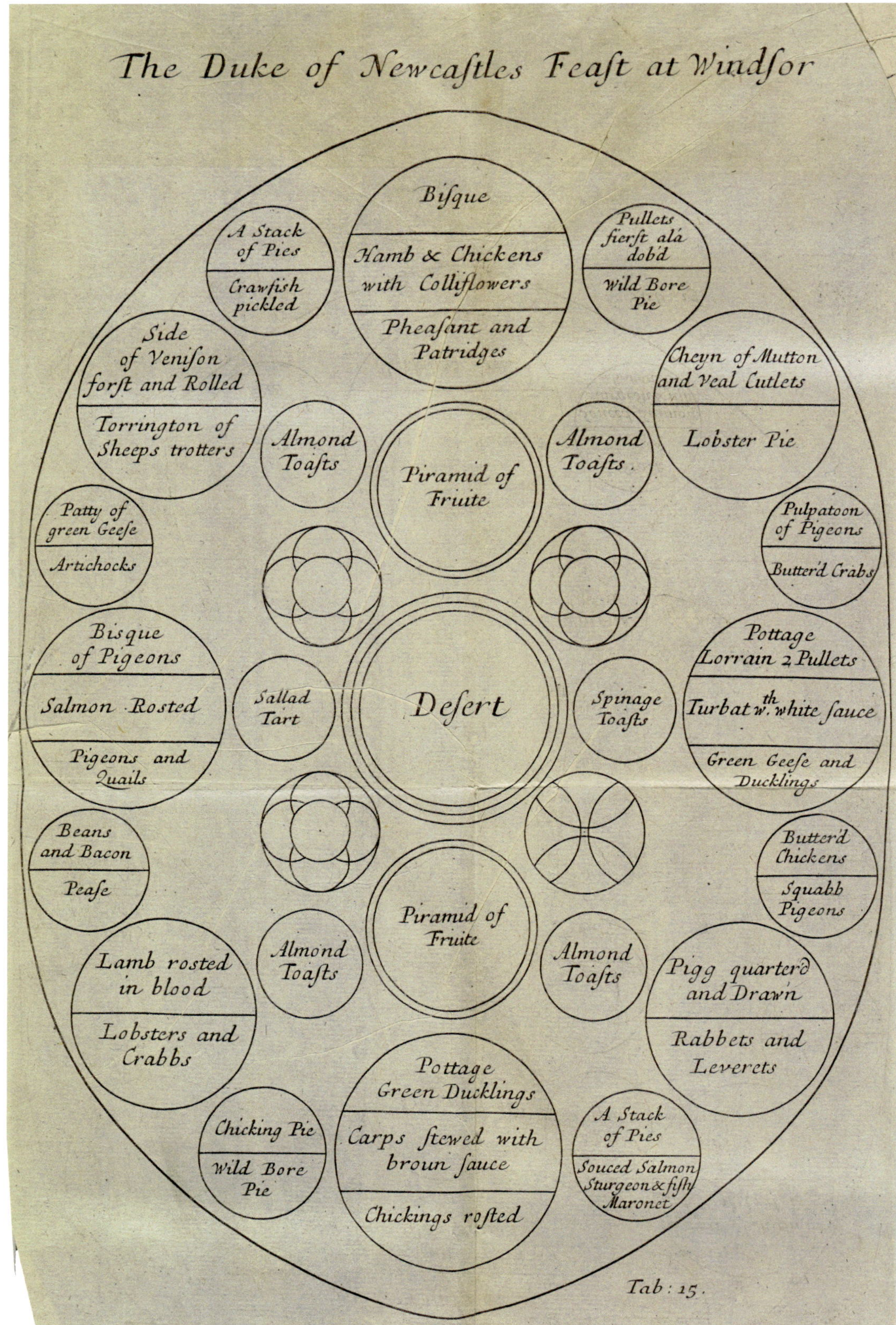

FIG. 17.

Patrick Lamb

(English, 1650–1708/9).

The Duke of Newcastle's Feast at Windsor, engraving, 26 × 17.3 cm (10¼ × 6¾ in.).

From *Royal Cookery; or, The Compleat Court-Cook* (London: Printed for Abel Roper, and sold by John Morphew, near Stationers-Hall, 1716), pl. 25.

Los Angeles, Collection of Anne Willan and Mark Cherniavsky.

jelly, crayfish, bologna sausages, collops and eggs, rabbit, pickled oysters, Portuguese eggs, mushrooms, beef, veal, hogs' tongues, cheesecakes, asparagus, salmon, pheasant, pigeon, chicken, artichokes, lamb, bacon, and pig. The meal also included table pieces in the form of square and circular pyramids, which rose above the serving platters.

An Account of His Excellence Roger Earl of Castlemaine's Embassy:

A Roman Banquet for the English King

One exceptional publication describes a festival banquet celebrating the rule of King James II. It did not take place in England but rather in Rome, on behalf of the embassy led by Roger Palmer, Earl of Castlemaine, to garner the support of the Papacy for the reestablishment of the Catholic Church in England. Pope Innocent XI and others neither respected nor liked Castlemaine for various personal reasons having to do with his reputation for having a volatile character. His wife's affair with King Charles II (said to be with Castlemaine's consent) was as problematic on moral grounds as for reasons of respectability. The ambassador presented several demands for ecclesiastical titles to which the pope did not wish to accede.[33] Of course, no difficulties of this sort are mentioned in the text, which skirts the complicated issues of religion and English politics during this period. Castlemaine's stay in Rome was brief, from April 1686 to June 1687, paralleling James II's short reign from 1685 until the Glorious Revolution in 1688. Although the political connection never sparked, the book and its images still astonish to this day (see Imorde, "Edible Prestige," figs. 1–3).

In this case, it was an entrepreneurial artist, John Michael Wright, who not only conceived and managed the festive events but also wrote two nearly identical illustrated books that record the banquet in Italian (1687) and English (1688).[34] Wright was an English artist (possibly with Scottish roots) who had previously spent time in Rome in the 1640s and 1650s; in 1648, he became a member of the Accademia di San Luca. Wright was an accomplished artist who painted for two English kings— Charles II and his brother James II. His forte was portraits, but he also produced religious subjects and copies. Wright collected prints, paintings, gems, shells, medals, and books. He had an extensive library. These collections were sold in 1694, the year of his death.[35] From the mid-1650s, he held a post in Flanders as an antiquary with Archduke Leopold, governor of the Spanish Netherlands; the archduke probably dealt occasionally in art and curiosities as well. Wright came back to London in 1656. He returned to Rome in 1686 to work as the majordomo at the Castlemaine embassy, possibly because of his extensive knowledge of Italian culture and language, not to mention the compatibility of his Catholic faith with his king's. As an engaged artist and author, Wright took extraordinary care with the production qualities of the book. In the context of festival books, Wright's multivalent role serves as a reminder that it is always important to determine who is behind the publication.

Wright's book is a firsthand account—no doubt idealized—that focuses on the integrated decorative arts created in approximately ten months for Castlemaine's festival, including opulent table sculptures and equally lavish carriage ornaments. Following the model of the French festivals, Wright employed established artists and printmakers to reproduce the sugar-paste designs, table settings, and banquet hall, as well as the richly decorated carriages. The illustrations convey the art and conspicuous luxury of Castlemaine's circumstances in Rome. Food is described in the texts, but it is not shown in the prints, which present the artistic frame of the banquet.

Not surprisingly, the book presents an optimistic view of the Castlemaine embassy. During his progress in 1686 from England to Italy, through France, the earl received enthusiastic welcomes and support for the English king while enjoying luxurious travel and fabulous dining. Although he was said to be traveling incognito, he was greeted and feted in every city he passed through. Stopping in Avignon, the party was welcomed and entertained extravagantly. A magnificent supper consisted of four services, with nine grand dishes and fourteen small *entremets*. In the middle of supper, Castlemaine toasted the health of His Holiness; the vice legate returned the favor to the English king. Six guns were fired, and then food was served to all.[36] The Avignon stay continued with several more meals, described by Wright:

> Not without particular Elogies, to the Lord Embassador, were the entertainment of the morning; and that over, the whole company return'd to the Palace, where, a Dinner, even superiour to the Supper, waited them, and that, So beautifully garnisht, with intermixt Figures, relating to the Triumphs of England, that the like, had been scarce there before, or to be seen any where again, if his Excellence the Lord Embassador, had made no entertainment at Rome.[37]

Looking ahead, Wright made special note of the table sculptures, which prefigured those to be designed for the forthcoming grand banquet he would oversee in Rome. After two more banquets, the party moved on to Livorno.

Arriving in Rome on Holy Saturday, the group settled into "the most troublesome part of the Embassy…the Equipage and preparations for the publick Entry."[38] The coaches of the papal court were known for their magnificence and splendor. The court members had the richest liveries, and the most valuable horses, all adorned with brocade, embroidery, gold lace, and fringe.

Nearly ten months after the arrival of the embassy, Castlemaine held a grand banquet and concert at his Roman residence, the Palazzo Pamphilj on Piazza Navona.

The party was held on 14 January 1687, just a week after the earl's papal reception on 8 January. Staged at a high time for Roman festivals, this Anglo-Roman festival aimed to integrate itself into local practices. Principal guests were the eighty-four cardinals and prelates, who are identified but never shown in the book.

Wright describes the heraldic devices of the king and the pope, which were created in great detail for the palace facade. There was an orchestrated progress of guests through the palace after they descended from their decorated carriages, shown on six plates in the first part of the book. Initially, they made their way through the Great Hall, which provided the showy preview of the foods and tableware essential to grand banquets. Wright comments:

> The Great, or outward Hall (which is one of the fairest and best proportioned Rooms, that can be seen anywhere) was surrounded with 53 long Tables, cover'd with excellent Linnen, and fill'd, with wonderful quantities of Fruit, Sweetmeats, Parmegian Cheese, and other delicacies, belonging to the Desert, or last Course; For thus are the Italians wont at their Solemn Feasts, that by exposing to the Spectators, one part of the Entertainment, they may better judge, what the whole will be.[39]

Beyond the dessert tables were familiar festival buffet displays: beneath a canopy, there was a cupboard, or credenza, on which were mounted shimmering round silver plates (an obligatory part of the ambassador's household goods), Venetian glass, and crystal vessels. In the last room before the dining room were the English gilt plates. For two days before the banquet, the decorations and some foods were on display for interested visitors. Between the sculptures and artfully folded napkins were two rows of salty, sweet, and sour *entremets,* including pickles, butter, delicate bacon slices, bologna sausages, and *tartufoli* (truffles).[40] Swiss Guards and thirty servants were in attendance to keep the food on the table and the parade of onlookers in order and away from the food. The eight-foot-wide table was set for eighty-four guests. The feast itself had twenty-four imperial dishes and a carver for every eight guests, and a server for each person. There was a service of ten courses, after which the table was cleared of all sculptures and dishes for the dessert (see Imorde, "Edible Prestige").

Tapestries were hung in the dining hall, which Wright modestly calls "a gay and pleasant Gallery" and which was notable for its frescoes by Pietro da Cortona.[41] Above the banquet table was a life-size portrait of King James II. However, the etching in the book is remarkably similar to Wright's painting of Charles II.[42] Such a grand royal portrait was an important element of the ambassador's residence. Centrally hung above the banquet table, the portrait served as a surrogate presence of the English king for whom the Earl of Castelmaine was the royal representative.

While this was an English diplomatic embassy seeking the support of the Catholic Church, the event featured classical mythology. Indeed, it was a Banquet of the Gods. Echoing the artistic themes of the grand festival carriages, the gods Cybele, Juno, Neptune, and Vulcan—the four elements—appear on the table in their chariots (see Imorde, "Edible Prestige," figs. 2, 3). Like the festival arts of Versailles and Vienna, decorative themes meld the rulers' emblematic virtues such as justice, peace, and valor, with myth, heraldry, and family symbols. Palm trees, for example, acknowledge the ambassador's family name. However, Wright is most proud of the sugar-paste table settings, describing them at great length. Down the middle of the table ran a range of "Historical Figures (some almost half as big as…Life) which the Italians, call Trionfi. They are made of a kind of Sugar-Pafte, but modeled to the utmost skill of a Statuary; So that they are afterwards, sent as Presents to the greatest Ladies; and their use at Entertainments, is to gratifie the Eye, as the Meat, Musique, and Perfumes, do the other Senses." Nature is present only in re-creations and marvelous reproductions of creatures who play a symbolic role: "Between these stood great Vases of Artificial Flowers and (to fill up the empty spaces of the middle) there were a wonderful Company of Birds in a flying posture, on lesser Plates and as many Lyons, Unicorns, and Eagles, on larger, alluding to the supporters, and bearings, of both their Majefties."[43]

As a comprehensive overview of the artistic designs created for the embassy—the carriages (called "machines"), the carved and painted heraldic plaques for the palace entry, and, most importantly, the decorations for the grand banquet setting—this festival book's great value resides in the considerable attention paid to the iconography of the table sculptures made of sugar paste, called *trionfi*. The dedicatory images of King James II, Pope Innocent XI, Laura Martinozzi, the Duchess of Modena (in the Italian edition), and her daughter Queen Mary (in the English edition) are finely etched prints, and the carriages and heraldic panels are depicted as ornament prints. The sugar-paste table pieces are reproduced as independent three-dimensional sculptures. The extraordinary triple-foldout plate of the banquet table set with *trionfi* echoes the depictions of coronation processions, which were usually seen in scrolls or long foldouts, showing the pageant wagons and participants as they passed through the city streets (see Imorde, "Edible Prestige," fig. 1). Possibly because he was an artist and connoisseur, Wright's book shows only the art, not edible works made of food or participants. The principal subjects are the beautifully designed, conspicuous display of rich fabric (brocade and velvet), gold, silver, crystal, and that expensive and rare commodity, sugar.

Wright concludes his book with descriptions of two receptions: one given by Christina of Sweden and another at the Palazzo Barberini. At the queen's palace in

February 1687, there was a performance of Italian lyrics and an encomium by Cardinal Francisco Albani in honor of the English king.[44] A quatrain closed the event with the words: "He's Great in Britain, even. Let Him be Great in Rome, and Great in Heaven."[45] Next, Cardinal Pamphilj invited Castlemaine to the performance of a tragedy at his palace, after which Cardinal Barberini, the pope's uncle, invited Castlemaine and seven other "English men of quality" to an entertainment on Shrove Tuesday, the eve of Carnival.[46] Displayed together with the ceiling painted by Pietro da Cortona and the tapestries, at the upper end of the gallery was "a full picture of his majesty on a sprightly horse, trampling the many-headed monster of rebellion, under his feet."[47] As for the banquet, the hall was set with crimson velvet chairs that had long golden fringes. In the middle, upon a small rise, was a table, thirty feet long and seven feet wide. Along its length were arrayed a procession of triumphs [*trionfi*], and beside them, smaller ones symbolizing the arts, peace, war, and victory. Wright comments, "Nor was the number of the services, the vastness of the dishes, the variety of the intermesses, and relishing plates round every Trencher, the plenty, and choice of wines, the nobleness of the dessert, excellence of the music, and great order of the whole, in any wise disproportionate to the magnificence of the place, or the person, that made it. And if it fell short in anything, of that of the Lord Ambassador's, it was not, that his Eminence's intention was not the same, but the company less."[48] In other words, Castlemaine's banquet was far more grand.

Despite the elaborate artistic program and Wright's earnest efforts to promote the effects of their stay in Rome, the Earl of Castlemaine's embassy was not a success. Yet, the artfully designed book has served well to perpetuate the memory of a very grand event. Wright's book gives both seventeenth-century readers and those who have viewed it over more than three centuries a sense of the ostentation customary for festivals. Like the Versailles *fête* publications, it is one of the most commonly found festival books. Produced to give as gifts, the Italian and English versions circulated widely among European courts. The book made its way to rare book and print collectors in its time, and then into royal or national libraries in the nineteenth and twentieth centuries.

A CIVIC BANQUET IN BOLOGNA

In Bologna, banquets were staged to mark the political terms of the city's elders and to confirm the solidarity of the city government.[49] On 28 February 1693, Senator Francesco Ratta gave an especially sumptuous dinner for sixty-four eminent persons in the Palazzo Vizzani. An unusually extensive amount of documentation—two booklets and at least nine prints—was published to record and interpret the artistic productions designed for the dinner that commemorated the end of Ratta's term as gonfalonier.[50] Senator Ratta was a member of an old and distinguished Bolognese family, and it was customary for patricians to open their palaces for public inspection. Luxurious accoutrements—paintings, sculptures, beautifully furnished rooms with decorative arts—were seen to ratify the magnificence and splendor of the dwelling and lifestyle, hence the power of the owner.[51] The frontispiece to *Disegni del convito* (Designs of the banquet) shows a circular table in the great hall of the Palazzo Vizzani (fig. 18). Unlike long banquet tables, this arrangement allowed all guests to be seated as equals, obviating the isolation of the head table or seating hierarchy.[52] Hanging above are Tommaso Laureti's paintings (now lost) of the history of another great leader, Alexander the Great. Several more engravings depict the beverage tables and the sideboard displaying silverware from different perspectives; and opposite them, mirrors were hung slanting down to reflect and aggrandize the artistic decorations (figs. 19, 20).

Featuring wonders of nature and art, the banquet hall displayed the wealth and good taste of Bologna as well as the genius of Senator Ratta. The table sculpture

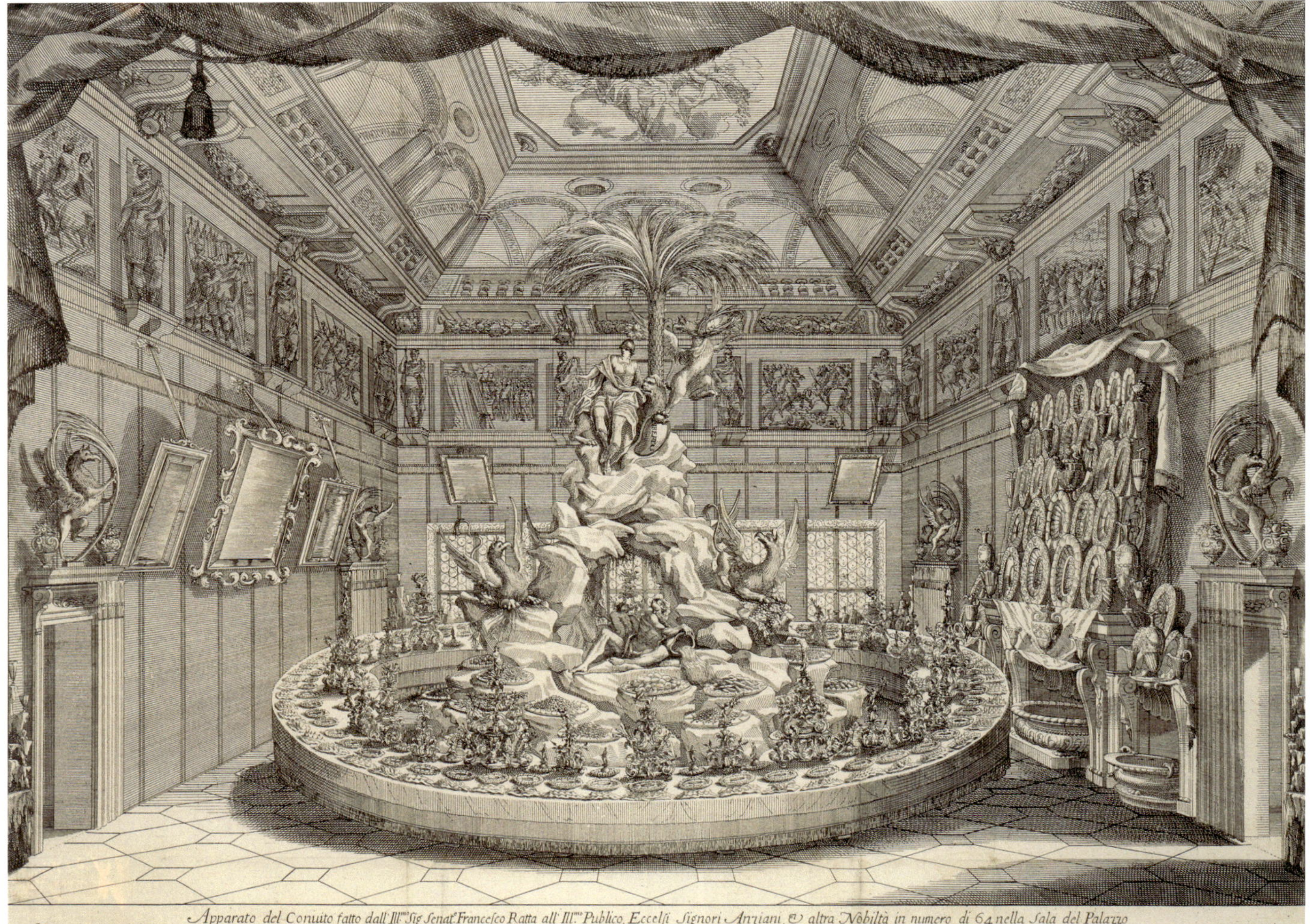

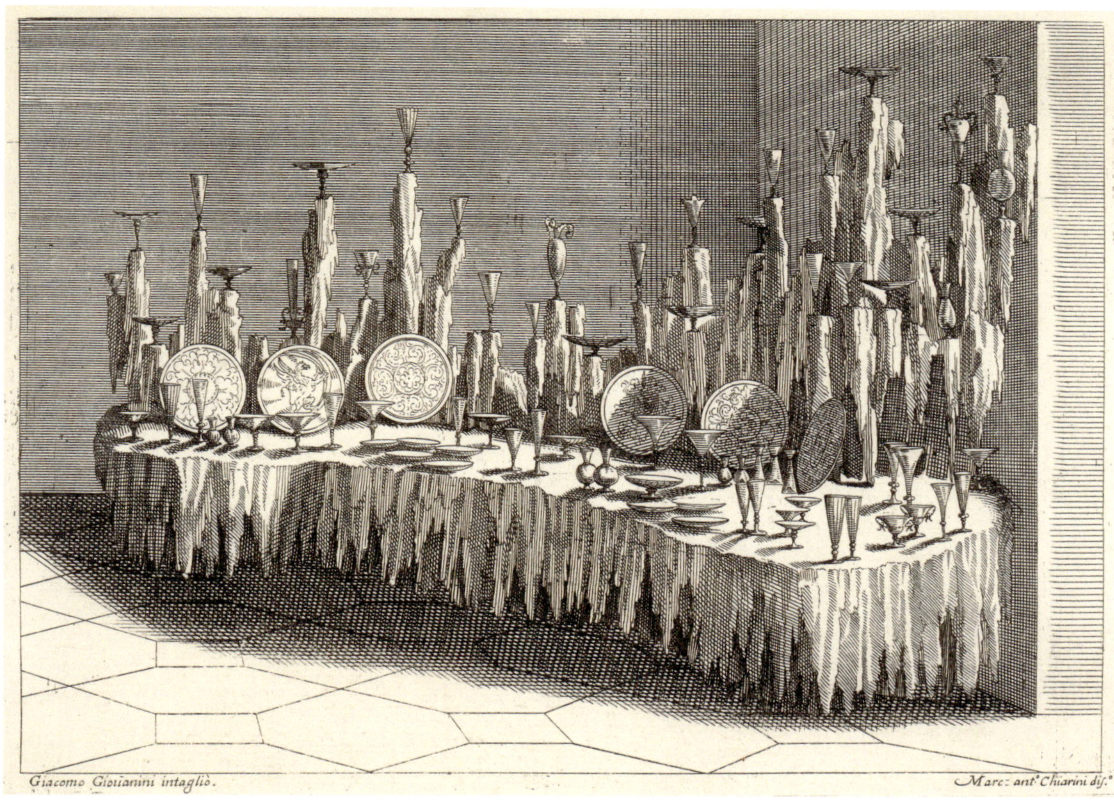

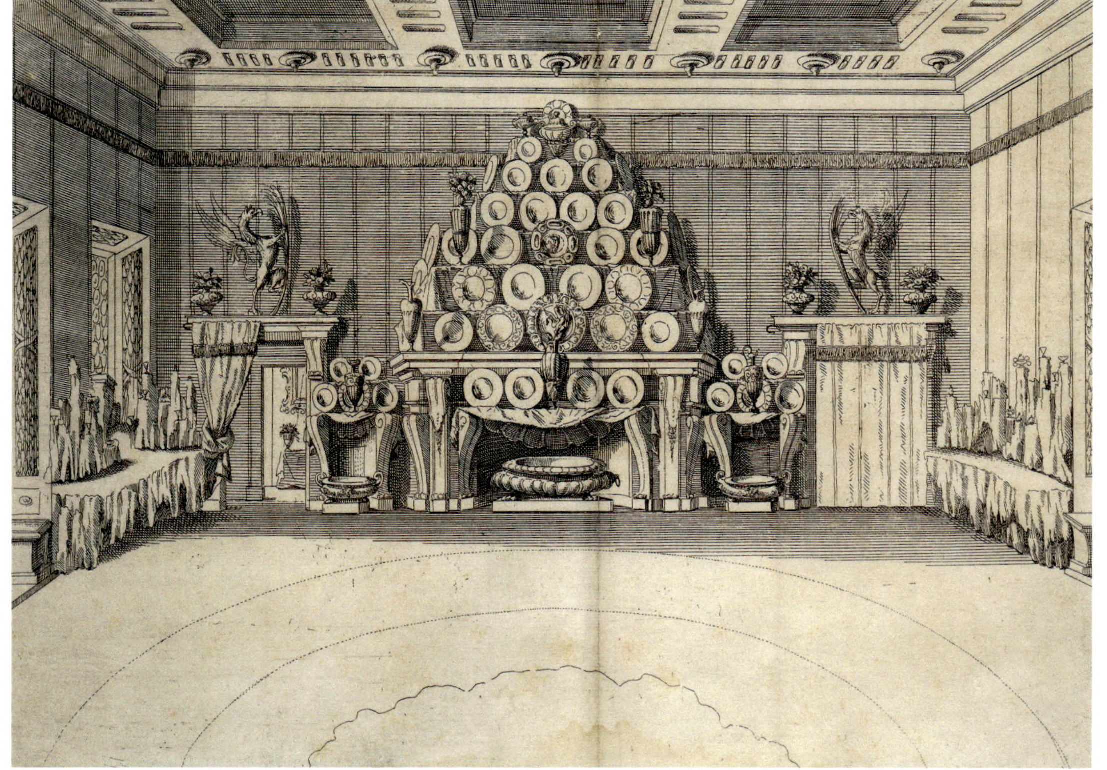

FIG. 19.

Giacomo-Maria Giovannini (Italian, 1667–1717), after Marc'Antonio Chiarini (Italian, 1652–1730).
Table with crystal, etching, 18 × 25.7 cm (7⅛ × 10¼ in.). From *Disegni del convito…* (Bologna: Per li Peri, 1693), pl. 1. Los Angeles, Getty Research Institute.

FIG. 20.

Credenza of silverware in the Palazzo Vizzani in Bologna.
Etching, 26 × 36 cm (10¼ × 14⅛ in.). From Giuseppe Mazza, *La cvstodia d'oro…* (Bologna: Per li Peri, 1693), pl. 2. Los Angeles, Getty Research Institute.

with four river gods seems to have been inspired by Gian Lorenzo Bernini's *Fountain of the Four Rivers* in the Piazza Navona in Rome.[53] The sculpture, with its silver palm tree, echoes the *trionfi* of Roger Palmer's Roman banquet. More than twenty-two feet high and almost sixty feet across, the sculpture was made to be seen from all sides; the rocky crag is made of silver and covered with green foliage like the palm tree.[54] In Bologna, civic emblems predominate. La Felsina, the crowned Etruscan warrior from whom the city derives its nickname, stands triumphant in the shelter of the palm, resting her left hand on the head of a lion. To the right, a griffin holds a leafy wreath. The lion supports a shield on which is inscribed "Libertas," alluding to Bologna's status as a free city under papal protection.[55] All the figural elements are gilt. Winged griffins stand on either side of the mounds of rocks and on four pedestals around the room. Both griffins and the lion are borrowed from the Ratta family coat of arms.

Shown as circles, the banquet table covers are a compact version of Wright's design for a long setting, while the monument is an indoor installation that echoes Louis's garden machines at Versailles, particularly the *Festin donnée dans le petit parc de Versailles* of 1668 (see fig. 11). Indeed, as the focus of the feast, this setting is a slightly more generous offering: unlike at Versailles, where guests were kept back from the tables by guards, edible features are clustered within reach of the guests. Around the base of the sculpture, smaller tables hold more than fifty silver plates filled to the brim with sweetmeats and candies. In addition, there are twenty-four plates of the most precious citrus fruits, called *agrumi* or *siti.* Toward the center of the table are twenty-four large, leafy, and figural sculptures. Standing at heights from two to six feet, these triumphs are made of sugar paste mimicking cast metal sculptures (fig. 21).[56] Above these are ninety-six golden figures with crowns of laurel, olive, oak, and rose branches that recall the protective powers of the gods. Among the *trionfi* are basins made of sugar surrounded by fine sugar laid down in patterns, like fine stonework in gardens. The golden figures were intended as gifts for the guests.

The expansive imagery folds in themes of wealth and power. A towering mountain supports the figure of La Felsina in the attitude of peaceful conquest—in other words, leadership (see fig. 18). Beneath her, the great rivers flow (a variation on a theme by a great artist), and the precious metals of gold and silver glitter. The small mounds clustering below the Appenine promontory are fertile hillsides where agriculture flourishes. The bowls of fruit are natural treasures to be admired. Taken away from its quotidian functions, the food designed as art is made to look rare and beautiful. Within this ornate scheme, the artwork proper—seen in the gallery of paintings above or the silverware, glass, and crystals—becomes an ornate frame for the *Wunderkammer* of the great hall that frames the scene, seen in fish-eye view, like a *vue d'optique.* Although the guests at this banquet were the city's elite, there was food

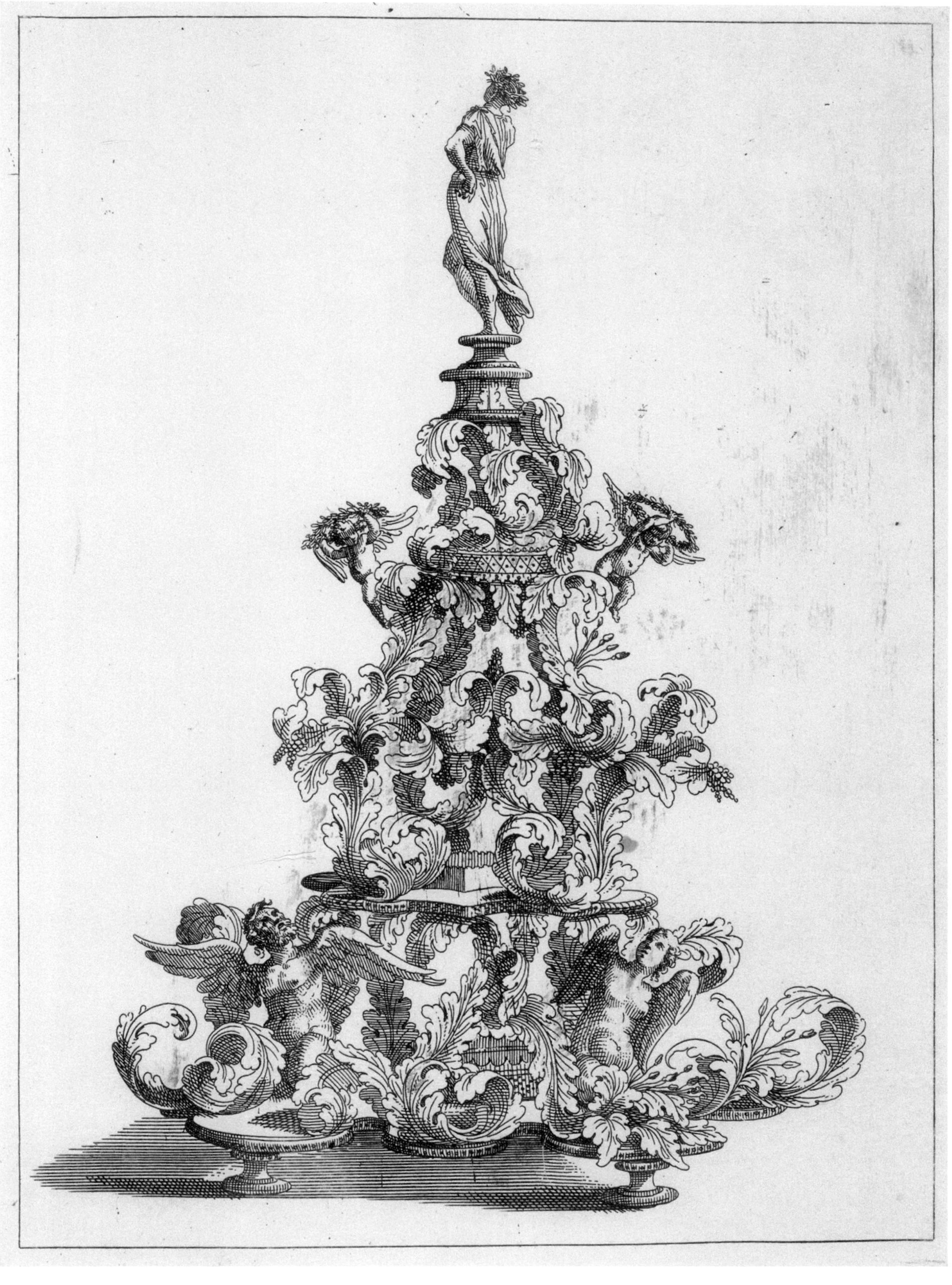

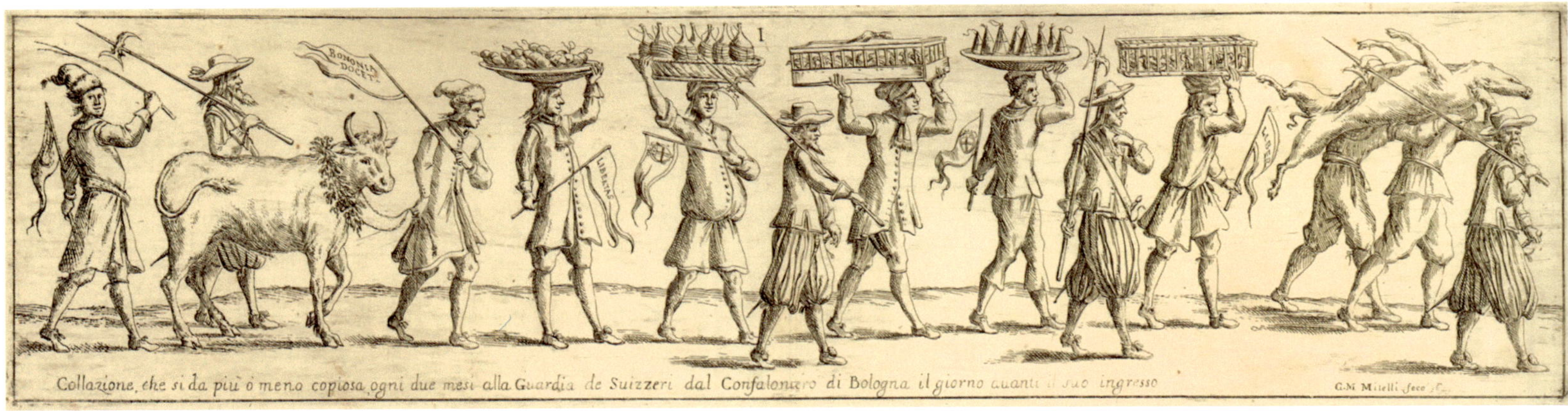

Collazione, che si da più ò meno copiosa ogni due mesi alla Guardia de Suizzeri dal Confaloniero di Bologna il giorno auanti il suo ingresso   G.M Mitelli fece C.

FIG. 22.

Giuseppe Maria Mitelli (Italian, 1634–1718).

Meal…Given Every Two Months to the Swiss Guard by the Gonfalonier of Bologna. Bologna, 1699, etching, 13.5 × 53 cm (5⁵⁄₁₆ × 20⁷⁄₈ in.). London, The British Museum.

FIG. 23.

Johann Andreas Pfeffel (Austrian, 1674–1748) and Christian Engelbrecht (Austrian, 1672–1735), after Johann Cyriak Hackhofer (Swiss, 1675–1731).

Banquet for the Ranking Lords of Lower Austria, on the Occasion of Emperor Joseph I's Oath of Allegiance, etching, 52 × 40 cm (21⅕ × 15½ in.). From Ludwig von Gülich, *Erb-Huldigung, so dem aller- durchleüchtigist- grossmächtigist und unüberwindlichsten Römischen Käyser…* (Vienna: Bey Johann Jacob Kürner, [1705]), pl. 7. Los Angeles, Getty Research Institute.

for all. The Bolognese printmaker G.M. Mitelli's series of six popular prints shows a procession of foods given by the *gonfalonieri* of Bologna to the Swiss Guards.[57] Held high above the marchers' heads, the platters and containers are paraded through the streets like booty during a triumphal procession, displaying the connections between public feasts and private celebrations (fig. 22).

IMPRINTING ROYAL HISTORIES

The Versailles *fête* books portray the world of the court of Louis XIV. The English and Italian books focus on the pageantry and decorative arts of the banquets as well as the guests, often showing the meal in progress and carefully elucidating the meanings of the iconography and the heraldry. Since festivals are intended to be publicized, it seems odd that the books depict only the designs and not the lavishly staged festival or those who attended and looked on. Texts describe them, but there is no visual equivalent.

Like the Versailles festivals and the Swedish carousel for Charles XI in 1672, it was seen as important to show who was in attendance at eighteenth-century Viennese imperial banquets. In a series of remarkably similar successive volumes, publishers took a notably economical approach in their depiction of the banquet scenes for the 1705, 1712, and 1740 court feasts on the occasions of the oaths of allegiance by Emperor Joseph I, Emperor Charles VI, and Empress Maria Theresa. In the first two volumes, different versions of the same copperplate, which was burnished and re-engraved, were used to document the new rulers and those in attendance (figs. 23–25). For the empress's banquet, a new image was created, introducing women into the banquet scene (fig. 26). Although scant attention is paid to the table settings or food, by means of such similar images, the illustrations crucially demonstrate how important repetitions were to ceremonial meanings, as new rulers moved into traditional positions and inserted themselves into history.

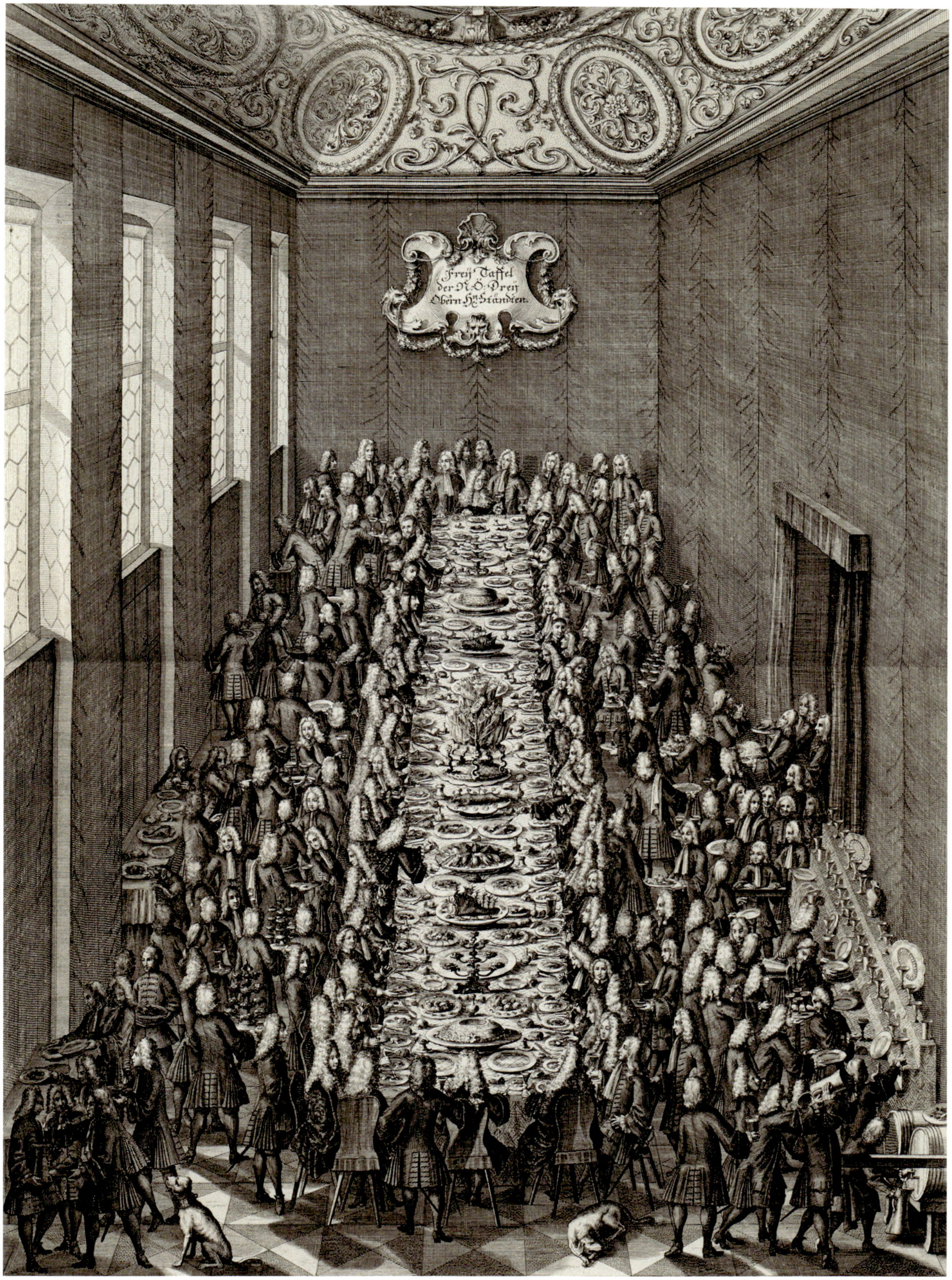

FIG. 24.

Johann Andreas Pfeffel (Austrian, 1674–1748) and Christian Engelbrecht (Austrian, 1672–1735), after Johann Cyriak Hackhofer (Swiss, 1675–1731).

The Emperor's Table in the Knights' Parlor, on the Occasion of Emperor Joseph I's Oath of Allegiance, etching, 33 × 46.5 cm (13 × 18¼ in.). From Ludwig von Gülich, *Erb-Huldigung, so dem aller- durchleüchtigist- grossmächtigist und unüberwindlichsten Römischen Käyser…* (Vienna: Bey Johann Jacob Kürner, [1705]), pl. 6. Los Angeles, Getty Research Institute.

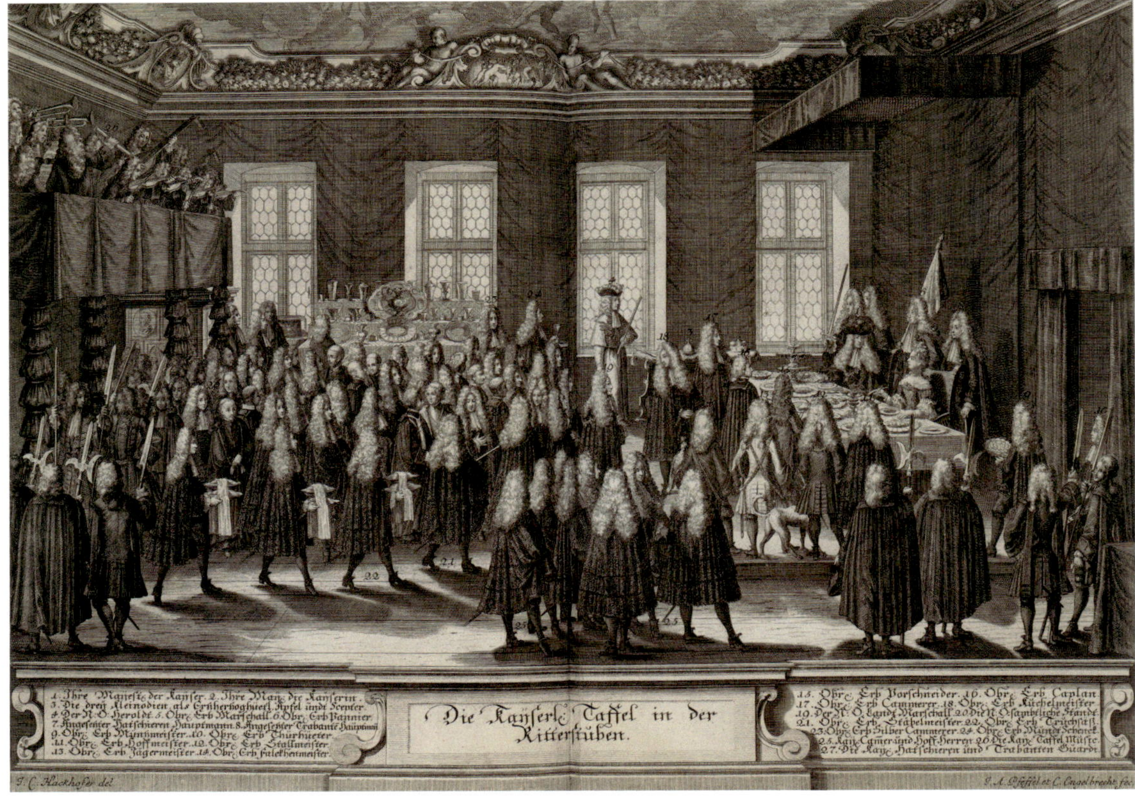

FIG. 25.

Johann Andreas Pfeffel (Austrian, 1674–1748) and Christian Engelbrecht (Austrian, 1672–1735), after Johann Cyriak Hackhofer (Swiss, 1675–1731).

The Emperor's Table in the Knights' Parlor, on the Occasion of Emperor Charles VI's Oath of Allegiance, etching, 33 × 46.5 cm (13 × 18½ in.). From Johann Baptist von Mairn, *Erb-Huldigung, welche der allerdurchleuchtigst-grossmächtigsten Frauen, Frauen Mariae Theresae zu Ungarn und Böheim Königin…* (Vienna: Bey Johann Jacob Kürner, [1712]), pl. 6. Los Angeles, Getty Research Institute.

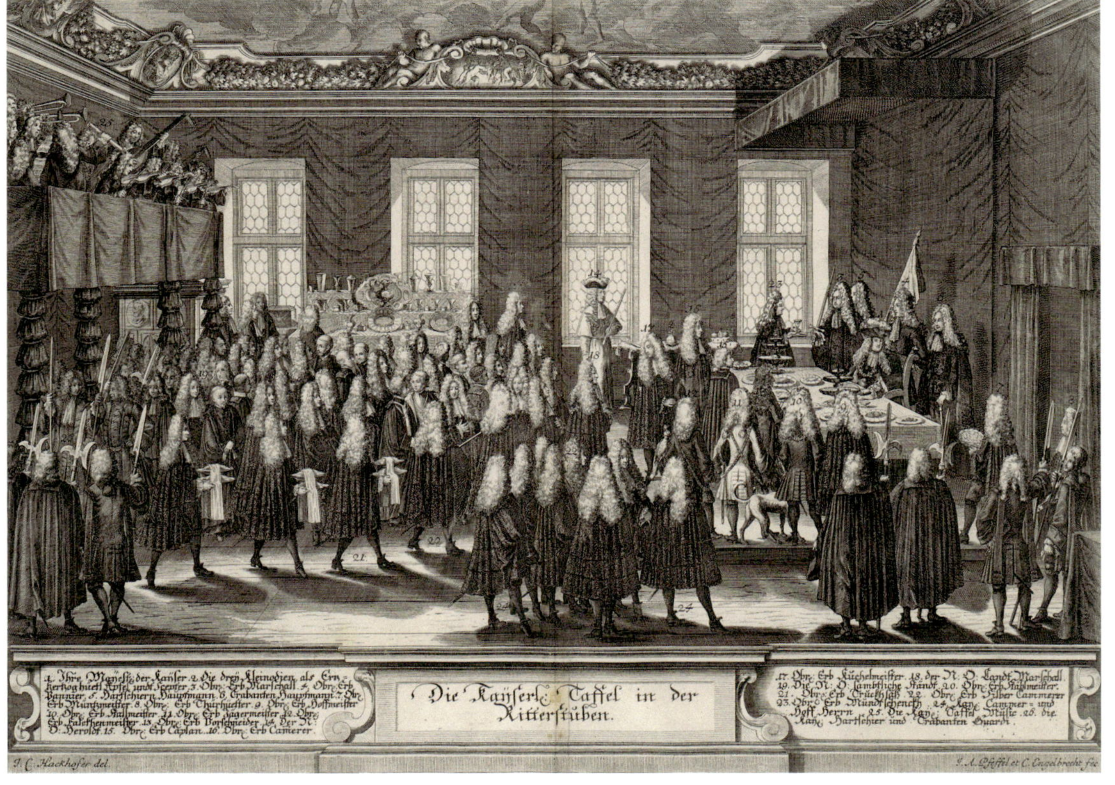

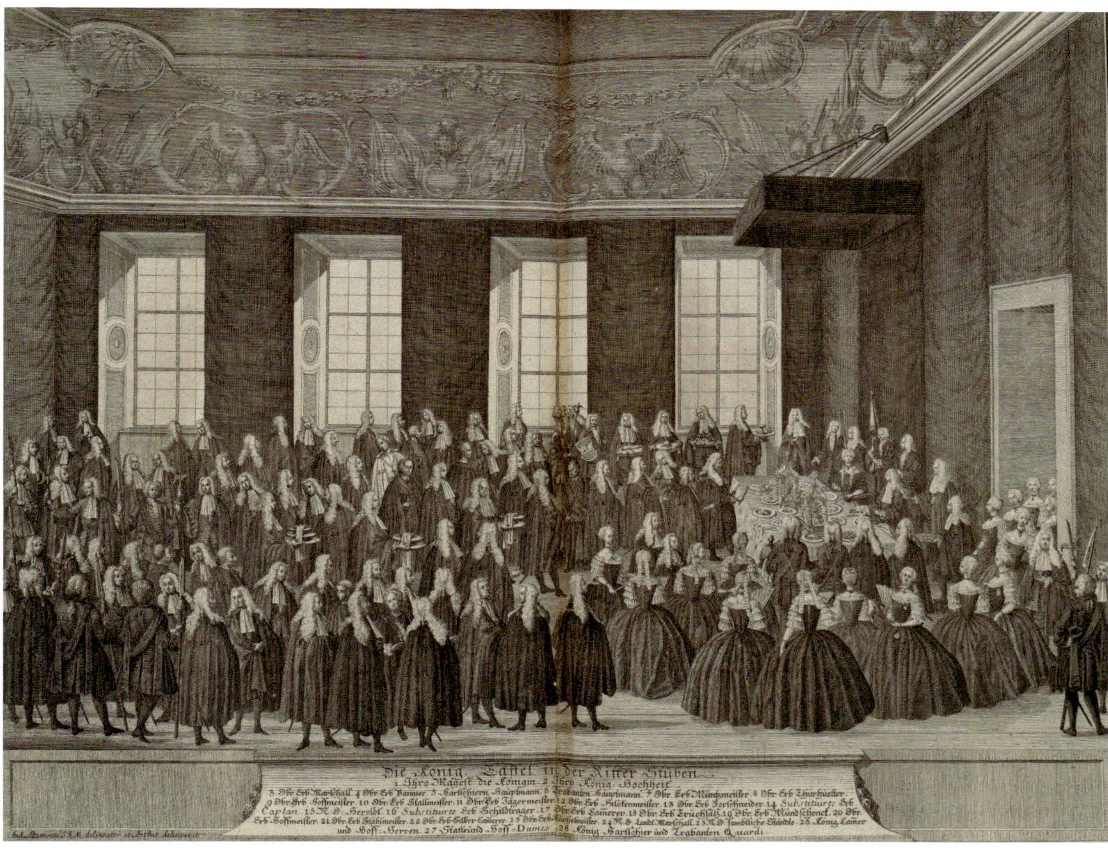

NOTES

Portions of this text were previously published in Marcia Reed, "The Edible Monument," in Harlan Walker, ed., *Food in the Arts: Proceedings of the Oxford Symposium on Food and Cookery, 1998* (Devon, England: Prospect, 1999), 141–50.

1. For more on the Cuccagna festival, see Reed, "Feasting in the Streets," this volume.

2. Homer, *Iliad* 24.25–30.

3. Ovid, *Fasti* 1.391–400; 6.319–41.

4. Anthony Colantuono, "*Dies alcyoniae:* The Invention of Bellini's *Feast of the Gods,*" *Art Bulletin* 73, no. 2 (1991): 237–56. The painting is now in the National Gallery, Washington, D.C.

5. Charles Perrault, *Le banquet des dieux: Pour la naissance de monsigneur le duc de Bourgogne* (Paris: Jean Baptiste Coignard, 1682).

6. Perrault, *Le banquet des dieux,* 6. All translations are mine, unless otherwise noted.

7. Perrault, *Le banquet des dieux,* 11.

8. For example, *Le triomphe de la France sur l'entrée royale de leurs maiestez dans leur bonne ville de Paris* (Paris: Jean Baptiste Loyson, 1660); Jean Tronçon, *L'entrée triomphante de leurs maiestez Louis XIV roy de France et de Nauarre, et Marie Therese d'Austriche son espouse: Dans la ville de Paris capitale de leurs royaumes, au retour de la signature de la paix generalle et de leur heureux mariage* (Paris: Les exemplaires se vendent a Paris chez Pierre Le Petit…Thomas Ioly…et Louis Bilaine…, 1662). See also Charles Perrault, *Festiva ad capita annulumque decursio: A Rege Ludovico XIV, principibus, summisque aulae proceribus edita anno M.DC.LXIII / scripsit Gallicè Carolus Perrault; Latinè reddidit e versibus heroïcis expressit spiritus Fléchier* (Paris: Typographia Regia, 1670); for the French edition of this publication on the Grand Carousel, an elaborately decorated and

costumed procession and tournament, see Charles Perrault, *Courses de testes et de bague faites par le roy et par les princes et seigneurs de sa cour, en l'année 1662* (Paris: Imprimerie royale, 1670).

9.   Baltasar de Beaujoyeulx, *Le balet comique de la royne…* (Paris: Par Adrian le Roy, Robert Ballard, & Mamert Patisson, imprimeurs du roy, 1582), n.p. Quoted by Benoît Bolduc, "La fête du papier (1549–1679): Des ateliers parisiens au Cabinet du roi," *XVIIe siècle,* no. 258 (2013): 15.

10.   Tronçon, *L'entrée triomphante.*

11.   André Félibien, *Les plaisirs de L'isle enchantée: Course de bague; collation ornée de machines…et autres festes galantes et magnifiques…* (Paris: Paris: Imprimerie Royale, 1673/74). The title page is dated 1673, but the colophon is dated 1674. The text is unsigned; some say it is by Charles Perrault.

12.   Félibien, *Les plaisirs de L'isle enchantée,* 4.

13.   See Alice Jarrard, "Vigarani, Italy, and Machine Marvel in France, circa 1668," in Walter Baricchi and Jérôme de La Gorce, eds., *Gaspare e Carlo Vigarani: Dalla corte degli Este a quella di Luigi XIV* (Milan: Silvana, 2009), fig. 1, p. 114.

14.   Félibien, *Les plaisirs de L'isle enchantée,* 4.

15.   The printed title page enumerates the events*: Les plaisirs de L'isle enchantée. Course de Bague; collation ornée de machines,* [etc.]. The engraved title reads: *Les plaisirs de L'isle enchantée, ou les festes et divertissements du Roy à Versailles. Diviséz en trois journées, et commencéz le 7me Jour de May de L'année 1664.*

16.   Félibien, *Les plaisirs de L'isle enchantée,* 18–19. Aside from the king and his brother, Monsieur (Philippe I, duc d'Orléans), there were only women at the table. Names of those in attendance are listed on these pages.

17.   Félibien, *Les plaisirs de L'isle enchantée,* 19.

18.   André Félibien, *Relation de la feste de Versailles du 18. juillet mil six cens soixante-huit* (Paris: Imprimerie royale, 1679), 4–5.

19.   Félibien, *Relation de la feste de Versailles,* 17–28.

20.   Félibien, *Relation de la feste de Versailles,* 52.

21.   Félibien, *Relation de la feste de Versailles,* 57.

22.   Félibien, *Relation de la feste de Versailles,* 60.

23.   André Félibien, *Les divertissemens de Versailles donnez par le roy à tout sa cour au retour de la conqueste de la Franche-Comté en l'année M.DC.LXXIV* (Paris: Imprimerie Royale, 1676), 4. He uses the word "promptitude."

24.   Félibien, *Les divertissemens,* 5.

25.   Félibien, *Les divertissemens,* 14.

26.   André Félibien, *Entretiens sur les vies et sur les ouvrages des plus excellens peintres anciens et modernes: Avec la vie des architectes* (Trevoux: De l'Imprimerie de S.A.S., 1725); idem, *Description de la grotte de Versailles* (Paris: De la Imprimerie royale, 1676); and idem, *La description du Château de Versailles* (Paris: Antoine Vilette, 1687).

27.   Peter Fuhring, Louis Marchesano, Rémi Mathis, and Vanessa Selbach, eds., *A Kingdom of Images: French Prints in the Age of Louis XIV, 1660–1715* (Los Angeles: Getty Research Institute, 2015).

28.   Although Leonello Spada is now believed to be the painter of *Aeneas Carrying His Father,* it was first attributed to Domenichino and then to Ludovico Carracci, as described in the *Mercure galant.* The painting was in the collection of Louis XIV and now resides in the Louvre. See Arnauld Brejon de Lavergnée, *L'inventaire Le Brun de 1683, La collection des tableaux de Louis XIV* (Paris: Ministère de la culture et de la communication, Editions de la Réunion des musées nationaux, ca. 1987), 97–98. I am grateful to Thomas Gaehtgens for this information.

29.   *Mercure galant,* December 1682, 36–41.

30.   David Klöcker Ehrenstrahl, *Das grosse Carrosel und prächtige Ring-Rännen…* (Stockholm: Joh. G. Eberdt, 1685), 12. The GRI's copy includes loose prints at the back of the 1662 French edition on the Grand Carsousel; see note 8.

31. *Ricettario fiorentino di nuovo illustrato* (Florence: Cecconcelli, 1623), see the recipes for "Conserva di fiori d'arancio" and "Conservi di fiori di cederno" on page 152 of the chapter "Del ricettario dell'arte et Vniversita de medici, e speziali della città di Firenze."

32. Perrault, *Courses de testes et de bague,* 44, 62.

33. See Richard E. Boyer, "English Declarations of Indulgence of 1687 and 1688," *Catholic Historical Review* 50 (1964): 341-42.

34. [John] Michael Wright, *Ragguaglio della solenne comparsa di…signor conte di Castlemaine, ambasciadore straordinario di…Giacomo secondo rè d'Inghilterra…alla…Papa Innocenzo undecimo* (Rome: Domenico Antonio Ercole, 1687); idem, *An Account of His Excellence Roger Earl of Castlemaine's Embassy: From His Sacred Majesty James the IId.…to His Holiness Innocent XI* (London: Tho. Snowden for the author, 1688).

35. *Mr. Michael Wright's Curious Collection of Philological Books* (4 June 1694), [100]; see Sara Stevenson and Duncan Thomson, *John Michael Wright: The King's Painter* (Edinburgh: Scottish National Portrait Gallery, 1982), [100].

36. Wright, *An Account,* 10.

37. Wright, *An Account,* 12-13.

38. Wright, *An Account,* 20.

39. Wright, *An Account,* 52-53.

40. Wright, *An Account,* 67.

41. Wright, *An Account,* 54.

42. See Stevenson and Thomson, *John Michael Wright,* 81-82.

43. Wright, *An Account,* 55-56.

44. Wright, *An Account,* 70-74.

45. Wright, *An Account,* 74.

46. Wright, *An Account,* 76.

47. Wright, *An Account,* 78.

48. Wright, *An Account,* 78-79.

49. See Giancarlo Roversi, *Palazzi e case nobili del '500 a Bologna* (Bologna: Grafis, 1986), 196-213.

50. *Disegni del convito…terminando il suo confalonierato li 28. febraro 1693. In Bologna, per li peri. All'insegna dell'angelo custode…[n.d.]* (Bologna 1693?); Gioseffo Mazza was responsible for the designs. And *La cvstodia d'oro godvta nel vigilantissimo confalonierato dell'illvstrissimo signor senatore Francesco Ratta* (1693?).

51. Pierangelo Bellettini et al., eds., *Una città in piazza: Comunicazione e vita quotidiana a Bologna tra cinque e seicento* (Bologna: Editrice Compositori, 2000), 155-56.

52. *Disegni del convito,* fol. 2r.

53. See Maurizio Fagiolo dell'Arco, *L'effimero barocco,* vol. 2 (Rome: Bulzoni, 1978), figs. 233-34.

54. "Contandosi l'altezza di questo fino à deciotto, e la circonferenza a quarant' otto piedi" (Calculating the height at its top to eighteen [feet], and [with a] circumference of forty-eight feet). "Feet" is not the same measurement used today. *Disegni del convito,* fol. [2r].

55. See Silvia Camerini, ed., *Il magnifico apparato: Pubbliche funzioni feste e giuochi bolognesi nel Settecento* (Bologna: Clueb, 1982), 9.

56. "Ventiquatro Trionfi di pasta di Zuchero finissimo: e sei di essi sono di piedi cinque di altezza, sei di tre, e dodici di due" (Twenty-four triumphs in very fine sugar paste: six of which are five feet high, six three feet high, and twelve two [feet high]). "Feet" is not the same measurement used today. *Disegni del convito,* fol. [2v].

57. Reproduced in *Il magnifico apparato,* 22.

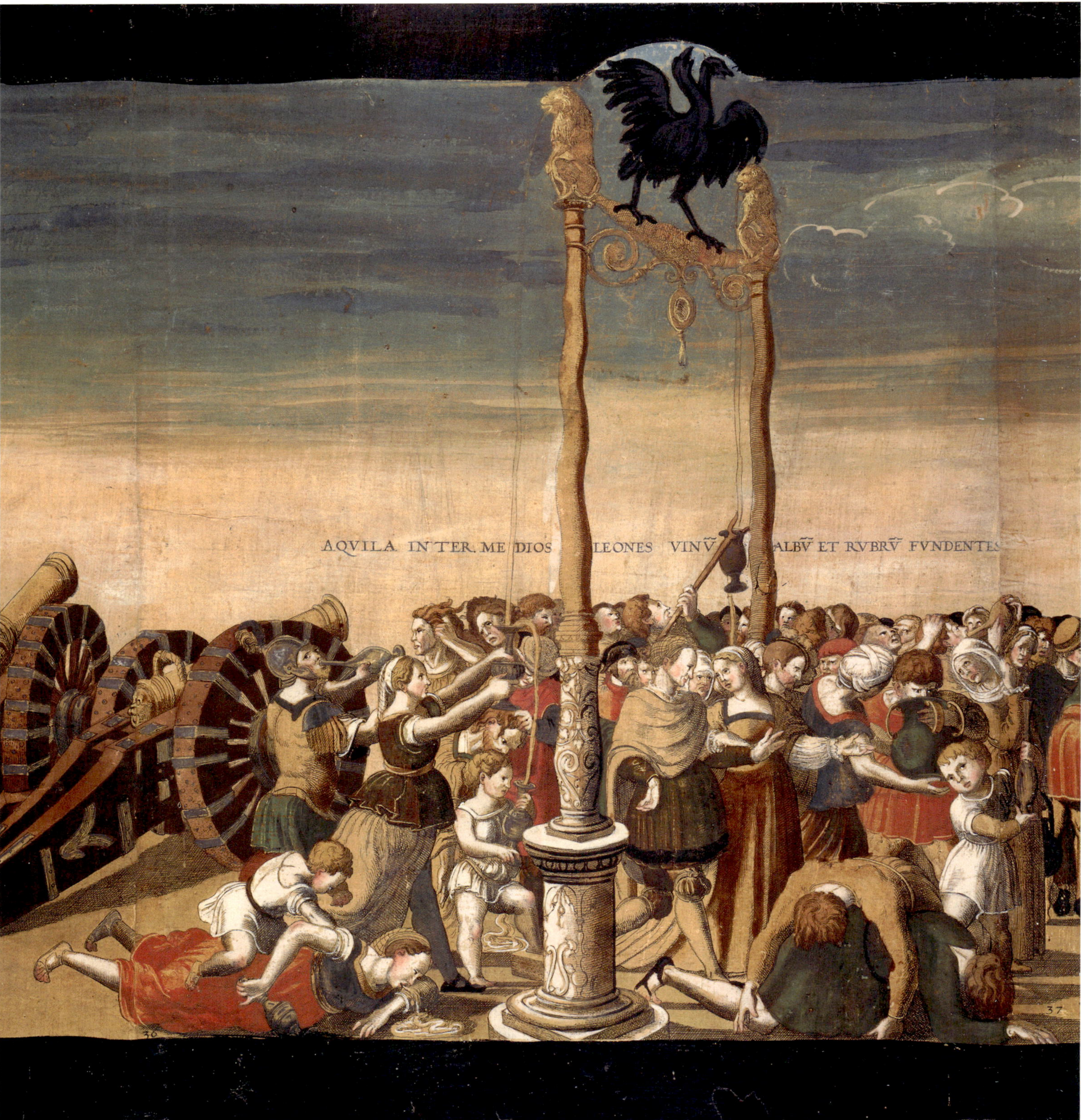
AQVILA. INTER. MEDIOS LEONES VINŪ ALBŪ ET RVBRŪ FVNDENTES

FEASTING IN THE STREETS
CARNIVALS AND THE CUCCAGNA

MARCIA REED

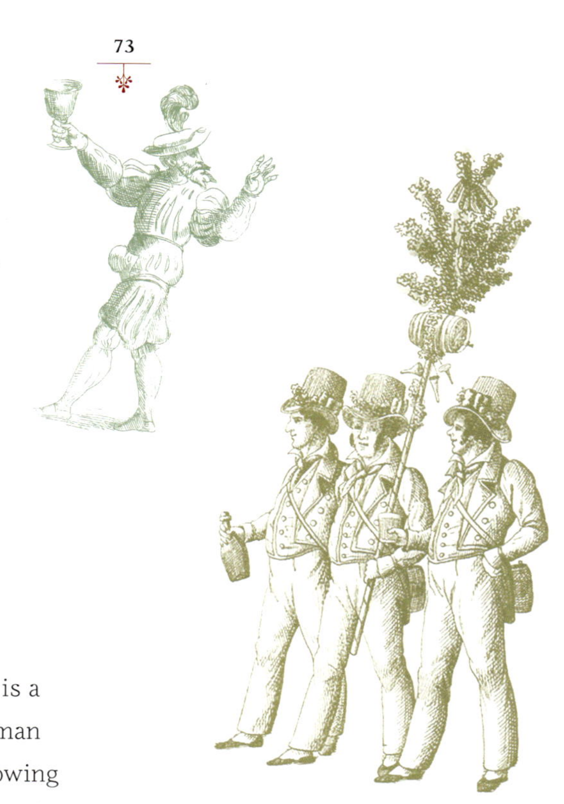

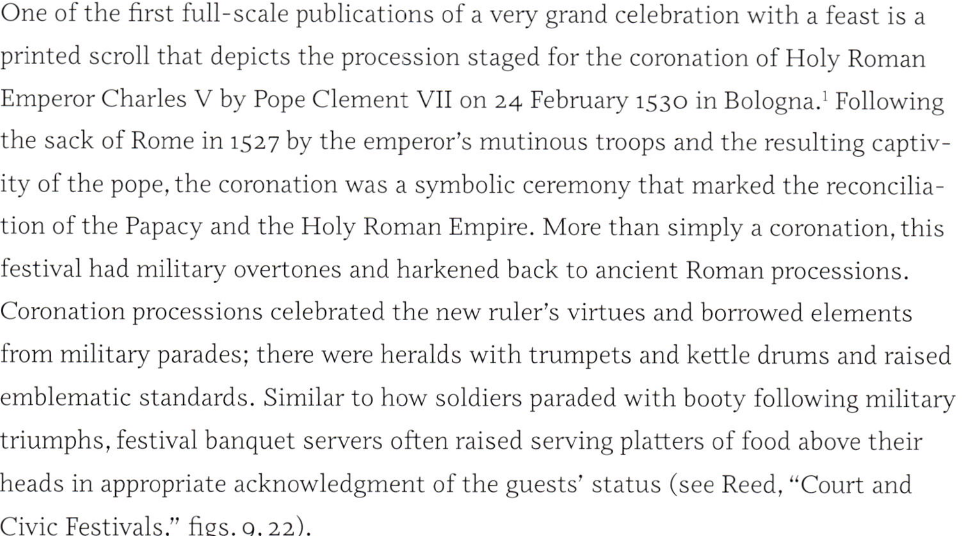

One of the first full-scale publications of a very grand celebration with a feast is a printed scroll that depicts the procession staged for the coronation of Holy Roman Emperor Charles V by Pope Clement VII on 24 February 1530 in Bologna.[1] Following the sack of Rome in 1527 by the emperor's mutinous troops and the resulting captivity of the pope, the coronation was a symbolic ceremony that marked the reconciliation of the Papacy and the Holy Roman Empire. More than simply a coronation, this festival had military overtones and harkened back to ancient Roman processions. Coronation processions celebrated the new ruler's virtues and borrowed elements from military parades; there were heralds with trumpets and kettle drums and raised emblematic standards. Similar to how soldiers paraded with booty following military triumphs, festival banquet servers often raised serving platters of food above their heads in appropriate acknowledgment of the guests' status (see Reed, "Court and Civic Festivals," figs. 9, 22).

On the scroll, engravings by Nikolaus Hogenberg portray the coronation procession. Single prints pasted together show the descending social order of participants, who are identified in texts below. Before and after the emperor and the pope, marchers snake along the street to the blasts of trumpets and the beats of drums. Following the parade, the emperor and prominent guests dined inside a large banquet hall, but this elite feast is not shown on the scroll. When the toasts and dinner were over, all the leftovers from the banquet were thrown out the windows onto the streets. Food is featured in street scenes of the hungry, drunken, and unruly crowd. Red and white wines flow from a temporary structure of two columns inscribed with the emperor's motto *Plus ultra* (Further beyond) (fig. 1). The columns support an architrave crowned by the two-headed imperial eagle and golden lions, whose mouths serve as spigots—effectively advertising both the ceremonies as well as the prospect of food and drink for the people. At the scroll's end, a large ox stuffed with small game and

FIG. 1.

**Nikolaus Hogenberg
(Dutch, 1500–1539).**

Red and White Wine Fountain
(detail), hand-colored etchings
on a scroll, 40.5 × 29.7 cm
(16 × 11⁷⁄₁₀ in.).
From *Divo et invicto Imperatori
Carolo V. P. F.* (Bologna: Hogenberg,
1535–39), pl. 36.
Los Angeles, Getty Research
Institute.

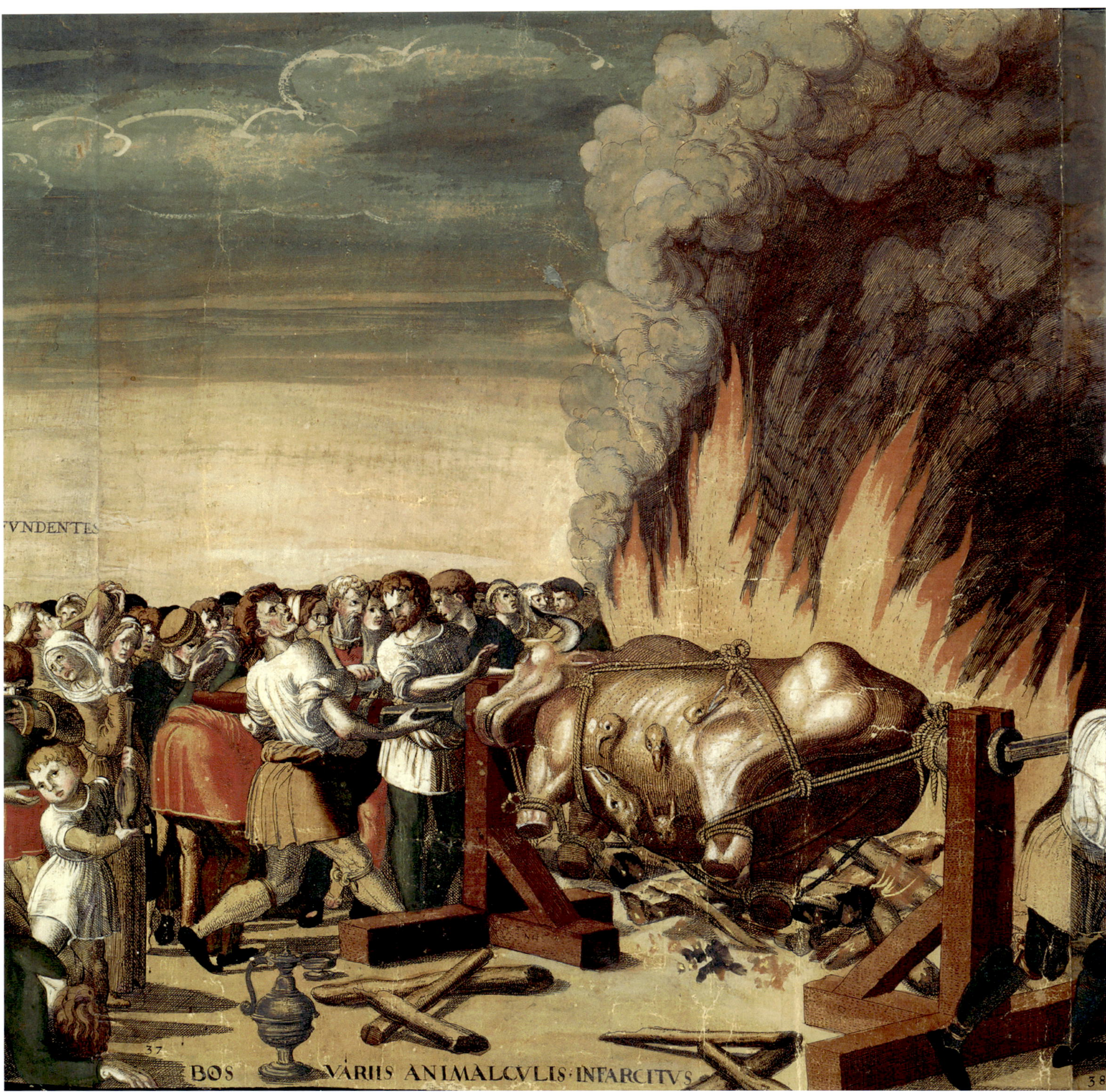
VNDENTES
37
BOS VARIIS ANIMALCVLIS INFARCITVS
38

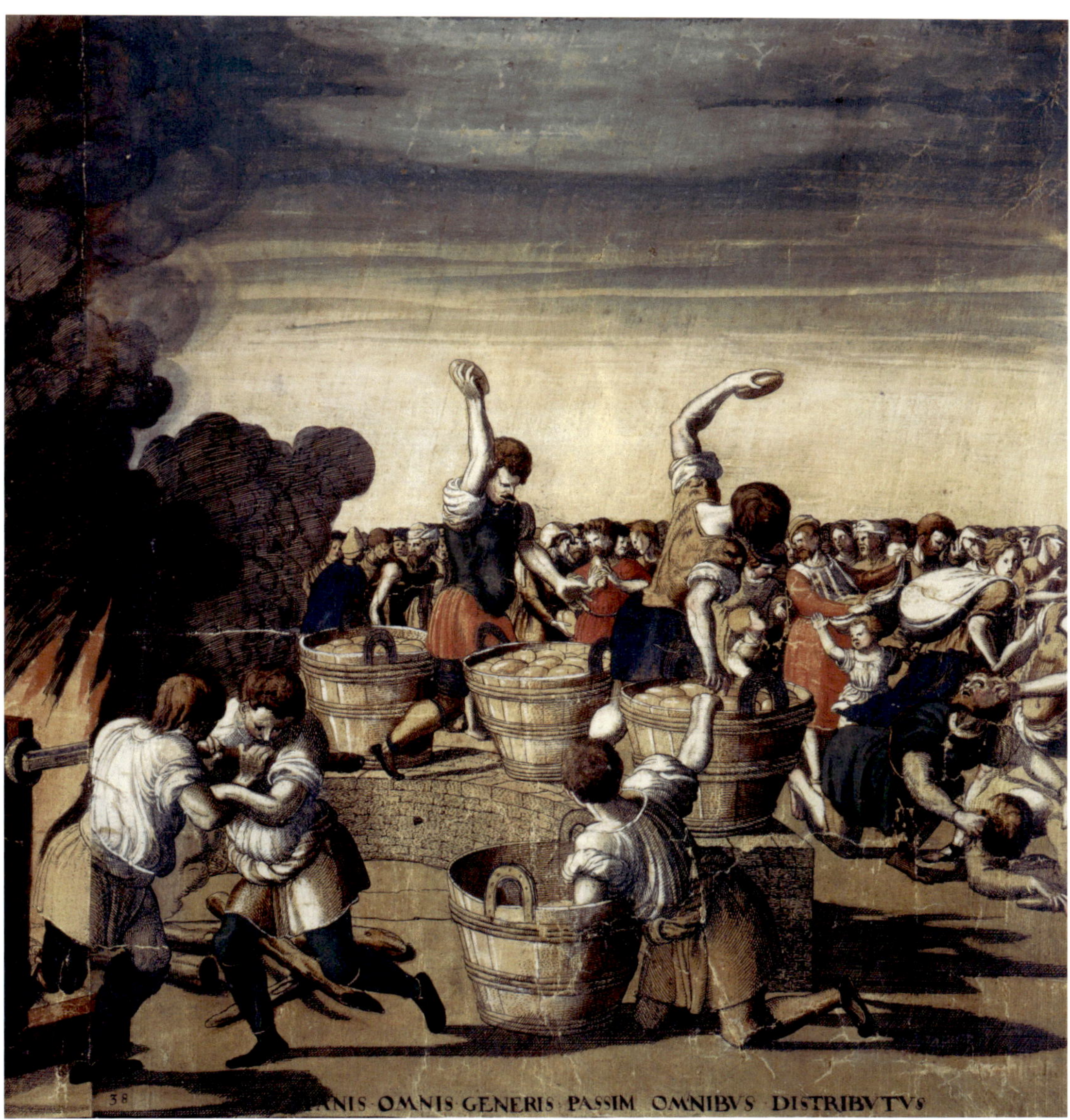

FIG. 2.

Nikolaus Hogenberg

(Dutch, 1500–1539).

Roast Ox Stuffed with Other Animals
(detail), hand-colored etchings
on a scroll, 40.5 × 29.7 cm
(16 × 11⁷⁄₁₀ in.).
From *Divo et invicto Imperatori*
Carolo V. P. F. (Bologna: Hogenberg,
1535–39), pl. 37.
Los Angeles, Getty Research
Institute.

FIG. 3.

Nikolaus Hogenberg

(Dutch, 1500–1539).

Bread Being Distributed to the People
(detail), hand-colored etchings
on a scroll, 40.5 × 29.7 cm
(16 × 11⁷⁄₁₀ in.).
From *Divo et invicto Imperatori*
Carolo V. P. F. (Bologna: Hogenberg,
1535–39), pl. 38.
Los Angeles, Getty Research
Institute.

fowl—including geese or ducks, pigs, lambs, and rabbits—is shown roasting on a spit
(fig. 2). Hogenberg engraved his initials on one of the supports. Soldiers heave bread
from baskets (fig. 3). Indeed, this is bread and circuses for the masses, but the prints
also show how all the people of the community were included and taken care of by
the government. Linked to similar paintings of the coronation, the scroll was testimony to the power of the Holy Roman Empire and the position of the Papacy following the sack of Rome. Unusual for a coronation festival, there is a concluding image of
cannons, alluding to the strength and successes of Charles V's military forces.

   This festival scroll was produced in a number of versions. The Getty's copy is
beautifully colored by hand. Special copies for dignitaries were printed on vellum and

illuminated. Black-and-white copies of the prints were bound as books. In addition to this impressive engraved scroll made to be hung on a wall, small pamphlets—libretti—were published in Bologna, Florence, and Rome. As news items, they describe the festival, reporting on this significant political event and recording the ceremonies, but they make no mention of the food. It is prints of street feasts that depict the triumph of food at the festive party for the people. Food is on the ground and made to be experienced. Street food is a gesture to community that testifies to the ruler's ability to nurture it. The scroll's final images demonstrate how food is increasingly featured in visual documents on festivals. Prints depict the presentations of food in compelling though admittedly limited ways, since we cannot smell or taste them. These images—some of the first published scenes of such celebrations—show how food was the draw and probably the main event for the people. The roasted ox was a luxury for those who were hungry and did not often eat meat. Such food was not part of the formal coronation ceremonies, hence very little is written in the official printed accounts. To learn more about this street food, we must go to other sources.

BOLOGNA'S FEAST OF THE ROASTED PIG

Festivals are often planned for specific times of the year, such as the pre-Lenten Carnival period or the seasonal harvest of a local crop. They amalgamate a mélange of local history and legends, referencing religion or myths in which local figures often took on roles that associated them with gods and heroes. The festivals rally the community together in celebration, creating anew social bonds with repetitive, exciting, and satisfyingly familiar activities.

As a free city under papal protection, Bologna was prosperous. Grand banquets like Senator Francesco Ratta's in the late seventeenth century were held in the city halls and palaces for elite guests (see Reed, "Court and Civic Festivals"). Bologna had many popular festivals to celebrate local holidays and history, and they were shown in prints featuring parades, fireworks, games, and, quite importantly, food. The city is associated with the sausage produced there: mortadella, better known to many as "baloney," which remains a favorite sandwich meat to this day.

Bologna was also known for its ephemeral decorations and popular prints of the city's festivals. During the August fair in the last weeks of summer, the culminating celebration was the Festa della porchetta. Sponsored by the city elders, this community food fest featured a roasted suckling pig. It took place on the feast day of Saint Bartholomew, August 24, and was held for more than five centuries until Napoleon's troops took over the city in 1796. As he traveled through Italy researching his book on music history, the English writer Charles Burney wrote about Bologna's Festa della porchetta.

After dinner upon the great piazza or square in the theater constructed for the fair
by the majistrates…the usual popular festival called the porchetta (or little pig) is
kept in memory of the extinction of the civil war about 1278 in which by accident of
a pig running across the street, the stout Antonin Lambertazzi, head of the Ghibel-
line faction, was killed. In this amphitheatre, after a popular spectacle diversified
every year, peacocks, cocks, hens and money are thrown to the people and lastly a
pig ready dressed. The Cardinal Legate attended in the balcony and threw money
to the mob. The crowd was prodigious—stages built all around—and the windows
and even tops of houses were crowded with people. It began by pageant, a kind of
mock triumphal carr, with ordinary girls dressed very fine in it, proceeded by others
in procession. There was next represented the palace of Armida into which she
conducted Rinaldo…a huge dragon comes out of the cave under the palace to attack
them together with 2 griffins all spitting fire and made hideously frightful. [Rinaldo
boards a vessels and sails away.]…More monsters appear all in flames and set fire
to the palace whiles Armida flies away on a fiery dragon. The whole of this was
comical enough—as it was all burlesque—sometimes the machinery of the monsters took fire and burnt the men underneath, upon which they throw off the whole
apparatus and appear half-naked to the spectators. The scrambling for money, the
poultry etc too afforded great diversion.[2]

According to Burney's account, the Festa della porchetta commemorated a thir-
teenth-century military victory. The public hunt and kill also had parallels with
ancient feasts featuring sacrificial slaughter.[3]

Among the graphic works that depict Bolognese festivals, the Festa della porchetta is by far the most popular subject. During the seventeenth and eighteenth
centuries, more than a hundred publications and prints documented this annual
celebration.[4] Framed by the heraldic devices of the city elders, these prints are not
intended to be realistic depictions; rather, they show the temporary architecture, the
theater with mythical figures such as Armida and Rinaldo, the pageant floats and
monsters, and, inevitably, Bacchus, the god of wine, as well as tournaments, games,
acrobatics, and fireworks.

The highlight of the festival was the spectacle of the people scrambling for food.
Rather than depicting the elite banquet that was held inside the palace on the day of
the Porchetta, the prints show pigs on the hoof and the scene of the central plaza in
front of the palaces and the church of San Petronio as roast pig, fowl, bread, cheeses,
and cakes were hung or thrown down from the balcony for the hungry Bolognese
to feast upon. Luigi Mattioli's 1691 print *Festa de vino à Bologna* (Wine festival in
Bologna) depicts the wine barrels.[5] Giovanni Antonio Belmondo's print shows the

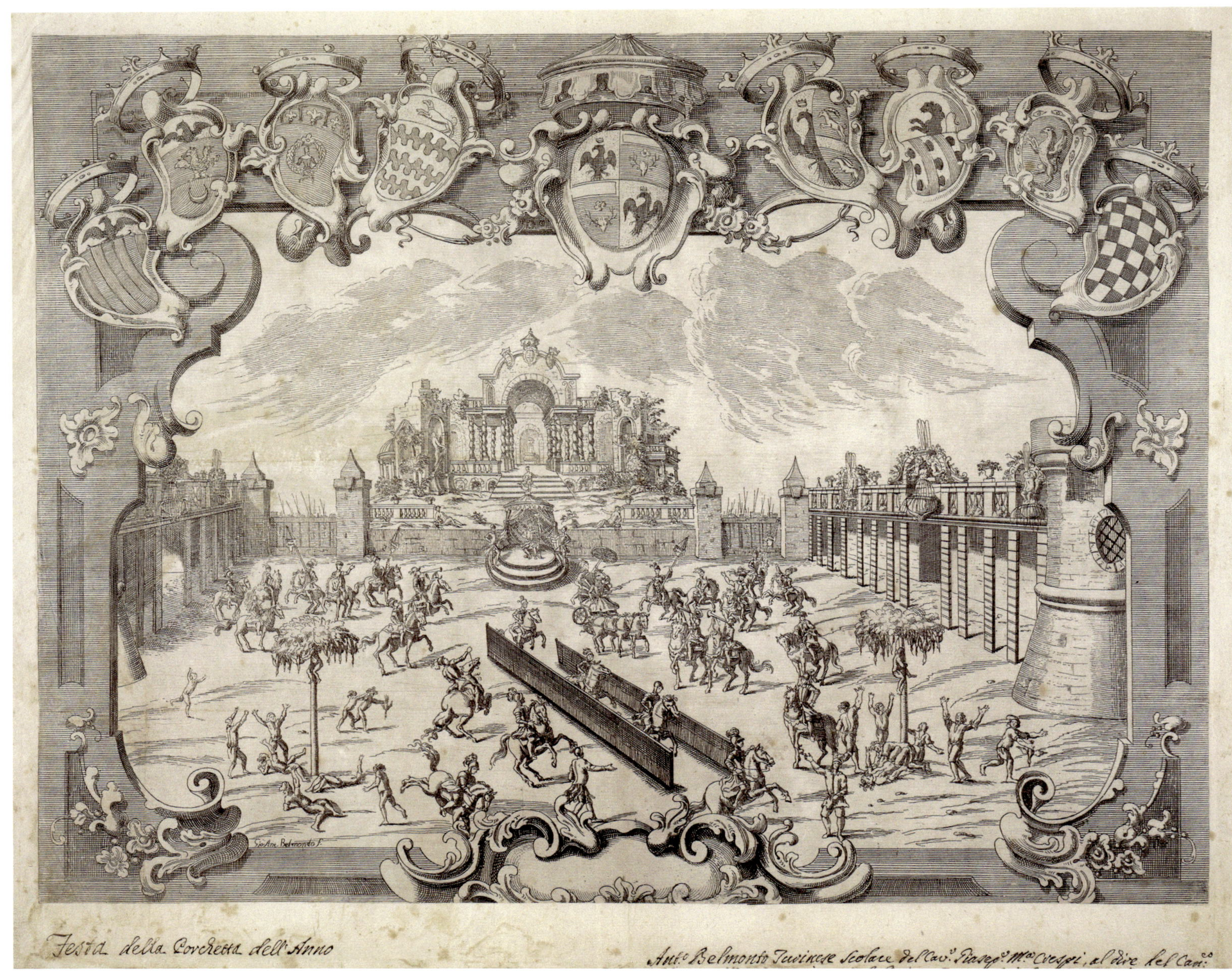

FIG. 4.

Giovanni Antonio Belmondo

(Italian, 1696–1775).

Festa della porchetta in Bologna,

Bologna, ca. 1735, etching,

35.3 × 48.1 cm (13⁹⁄₁₀ × 18⁹⁄₁₀ in.).

Los Angeles, Getty Research

Institute.

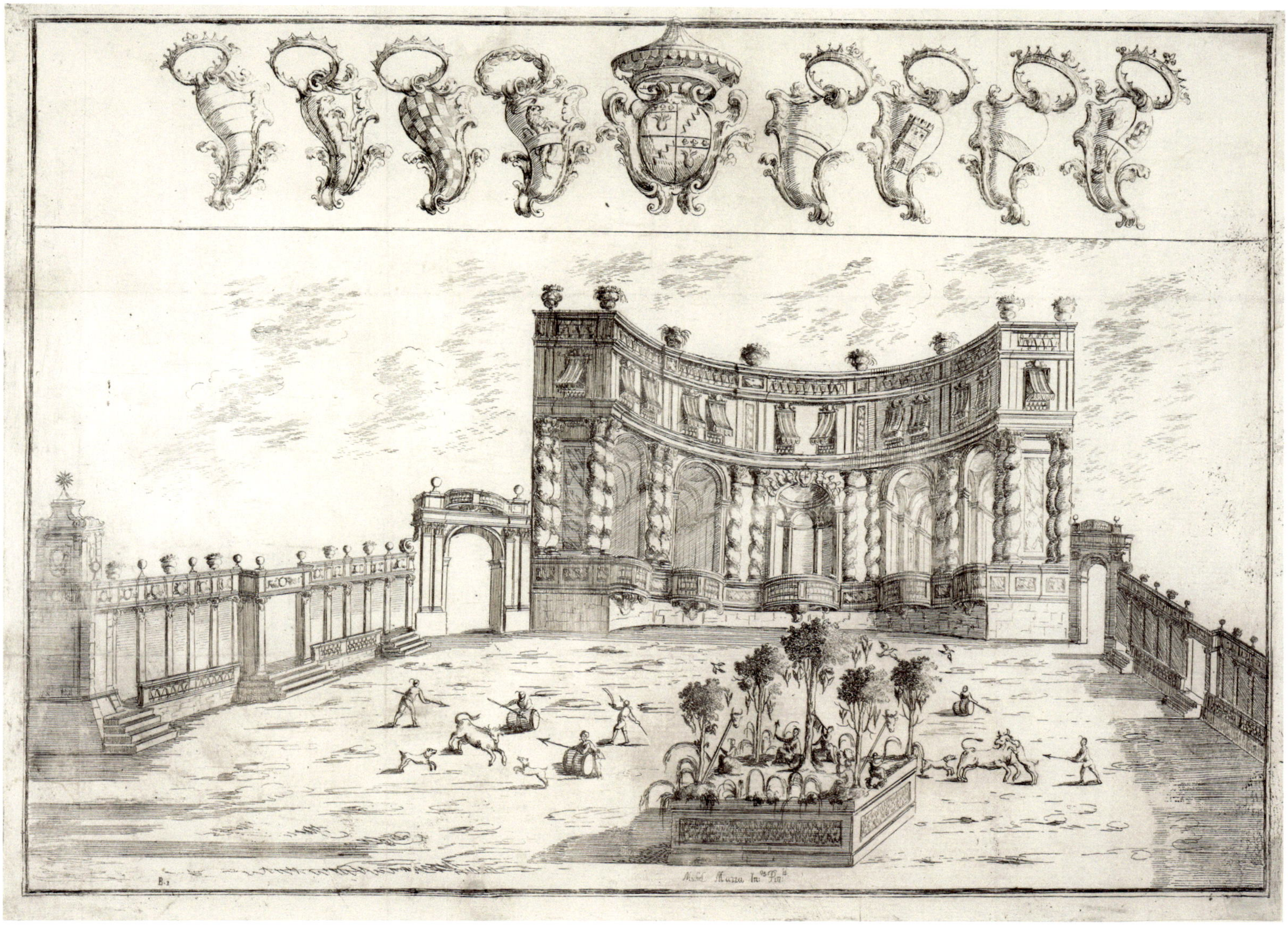

temporary architecture staged in the Piazza Maggiore (fig. 4). Amid the dances, jousts, and theater, the primary entertainment was the chase of livestock—pigs, wild boars, bulls, and birds—let loose among the temporary architecture and sculpture. Michele Mazza's print depicts an enclosed space with festival structures in the background and Cuccagna trees hung with birds (fig. 5). Here, there is no edible table monument laden with symbols to be admired like those designed for the elite banquets of the *gonfalonieri* (city elders). Cuccagna trees (seen in the foreground of both figures) were greased poles with fowl and other foods hung to reward the climbers who successfully scaled them.[6] Borrowed from Cuccagna festivals, the tall, ephemeral trees signaled festival games that were sporting for those who tried to shinny up the poles and entertaining for those who watched the climbers, laughing and cheering them on.

FIG. 5.

Angelo Michele Mazza (Italian, d. 1726).

Festa della porchetta in Bologna, Bologna, ca. 1716, etching, 36.4 × 52.1 cm (13⅗ × 20½ in.). Los Angeles, Getty Research Institute.

CARNIVAL IN NUREMBERG

Well into the sixteenth century, festivals were still recorded in manuscripts and sketches. Although they were frequently copied, manuscripts, as unique works, did not circulate widely. Instead of employing the new media of letterpress, woodcut, or engraving, traditional handwritten accounts and gouaches were deemed appropriate for historic reenactments on holidays, recording times spent with family and friends.

In late medieval Nuremberg (1449-1539), the Schembart festival took place during Carnival. Dating from the sixteenth century and later, *Schembartbücher* (illustrated festival manuscripts) presented detailed retrospectives of the festival during the fifteenth and sixteenth centuries. They are organized in standard formats by the years in which celebrations took place, naming the sponsoring families and showing the specially designed costumes with their heraldic colors. Not until the end of the eighteenth century was there a printed publication on the Schembart festival. But, in contrast to the lively and vivid depictions in the manuscripts, it was a dull little volume with postage stamp-size prints that conveyed the history but no sense of the excitement.[7]

Like the Festa della porchetta in Bologna, the Schembart festival was a civic event associated with prosperous families in the southern German city of Nuremberg. Originally, the festival was sponsored by the butchers' guild, and, as festivals often are, it was anchored in a historic event. Schembart books trace the event's origins to an artisans' revolt in 1348. The butchers did not take part in the unrest. For their loyalty, Holy Roman Emperor Charles IV and the city council gave the guild permission to hold a butchers' dance on Shrove Tuesday (*Fastnacht*). The costumed procession of *Schembartlauf* was added to the festival a century later, and eventually became the main event.[8] For the dance, the butchers hired young men to run ahead of them and clear the way. By the mid-fifteenth century, the masked runners (*Läufer*) were predominately sons of wealthy families, resulting in extravagant costumes. The runners from the years 1449 to 1456 have an image of a butcher's knife on the breast of their garments.[9]

For Fat Tuesday, we might expect more than just a hint about the food in the *Schembartbücher,* but the only information about edibles is provided by the fish in baskets and nets that hung from the Schembart runners' waists (fig. 6).[10] Marking the onset of the Lenten fasts, fish were strung on poles or collected in baskets at the runners' feet; these are never shown after the first several years of festivals in the mid-fifteenth century. Just one feast appears among all the scenes illustrating festival floats and temporary monuments along the parade route: the opening for 1518 shows a round table set with four plates and a central platter (fig. 7).[11] Two runners, still in costume and masks (it must have been difficult to eat while wearing a

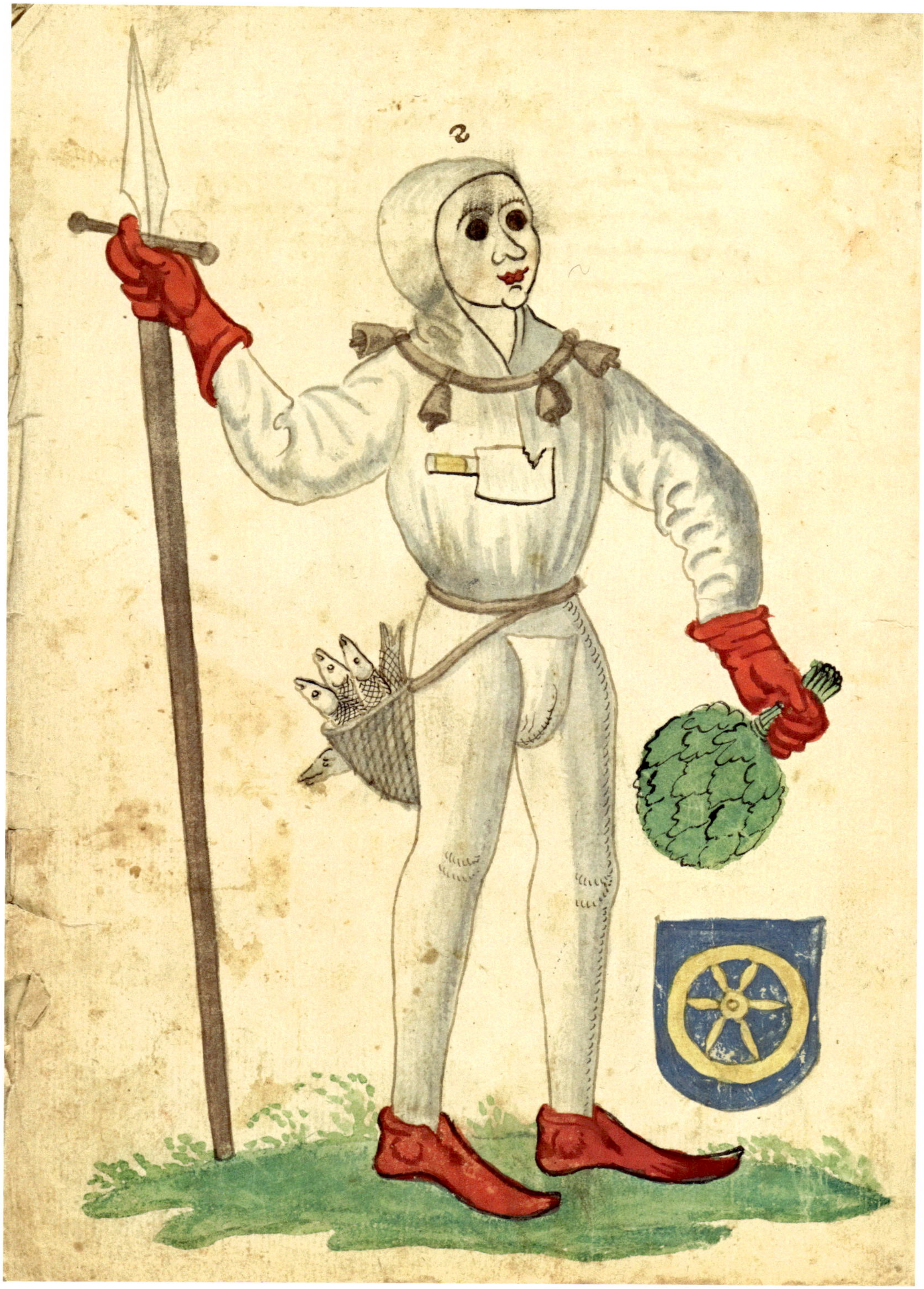

FIG. 6.

Läufer with butcher's knife on his doublet and fish basket from the first Schembart festival, in 1449.

Schembard Büch, Nuremberg, 16th century, manuscript with gouache sketches on paper, 6v, 21 × 15 cm (8¼ × 6 in.).

Los Angeles, Getty Research Institute.

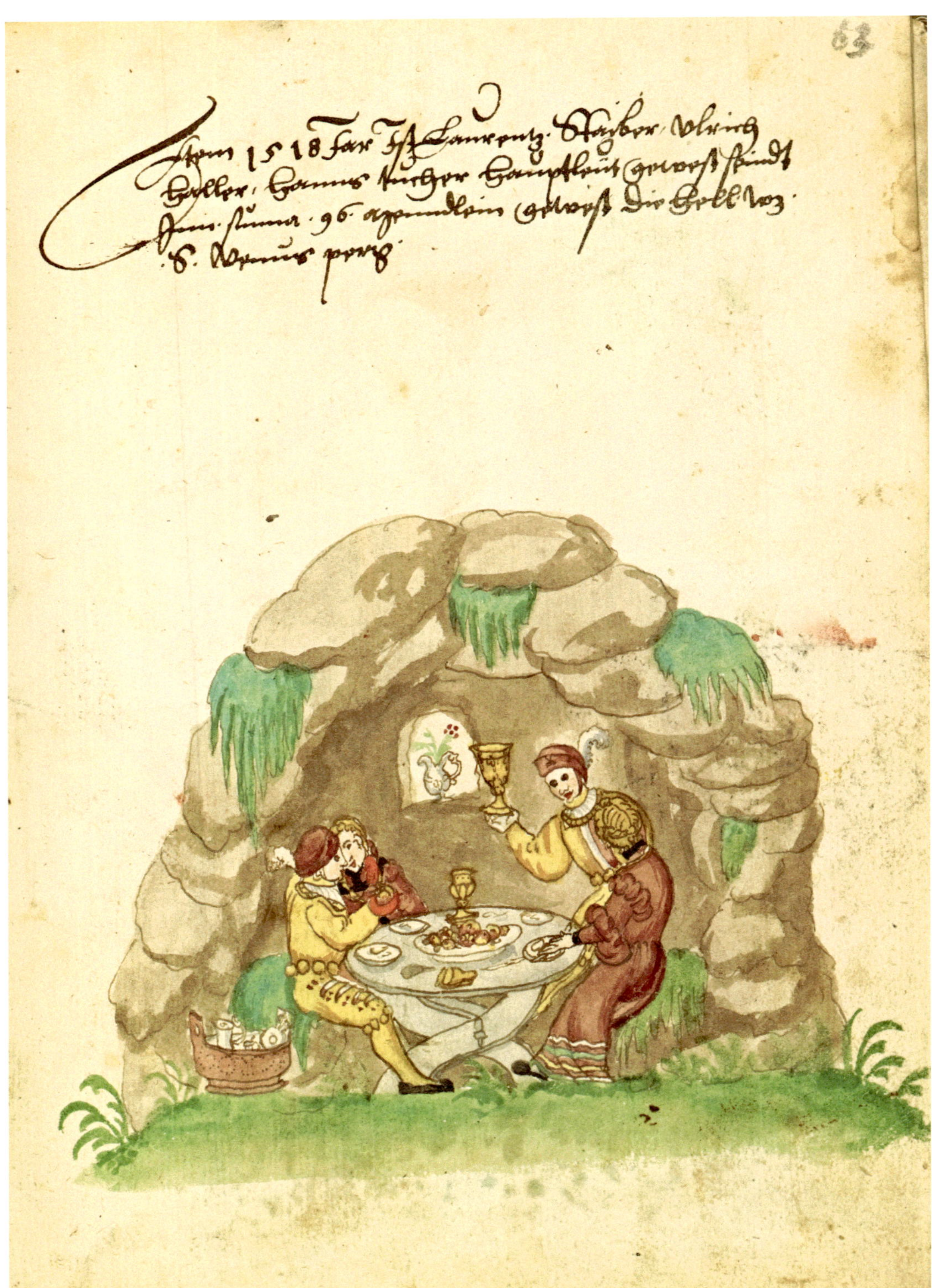

FIG. 7.

A tableau of a lascivious banquet in Venusberg mounted for the Schembart festival in 1518.

Schembard Büch, Nuremberg, 16th century, manuscript with gouache sketches on paper, 63r, 21 × 15 cm (8¼ × 6 in.).
Los Angeles, Getty Research Institute.

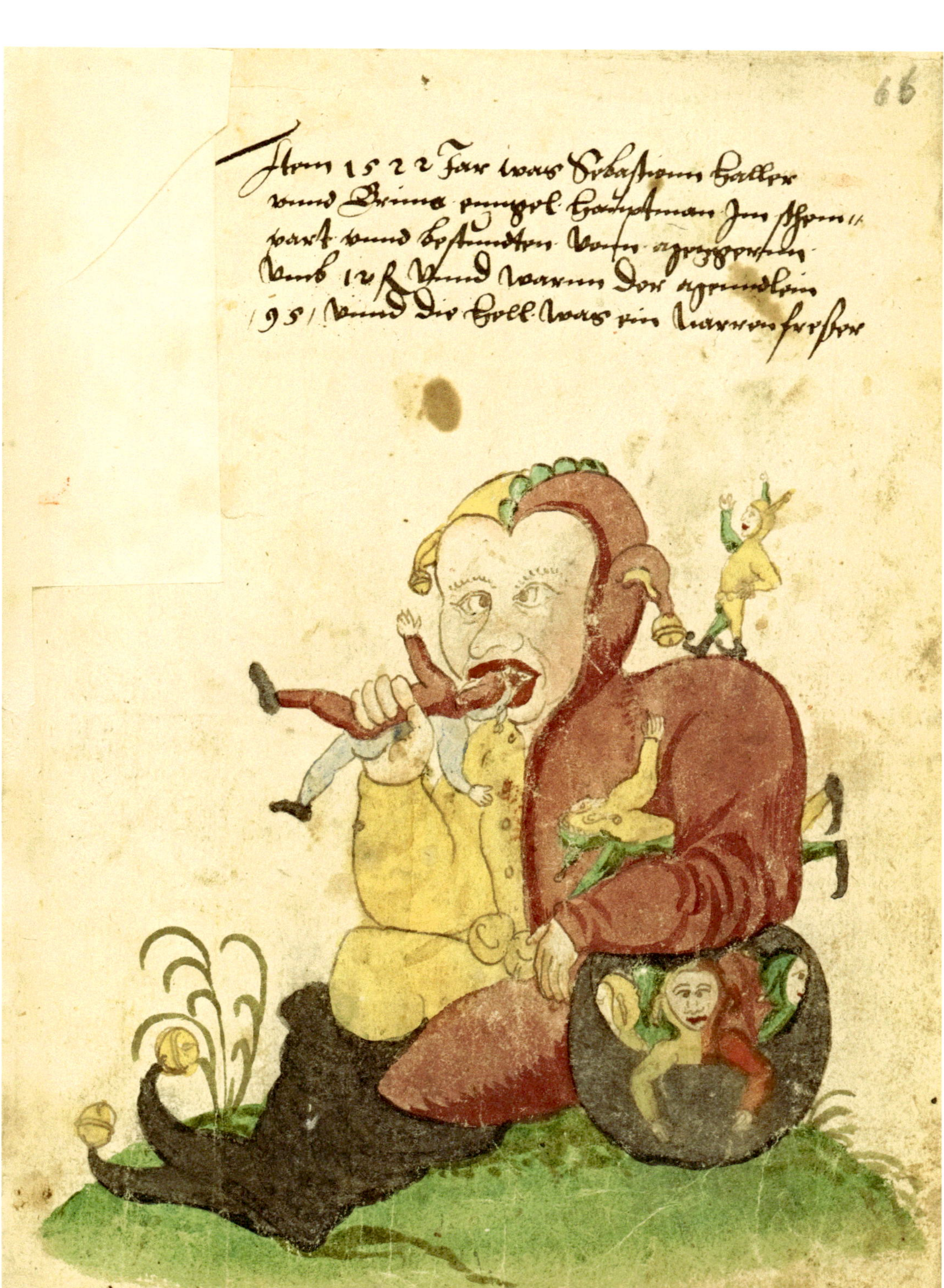

FIG. 8.
The "Hell" staged for the 1522 Schembart festival with a brightly garbed monster eating fools (*Narrenfresser*).
Schembard Büch, Nuremberg, 16th century, manuscript with gouache sketches on paper, 66r, 21 × 15 cm (8¼ × 6 in.).
Los Angeles, Getty Research Institute.

facemask), and two women dine in a grotto; one runner is making a toast with a large glass. It is a meager meal. The spare representation of food follows the tradition of medieval illuminated manuscripts. In the Schembart books, the festival floats (called *Höllen,* or "hells"—they were burned at the end of the procession) represent eating as demonic entertainment and feature monsters, dragons, and fools. With devilish humor, the image for the year 1522 shows a plump giant biting the head off a small fool while holding his next victim (and meal) under his arm (fig. 8).[12]

CARNIVALS AND MASQUERADES

Feasts alternate with fasts. Pre-Lenten celebrations continue through the centuries, allowing revelers the opportunity to step away from daily routines and enjoy the sensuous offerings of festivals: food and drink, music and dancing, decorations, parades, and games. Carnival festivals take place around the world, connecting with local customs and holidays. In mid-nineteenth-century Bamberg, another southern German city, the great public masquerade took place on Shrove Monday (the day before Mardi Gras) (fig. 9). Participants in the procession rode on horseback and in pageant wagons. They dressed as pirates brandishing bayonets, foreigners turbaned like Turks, and Commedia dell'arte characters from the street theater. They ate, drank from tankards, and distributed food as they rode through the city on elaborately decorated pageant wagons, some of which featured trees hung with sausages. Such traditional festivals frequently combine costumes—the crazier and sillier the better—and holiday foods. Sausages are favorites in both Italy and Germany. Special menus and foods served to enhance the extraordinary celebrations.

Eating was an essential part of festival entertainment, and drinking was not far behind. According to reports published in the *Mercure galant* during the reign of Louis XIV, from the 1680s on, wine fountains were featured at parties and receptions in Paris and Versailles. In city plazas and gardens, bread was distributed to people in the streets as illuminations were lit and fireworks were set off. In August 1682, as "Mademoiselle d'Orleans and Madame de Guise celebrated with illuminations in the dome and windows of this great palace, a grand meal was served to the ladies with music, and with bread and wine distributed to all who came to receive them."[13] Remarkably, for the next sixty pages, the *Mercure* attests to the regular offerings of wine and occasionally other foods proffered by court figures as well as the merchants in the streets of Paris.

In December 1700, there was an extraordinary court carnival held at Versailles. It was celebrated with "gallant collations" in the Chinese style. Buffets displaying fruits—oranges and sweet limes—dragées, pastries, and abundant liqueurs were accompanied by interior decorations and ornaments of crystal, gold, silver, and

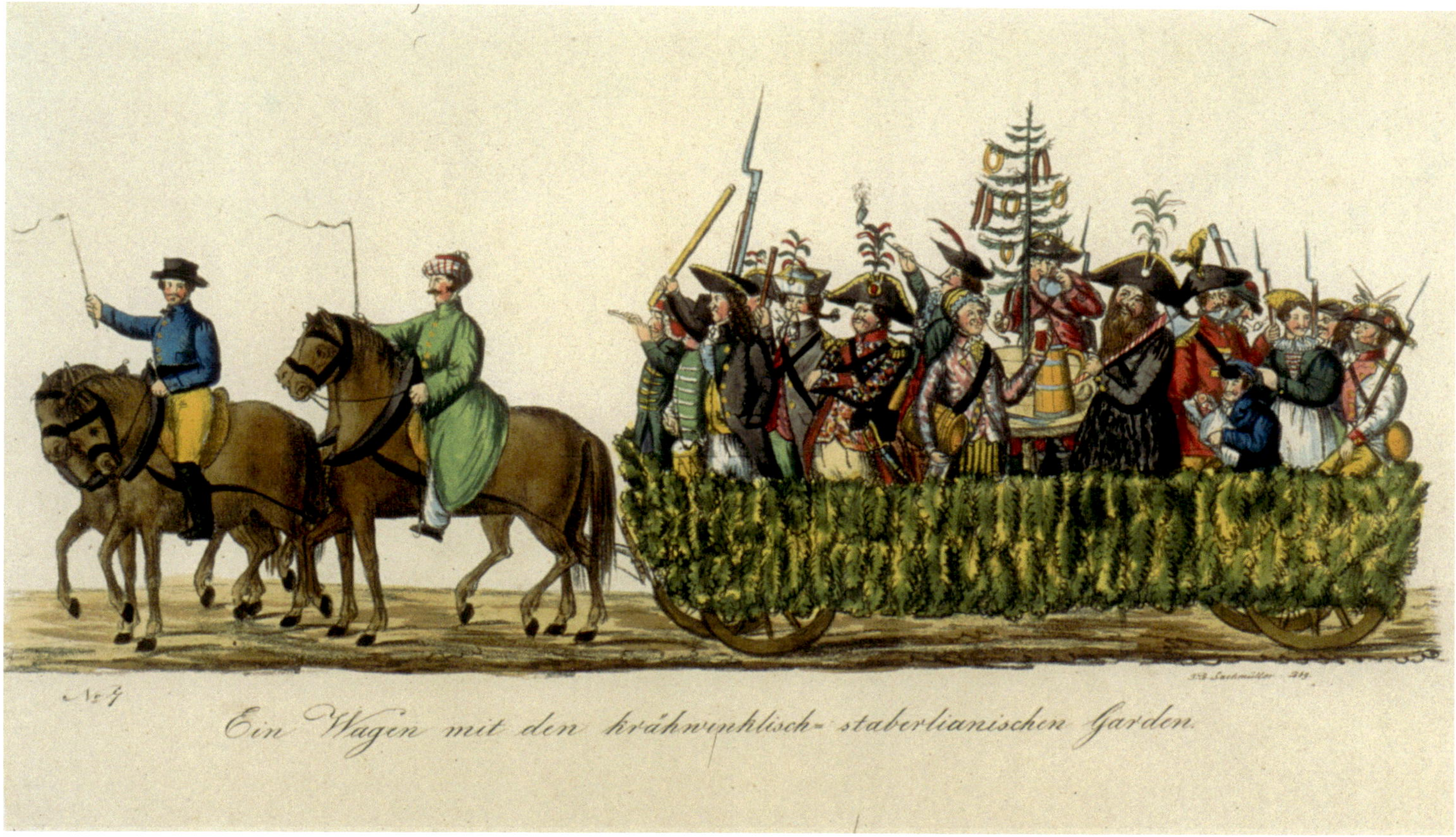

Ein Wagen mit den krähwinklisch-staberlianischen Garden.

porcelain.[14] One enormous buffet setting had five ascending glass tiers, each decorated with varied colored brocades of silver and gold, displaying fruits, sweets, and an astonishing amount of real flowers. At the fifth level, there was a royal Chinese throne for a seated figure and two smaller thrones beside him. The thrones were surrounded by four flowering orange trees heavy with fruit; caramels were placed on the branches among the leaves. On the buffet was a heavily decorated Indian tablecloth with gold and a variety of colors. Twelve officers of Louis, duc de Bourgogne and future dauphin of France, served; they were dressed as pagodas and seated between each table. When Marie Adélaïde of Savoy, duchesse de Bourgogne, came into the room, the living pagodas rose to acknowledge her. Although other participants in this masquerade wore masks, the duke and duchess did not. According to the *Mercure* writer, everything was so well organized and orderly that there was no hurry, allowing time for the guests to admire the magnificence and good taste of the duke. When the duke and duchess had left, there was a prodigious distribution of the liqueurs, sweets, and fruits. The ball began at two and went until four in the morning, after which coffee and chocolate were served from great trays (*cabarets*) carried by two men on their shoulders.[15]

FIG. 9.

J. B. Lachmüller

(German, fl. mid-19th century).

Pageant wagon for Shrove Monday, hand-colored lithograph, 27 × 43 cm (10³⁄₅ × 16⁹⁄₁₀ in.).

From Die grosse offentliche Maskerade zu Pferde und zu Wagen in Bamberg am Fastnachts Montage 1837 (Bamberg: Lachmüller, 1837), no. 7.

Los Angeles, Getty Research Institute.

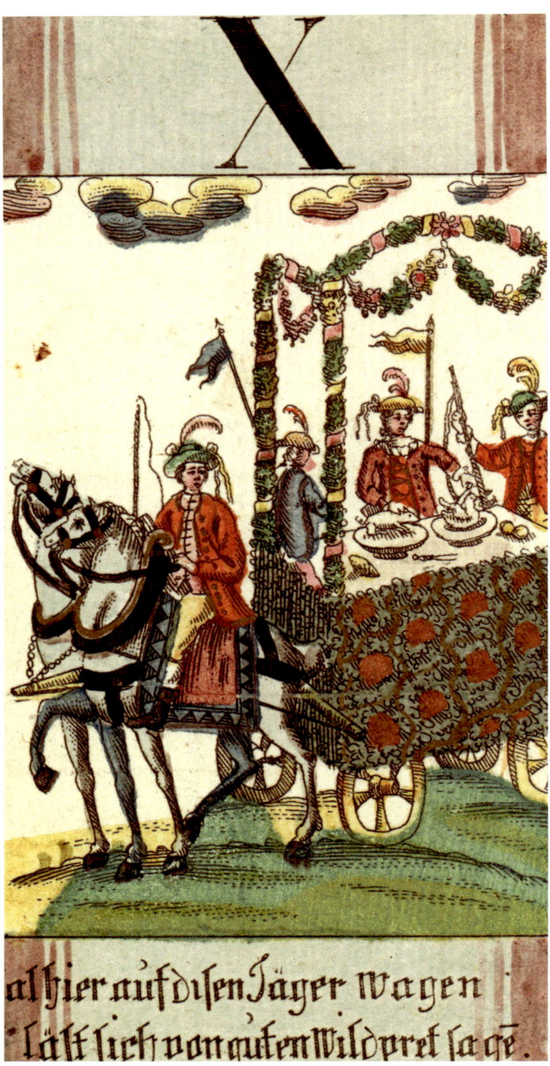

Court ceremonies and street festivals often came together in unique, occasionally bizarre, and often humorous ways. A set of seventy-eight playing cards depicts a *Baurnhochzeit* (peasants wedding) procession (fig. 10). This festival, which commemorates the wedding of Bavarian princess Josefa to Joseph II of Austria in 1765, was typically held at the end of Carnival celebrations. A variation on popular street festivals, this elite masquerade recalls the costumed entertainments and horse carousels at Versailles a century before. Members of the Munich court "dressed down" in costumes of farmers, shepherds, shopkeepers, and merchants as they rode through the city on horseback and pageant wagons, drinking and feasting. Appropriately for the wedding theme, cards show characters who personify social types and tradesmen. Satirical verses below the pictures comment archly on this social role-playing: "Ein baur bin ich nach den gwand, iedanooch gros von adlstand" (Although I am a farmer by my costume, by birth I am grand).[16]

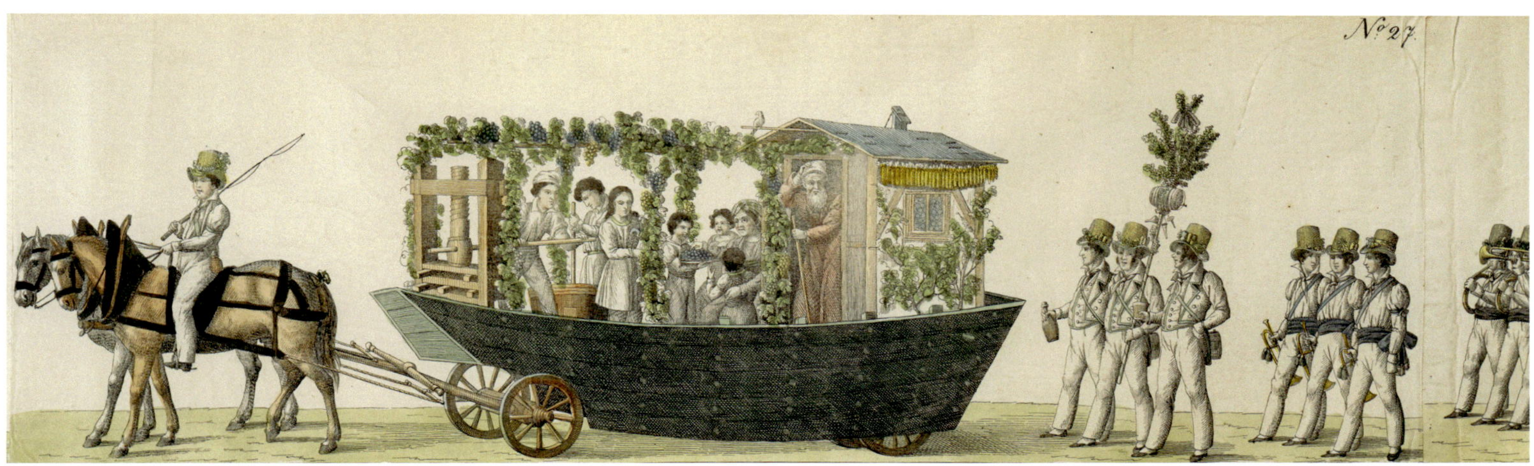

In agricultural regions, particularly where grapes were grown, popular festivals and processions celebrated the harvest. Many vineyards had originally belonged to local abbeys and monasteries, and the celebrations combined religious subjects, folklore, and myths. On a scroll depicting the "Feast of the Winegrowers," the ark of Noah (who was considered to be the first vintner) is preceded by Ceres (the Roman goddess of agriculture) and Silenus (the Greek companion to Dionysus), riding a donkey (fig. 11). The townspeople are dressed as ancients, wearing togas and laurel wreaths. Many festivals have long lives and continue to be enacted on a regular basis. This celebration still takes place approximately every twenty years in the Swiss town of Vevey.

PARADISE ON EARTH: THE CUCCAGNA

Cuccagna festivals hark back to legends of the Land of Cockaigne. According to medieval folktales, it was a paradise on earth. Cockaigne is a mythical land where no one ever goes hungry, grows old, or must work hard. Whoever works the least earns the most (fig. 12). This was the perfect theme for festival celebrations that sought to distract poor and hungry people from the hardships of their daily lives, if only for a moment. A French broadside from the mid-sixteenth century gives a humorous description of this fabulous land, calling it "The Island of Bustbelly."[17] It is a paradise made of porridge and other edibles—rocks of melted cheese and trees of butter. A house is shingled with cheese tarts and has doors of cakes. Men grow ripe on trees, falling fully grown and well dressed to lead a lazy life of eating, playing games, and making love.

In Italy, this mythical place blended with Carnival themes. Ferando Bertelli's Venetian print, *Il trionfo de carnavale nel paese de Cucagna* (The triumph of Carnival in the Land of Cockaigne), tells the story from a poor man's perspective in texts accompanying the vignettes (fig. 12). Combining the Festa della porchetta with this

FIG. 11.

Gustave Spengler (Swiss, 1818–76).

Pageant Wagon of Noah's Ark in the Procession of the Vintners, hand-colored lithographs on a scroll, 19 × 50 cm (7½ × 19¾ in.). From Christian Gottlieb Steinlen, *Fête des vignerons* (Vevey: G. Blanchaud, 1833), pl. 27. Los Angeles, Getty Research Institute.

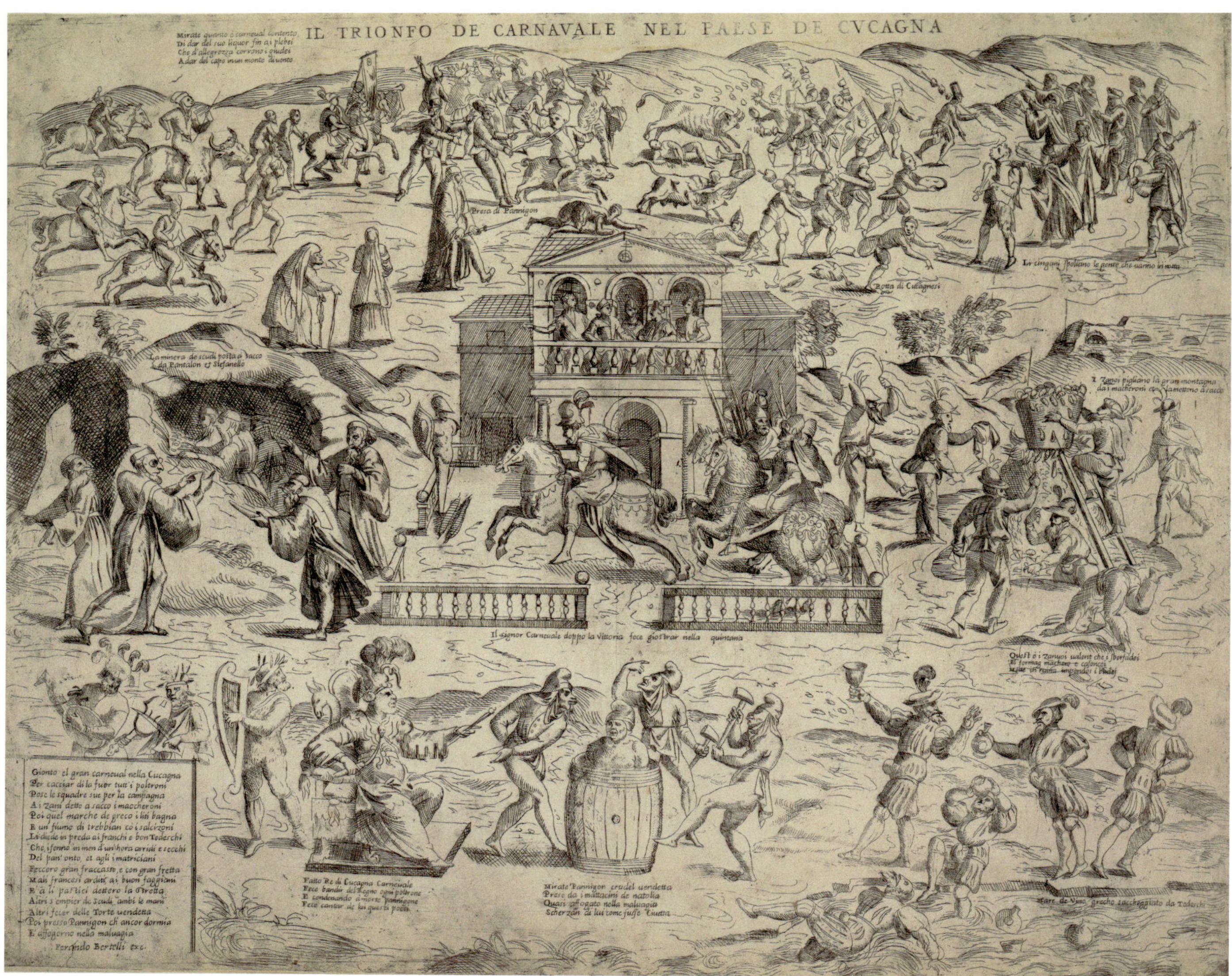

FIG. 12.

Ferando Bertelli (Italian, fl. 1563).

The Triumph of Carnival in the Land of Cockaigne, Venice, ca. 1560s, etching, 39 × 49.5 cm (15⅓ × 19½ in.). Los Angeles, Getty Research Institute.

earthly paradise, Giuseppe Maria Mitelli's 1703 narrative print *La Cucagna nuova* (The new Cuccagna) depicts the landscape of "Porcolandria."[18] With mountains covered with gold and silver (like Senator Francesco Ratta's banquet sculpture or Louis XIV's gilded garden grottoes at Versailles), the Land of Cockaigne is a pastoral place where all kinds of animals graze and the trees are filled with fruits. There are birds that drop into people's hands, hens that lay thirty eggs per day, rivers of fine wines, lakes of milk and honey, mountains made of cheese, and rainstorms of cakes and candies. On one of the mountains, there is a beautiful palace decorated with delicacies. Everyone is dressed superbly and occasionally visits a fountain of youth. Life presents itself as easy, full of sensual pleasures and no responsibilities. Similar to the heavenly vision described in the book of Isaiah, which tells of a feast of rich food on a mountain, the Land of Cockaigne was the opposite of the hard life of the hungry poor in cities and peasants in the country.[19] It was the perfect theme for festival celebrations that sought to take people away from the rigors and deprivations of everyday life (fig. 13).

FIG. 13.

Description of the Land of Cockaigne, Where Whoever Works the Least Earns the Most. Bassano: Remondini, 1606, hand-colored etching, 41.5 × 55.5 cm (16⅓ × 21⁵⁄₇ in.). Los Angeles, Getty Research Institute.

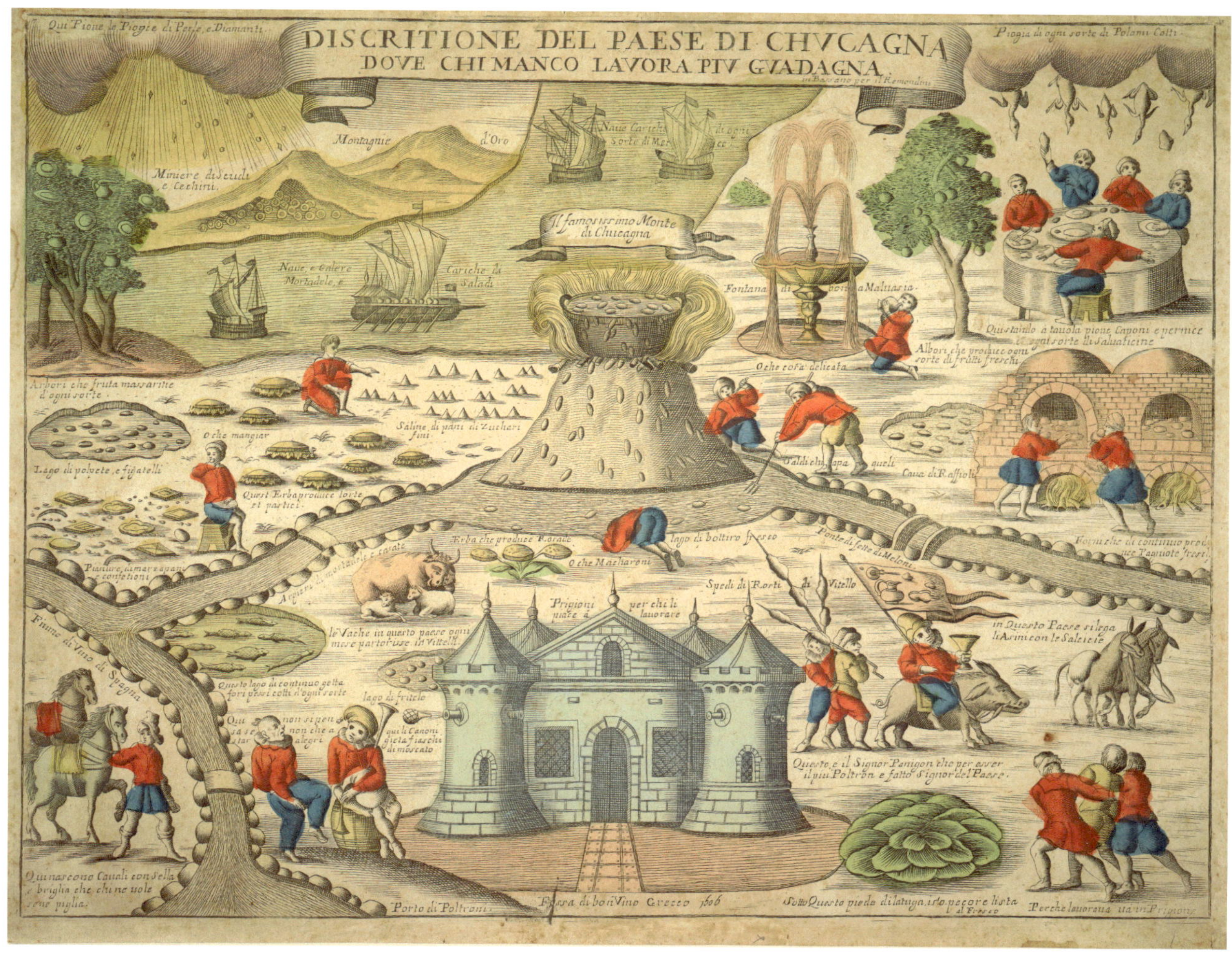

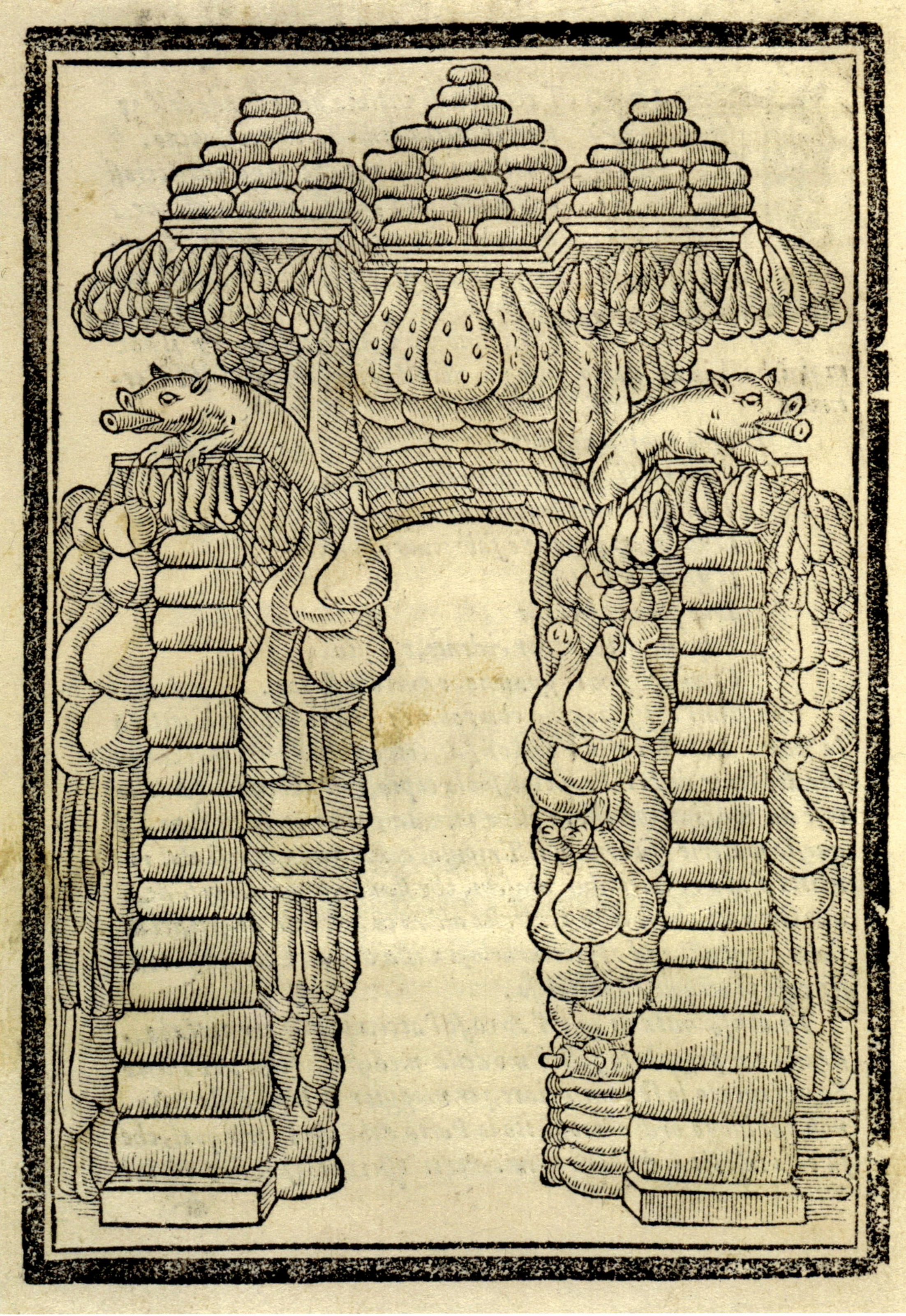

Artistic designs based on the Cuccagna legend took many forms. Most often, they became decorative elements or were built into large temporary structures made of food. In a book-length account of the Feast of Saint John the Baptist in Naples on 23 June 1629, a woodcut shows a triumphal arch in the Porta della Caputo (fig. 14).[20] Inspired by the wares of neighborhood stores, this Cuccagna monument is completely covered with fruits, vegetables, breads, salami, and roasted pigs. Poets and artists fabricated images and combined them with real edibles. Fireworks spewed out of the mouths of the pigs. Some decorations were varnished and painted and not intended for consumption. The Cuccagna arch is only one among many decorations with emblems, notable figures, and architecture mounted to celebrate the heroic virtues of Antonio Alvarez di Toledo, the Duke of Alba. The bountiful display of edibles in the Cuccagna arch alludes to one of the duke's virtues: the generous provision of sustenance for the people of the city.[21]

Not always a proper festival, a *Cuccagna* was also an ornamental public display of food—a temporary monument, or "machine," made for festivals such as Carnival or the Porchetta. Cuccagne were featured in the eighteenth-century Chinea festivals given in homage to the pope by the people of Naples in Rome. (Beginning in the middle ages, this tribute was delivered on the back of a white mare, or *chinea*.)[22] Over the course of the eighteenth century, most notably in Naples, the Cuccagne became monumental set pieces, with freestanding architecture and sculpture constructed in central plazas. These food monuments, *macchine della Cuccagna,* were designed for royal visits and entries or for court celebrations such as birthdays. Michelangelo De Blasio's *Machina della Cocchagna* was created to celebrate the name day of Elizabeth Christina, the consort of Charles VI, in 1722 (fig. 15). The Neapolitan engraver Francesco de Grado's large print on three sheets records the ephemeral architecture built in the showy style of the Neapolitan baroque monuments. Decorations made of food—breads, pastries, swags of fruits and vegetables, livestock and fowl—appear like ornamental studs on the surface of the monument. De Blasio's design combines the edible features of the Cuccagna with traditional festival architecture such as triumphal arches and arcades, classical monuments such as obelisks, fountains and river gods with heraldic devices, and portraiture alluding to the political regime in Naples. Another large engraving of theater performed during a banquet for Elizabeth in 1724 shows how traditional feasts were staged and combined with other festival pieces. Two years later, in November, De Blasio designed another Cuccagna monument to honor the name day of Charles VI (fig. 16). It is embellished with food in a design that is similar to the earlier *macchina,* though simpler.

De Grado's engravings record another pair of Cuccagna monuments designed by Domenico Antonio Vaccaro for Charles and Elizabeth in 1728. Both monuments

FIG. 14.

Cuccagna arch of bread, cheese, and suckling pigs, made in honor of Duke Antonio Alvarez di Toledo, Viceroy of Naples, on the Feast of Saint John the Baptist, 23 June 1629. Woodcut, 21.8 × 15.9 cm (8½ × 6¼ in.). From Francesco Orilia, *Il zodiaco* (Naples: Ottavio Beltrano, 1630), 456. Los Angeles, Getty Research Institute.

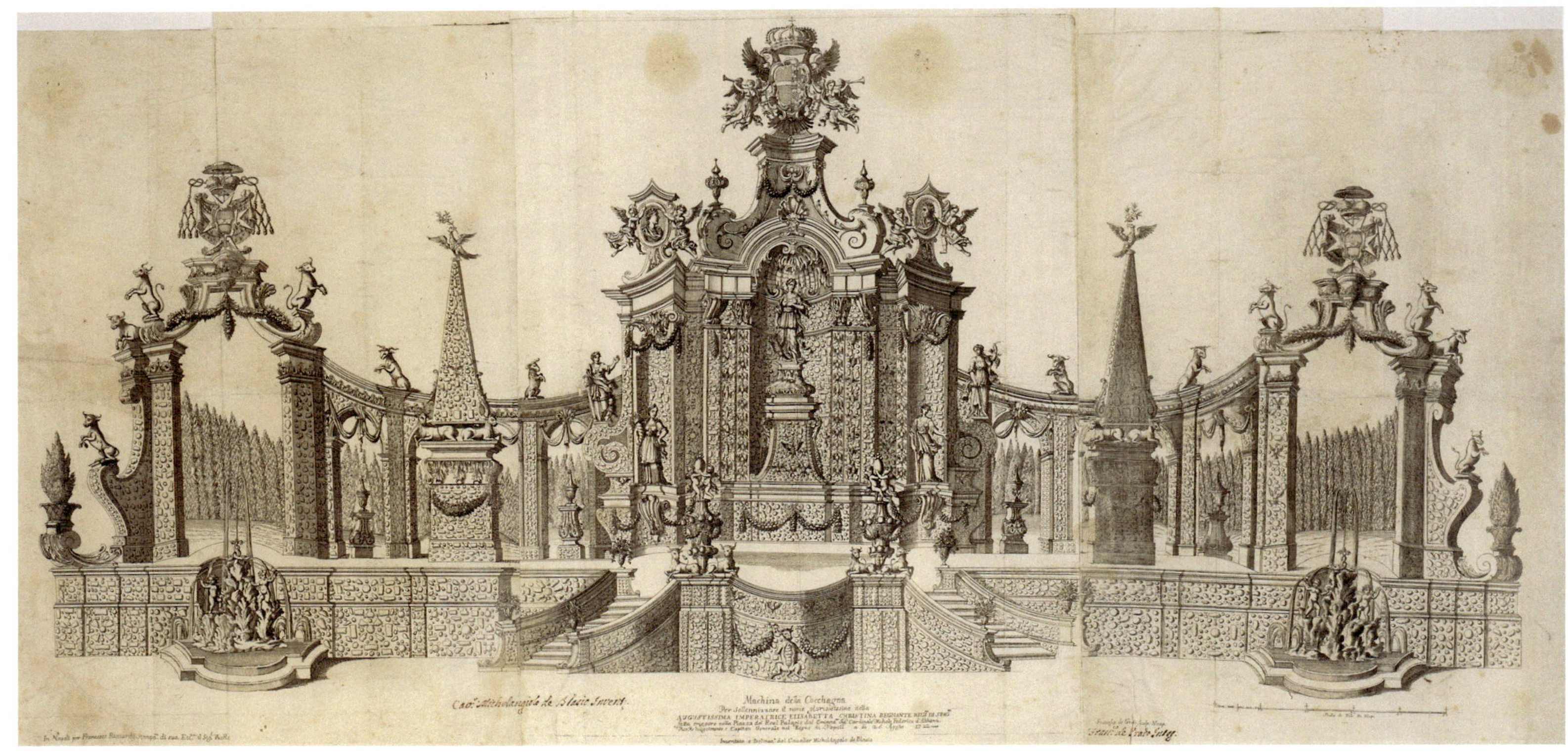

return to the basic theme of the Land of Cockaigne and feature ascendant mountains of pastoral meadows—a fertile paradise with birds, animals, and flowing fountains. The *macchina* for Charles VI depicts a battle of the Titans at its crest. Vaccaro's second machine, for Elizabeth, is more complex (fig. 17). Its central focus is a tree crowned by a ram's head from which fireworks are shot. Below, at the base of the trunk, are cavorting, rampant bulls, their backs decorated with food. In lower sections are fountains whose walls are decorated with edible pastries and confections. Birds fly in and out of the fountains of falling water; warriors stationed at gates on either extremity of the monument appear to guard the water's flow. Set in the landscape of eighteenth-century Naples, the mountainous profile of the Cuccagna would have echoed that of Mount Vesuvius, looming in the distance. In Naples, the art of the festival conjured another kind of magic mountain—that is, a paradise of food to be consumed and eventually destroyed by the people.

Most often associated with Naples, the Cuccagna monuments made of food and the celebrations that culminated in sacking were described and illustrated in travelers' accounts.[23] Yet temporary Cuccagna monuments were also featured in other Italian city festivals. In Milan, an elaborate illuminated structure was erected on Corso di Porta Orientale, otherwise known as Corso di Porta Venezia, for the wedding celebration in 1771 of Maria Beatrice Ricciarda d'Este of Modena and Archduke Ferdinand

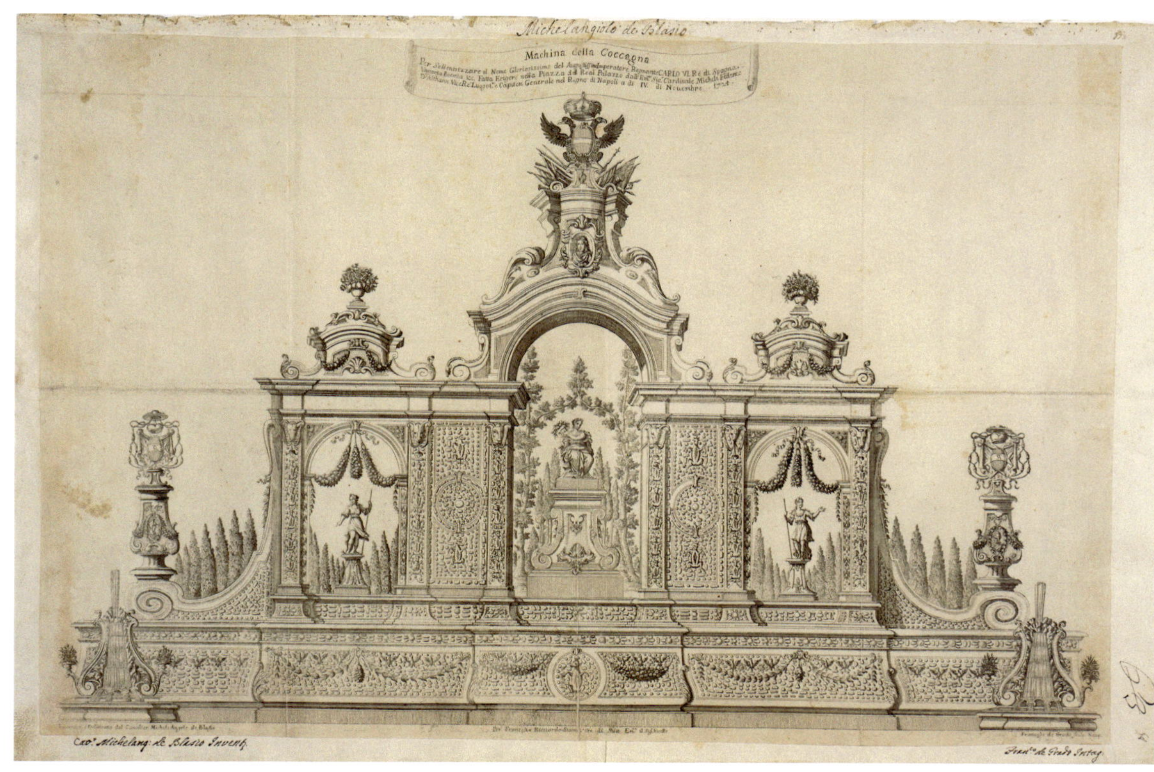

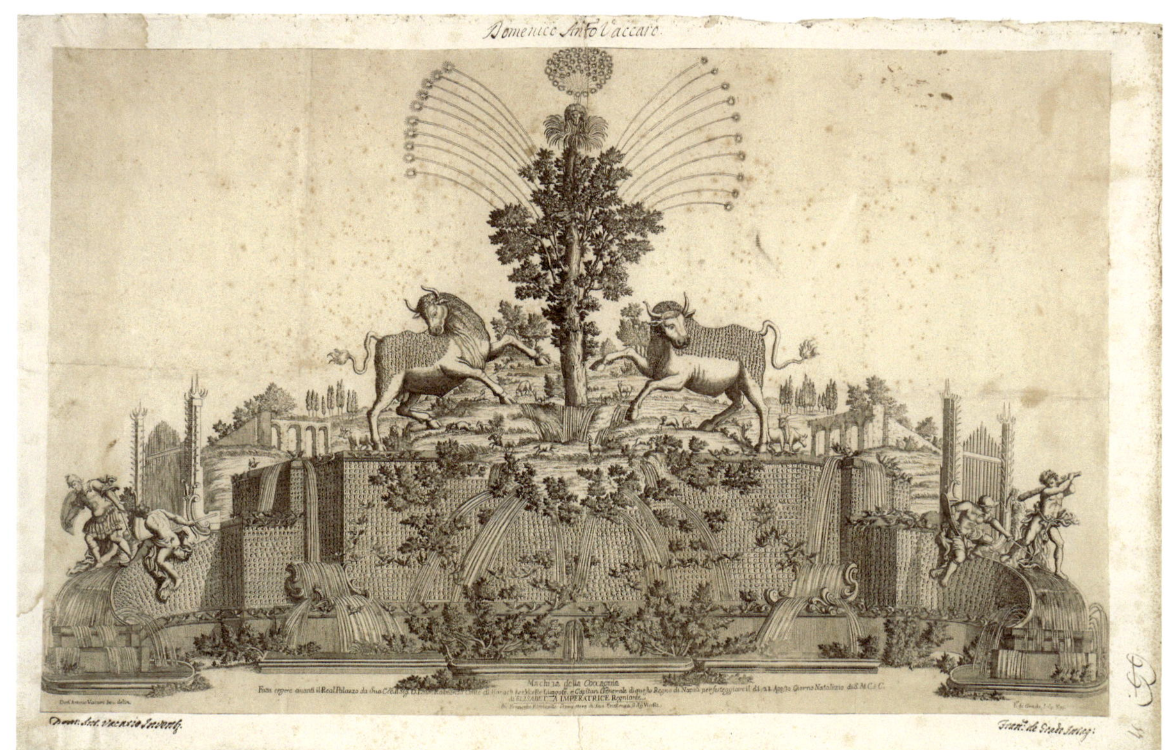

FIG. 16.

Francesco de Grado (Flemish, 1663–ca. 1733), after Michelangelo De Blasio (Italian, fl. 1721–42). Cuccagna monument for the name day of Emperor Charles VI, Naples, 1724, etching, 46.7 × 71.8 cm (18⅓ × 28¼ in.). Los Angeles, Getty Research Institute.

FIG. 17.

Francesco de Grado (Flemish, 1663–ca. 1733), after Domenico Antonio Vaccaro (Italian, 1678–1745). Cuccagna monument for the birthday of Empress Elizabeth Christina, Naples, 1728–33, etching, 44.5 × 71.5 cm (17½ × 28 in.). Los Angeles, Getty Research Institute.

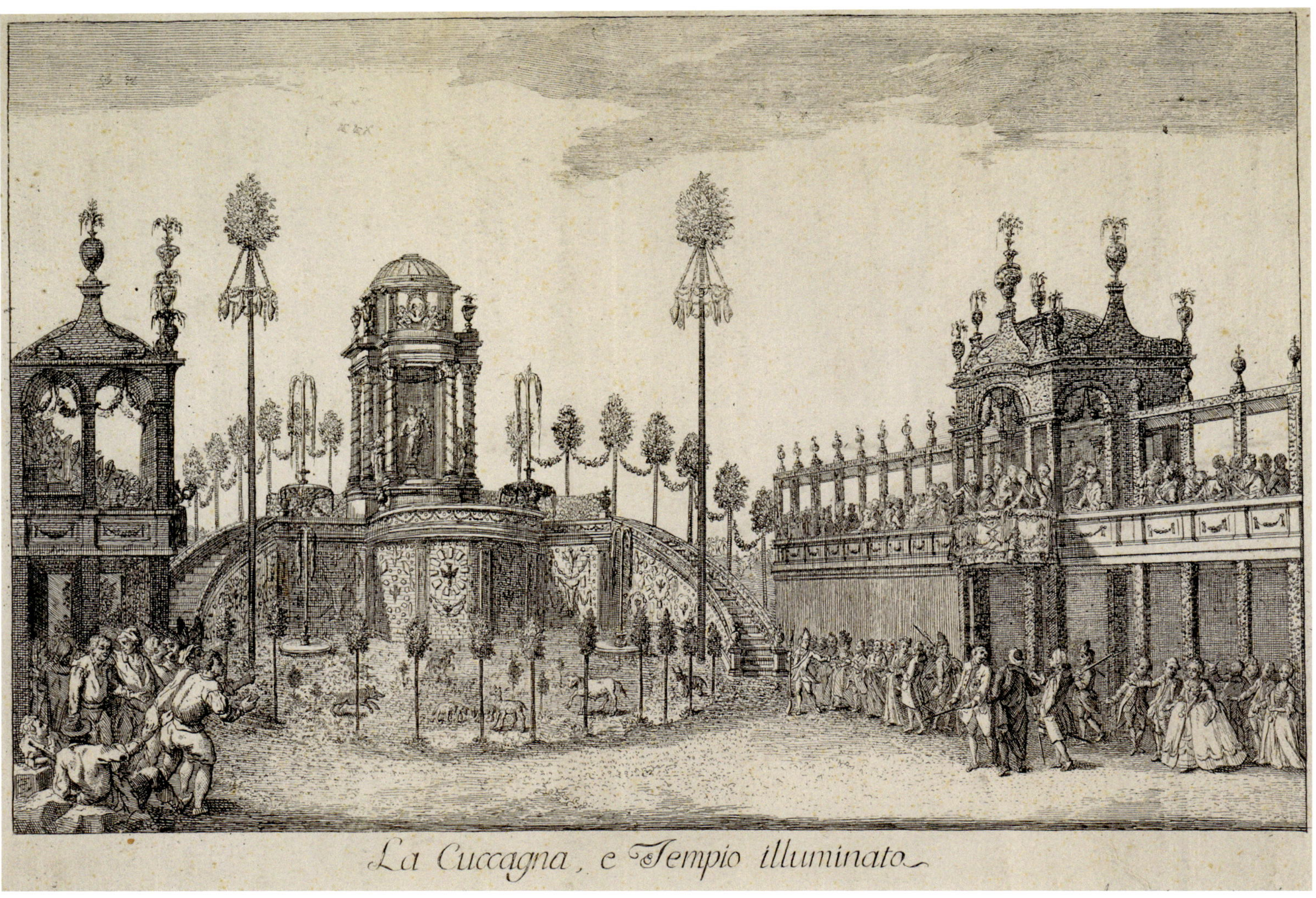

FIG. 18.

Giulio Cesare Bianchi

(Italian, fl. ca. 1760–71).

The Cuccagna, and Illuminated Temple, Milan, ca. 1771, etching, 28.4 × 40.2 cm (11¼ × 15⅘ in.). Los Angeles, Getty Research Institute.

Karl of Austria-Este (fig. 18). A *tempietto* (little temple) flanked by two semicircular flights of stairs is adorned with fowl and game. Animals run about near two Cuccagna trees. Courtiers appear at the right on the ground or on a stand, watching from balconies, while musicians and the populace are shown on the left.

A lavish folio, the *Narrazione delle solenni reali feste* (Narrative of solemn royal feasts), was published to celebrate the birth of Prince Philip, the eldest son of Charles VII, the king of Naples (later Charles III of Spain), and Maria Amalia, in Naples on 13 June 1747. Following the model set by the French Imprimerie royale at the end of the seventeenth century, this stylish volume adheres to the high quality of publications and prints for which Naples became well known in this period, epitomized by the eight-volume *Antichità di Ercolano* (1757-92; Antiquities of Herculaneum). The wide-ranging festival program for the Neapolitan people combined elite banquets and court ceremonies with illuminations, fireworks, and edible monuments made for feasts. Staged in the city plaza, these public events also served as entertainment for the court. Providing a detailed description of the events, the festival book tracks the progress inside the palace and out on the streets. Like the Versailles *fête* books, it is a beautifully produced volume, in this case, with double-page engravings of designs by Vincenzo dal Ré.

As a political statement, the festival "narration" appears to be both a highly positive historical account and a bit of civic public relations on behalf of the magnificence of the Neapolitan court and the city. It comprises an emblematic frontispiece that shows the prince escorted by the gods as he descends from heaven. There are fifteen double-page prints and twenty pages of unsigned official description.[24] Like the Versailles festival engravings, these prints show people enjoying the entertainments; but they also make clear the closed nature of court events, which were private parties for elite guests. Unlike most festival books, however, this one illustrates all the celebrations, including those in the streets and city plazas. The public, who in many cases had been employed in the considerable work of festival preparations, watched the grand carriages drive through the city, waiting in anticipation. Plate VII, a cross section of the royal palace, demonstrates how the interior architecture guided the progress of the festival. It shows how elite guests entered on the street level, climbing the grand stairway to the Camera del Guochi (Hall of Games) and to the Camera dei Rinfreschi (Hall of Refreshments) for entertainment, food, and drinks. The last plates show external views of the street festival, decorated for the finale of fireworks; a machine known as the "Temple of Felicity"; and the moment before the sacking of the Cuccagna monument (fig. 19).

Designed by dal Ré as the final entertainment in the festival for the birth of the prince, the Cuccagna in Giuseppe Vasi's engraving elegantly brings together themes that have been associated with Cuccagna festival designs. At the base of the structure is a formal garden with a large central fountain flowing with wine. The smaller

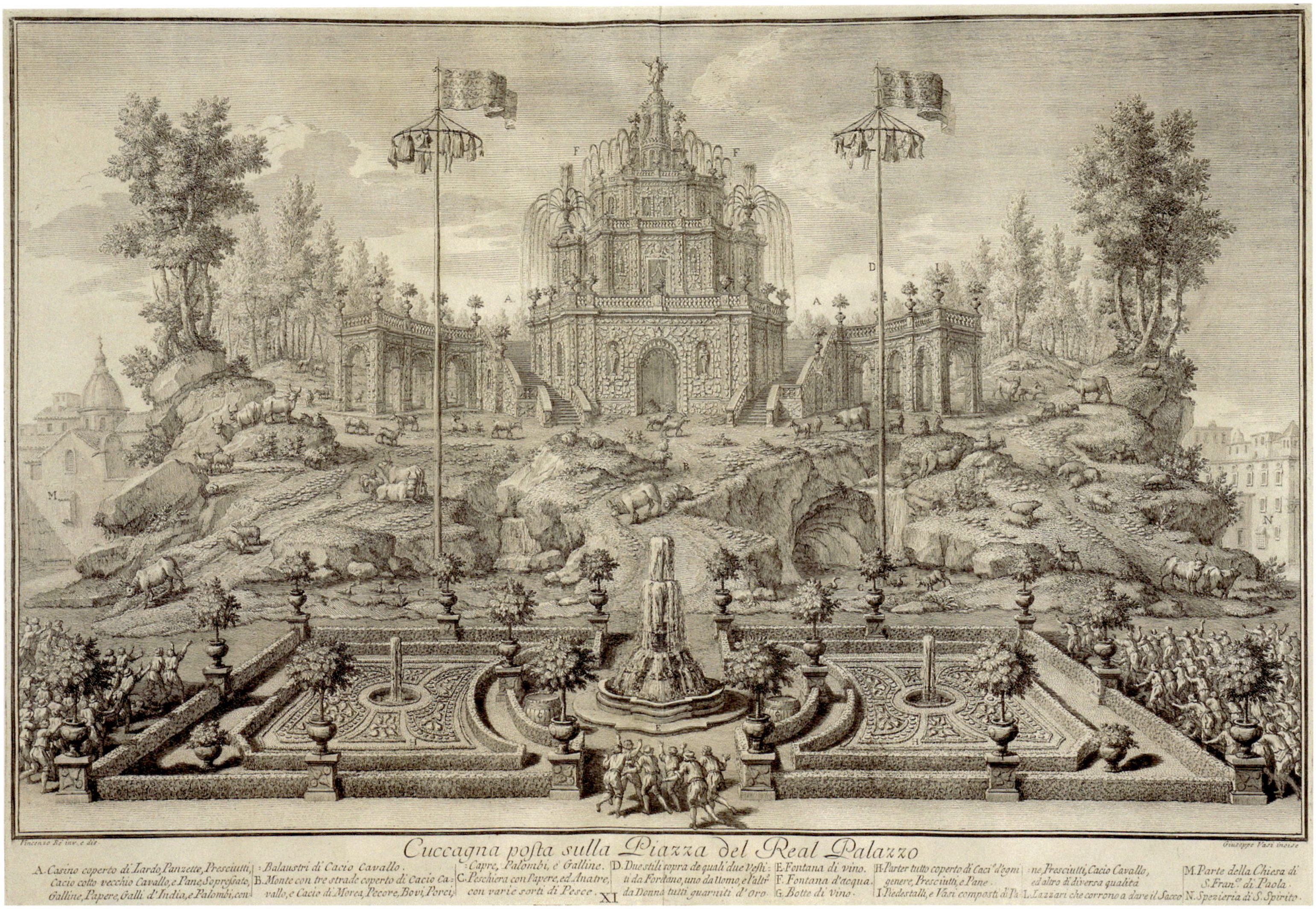

Vincenzo Ré inv. e dis.
Giuseppe Vasi incise.
Cuccagna posta sulla Piazza del Real Palazzo
A. Casino coperto di Lardo, Panzette, Presciutti, Cacio cotto vecchio Cavallo, e Pane Sopressato, Galline, Papere, Galli d'India, e Palombi, con
Balaustri di Cacio Cavallo.
B. Monte con tre strade coperto di Cacio Cavallo, e Cacio di Morea, Pecore, Bovi, Porci, Capre, Palombi, e Galline.
C. Peschiera con Papere, ed Anatre, con varie sorti di Pesce.
D. Due stili sopra de quali due Vesti ti da Fortuno, uno da Uomo, e l'altr da Donna tutti guarniti d'oro.
E. Fontana di vino.
F. Fontana d'acqua.
G. Botte di vino.
H. Parter tutto coperto di Caci d'ogni genere, Presciutti, e Pane
I. Piedestalli, e Vasi composti di Pa
ne, Presciutti, Cacio Cavallo, ed altro di diversa qualità
L. Lazzari che corrono a dare il Sacco
M. Parte della Chiesa di S. Fran.co di Paola
N. Spezieria di S. Spirito.
XI

FIG. 19.
Giuseppe Vasi (Italian, 1710–82),
after Vincenzo dal Ré (Italian,
d. 1762).
Cuccagna on the Square before
the Royal Palace, etching, 49 × 71.5
cm (19¼ × 28¼ in.).
From Narrazione delle solenni reali
feste…(Naples: s.n. 1749), pl. XI
Los Angeles, Getty Research
Institute.

fountains on either side are filled with water. On all three sides outside the garden, groups of the *lazzari* (the street beggars of Naples) are seen running, arms flailing and bodies leaning forward, nearly stumbling as they approach the wondrous vision of the Cuccagna. In utter contrast to these poor wretches from the Neapolitan streets, a peaceable kingdom of grazing animals looms on the mountain above. Two very tall, graceful Cuccagna trees just behind the garden punctuate the scene. These stand in small pools of water that flow under the bridge with ducks swimming in them. At the summit is an arcaded building with two grand stairways; fireworks spew like fountains from the upper porches. As in the earlier *macchine della Cuccagna,* all of the architectural elements are studded with meats, fowl, cheeses, and breads. Both the balustrades and the mountain paths are made of *caciocavallo* cheese. All this is made clear by the captions on the lower edge of the print. Dal Ré's conception is a high point of Cuccagna design, which amalgamates folkloristic themes with traditions of Italian baroque festival architecture.

For the Neapolitan people, the *macchine della Cuccagna* must have appeared like dreams that beckoned and promised an end to hunger and poverty. Two accounts of Neapolitan festivals published in Rome later in the century provide further ideas about what took place.[25] Both describe Maria Carolina's voyage through the countryside on her way to a grand entry into Naples to celebrate her marriage to King Ferdinand in 1768. These accounts tell of grand banquets, illuminations, and processions along the way. After she arrived in Naples, the festival celebrations went on for more than two weeks. They included fireworks, dances, musical concerts, and theater. However, according to the *Narrazione,* the most pleasing spectacle took place on the fifth of June in the plaza in front of the royal palace, where a Cuccagna was built to resemble a fortress and decorated with food. While the king, queen, grand duke and duchess of Tuscany, and others looked down on the crowd from the royal palace, the base of the Cuccagna was flooded with water filled with live fish. When King Ferdinand gave the signal, people from the crowd attempted to scale the fortress. With laughter, the noble spectators watched their efforts to swim through the water and then to climb with difficulty up the muddy mountain. On a final signal from the king to the successful ones, the Cuccagna was attacked and completely destroyed.

The Festa della porchetta and the Cuccagna had dual levels of meaning. They served as civic spectacles for the people and as street theater staged as entertainment for nobility and others who looked on from above. Although we may think of festivals as celebratory occasions, there were other aspects. The progress of the festival created a tension between the depicted ephemeral paradise where no one ever went hungry and the awkward earthbound scramblings of the street people for sustenance and survival in the face of edible temptations.

NOTES

Portions of this text were previously published in Marcia Reed, "The Edible Monument," in Harlan Walker, ed., *Food in the Arts: Proceedings of the Oxford Symposium on Food and Cookery, 1998* (Devon, England: Prospect, 1999), 141-50.

1. See Nicolas Hogenberg, *The Procession of Pope Clement VII and the Emperor Charles V after the Coronation at Bologna on the 24th February MD.XXX* (Edinburgh: Edmonston & Douglas, 1875), 18.

2. See Charles Burney, *Music, Men, and Manners in France and Italy, 1770,* ed. H. Edmund Poole (London: Eulenberg, 1969), 93.

3. See Selma Aslaoui, *Alle origini della festa bolognese della porchetta* (Padua: Clueb, 2005).

4. See Silvia Camerini, ed., *Il magnifico apparato: Pubbliche funzioni feste e giuochi bolognesi nel Settecento* (Bologna: Clueb, 1982), 150-53, which lists 115 prints, and surely there are more examples, as well as additional libretti. See also Achille Bertarelli, *Le incisioni di G.M. Mitelli* (Milan: Comune di Milano, 1940), 54-55.

5. Angelo Michele Mazza, [Festa della porchetta], ca. 1716. Getty Research Institute, 91002.

6. For examples, see G.M. Mitelli, "Festa della porchetta 1665"; and G.A. Belmondo, "Festa della porchetta 1735," Getty Research Institute, 91002.

7. Georg Andreas Will, *Nürnbergisches Schönbart-Buch und Gesellenstechen* (Jena: Mullerianis, 1765).

8. Marcia Reed, "Fireworks and Fish Baskets: The Schembart Festival in Nuremberg," *Getty Research Journal* 4 (2012), 145-52; and Keith Moxey, *Peasants, Warriors, and Wives: Popular Imagery in the Reformation* (Chicago: University of Chicago Press, 1989). The first chapter provides a summary of city politics at the time of the Schembart festival; see pages 11-18.

9. Guild members were the *Metzgers* or *Flaischhackern* (butchers) and the *Messeren* (knife sharpeners).

10. *Schembard Büch,* sixteenth century, Getty Research Institute, 2009.M.38. See leaves 5v for the fish basket by the runner's feet; 6v has a fish basket around the runner's waist; 7v shows fish carried on a pole; and 8v has fish held in a net from the runner's waist. Later portraits of the runners show the guild sign of a butcher's knife on the runners' costumes.

11. *Schembard Büch,* Getty Research Institute, 2009.M.38, l. 63 recto.

12. *Schembard Büch,* Getty Research Institute, 2009.M.38, l. 66 recto.

13. *Mercure galant,* August 1682, 100-101.

14. *Mercure galant,* December 1700, 187, 191.

15. *Mercure galant,* December 1700, 197-209.

16. Andreas Benedictus Göbl, *Baurn Hochzeit,* Munich, ca. 1765, trump/tarot card III. Los Angeles, Getty Research Institute, 93-F106.

17. For an earlier French version of this mythical land, see Pierre de la Maison Neuve's *Familière description du très vinoporratimalvoisé et très envitaillegoulmenté Royaume Panigonnois…*, ca. 1560, Collection Hennin, no. 1210, Bibliothèque nationale de France, Paris; reproduced in *The French Renaissance in Prints from the Bibliothèque nationale de France,* exh. cat. (Los Angeles: Grunwald Center for the Graphic Arts, University of California, Los Angeles, 1994), 400-401.

18. See Bertarelli, *Le incisioni,* 110-11, table XV, no. 553.

19. Isaiah 25:6.

20. Francesco Orilia, *Il zodiaco; o, Ver idea di perfettione di prencipi formata dall'heroiche virtù dell'illvstriss. et eccellentiss. Signore d. Antonio Alvarez di Toldeo…celebrata à 23 di giugno 1629 per il settimo anno del suo gouerno raccolta per Francesco Orilia* (Naples: Ottavio Beltrano, 1630).

21. "Con simil artificio, ma con roba di grascia, fù architettata la Porta dedicata alla Vigilanza, come che la principal cura, che dee tener desto il Prencipe, sia la copia, & l'abbondanza delle cose da mangiare, perche la plebe minuta è più ventre, che capo" (With such artifice, but with foods [or victuals], was developed the city gate dedicated to Vigilance, because the Prince's main task and concern were to ensure plentitude and abundance of things to eat, since the common people have bigger bellies than heads). Orilia, *Il zodiaco,* 455.

22. Mario Gori Sassoli, *Della Chinea e di altre "macchine di gioia": Apparati architettonici per fuochi d'artificio a Roma nel Settecento* (Milan: Charta, 1994); and John E. Moore, "The Chinea: A Festival in Eighteenth-Century Rome" (PhD diss., Harvard University, 1992). "Festival of the Chinea," Canadian Centre for Architecture, http://www.cca.qc.ca/en/collection/1244 -festival-of-the-chinea.

23. See Jean Claude Richard de Saint Non, *Voyage pittoresque; ou, Description des royaumes de Naples et de Sicile* (Paris: Imprimerie de Clousier, 1781), 1:249-50.

24. Alden Murray, "The Court and the Cuccagna," *Metropolitan Museum of Art Bulletin* 18, no. 5 (1960): 157-67, states: "There was no Neapolitan vedute factory"; but there actually were spectacular city views published by Antonio Cardon, Antonio Joli, Filippo and Raffaello Morghen, and Gabriele Riccardelli, among others.

25. *Relazione del pubblico solenne ingresso fatto nella città di Napoli* (Rome: Chracas, 1768); and *Continuazione del viaggio di Sua Maestà Maria Carolina* (Rome: Chracas, 1768).

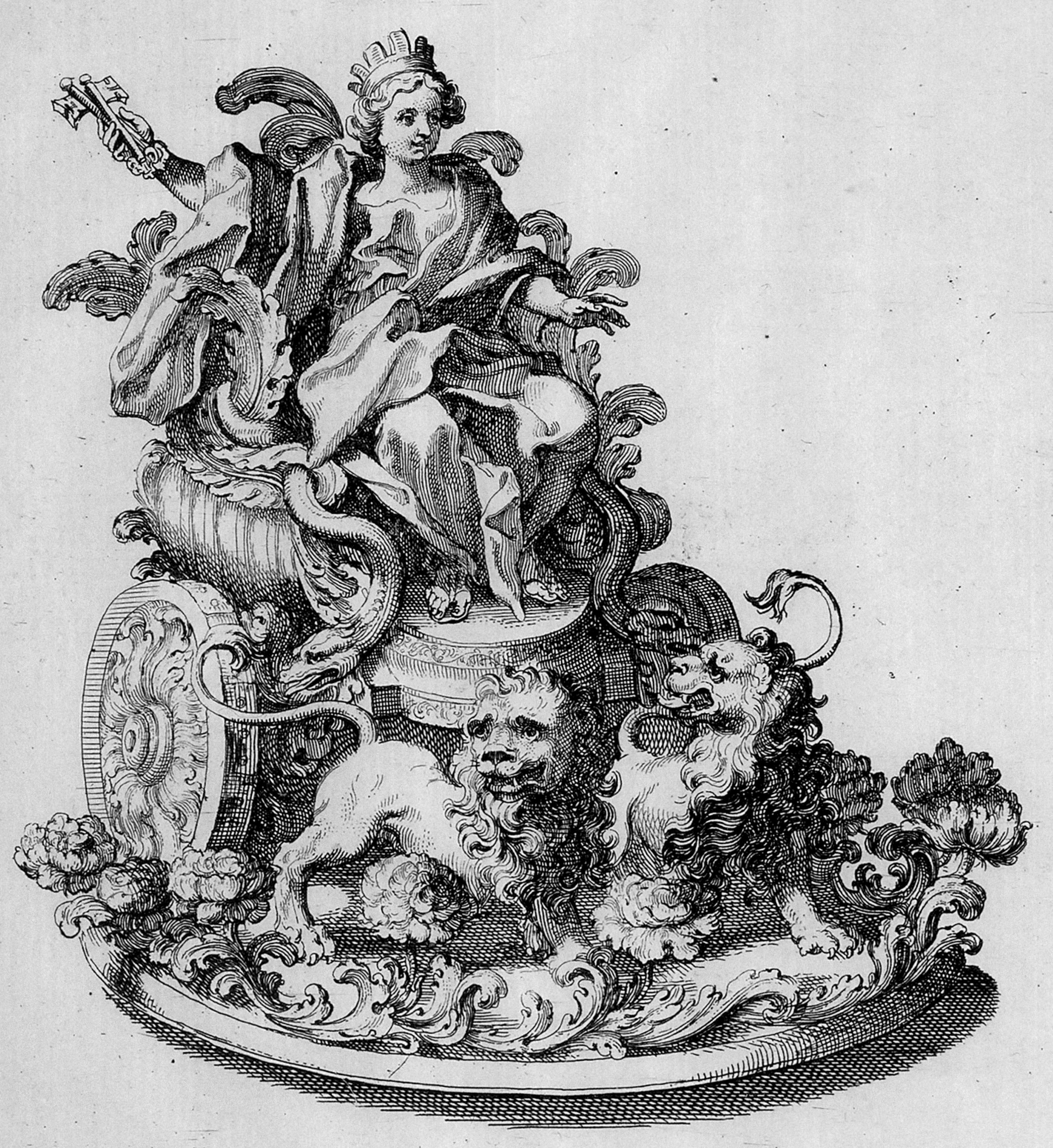

Gio. Batta. Lenardi delin.

EDIBLE PRESTIGE

JOSEPH IMORDE

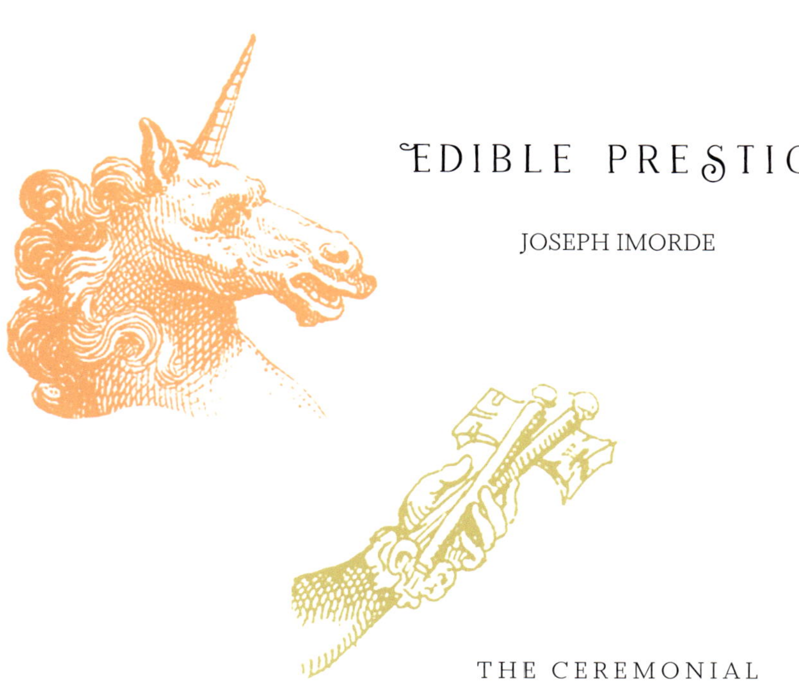

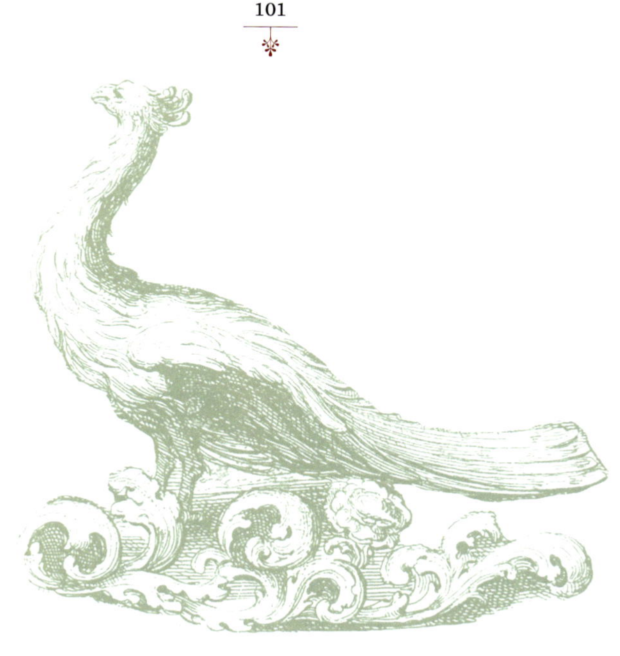

THE CEREMONIAL

The ceremonial is an order. All things in the world have their true and certain order, and one is always subordinated to the other. Why? They originate from a being of such perfection who cannot but proceed in order. The great work of the creation of the world represents a perfect example of the most beautiful order.[1]

—Johann Christian Lünig

Rulers and governing bodies used ceremonials—a specific series of events or rituals with an overarching formal order—to express political goals and accomplishments and to establish political hierarchies. These highly codified programs included the exhibition and consumption of luxury goods, which played a crucial role in defining social distinction and political regard.[2]

The complex dramaturgy and choreography of the ceremonial presented an image of the divine order as it was transferred to the mundane world. The divine was allegorized into human form and thus made accessible to the senses. In the ceremonial, this world order became fused with concepts of respect and authority.[3] According to Johann Christian Lünig, "great men" should strive to become as similar to the Almighty as possible. What created likeness and made the comparison perceptible was the power of the ruler, which gave order to everything and everybody: "GOD is a GOD of order which proves perfect in all created things…. The more those who want to follow His likeness here on earth desire to resemble it, the more order they have to establish in themselves and in their works."[4]

Representing the hierarchical order of the beyond in this life demanded the staging of distance—that is, the designation of external marks of social distinction.[5] In order to display prestige, the ruler's duty was to establish a court in which "his power

Arnold van Westerhout (Dutch, 1651–1725).

Trionfi (sugar sculptures) of Cybele and Juno (detail). See p. 113, fig. 2.

and authority may be recognized through it."[6] In this context, the displays of grandeur were understood, theoretically and practically, as signs that defined the host's rank. Prestige developed in the interplay of performance and reception. Only the scale of the ruler's exhibited virtues of generosity and magnificence made the authority of the sovereign perceptible.[7]

The staging of objects and the corresponding theatrical acts, especially for dining ceremonials, were necessary to make status material and to constantly remind the subjects of the majesty of their ruler: "Since everyone should eat and drink according to his rank, and dress and dwell accordingly, so must a king and ruler of a country eat and drink according to his majesty, and dress and dwell accordingly, too. And thus the royal table, in number and preciousness of the dishes, the garments in their splendor, and the castle in which he dwells in its size and beauty, must surpass all other tables, garments and buildings."[8]

One way in which a ruler could exhibit social distinction was in the festive decoration of the table with so-called *Schau-Essen,* defined literally as "show food." The word *banquet* was only used to designate the highest form of public dining.[9] The task of such feasts was to appeal to all the human senses. As early as 1657, Georg Philipp Harsdörffer described the sumptuousness of festive dinners in his carving book:

> Not only are the ears amused with charming and joyful music, and with poems and songs of praise, the brain is also fortified with fragrant waters and incense, the mouth pleasantly delighted with the most delicious dishes and sweet drink, the hands applied to choosing the best morsels; but sight as well, as the most splendid of all senses has been regaled with the sophisticated table pieces [*Schaugerichte*]; thus disposing to good conversation, and such food for the eyes is not only for the adornment of the table, but in this case directed at the memory of the glory and names of the invited guests; since the caressing world in this case also does not omit anything that seems beneficial to the appropriate praise of the great lords often keeping them in memory not as they are but as they should be.[10]

Harsdörffer noted that special care should be taken to ensure that centerpieces made from sugar, butter, or turnips were created not only to adorn the table but also to proclaim the glory of the "highly distinguished invited guests."[11] An important purpose of these table decorations,[12] "which, according to the circumstances of the guests and the time, intimate more than they show," was to stimulate intellectual debate.[13] Schau-Essen were dishes made by hand. First they pleased the eyes and only then the mouth, and were, for the most part, placed upon the table when the guests had already eaten their fill of other dishes.[14]

During this last part of the festive meal, the focus was no longer on food but rather on sheer opulence, in order to astonish and thus delight the guests. What Schau-Essen had to demonstrate was first and foremost the lavishness of the material extravagance and the beauty of the intricate preparation, but there was also a more concrete layer of meaning in these centerpieces.[15] Giving appropriate credit, Harsdörffer places the origins of elaborate table decoration in Italy: "The clever Italians have shown their reason especially when it comes to splendor, and we Germans must learn from them both the art of setting the table and that of carving."[16]

SUGAR DIPLOMACY

In his treatise, *De conviventia* (On conviviality), written in 1494 and first published in 1498, the Neapolitan humanist Giovanni Pontano explains that edible table decorations were closely connected to the increasing availability and consumption of sugar. His introduction on sugar collations describes this innovation as essential to the display of a ruler's prestige. Pontano writes:

> The second part of the meal lends great splendor to the banquets, to which splendor, it seems to me, much attention should be devoted. For, as the best poets care most about the last act, so to ourselves, who prepare banquets, the second part should be a matter of diligent concern. Since the discovery of sugar, which is used in a variety of ways, banquets and dinners have acquired a great complement that is elegant and magnificent. Many things prepared from it appeal not only to taste but to the pleasure of the eyes of the guests, for example the confections made for "little meals" that we now call "collations," which, since they afford an opportunity for magnificence, I see that the princes themselves greatly appreciate; this began with Alfonso, whom we know to have had the greatest enthusiasm for these things as for other forms of splendor.[17]

Pontano was one of the first to theorize the banquet as a whole as a medium of princely self-representation.[18] He emphasized just how much the second part of the feast could contribute to displaying noble virtues such as wealth and magnificence.[19] He stressed that the different components of the banquet should not be separate but should enter into increasing competition, finally achieving an orderly unison that is the quality of splendor, the essence of all ceremonial aesthetics.[20] Such sugar collations—which Pontano understands as an assortment of diverse confectionery and sweets—first emerged during the reign of King Alfonso V of Aragon (Alfonso I of Naples) in the first half of the fifteenth century.

While sugar in the context of festivals has already been documented by this time,[21] the term *collazione* appears only after 1470 to indicate an independent part of an orchestrated meal. Eleanor of Aragon, the granddaughter of Alfonso V, uses the word in a letter of 10 June 1473.[22] The Neapolitan princess and bride also describes her stay in Rome to her fiancé, Ercole d'Este of Ferrara, mentioning in particular a banquet held in her honor during which there was an almost incredible amount of sugar.[23] Famous for his extravagance, Cardinal Pietro Riario, nephew of Pope Sixtus IV (Francesco della Rovere), held the banquet in his palace, near the church of Santi Apostoli,[24] welcoming guests from Naples and Ferrara on Whit Monday, 7 June 1473. Eleanor writes:

> On Monday the aforementioned cardinal of San Sisto invited us together with those mentioned below, and he held this banquet in the said chamber, and the credenza mentioned above was well furnished with silver for all its shelves. Once at table, we stood a while with our backs to the table, and a sugar course arrived on ten trays with some imperial eagles made of sugar, and it was an array of sweets and gilded candied oranges and cups of malvasia to drink.[25]

In the sugar eagles, it is easy to recognize the diplomatic gesture by the pope's nephew to the heraldic birds of the Este family.[26]

After the guests were seated, the more than sumptuous succession of dishes was repeatedly interrupted by surprises.[27] There was singing, music and dancing, more confectionery, and many sugar sculptures (also intended as political allegories). Astonishment was caused by the appearance of "ten trays with ten ships made of sugar, containing acorns and roses made of sugar, and ten cups with *pinocchiate* [sweets made from pine nuts, egg whites, and sugar] in the shape of fish of different kinds."[28] The sugar acorns recalled the coat of arms of the helmsman of the *navicella Petri* (ship of salvation), Sixtus IV.[29] After many more platters of fish, capons, calves' feet, mutton, venison, and pork, another sweet course was served to refresh the guests and aid digestion and convivial conversation. The main attraction now was the life-size sugar sculptures.[30] Guests viewed heroic virtues shaped from sugar paste, notably three different sculptures depicting the labors of Hercules, that were made to be eaten: Hercules strangling the Nemean lion, capturing the Erymanthian boar, and taming the Cretan bull.[31] Interpretation of these centerpieces put no great demands on the guests. The fact that Eleanor's future husband, Ercole d'Este, was the namesake of the antique hero was all too evident.

This staging of resplendent wealth—unparalleled in Rome and even Italy up to that moment—was based on political calculation.[32] The goal was to create closer ties between the House of Este and the pope and his nephew. At the same time, it was intended to strengthen the existing alliance of the Roman Catholic Church with Ferdinand I, king of Naples. What was crystallizing—as one might say—in the different confections was a draft treaty discussing the ways in which Ercole d'Este's martial feats in the service of the church would be lavishly rewarded by what Sixtus IV and his nephew had to offer: dignities, offices, and sinecures, along with their attendant and highly desirable opulent magnificence.

In summary, one could say that from 1470 sugar courses with their sculptures became a necessary form of display for those who saw themselves as "great lords." They established a hitherto unknown kind of political iconography on princely tables; their main purpose was to translate diplomatic content into symbolic images and thus display political claims.[33] As Pontano suggests and Harsdörffer confirms, things cast from the luxury commodity of sugar were prepared to please the palate, but more and more they were displayed for the eyes of the guests. Thus, the second part of the banquet served to accentuate the prestige of the great lords and to appropriately represent the host's rank through the splendor of the meal and the sophistication of the attractions on offer.

Sugar collations undertook the imitation of every conceivable dish, culminating in trompe l'oeil-like creations and elaborate sculptural programs, often with mythological or historical themes, that became fashionable all over Europe.[34] As the second part of a banquet or an intermediate course, the sugar pieces became an important medium of entertainment and an indirect expression of princely magnificence.[35] From the beginning of the sixteenth century, the success of a banquet was measured by the size and complexity of the confections. Today, the degree of astonishment provoked by this can be reconstructed only from documentary sources, such as the numerous descriptions of banquets organized for various festive occasions and the commentaries written by guests. Reports about such festivities offer today's reader a privileged position, because the narrative distance allows an overview of the whole event.[36] Descriptions of festivals monumentalize ephemeral objects into a sphere of textual eternity through a change of media;[37] but at the same time, they reduce the complexity of the interrelated fields of the ceremonial.[38] Texts are added to the events as historical evidence, and their task is to proclaim the successful order of the ceremonial actions to the world. These descriptions are also linked to political interests; and the necessary display of social distinction, manifested in the ephemeral sign systems (the direct or indirect declaration of the order of rank of participants), often plays the decisive role.[39] Texts increased the prestige of the ruler, and they saluted his glory through the historicization of ephemeral grandeur, recording a worldly and transcendent order for posterity.[40]

The following sections describe the use of edible monuments in the context of diplomatic ceremonial aesthetics.

PRESTIGE ON DISPLAY

The banquets given in 1574 by the city of Venice to honor the entry and state visit of Henry of Valois, the elected king of Poland and soon-to-be king of France (as Henry III), were especially lavish, as documented by an unprecedented number of festival accounts. The Venetian festivities for Henry have attracted the attention of art historians, particularly because the famed architect Andrea Palladio erected a loggia and a temporary triumphal arch on the Lido to celebrate the king's entry. The loggia was decorated with paintings by artists such as Veronese and Tintoretto.[41] The architecture and the paintings are mentioned in the numerous festival accounts, yet it was other performances and ephemeral displays of opulence staged by the republic for the honored guest that made a stronger impression. The festivities organized for the entry of the king radically reshaped the city as a whole. It was as though, for Venice, the foreign monarch had become a new, movable center whose body, thanks to his rank and the gravity that accompanied it, could redirect spaces, things, and people—that is, the entire life of the city—toward himself for the duration of his stay.[42]

Wherever the ruler went, performances of distinction were staged. Signs and sounds continuously accompanied him:[43]

When the bucentaur stopped right in front of the Doge's Palace at San Marco, the galleys were all lined up in formation, and as it reached the entrance to the Grand Canal, all of a sudden artillery fired, each galley firing simultaneously, and there were another five decommissioned galleys at the banks, and the fustas and the brigantines, and many ships and vessels of all kinds. Many shots were fired in the piazza; trumpets, wind instruments [*piffari*], and drums were played on the galleys and brigantines; the bells of San Marco and those of all the bell towers of the city rang out, and all around everyone cheered. No greater uproar has ever been heard—I believe—at a sea battle, nor greater applause for a triumph.[44]

One chronicler felt that the thundering echo of such well-coordinated and therefore terrifying noise would make the whole world fall into ruins.[45]

The ceremonies and festivities lasted for more than a week. They might best be described in two words: *order* and *propaganda. Order* because the republic subordinated itself to the king in every way; *propaganda* because, during the king's visit, the city exhibited everything that it had to offer. No matter what wares Venice produced or which luxury item the city was the first to import, refine, and then export again, everything was displayed before the eyes of the king. He was potentially a very important client, and in the midst of the lavish entertainment, there were goods offered for sale. Lively exchanges of greetings and homages took place between the key players that required the purchase and distribution of gifts.[46] The king presented the doge with a diamond ring; the other dignitaries of the republic received mostly gold chains and noble titles. Appropriate liberality was displayed here as a princely virtue, but at the same time, through the fulfillment of high expectations, it also represented a diplomatic obligation.[47]

In this complex material culture of diplomacy, the visit to the Venetian Arsenal on 24 July 1574 was one of the high points. For more than three hours, Henry looked at the wondrous order in the shipyards and workshops. He marveled at the many ships of all kinds that were being built, and he took the greatest interest in the production of cannons in the foundry.[48] Everything that Venice had on offer in terms of armaments was being closely examined, admired, and judged. As an integral part of this presentation of military and economic strength, the king and his company, while still in the Arsenal, were offered a refreshment, described as a sugar collation. It was presented as a kind of sweet contrast to the bitter craft of war.[49] Having just admired war machinery of all kinds, the eminent state guest now stood in astonishment before elaborate creations in marzipan and an immeasurable quantity of confectionery. Awe at the scale of the confectioners' artistry turned to bafflement when Henry tried to lift one of the napkins; it broke and fell to the ground. Amazed and amused, the king and his courtiers saw that not only the napkins but also all the crockery and cutlery, and even the breads, were cleverly crafted from sugar. This impressive deception was followed by the merciless plundering of the buffet, according to the established custom of the court.[50]

The state banquet proper was held the following day in the Sala del Maggior Consiglio (Hall of the Great Council) of the Palazzo Ducale (Doge's Palace). The city showed its best face by presenting, like delicacies, two hundred of the most beautiful Venetian noblewomen to the French guests. All the women were clad in white silk, and all had blond hair as a badge of their beauty.[51] After they had performed a dance before the monarch, and he was able to look closely at them, the company went to the Sala dello Scrutinio (Voting Hall).[52] In a closed-off area called the seraglio, a collation of more than three hundred figures made of the whitest sugar was displayed on several tables.[53] Without noise or disorder, the women were led through the doors of the room, entering into beauty competition with the statuettes. Breaking protocol, the king walked through this "sweet seraglio"; he finally took a seat at a small table that displayed even larger sugar sculptures.[54] The most conspicuous was a queen who looked particularly lifelike in offering two crowns to Henry; she was flanked by tigers bearing the coats of arms of France and Poland on their breasts. Various figures represented Saint Mark, King David, Athena and Iustitia, as well as other allegories and personifications.[55] All these figures were produced by a certain spice merchant or apothecary named Nicolò della Pigna; the sketches and models, however, came from the sculptor Jacopo Sansovino.[56] The great and beautiful golden room was so resplendent with decorations and divine draperies of yellow and deep blue silk that it resembled the Banquet of the Gods, as described by the poets. Yet again, the French guests plundered the buffets at the end, giving the sugar sculptures to the assembled Venetian beauties and carrying the artistic confections away in special bags provided for that purpose. After this sweet experience, the king ordered thirty-nine smaller sugar figures to take back to France.[57]

Art historians have emphasized how much these unprecedented festivities were politically motivated by the desire to put Venice's relationship to France on firmer footing. In wooing the new French ruler, Venice seemed to be seeking a way to test the Spanish dominance in Italy. At the same time, the Venetians were trying, through rituals and ceremonies with symbols and allegory, to win an ally who would be ready to invest and possibly even intervene in the struggle against Turkish expansionism in the Mediterranean and the Balkans. While these broad political aims can be deduced only indirectly from the ceremonial program, the economic intentions of the republic are starkly displayed in accounts of the festival. That the festivities were staged especially to further trade with France became clear, for example, when upon arrival, the brigantines of the Venetian trade and craft guilds greeted the king. The boats were covered with advertisements for their wares from stern to forecastle, on masts and sails. One richly decorated boat clearly presented the sponsoring guild in large letters: "tessitori di panni di seta" (silk weavers). In comparison, the painted boat of the goldsmiths and jewelers, from whom Henry would commission gifts, carried the ambiguous message of "corona atrium" (crown of the arts).[58] Henry was staying at the Ca' Foscari. On the evening after his arrival, the brigantines, accompanied by lilting music, floated by the palace in a long line offering the sovereign a display of the skills of the Venetian artisans.[59] Throughout his stay, the king was given every possible opportunity to familiarize himself with the most desirable luxury goods of Venice, including the latest cannons of the Arsenal, silk fabrics, glass and jewelry, and the Venetian beauties, not to mention the symbol-laden sugar products.

At this time, Venice was still the center for the trade and processing of sugar in Europe.[60] The raw material came mainly from Egypt and was refined and further processed in the city. No one who wanted to purchase large quantities of sugar in the sixteenth century could do so without Venice as a trading partner. The important role of the city in the sugar trade and refining was also reflected in the great skill of the local confectioners, whose most famous specialty was the imitation of foods and objects of all kinds.[61] Every imaginable sea creature could be commissioned in sugar and then, at the end of a fish banquet, presented as a surprise on a second table. The deceptively

genuine-looking plates and cups, knives and forks, napkins and tablecloths—all made
to be eaten—also became an extremely successful Venetian export.[62]

A century after their invention, sugar collations had become so well established
on the princely table that they were an indispensable part of festival culture, even
at minor courts and in smaller cities and towns. The size and caliber of the confections—like the height of the obligatory credenza and the quality of the wares displayed—reflected very clearly how much effort and finance had been contributed to a
banquet and therefore how much respect one was prepared to offer a guest or guests.
The success of this display of splendor developed further at the beginning of the
seventeenth century, when sugar prices started to fall as a result of the successful
cultivation of sugar cane in South America and the beginning of large-scale overseas
trade. The consumption of exquisitely crafted sugar products increased to hitherto
unknown levels. Ever larger quantities of the purest sugar were processed in court
kitchens, and the ephemeral centerpieces, with their political meanings, became more
and more sophisticated.

POLITICAL SUBTLETIES

Another well-documented example of the attempt to gain political influence through
allegorical sugar sculptures was the 1687 banquet in honor of Pope Innocent XI,
during the first week of Carnival, in Rome. Roger Palmer, Earl of Castlemaine, in
his role as ambassador to the Holy See and surrogate for King James II, sought to
increase English prestige with the Vatican.[63]

The centerpiece of Castlemaine's stay in Rome was a banquet held in the gallery of the Palazzo Pamphilj, beneath the frescoes by Pietro da Cortona depicting
the life of Aeneas. Sugar sculptures are not often illustrated in detail; fortunately,
the publication by the artist and majordomo John Michael Wright features intricate
engravings of the table decorations with explanatory texts. In the middle of the
banquet table, which was nearly one hundred feet long, stood a sculpture made from
the finest sugar, several feet in height (fig. 1).[64] In his treatise, Wright gives a description of a female figure, the personification of the Roman Catholic Church, that stands
on a cloud bank above the sun. A second figure—the religious genius of the British
monarch—is introduced to the Church by the unveiled Truth. On the other side of
the sculpture, a winged warrior with a spear in his hand—the personification of the
valor of the king—chases away Fraud and Discord. Below the warrior lies the hydra
of rebellion, which he has decapitated.[65] More sugar sculptures are displayed on the
table in exquisite order (figs. 2, 3). They include the divine personification of the four
elements and various virtues arranged in pairs or standing in groups around a palm,
recalling the heraldic tree of the Palmer family. There were two mythological scenes

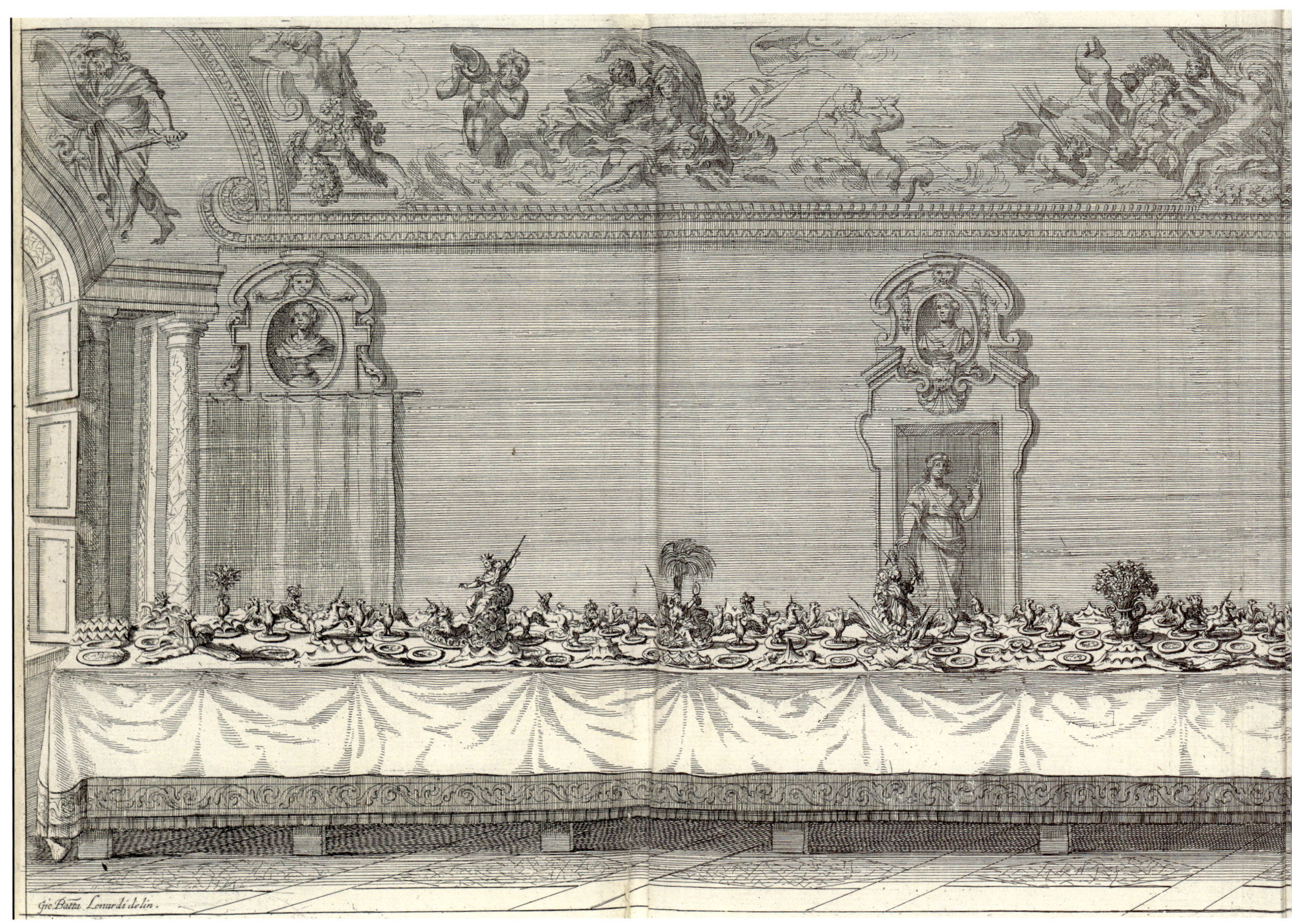

FIG. 1.

Arnold van Westerhout (Dutch, 1651–1725), after Giovanni Battista Lenardi (Italian, 1656–1704). Banquet table, etching, 26 × 110.5 cm (10¼ × 43½ in.). From John Michael Wright, *Raggvaglio della solenne comparsa,* *fatta in Roma gli otto di gennaio* *MDCLXXXVII. dall'illvstrissimo,* *et eccellentissimo signor conte* *di Castelmaine…* (Rome: Domenico Antonio Ercole, 1687), unnumbered plate. Los Angeles, Getty Research Institute.

FIG. 2.

Arnold van Westerhout (Dutch, 1651-1725), after Giovanni Battista Lenardi (Italian, 1656-1704).

Trionfi (sugar sculptures) of Cybele and Juno, etching, 16.5 × 26 cm (6½ × 10¼ in.).

From John Michael Wright, *An Account of His Excellence Roger Earl of Castlemaine's Embassy: From His Sacred Majesty James the IId….,to His Holiness Innocent XI* (London: Printed by Tho. Snowden for the author, 1688), pl. 11.

Los Angeles, Getty Research Institute.

FIG. 3.

Arnold van Westerhout (Dutch, 1651-1725), after Giovanni Battista Lenardi (Italian, 1656-1704).

Trionfi (sugar sculptures) of Vulcan and Neptune, etching, 16.5 × 26 cm (6½ × 10¼ in.).

From John Michael Wright, *An Account of His Excellence Roger Earl of Castlemaine's Embassy: From His Sacred Majesty James the IId….,to His Holiness Innocent XI* (London: Printed by Tho. Snowden for the author, 1688), pl. 12.

Los Angeles, Getty Research Institute.

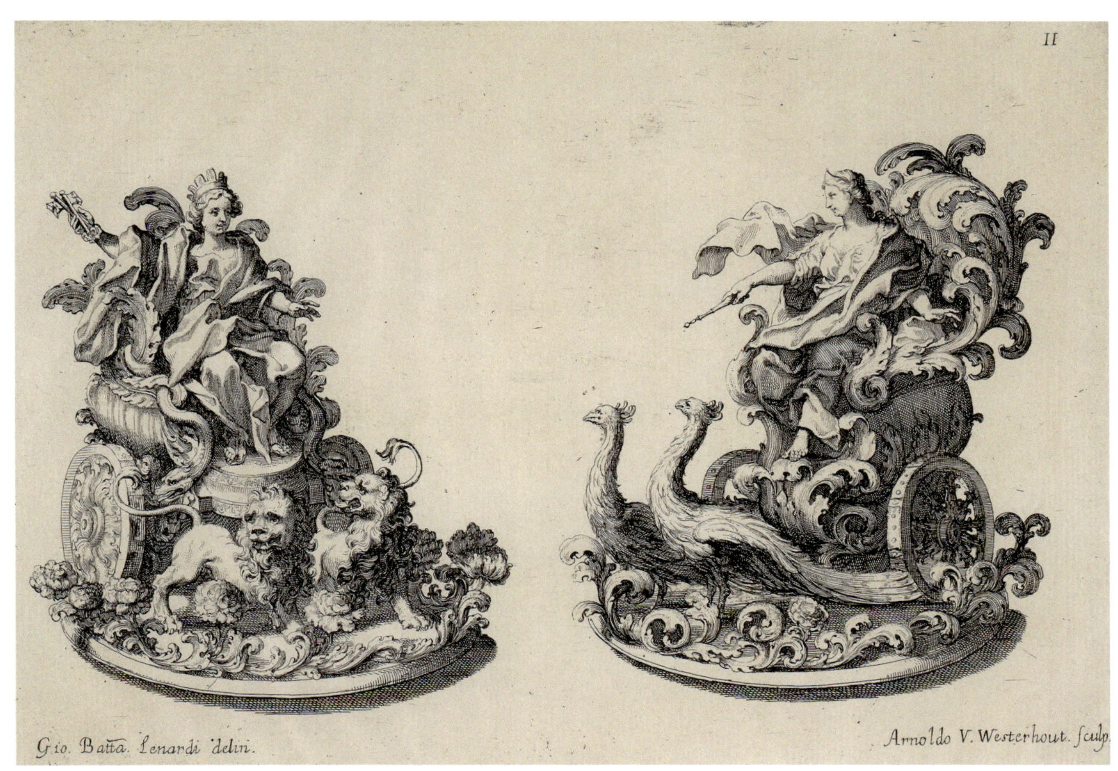

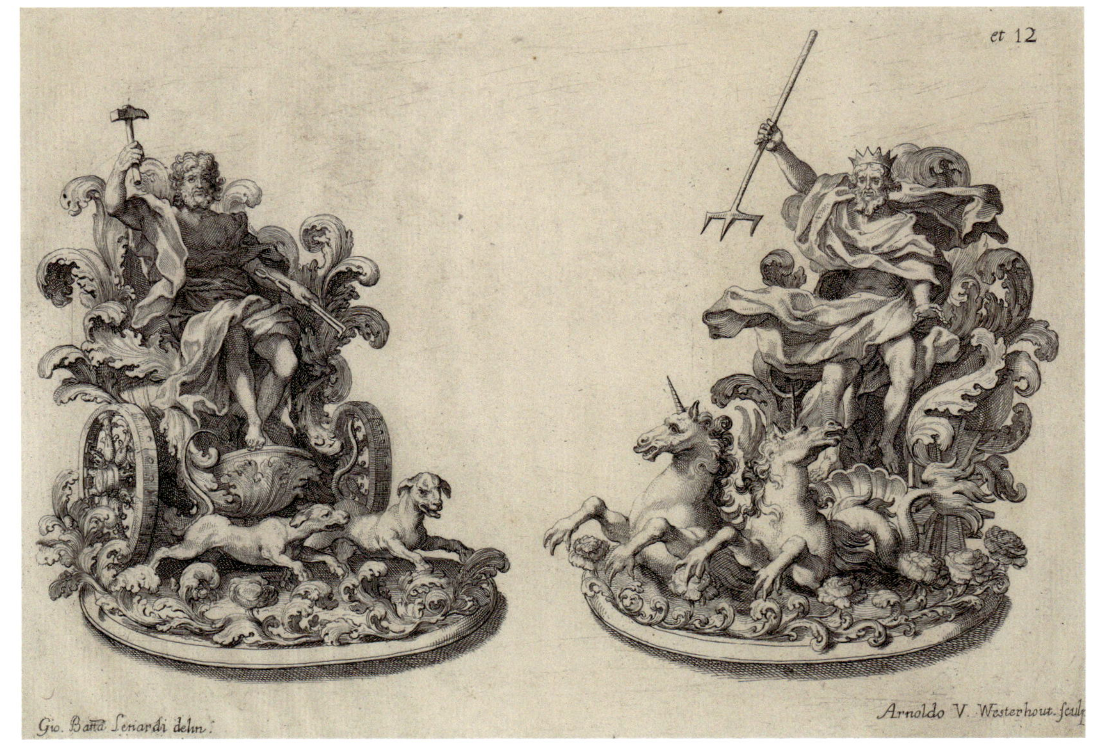

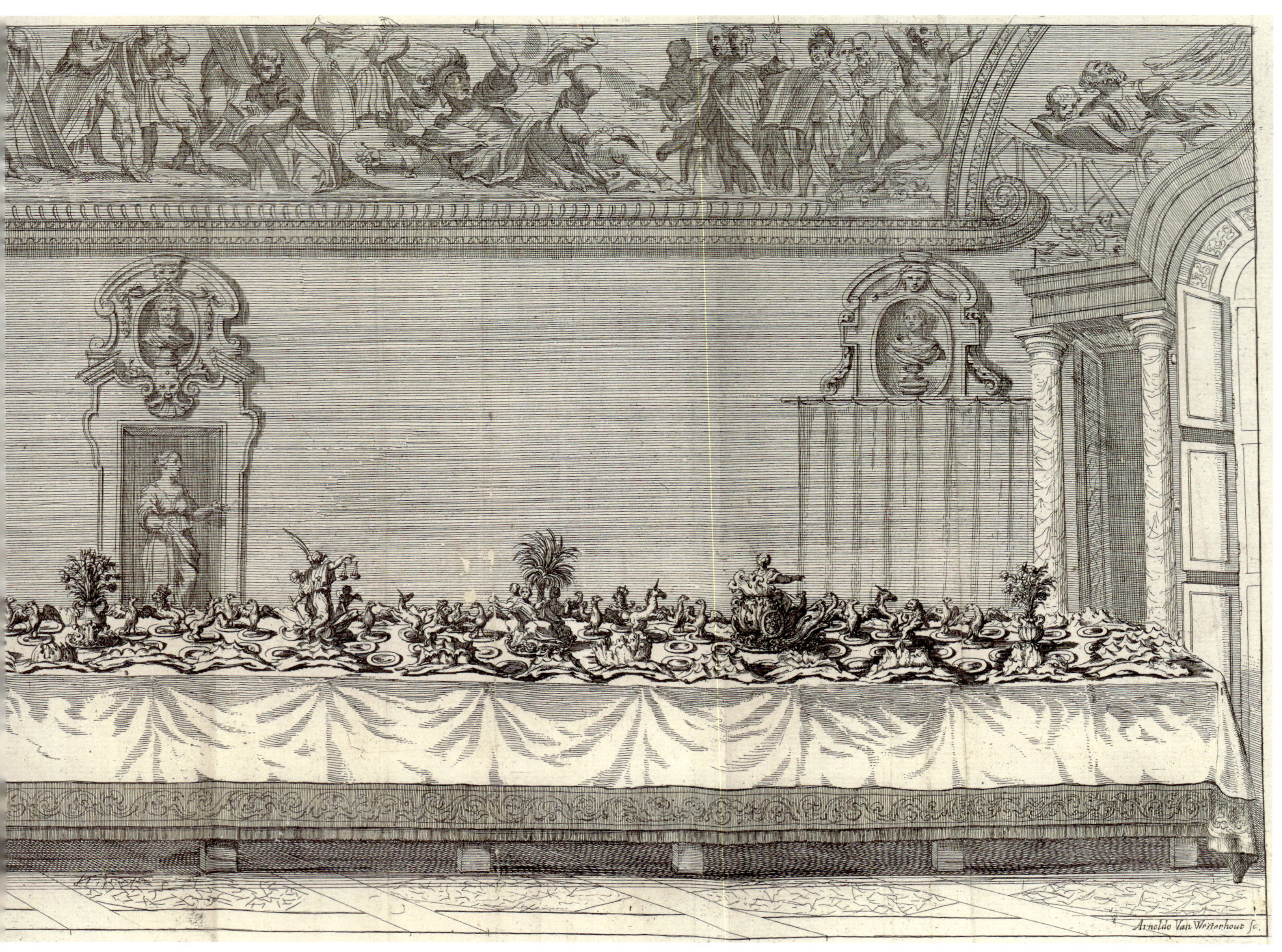

Arnoldo Van Westerhout Sc.

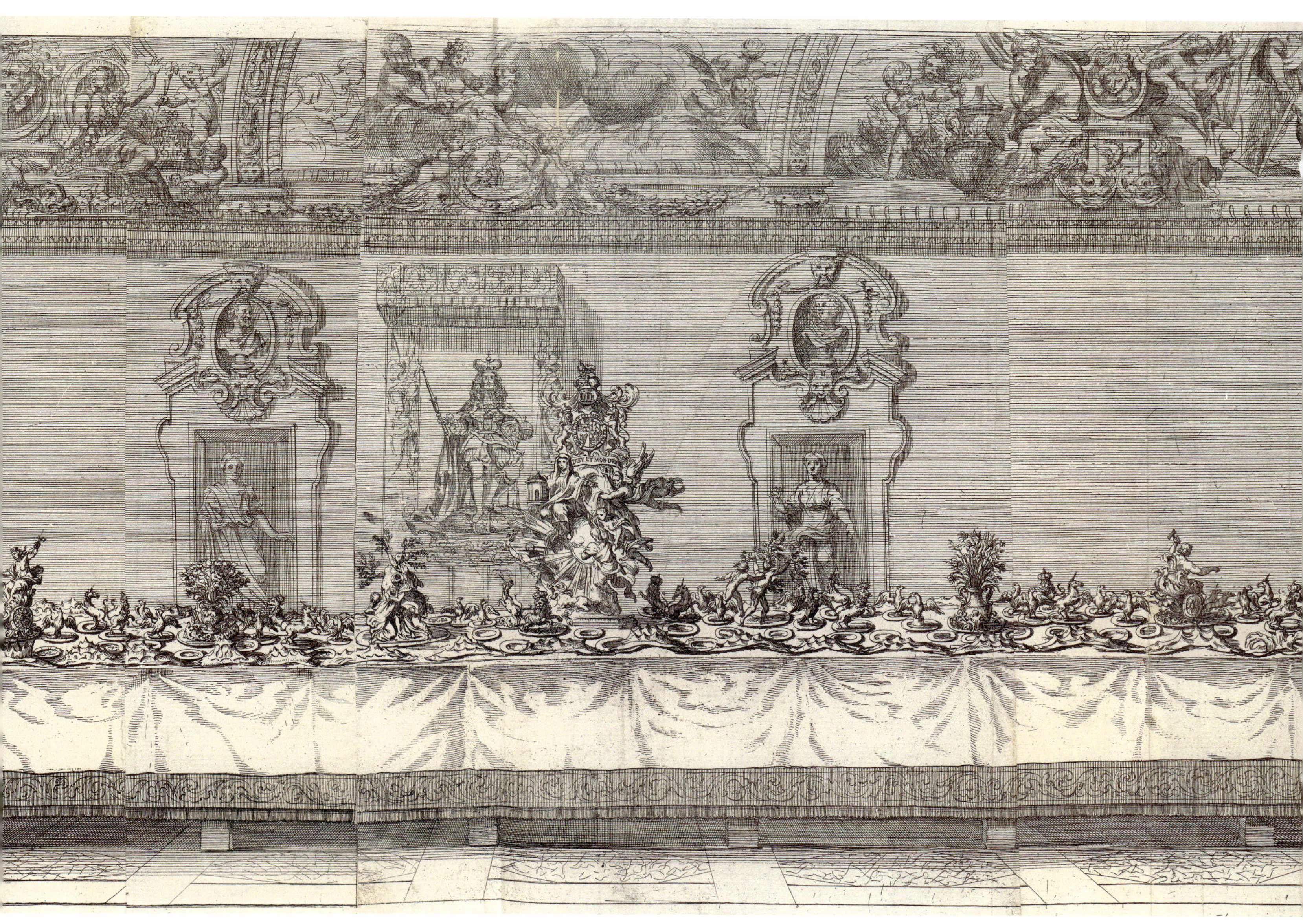
DIEU ET MON DROIT

from Ovid's *Metamorphoses* and innumerable smaller statuettes—lions, unicorns, and eagles. In short, the table displayed the heraldic supporters of the pope and the English king cast in sugar paste.

This ambitious sugar sculpture program summarizes political messages that were already expressed in two large, colored epitaphs on the facade of the Palazzo Pamphilj. Letters reached England telling of Castlemaine setting up "the armes of the Pope and His Majestie over his pallace, with several devices of the catholick religion triumphing over heresy" and of "the great splendor and magnificence of his reception."[66] The British king's achievements in ecclesiastical politics were presented in allegorical form—including the suppression of rebellion in England, the expected return of the Catholicized kingdoms into the bosom of the Roman Catholic Church, and the submission of the British royal house to the primacy of the pope.[67] With this lavish display, the ambassador publicly formulated a political claim for the pope to compensate the British king for services that he had already rendered or would render. The British delegation demanded that the pope elevate one of the closest royal advisers, Jesuit Edward Petre, to the post of bishop. With the greatest insistence, Castlemaine made public what had not been achieved by diplomatic means up to this date; and it was hoped that the support of the eighty-six cardinals and prelates who had been invited to the banquet might still achieve a good outcome.[68] But even this attempt to influence public opinion did not alter the pope's position on the matter. Only a few weeks before Castlemaine's mission was judged to have failed and the king recalled him to England, the Italian version of Wright's festival account was published in April 1687 in Rome. It is essentially a political report whose purpose was to show that the ambassador to the Holy See had spared no effort to reach his goal, pursuing it on a grand scale and using all available media.

This sumptuous book that monumentalizes the sugar sculptures appeared in an English version in spring 1688, with additions concerning Castlemaine's diplomatic resolution of an impasse concerning Mediterranean piracy. The book played its own political role, since the Protestant and Parliamentarian camp regarded the king's expenditure as an affront, viewing the embassy as kowtowing to the pope. The boastful documentation of the sugar sculptures produced in Rome gave ammunition to the English opposition and demonstrably strengthened the front against the king with his absolutist leanings and his gradual catholicization of the country. The book would be another mistake by Castlemaine, who during the Glorious Revolution had to pay for his close relations to the king and failed mission in Rome with two years in the Tower of London.

Comparing these different examples of sugar collations, it might be said that their main function had hardly changed since they were first created in the fifteenth century. Even in the late seventeenth century, the purpose of the sugar figures was to demonstrate princely magnificence and to stand as impressive evidence of opulence; all the while, they continued to serve specific diplomatic ambitions and initiatives. What did change in these two hundred years of sugary political iconography, however, was the framework of the European sugar economy. Thanks to increased land available overseas and the new trade routes via Portugal and Spain, the center of the sugar trade shifted from the Mediterranean to the Atlantic, and prices dropped, leading to an increase in consumption. The concrete effect of this on table displays may be gleaned from a passage in Julius Bernhard von Rohr's 1729 volume on the ceremonial of great men. He reflects on the gradual disappearance of sugar collations from the princely tables but at the same time stresses that these edible monuments had not lost their appeal:

> The "Schau-Essen" were in olden times more fashionable than nowadays. Occasionally, as the ancient historians tell us, during former great festivities, where everything was resplendent, more Schau-Essen were presented on display than other dishes for carving and serving. Today they are rarer but all the more inventive and devised in a more ingenious manner; the sugar-pieces especially are oftentimes set up according to specific rules of art. Sometimes entire stories are depicted. All columns, cornices and fixtures, all statues and figures, and whatever else belongs to architecture, all flowers, trees and leaves, all dresses and garments on the personages, the translucent clouds and everything visible are cast entirely from sugar in such a manner that the colors make the marble, bronze, personages, flowers, leaves and fruits appear most naturally and perfectly.[69]

Although such table pieces continued to appear on banquet tables well into the nineteenth and even the twentieth century, sugar sculptures increasingly lost their aura of luxury and extravagance; and from the mid-seventeenth century, they were gradually replaced by other table decorations, moving from edible festive decorations to larger, inedible centerpieces.[70] During the eighteenth century, ephemeral sugar sculptures were replaced, for example, by elaborate porcelain pieces, which were originally produced in Meissen and Nymphenburg, as well as other places.[71] Another reason why court culture switched to durable table decorations made of porcelain was that from roughly 1750 sugar became affordable even for Europe's urban bourgeoisie. This growing middle class now sweetened the bitter drinks of tea, cocoa, and coffee with imported cane sugar and increasingly indulged in the consumption of confections and sweetened dishes.[72] They sought to catch up with the nobility when it came to festive dining.[73] As a result, sugar collations gradually disappeared from princely tables because they no longer signified material distinction and courtly prestige.

SWEETNESS AND DECADENCE

Luxurious banqueting practices of the early modern era were also sharply criticized by contemporaries. Writers took issue with the content of convivial ceremonial aesthetics, with the imperative for social distinction, and they objected to widespread vices such as gluttony. Referring back to antiquity, they repeatedly urged rulers to practice moderation.[74] In the context of the pernicious effects of unrestrained eating and drinking, there were cautions against excessive consumption of sweets. In 1637, the physician Angelo Sala described in detail what would happen to those who over-indulged in sugar. If sugar was not used "in the correct way," it could "do as much damage to the body as good. For firstly if somebody eats excessive sugar it causes his cardia to soften, weakens the digestion, causes wind and bloating, befogs the head, stimulates the flow of humors, damages the face, rots the palate, weakens and black-ens the teeth and loosens them so that they fall out."[75]

The dire consequences of excessive sugar consumption were general medical knowledge;[76] to have bad teeth was—as the Austrian imperial court preacher Abra-ham a Sancta Clara knew—God's punishment, and toothache had come into the world only when Adam bit into the apple of paradise.[77] The popularity of refined sugar in connection with ceremonial aesthetics brought with it a considerable increase in tooth disease in the highest circles.[78] Those who continuously indulged in sweets and ate them in large quantities—in the Renaissance and baroque periods, these were the rulers and their courts—were punished by fate with considerable tooth decay. The predilection for confectionery not only blackened the teeth of Elizabeth I of England,[79] but for Louis XIV, too, the regular enjoyment of large quantities of sweet confections brought bitter consequences. According to a study on the tooth diseases of the Sun King, Louis was advised by his personal physicians to have all his decayed teeth extracted at an early age. This led to an abscess in his upper left jaw and, as a consequence, to an inflammation of the paranasal sinuses and the bone tissue. To alleviate the pain, the remaining upper teeth were also extracted. When the physi-cians did this, they broke off a part of the palatine bone; and, for the purpose of disin-fection, the hole in the palate was burnt with a glowing iron rod. A little later, all the lower teeth were also extracted, and, if this was not quite enough already, the jawbone was broken on the occasion.[80]

The expanded production and increased consumption of sugar diminished the prestige value of edible table decorations. Sugar itself inevitably lost the status of a rare commodity or a luxury good. This devaluation accelerated with the onset of sugar beet cultivation in Europe and industrial production from 1850.[81] A flood of affordable new products soon appeared on the market. These new foods played an important social role, becoming an indispensable, energy-rich part of the everyday diet of large parts of the population within a short time. Sugar became a "staple food of the underclass" and has remained as such to this day.[82]

That only a few scholars have focused on the ephemeral sugar compositions of the early modern era may be a result of the cursory rejection of everything sweet and cheap in art history.[83] This bourgeois-academic imperative of distinction is expressed with surprising candor in Ernst Gombrich's *Meditations on a Hobby Horse:*

> The child is proverbially fond of sweets and toffees, and so is the primitive, with his Turkish delight and an amount of fat meat that turns a European stomach….My guess is, for instance, that small children and unsophisticated grown-ups will be likely to enjoy a soft milk chocolate, while citified highbrows will find it cloying and seek escape in the more bitter tang or in an admixture of coffee or, preferably, of crunchy nuts.[84]

If something can be learned from the history of the *collationi di zuccaro,* it is that a material ceremonial aesthetic needs a complex cultural and historical context to establish itself. But perhaps the present exploration of the representative function of sugar sculptures in early modern Europe will extend our perspective beyond the different historical contexts toward the conditions under which social, economic, and political mechanisms of social distinction are negotiated today. For it is certain that since the times of Giovanni Pontano, almost everything may have changed except for the human urge to define a social order through material culture.

NOTES

Martina Dervis translated this essay from the German. William Michael Short translated some Italian and Latin quotations. Chris Miller consulted on the Renaissance Latin.

1. Johann Christian Lünig, *Theatrum Ceremoniale…*(Leipzig: Weidmann, 1719), 2; and Jörg Jochen Berns and Thomas Rahn, "Zeremoniell und Ästhetik," in idem, eds., *Zeremoniell als höfische Ästhetik in Spätmittelalter und Früher Neuzeit* (Tübingen: Max Niemeyer, 1995), 650-65, here 657-58. Translation mine.
2. See Gottfried Stieve, *Europäisches Hoff-Ceremoniel…Nebst vollstänigem Register* (Leipzig: Joh. Friedr. Gleditsch & Sohn, 1715), 2; Lünig, *Theatrum Ceremoniale,* 2; Ulf Christian Ewert and Jan Hirschbiegel, "Nur Verschwendung? Zur sozialen Funktion der demonstrativen Zurschaustellung höfischen Güterverbrauchs," in Werner Paravicini, *Luxus und Intergration: Materielle Hofkultur Westeuropas vom 12. bis zum 18. Jahrhundert* (Munich: Oldenbourg, 2010), 111-12; and Thomas Rahn, "Sinnbild und Sinnlichkeit: Probleme der zeremoniellen Zeichenstrategie und ihre Bewältigung in der Festpublizistik," in Peter-Michael Hahn and Ulrich Schütte, eds., *Zeichen und Raum: Ausstattung und höfisches Zeremoniell in den deutschen Schlössern der Frühen Neuzeit* (Munich: Deutscher Kunstverlag, 2006), 39.
3. Volker Bauer, "Zeremoniell und Ökonomie: Der Diskurs über die Hofökonomie in Zeremonialwissenschaft, Kameralismus und Hausväterliteratur in Deutschland, 1700-1780," in Berns and Rahn, *Zeremoniell als höfische Ästhetik,* 34-35.
4. Lünig, *Theatrum Ceremoniale,* 292. See Bauer, "Zeremoniell und Ökonomie," 34-35.
5. Lünig, *Theatrum Ceremoniale,* 5.

6. Christian Wolff, *Vernüfftige Gedanken von dem gesellschaftlichen Leben der Menschen…Den Lieb-habern der Wahrheit* (Frankfurt and Leipzig: Rengerische Buchhandlung, 1725), 504.

7. Nicolas Le Roux, "Luxus, Freigebigkeit, und Macht in Krisenzeiten: Die Politik der Prachtent-faltung am Hof der letzten Valois," in Paravicini, *Luxus und Intergration,* 241. Le Roux cites a statement by Henry III: "La libéralité et magnificence est le propre d'un grand prince" (Liberality and magnificence are proper to a great prince). Quoted there from: Pierre Champion, ed., *Lettres de Henri III,* vol. 2 (Paris: C. Klincksieck, 1965), 133 (Henry III to Gilles de Noailles, abbé de l'Isle, Paris, 27 April 1575). See Hubert Christian Ehalt, *Ausdrucksformen absolutistischer Herrschaft: Der Wiener Hof im 17. und 18. Jahrhundert* (Munich: R. Oldenbourg, 1980), 122-25.

8. Wolff, *Vernüfftige Gedanken,* 504-5. See Marian Füssel, "Rang und Raum: Gesellschaftliche Kartographie und die soziale Logik des Raumes an der vormodernen Universität," in Christoph Dartmann, Marian Füssel, and Stefanie Rüther, eds., *Raum und Konflikt: Zur symbolischen Kon-stituierung gesellschaftlicher Ordnung in Mittelalter und Früher Neuzeit* (Münster: Rhema, 2004), 175-97, here 177.

9. See Friedrich Carl von Moser, *Teutsches Hof-Recht…* (Frankfurt: Johann Benjamin Andreä, 1754-55), 2:497-98:

> §. 1. The tables at which a person of high nobility, from Emperor to Imperial Count, takes the role of host or commissions such at his cost, are given the name 'Tafel'… §. 2. The dif-ferent 'Tafeln' can be distinguished from each other in various ways, as will be shown with several examples. The first difference lies in the extent to which the persons who live in the residence or the court participate in it. According to this the Tafel is subdivided into public, common and secret dining. §. 3. The public Tafel has different gradations again. The highest is the one which is called banquet. This is distinguished from the 'Speisen en Ceremonie' by the quantity of the guests, the extravagant number of dishes and by the fact that they nor-mally last a whole day and often several days.

10. Georg Philipp Harsdörffer, *Vollständig und von neuem vermehrtes Trincir-Buch…und mit Kupffern lehrartig außgebildet* (Nuremberg: Christoff Gerhard, 1657), 201-2. See also Andreas Gugler, "Speisen der Augen: Allegorische Schaugerichte bei den Krönungen von Kaiser Karl VI," in Lothar Kolmer and Christian Rohr, eds., *Mahl und Repräsentation: Der Kult ums Essen; Beiträge des internationalen Symposions in Salzburg 29. April bis 1. Mai 1999* (Paderborn, Germany: Ferdinand Schöningh, 2002), 125-34, here 125; and Stefan Bursche, *Tafelzier des Barock* (Munich: Editions Schneider, 1974), 43-45.

11. Harsdörffer, *Vollständig und von neuem vermehrtes Trincir-Buch,* 211.

12. *Schau-Essen* (show foods) are to be distinguished from *Schaugerichte* (table pieces). See Harsdörffer, *Vollständig und von neuem vermehrtes Trincir-Buch,* 212: "The Schaugerichte are displayed to be looked at and not to be eaten consisting in all kinds of creations, made from wax, linen, wood and the like, which shall give the banquet glory and lead those present to intelli-gent reflection." See Bursche, *Tafelzier des Barock,* 43-44. See also Emanuel Schmid and Ulrike Staudinger, "'Die Kurfürstin liess Katzen und Mäuse braten…' Tafelfreuden am Münchner Hof," in Ulrike Zischka, ed., *Die anständige Lust: Von Esskultur und Tafelsitten* (Munich: Spangen-berg, 1993), 80-112, here 106.

13. Harsdörffer, *Vollständig und von neuem vermehrtes Trincir-Buch,* 213. See also Julius Bernhard von Rohr, *Einleitung zur Ceremoniel-Wissenschafft der großen Herren…* (Berlin: Rüdiger, 1733), 103: "The Galanterie-Speisen or figures sometimes represent various pagan gods, which suit the individual feast; they are at times several feet high and are placed among the confections."

14. Harsdörffer, *Vollständig und von neuem vermehrtes Trincir-Buch,* 210.

15. See *Das verdeckte Schauessen an das Publicum über die gegenwärtigen Zeitläufte* (Petersburg: 1757), 3: "Show-food is a special food or dish which is displayed on a stately table, partially to please the eyes, partially to occupy the empty space, partially for other intentions…The word 'schauen' (to look) indicates that dishes brought to the table are there more to be looked at than to be enjoyed."

Edward Muir, *Ritual in Early Modern Europe,* 2nd ed. (Cambridge: Cambridge University Press, 2005), 139-40. See Michel Jeanneret, *A Feast of Words: Banquets and Table Talk in the Renaissance,* trans. Jeremy Whiteley and Emma Hughes (Chicago: Chicago University Press, 1987), 45.

16.   Harsdörffer, *Vollständig und von neuem vermehrtes Trincir-Buch,* 206.

17.   Giovanni Pontano, "De conviventia," in idem, *I trattati delle virtù sociali,* ed. Francesco Tateo (Rome: Bulzoni, 1999), 245-69, here 262.

18.   See Claudio Benporat, *Feste e banchetti: Convivialità italiana fra tre e quattrocento* (Florence: Leo S. Olschki, 2001), 93-99.

19.   In absolutism, magnificence and splendor became almost obligatory. See Ehalt, *Ausdrucksformen absolutistischer Herrschaft,* 137-39. Also, Guido Guerzoni, "Liberalitas, Magnificentia, Splendor: The Classic Origins of Italian Renaissance Lifestyles," in Neil De Marchi and Craufurd D. W. Goodwin, eds., *Economic Engagements with Art* (Durham, N.C.: Duke University Press, 1999), 332-78.

20.   Pontano, "De conviventia," 260: "It is considered proper and splendid that trumpets and pipes should precede the courses as they arrive, to delight the guests and those present with their music and give the signal for the next course, so that order is adjoined to mere pleasure, which, were it lacking, would inevitably unsettle and confound everything."

21.   See Edmund O. von Lippmann, *Geschichte des Zuckers seit den ältesten Zeiten bis zum Beginn der Rübenzucker-Fabrikation: Ein Beitrag zur Kulturgeschichte von Professor Dr. Edmund O. von Lippmann* (Berlin: Springer, 1929; reprint, Niederwalluf bei Wiesbaden, Germany: Dr. Martin Sändig, 1970), 339, 355-56.

22.   Republished in Benporat, *Feste e banchetti,* 167-71: Eleanor of Aragon, letter from Campagnano to Diomedes Carafa, dated 10 June 1473.

23.   Ercole d'Este lived at the court of Alfonso of Naples for an extended period. See Thomas Tuohy, *Herculean Ferrara: Ercole d'Este, 1471-1505, and the Invention of a Ducal Capital* (Cambridge: Cambridge University Press, 1996), 13-16; and Stefano Infessura, *Diario della Città di Roma* (Rome: Forzani & C. Tipografi del Senato, 1890), 77.

24.   Ferdinand Gregorovius, *Geschichte der Stadt Rom im Mittelalter V. bis zum XVI. Jahrhundert,* 2nd ed., 8 vols. (Stuttgart: J.G. Cotta, 1869-72), 7:239-41. This banquet was previously mentioned by Jacob Burckhardt, *Die Kultur der Renaissance in Italien* (Berlin: Th. Knaur Nachf, 1928), 412. See Ulrich Pfisterer, *Lysippus und seine Freunde: Liebesgaben und Gedächtnis im Rom der Renaisance; oder, Das erste Jahrhundert der Medaille* (Berlin: Akademie, 2008), 2-4.

25.   Benporat, *Feste e banchetti,* 167-71, here 167-68.

26.   Benporat, *Feste e banchetti,* 167-68.

27.   Benporat, *Feste e banchetti.* For a more critical perspective, see Gregorovius, *Geschichte der Stadt Rom,* 240-41, which is based on Corio's account.

28.   See Ludwig Pastor, *Geschichte der Päpste seit dem Ausgang des Mittelalters* (Freiburg: Herder, 1893-1930), 2:486-87. Benporat, *Feste e banchetti,* 169.

29.   Bernardino Corio, *Storia di Milano,* ed. Anna Morisi Guerra (Turin: Unione Tipografico-Editrice Torinese, 1978), 2:1391.

30.   Corio, *Storia di Milano,* 2:1391.

31.   How this was staged is described a hundred years later by Giovanni Battista Rossetti, *Dello scalco del Sig. Gio. Battista Rossetti, scalco della Serenissima Madama Lucretia da Este Duchessa d'Urbino…in tempo di guerra* (Ferrara: Domenico Mammarello, 1584), 215-18, here 215.

32.   See Pastor, *Geschichte der Päpste,* 487.

33.   See Sidney Wilfred Mintz, *Sweetness and Power: The Place of Sugar in Modern History* (New York: Viking, 1985), 91-94.

34.   Sugar sculptures also appear at the wedding celebrations for Eleanor of Aragon and Ercole d'Este in Ferrara. See Tuohy, *Herculean Ferrara,* 272; and also Benporat, *Feste e banchetti,* 224-36: Rimini, 24 June 1475, Festivities for the wedding of Roberto Malatesta and Isabella di Montefeltro.

35. Katharine J. Watson, "Sugar Sculpture for Grand Ducal Weddings from the Giambologna Workshop," *The Connoisseur* 199, no. 799 (1978): 20.

36. Margaret M. McGowan, "The French Royal Entry in the Renaissance: The Status of the Printed Text," in Nicolas Russell and Hélène Visentin, eds., *French Ceremonial Entries in the Sixteenth Century: Event, Image, Text* (Toronto: Centre for Reformation and Renaissance Studies, 2007), 29-54, here 29.

37. Ulrich Schütte, "Die Räume und das Zeremoniell, die Pracht und die Mode: Zur Zeichenhaftigkeit höfischer Innenräume," in Hahn and Schütte, *Zeichen und Raum,* 167-204, here 186. See also Axel Stähler, *"Perpetuall Monuments": Die Repräsentation von Architektur in der italienischen Festdokumentation (ca. 1515-1640) und der englischen court masque (1604-1640)* (Münster: Lit, 2000), 11-44.

38. See Rahn, "Sinnbild und Sinnlichkeit," 44-45.

39. Helen Watanabe-O'Kelly, "The Early Modern Festival Book: Function and Form," in J. R. Mulryne, ed., *Europa triumphans* (Aldershot, UK: Ashgate, 2004), 6-10.

40. Karl Möseneder, *Zeremoniell und monumentale Poesie: Die "Entrée solonnelle" Ludwigs XIV. in Paris* (Berlin: Gebr. Mann, 1983), 34-35; Rahn, "Sinnbild und Sinnlichkeit," 46-47; and Schütte, "Die Räume," 186.

41. Pier De Nolhac and Angelo Solerti, *Il viaggio in Italia di Enrico III Re di Francia e le feste a Venezia, Ferrara, Mantova, e Torino* (Rome: L. Roux, 1890); Bonner Mitchell, *The Majesty of the State: Triumphal Progresses of Foreign Sovereigns in Renaissance Italy (1494-1600)* (Florence: Leo S. Olschki, 1986), 112-26; and Iain Fenlon, *The Ceremonial City: History, Memory, and Myth in Renaissance Venice* (New Haven, Conn.: Yale University Press, 2007), 193-215.

42. Tommaso Porcacchi, *Le attioni d'Arrigo terzo, re di Francia et qvarto di Polonia…ch'altre volte sono stati riceuuti in Vinetia* (Venice: Giorgio Angelieri, 1574), 27r: "If one wanted to extend the hyperbole even further, one could say that the Majesty of the King (speaking as a Christian) resembled the Majesty of the highest Lord of the Heavens and universe, because to us this earthly grandeur seems to imitate the divine." For Italian text and English translation, see Mulryne, *Europa triumphans,* 1:140-83, here 158 and 159.

43. Thomas Weigel, "Der Venedig-Besuch des polnisch-französischen Königs Heinrich IV./III. in Text und Bild," in Barbara Stollberg-Rilinger, ed., *Die Bildlichkeit symbolischer Akte* (Münster: Rhema, 2010), 269; and Jörg Jochen Berns, "Herrscherliche Klangkunst und höfische Hallräume: Zur zeremoniellen Funktion akustischer Zeichen," in Hahn and Schütte, *Zeichen und Raum,* 49-64, here 49.

44. Quote in translation from Rocco Beneditti, *Le feste, et trionfi fatti dalla sereniss[ima] signoria di Venetia nella felice venuta di Henrico III* (Venice: 1574), third unnumbered page.

45. Marsilio Della Croce, *L'historia della pvblica et famosa entrata in Vinegia del serenissimo Henrico III, re di Francia et Polonia* (Venice: 1574), 15.

46. Le Roux, "Luxus, Freigebigkeit, und Macht in Krisenzeiten," 238-39.

47. See Evelyn Korsch, "Geschenke im Kontext von Diplomatie und symbolischer Kommunikation: Der Besuch Heinrichs III. in Venedig 1574," in Mark Häberlein and Christof Jeggle, eds., *Materielle Grundlagen der Diplomatie: Schenken, Sammeln, und Verhandeln in Spätmittelalter und Früher Neuzeit* (Konstanz: UVK, 2012), 103-22, here 113-16.

48. Porcacchi, *Le attioni d'Arrigo terzo,* 34r. The Italian text and the English translation can be found in Mulryne, *Europa triumphans,* 1:140-83, here 177.

49. Mulryne, *Europa triumphans,* 1:140-83, here 179:

> On Saturday [afternoon], after he had dined, his Majesty with many nobles went to the Arsenal, accompanied by the four ambassadors and by many Venetian gentlemen, who showed him all of it in every detail. The great Antonio Canale and the magnificent Patroni [one of the governing boards] of the Arsenal, and his Majesty all displayed the greatest admiration in seeing a place so grand, of almost two miles in circumference, surrounded by

the highest walls, which have many towers, with such a great number of light and heavy galleys, with so great a quantity of rigging, so many armories, enough to arm thirty thousand men in one hour, so many magazines of artillery, and so many other rooms full of such an abundance of munitions, and other things necessary to arm a great fleet, and a great army, all arranged in such beautiful order, in short, a workforce of twelve hundred brave craftsmen, paid for life, fully prepared whenever there is need to build a galley a day, and all willing as one, ever faithful to their prince, and ready at any time to serve him. After this beautiful sight, a sumptuous repast was prepared for His Majesty, of exquisite confections, and sugared fruits; and what is even more marvelous, and what has never since been seen with all the knives, forks, plates, and tablecloths made of sugar, and upon his departure, as upon his arrival, there was fired a great salvo of artillery.

50. Della Croce, *L'historia della pvblica,* 23. See De Nolhac and Solerti, *Il viaggio in Italia,* 143.

51. Porcacchi, *Le attioni d'Arrigo terzo,* 34r. The Italian text and the English translation can be found in Mulryne, *Europa triumphans,* 1:140-83, here 177.

52. Henry III is known for a "vita voluttuosa." See Weigel, "Der Venedig-Besuch," 311n88, citing an account of the Venetian envoy Giovanni Michiel of 11 November 1572: "he is entirely dedicated to a 'life of pleasure' always among 'women.'"

53. Porcacchi, *Le attioni d'Arrigo terzo,* 35r. The Italian text and the English translation can be found in Mulryne, *Europa triumphans,* 1:140-83, here 179.

54. Porcacchi, *Le attioni d'Arrigo terzo,* 34v-35r. The Italian text and the English translation can be found in Mulryne, *Europa triumphans,* 1:140-83, here 179.

55. See De Nolhac and Solerti, *Il viaggio in Italia,* 148-49; and Beneditti, *Le feste,* fifth and sixth unnumbered pages.

56. Planerio Quintino, *Felicissimi adventus Henrici galliarvum, et poloniae regis christianissimi, et avgvstissimi ad vrbem Venetam* (Venice: Jacobum Vitalem, 1574), fol. 6v, Venice, Biblioteca Naztionale Marciana: Misc.1226.18.

57. De Nolhac and Solerti, *Il viaggio in Italia,* 149.

58. Della Croce, *L'historia della pvblica,* 7-8.

59. De Nolhac and Solerti, *Il viaggio in Italia,* 107.

60. Lippmann, *Geschichte des Zuckers,* 355-57; and Noel Deerr, *The History of Sugar,* vol. 2 (London: Chapman & Hall, 1949), 451-53.

61. See Alessio Ruscelli, *The Secretes* [1558] (Amsterdam: Walter J. Johnson, 1975), fols. 62r-62v.

62. Giovanni Battista Rossetti, *Dello scalco…* (Ferrara: Domenico Mammarello, 1584), 159-62; and Maria Attilia Fabbri Dall'Oglio, *Il trionfo dell'effimero: Lo sfarzo e il lusso dei banchetti visti nella cornice fastosa delle feste nella Roma barocca, lungo il percorso storico dell'evoluzione del gusto e della tavola nell'Italia fra Sei e Settecento* (Rome: Ricciardi, 2002), 79-80.

63. Stieve, *Europäisches Hoff-Ceremoniel,* 232-33:

An ambassador is wont to and arguably must make a show or cut an impressive figure according to the instructions of a distinguished prince; it is certainly essential for him to behave magnificently and splendidly, for he must demonstrate the majestic dignity and affluence of his sovereign to the world and to represent his person extra Teritorium: for therewith a sovereign acquires standing and veneration among foreign nations, since such outward splendor engages the eye rather than the mind and convinces particularly common folk that such an ambassador, who presents himself magnificently and in liveries and coaches etc. of gold and silver aplenty, must be sent from a country in its Golden Age.

Accordingly, the magnificence of an ambassador appears in his "lodgings, table and household attendants."

64. John Michael Wright, *Raggvaglio della solenne comparsa, fatta in Roma gli otto di gennaio MDCLXXXVII. dall'illvstrissimo, et eccellentissimo signor conte di Castelmaine…* (Rome: Domenico Antonio Ercole, 1687), 64-65. See also the English version, idem, An Account of His Excellence

Roger Earl of Castlemaine's Embassy: From His Sacred Majesty James the IId.…to His Holiness Innocent XI (London: Tho. Snowden, 1688), 65.

65. Wright, *Raggvaglio della solenne comparsa,* 65.

66. See Philip W. Sergeant, *My Lady Castlemaine: Being a Life of Barbara Villiers, Countess of Castlemaine, afterwards Duchess of Cleveland* (London: Hutchinson, 1912), 267.

67. Sergeant, *My Lady Castlemaine,* 267: "In January 1687 he was sent by the King as Ambassador Extraordinary to the Pope, with a mission to "reconcile the kingdoms of England, Scotland, and Ireland to the Holy See from which, for more than an age, they had fallen off by heresy."

68. See Pastor, *Geschichte der Päpste,* 1028-31. On the diplomatic abilities of Castlemaine, all extant judgments are damning. See, for example, John Miller, *James II: A Study in Kingship* (Hove, UK: Wayland, 1977), 152: "a man of great religious enthusiasm, little common sense and no diplomatic experience." On Castlemaine's activities in Rome, see Francis Joseph Rigney, *Die Geschichte der Indulgenzerklärung Jakobs II. von England vom 4 April 1687* (Berlin: Buchdruckerei J. Särchen, 1940), 53-60.

69. Rohr, *Einleitung zur Ceremoniel-Wissenschafft,* 101-2. See Hans Sonntag, "Zur 'Tragant-Zucker-Kunst' der Conditoren als eine der Quellen des plastischen Porzellanschaffens in Europa," *Keramos* 172 (2001): 19-20.

70. Josef Cachée, *Die Hofküche des Kaisers: Die k. u. k. Hofküche, der Hofzuckerbäckerei und der Hofkeller in der Wiener Hofburg* (Vienna: Amalthea, 1985), 109-38 (Die k. u. k. Hofzuckerbäckerei), here 130 (Neuigkeits-Welt-Blatt, 25 December 1915): "The Christmas tree is richly decorated with figures made of tragacanth and sugar from the Court Confectionery, and also with ribbons and so-called angel hair."

71. Schnorr von Carolsfeld, *Porzellan der europäischen Fabriken des 18. Jahrhunderts* (Berlin: Richard Carl Schmidt, 1912), 75. See Bursche, *Tafelzier des Barock,* 52-55.

72. Wendy A. Woloson, *Refined Tastes: Sugar, Confectionery, and Consumers in Nineteenth-Century America* (Baltimore: Johns Hopkins University Press, 2002), 1.

73. Rohr, *Einleitung zur Ceremoniel-Wissenschafft,* 99: "The current Orders for Dining and the presentation of the courses are very different from those of times long past. Nowadays, some commoners at their solemn feasts have more dishes on their tables than princely personages had one or several hundred years ago."

74. Ken Albala, *The Banquet: Dining in the Great Courts of Late Renaissance Europe* (Chicago: University of Illinois Press, 2007), 159-72.

75. Angelo Sala, *Saccharologia darinnen erstlich von der Natur…zoilorum virus propria virtute sopire* (Rostock, Germany: Nicolao Keyl., 1637), 27.

76. Joseph Du Chesne, *Le povrtraict de la santé…philosophes et historiens, tant Grecs que Latins, les plus celebres* (Paris: Claude Morel, 1620), 484: "All those who eat a lot of sugar and fruit preserves burn their blood & their health is usually impaired & their teeth get corrupted from it & become black: it is especially noxious for young people & those of a hot and bilious humor."

77. Robert Jütte, "La douleur des dents est la plus grande: Zur Geschichte des Zahnschmerzes in der Frühen Neuzeit," *Jahrbuch des Instituts für Geschichte der Medizin der Robert Bosch Stiftung* 15 (1996): 37-54, here 50, referring to the book by Abraham a Sancta Clara, *Kurtze Beschreibung aller Stands-Ambts und Gewerbs-Persohnen…* (Nürnberg: Weigel, 1699), as cited in Norbert Nechwatal, *Zahnweh: Die Zahnheilkunde in der Dichtung* (Wiesbaden: Wittal, 1992), 70.

78. Paul Wiegel, *Zahnärzte und Zahnbehandlung im alten Frankfurt am Main bis zum Jahre 1810* (Munich: Barth, 1957), 76: "Tooth decay was not as widespread in the Middle Ages as in the modern age. The steep increase only occurs in the seventeenth and eighteenth centuries. For this reason fewer people were necessary to treat teeth than in later times."

79. Lippmann, *Geschichte des Zuckers,* 444.

80. See Ute Weidmüller, *Die Zahnkrankheiten Ludwig XIV.* (PhD diss., Rheinisch-Westfälische Technische Hochschule Aachen, 1985); and Claudia Kluckhuhn, "Mona Lisa hatte nichts zu lachen," *Zahnärztliche Mitteilungen* 19 (2003): 34-36.

81. Mintz, *Sweetness and Power,* 95: "As sugar became cheaper and more plentiful, its potency as a symbol of power declined while its potency as a source of profit gradually increased." See also Mintz, *Sweetness and Power,* 122, 133.

82. Ira Sibÿlle Bachmann, "Gaben Asiens, Tribute Amerikas," in Zischka, *Die anständige Lust,* 418-24. here 423.

83. Especially Jennifer Montagu, *Roman Baroque Sculpture: The Industry of Art* (New Haven, Conn.: Yale University Press, 1990).

84. Ernst Gombrich, "Psycho-Analysis and the History of Art," in idem, *Meditations on a Hobby Horse and Other Essays on the Theory of Art* (London: Phaidon, 1963), 30-44, here 39.

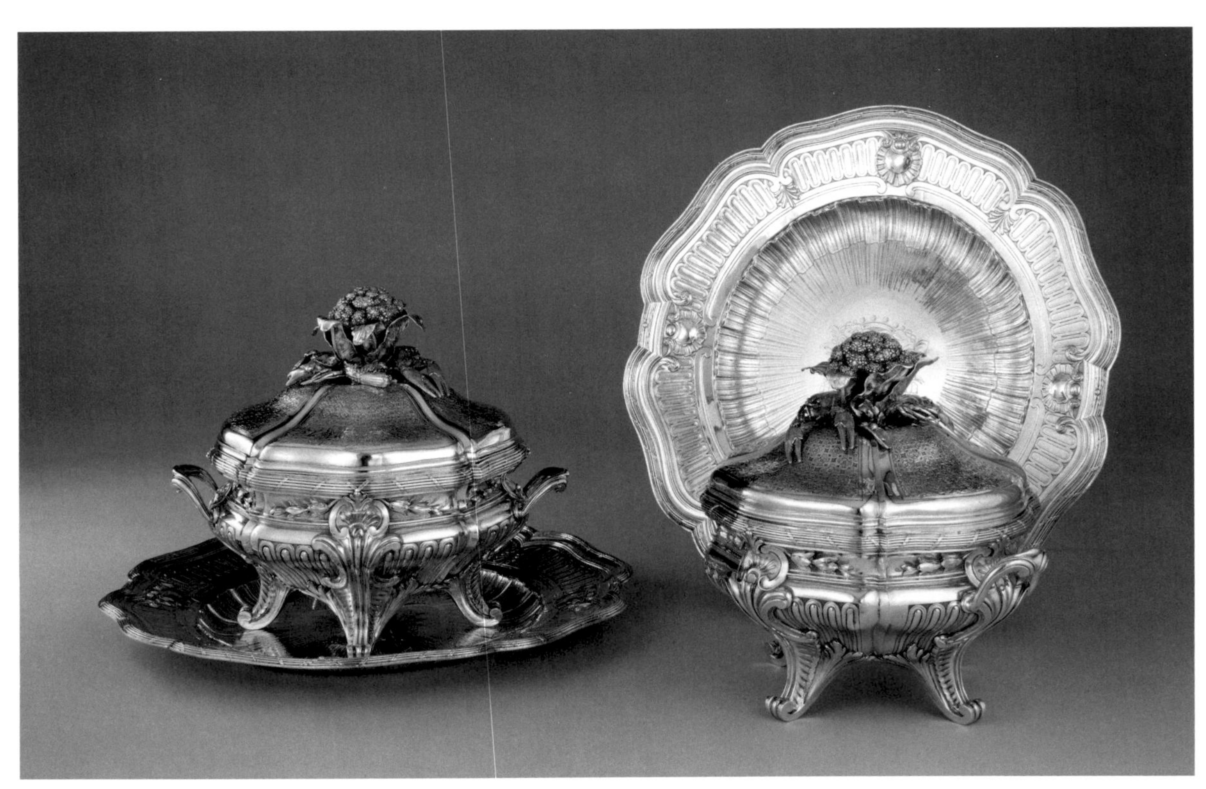

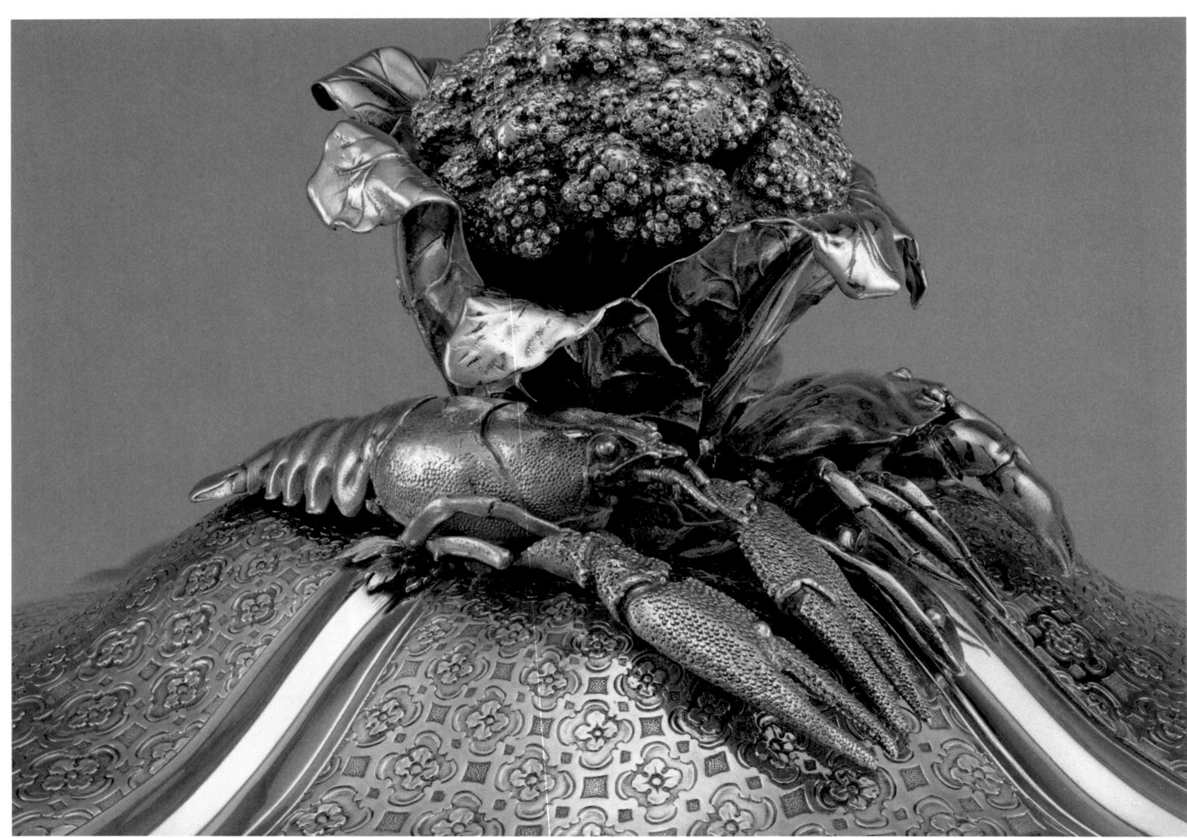

OF CAULIFLOWER AND CRAYFISH
SERVING VESSELS TO AWAKEN THE PALATE

CHARISSA BREMER-DAVID

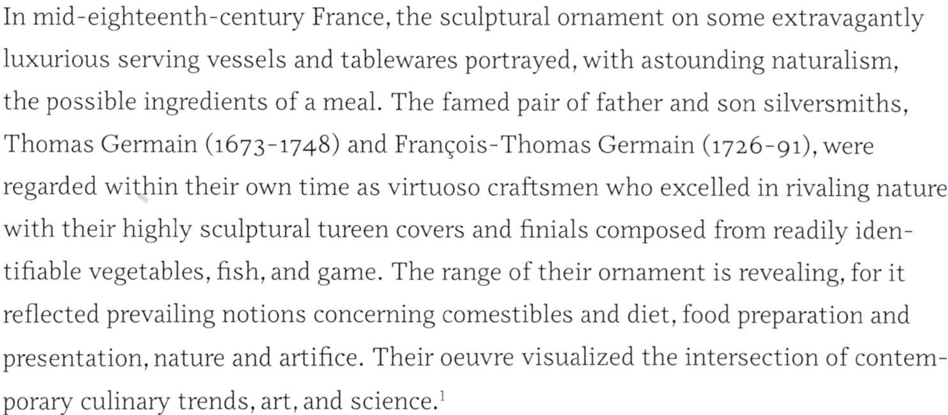

In mid-eighteenth-century France, the sculptural ornament on some extravagantly luxurious serving vessels and tablewares portrayed, with astounding naturalism, the possible ingredients of a meal. The famed pair of father and son silversmiths, Thomas Germain (1673-1748) and François-Thomas Germain (1726-91), were regarded within their own time as virtuoso craftsmen who excelled in rivaling nature with their highly sculptural tureen covers and finials composed from readily identifiable vegetables, fish, and game. The range of their ornament is revealing, for it reflected prevailing notions concerning comestibles and diet, food preparation and presentation, nature and artifice. Their oeuvre visualized the intersection of contemporary culinary trends, art, and science.[1]

The remarkable naturalism of some decorative elements found on serving vessels made in France from the 1720s to the 1770s stirs our modern-day awe and admiration. Elements seemingly cast from plant and animal specimens are recognizable because of their lifelike proportion, scale, and minute detailing. Consider, for instance, the finials on the lids to the pair of round tureens made by Thomas Germain in the mid-to-late 1740s and possibly completed by his son, François-Thomas Germain (figs. 1, 2). Each is composed of a miniature head of cauliflower still nestled within the plant's curling broad and thick leaves. The whole vegetable has been shaped into a slightly bulbous form and reduced in scale so as to accommodate the grasp of a human hand. The ungainly stalk of the cauliflower stem has been hidden behind an array of other plant elements (open pea pods, a gherkin, a morel mushroom, and a few broken sprays of parsley) and two whole crustaceans (a crayfish and a crab), all fixed to the center of the gently sloping lid. Excepting the cauliflower, the size of each individual form is true to nature and quite realistically rendered. Such naturalism—or human artifice, as an eighteenth-century critic would have called it—raises many questions.[2]

FIG. 1.

Thomas Germain (French, 1673-1748), and possibly finished by François-Thomas Germain (French, 1726-91).

Pair of lidded tureens, liners, and stands, engraved with the (partially effaced) arms of Archbishop Gaspar de Bragança, Paris, 1744-50, silver, tureen: 28.4 × 34.9 × 28.3 cm (11³⁄₁₆ × 13¾ × 11⅛ in.); stand: 4.1 × 46.2 × 47.1 cm (1⅝ × 18³⁄₁₆ × 18⁹⁄₁₆ in.). Los Angeles, J. Paul Getty Museum.

FIG. 2.

Detail of figure 1, showing the finial from the lidded tureen.

What motivated the *sculpteur-orfèvre* (sculptor-silversmith) to achieve this degree of realism in three-dimensional form, even when the choice of material—cold, lifeless, and monochromatic, albeit precious, metal—visually denied his efforts to imitate nature?[3] What was the intention of the silversmith when he applied such lifelike flora and fauna to functional serving vessels and tableware? By these artfully constructed still-life compositions, did he attempt to prove his power to invent and control form or to highlight his virtuosity in rendering different shapes and textures (figs. 3, 4)? Beyond demonstrating his quasi-alchemist mastery and transformative

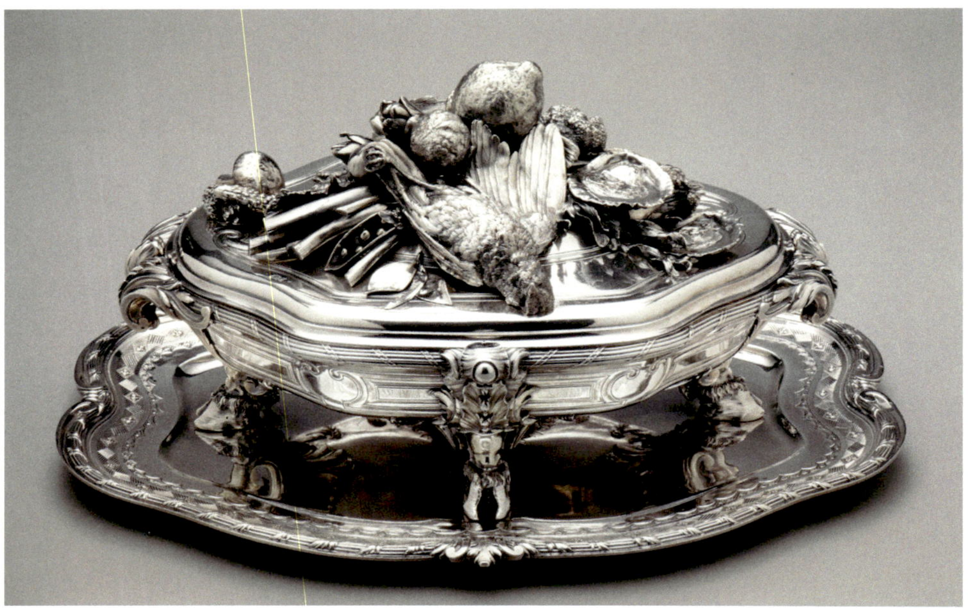

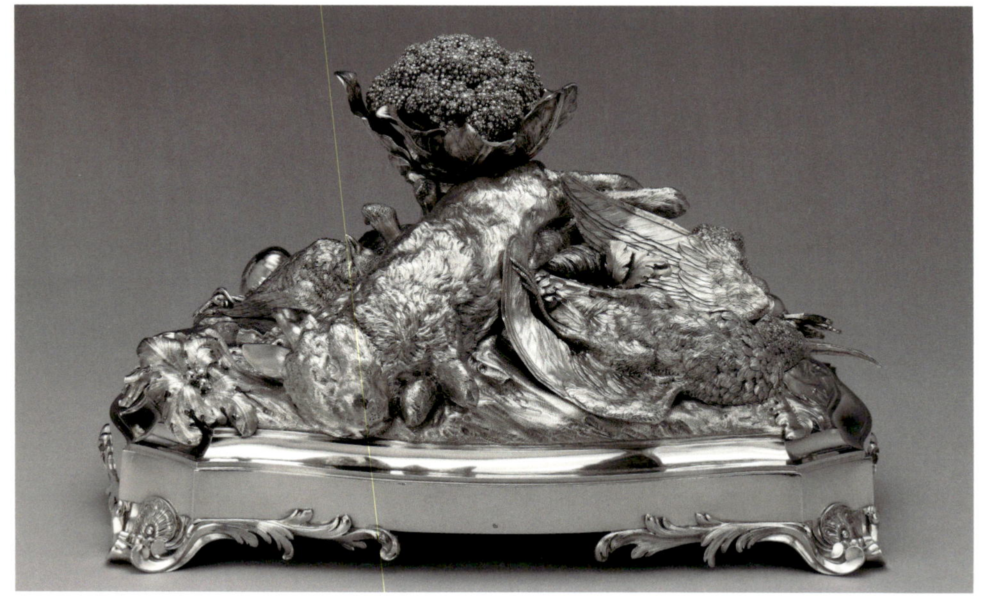

FIG. 3.

Thomas Germain

(French, 1673–1748).

Lidded tureen and stand, Paris, 1729–30, silver, overall: 21.6 × 43.6 × 35.2 cm (8½ × 17¼ × 13⅞ in.). Detroit, Detroit Institute of Arts.

FIG. 4.

François-Thomas Germain

(French, 1726–91).

Centerpiece for a table (*surtout de table*), or *La machine d'argent,* Paris, 1754, silver, 21 × 36.8 × 23.2 cm (8¼ × 14½ × 9⅛ in.). Los Angeles, J. Paul Getty Museum.

creativity with molten metal, did the sculptor-silversmith intend to rival the cook by visually suggesting the possible contents of the serving vessel? Or allude to food procurement and preparation activities such as harvesting, fishing, or hunting?

Consider the pair of children who gather ingredients, playfully grasping the stems of artichokes and leafy greens while resting upon celery stalks, mushrooms, and crustaceans, including a lobster and crayfish. First modeled in terracotta, the children reappear cast in silver as the protagonists on the allegorical finial of yet another round tureen, made in 1756-58 by Robert-Joseph Auguste (1723-1805), intended to contain a stew of shellfish and vegetables (figs. 5, 6).[4] Mimicking a cook and his assistant, the children enact the very processes of selecting and combining ingredients that took place in the kitchen. Forms and figures such as these, relevant for their subject matter and narrative possibilities, did not stifle nor constrain but rather enhanced the inventiveness and functionality of the vessel. It should be noted generally, however, that the applied ornament did not accord, always and consistently, with the edible contents contained within. For, just as today's hosts, *maîtres d'hôtel* (household managers) and kitchen stewards of the eighteenth century chose the most fitting and appropriate vessel from the available reserves, regardless of whether the decoration corresponded with the ingredients of the day.

FIG. 5.

Attributed to Robert-Joseph Auguste (French, 1723-1805).

Children with Vegetables and Shellfish, model for the finial for a tureen, Paris, ca. 1756, terracotta, height: 17.2 cm (6¾ in.). New York, The Metropolitan Museum of Art.

FIG. 6.

Robert-Joseph Auguste (French, 1723-1805).

Tureen (detail showing the finial from the cover), Paris, 1756-58, silver, height: 43.2 cm (17 in.). Copenhagen, The Royal Silver Vault, Danish State Collection, Christiansborg Palace.

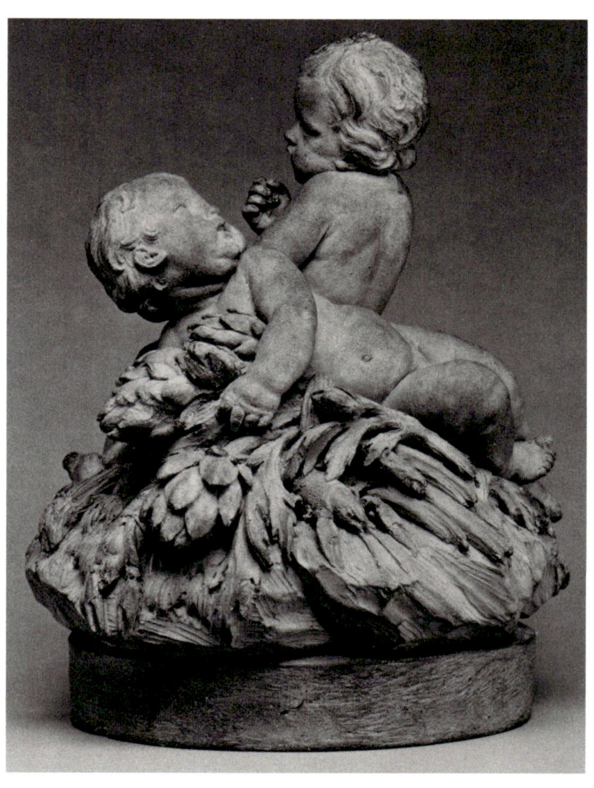

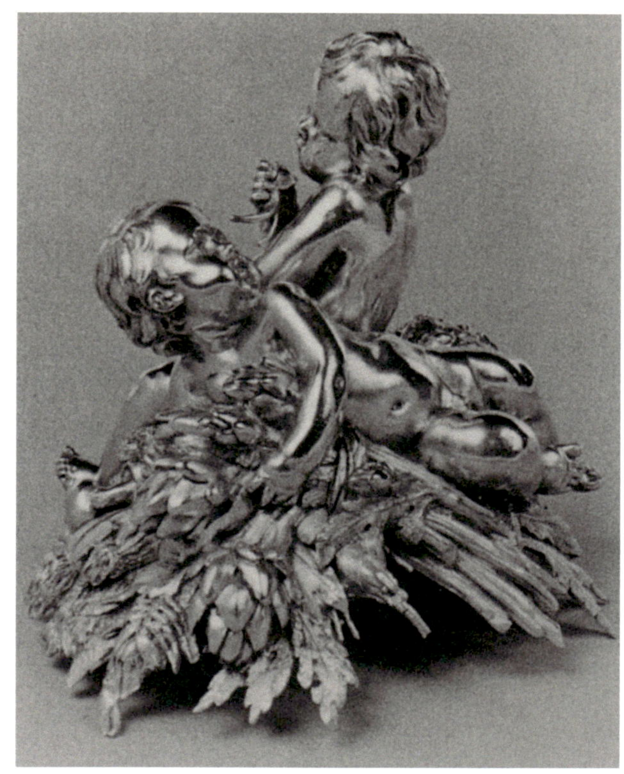

Silversmiths, however, did make deliberate and conscious choices in creating models for food-related ornament. Which aesthetic or culinary factors influenced these decisions? Why did the Germain silversmiths, for instance, choose to make casts of cauliflower rather than broccoli (see figs. 2, 4)? After all, both vegetables were known and available in eighteenth-century France.[5] In terms of execution, both posed an equal challenge to the craft, yet there was neither mention of broccoli among the lists of the Germain workshop models nor casts of broccoli in all of their surviving oeuvre. Instead, there were several recurrences of cauliflower, each distinctive curd finely and repeatedly punched with ringed-shaped tools in simulation of the vegetable head's friable and grainy surface.[6] Contemporary culinary preferences must have been at play, as horticulturalists esteemed cauliflower more highly than broccoli.[7] As early as 1600, the French soil scientist Olivier de Serres (1539–1619) commented on cauliflower in his volume titled *Le théâtre d'agriculture* (The theatre of agriculture), "*Cauli-fiori,* as the Italians say, are still rather rare in France, they hold an honorable place in the kitchen garden because of their delicacy of flavor."[8] His observation seemingly held true for mid-eighteenth-century Paris, as broccoli was not a common ingredient in cookbooks printed then and there, though cauliflower was; and representations of it, consequently, found their way onto serving vessels.[9] This point alone shows that the Germains were current with and sensitive to culinary trends in food preparation and presentation (fig. 7).

The Germain father-and-son team constituted the third and fourth generations in a dynasty of Parisian silversmiths.[10] Thomas Germain built upon and benefited from the successes of the family. He first studied painting with Bon Boullogne (1649–1717) before leaving Paris around 1688 to pursue bronze casting and chasing while attending the Académie de France in Rome. Before quitting the Eternal City, he trained as a silversmith and attained a high level of technical skill. He returned to Paris by 1706 with a reputation based upon his firsthand experience of the Roman baroque.[11] But he was not admitted as a master in the Paris guild of silversmiths until January 1720.[12]

A pivotal year for Thomas Germain was 1723, for in that year the French crown under Louis XV (1710–74) recognized and rewarded his talent with a brevet, or warrant, naming him *orfèvre ordinaire et sculpteur du roi* (silversmith and sculptor to the king).[13] With this royal appointment, the prestige and fame of the workshop increased, attracting the patronage of private clients from among aristocrats and courtiers, financiers and wealthy bourgeoisie, foreign princes and diplomats. Significantly, the appointment granted him gratis lodging in the Galeries du Louvre, where his son François-Thomas was born, and a workshop on the nearby rue des Orties, where he established both a forge and foundry.[14] Within the community of artists

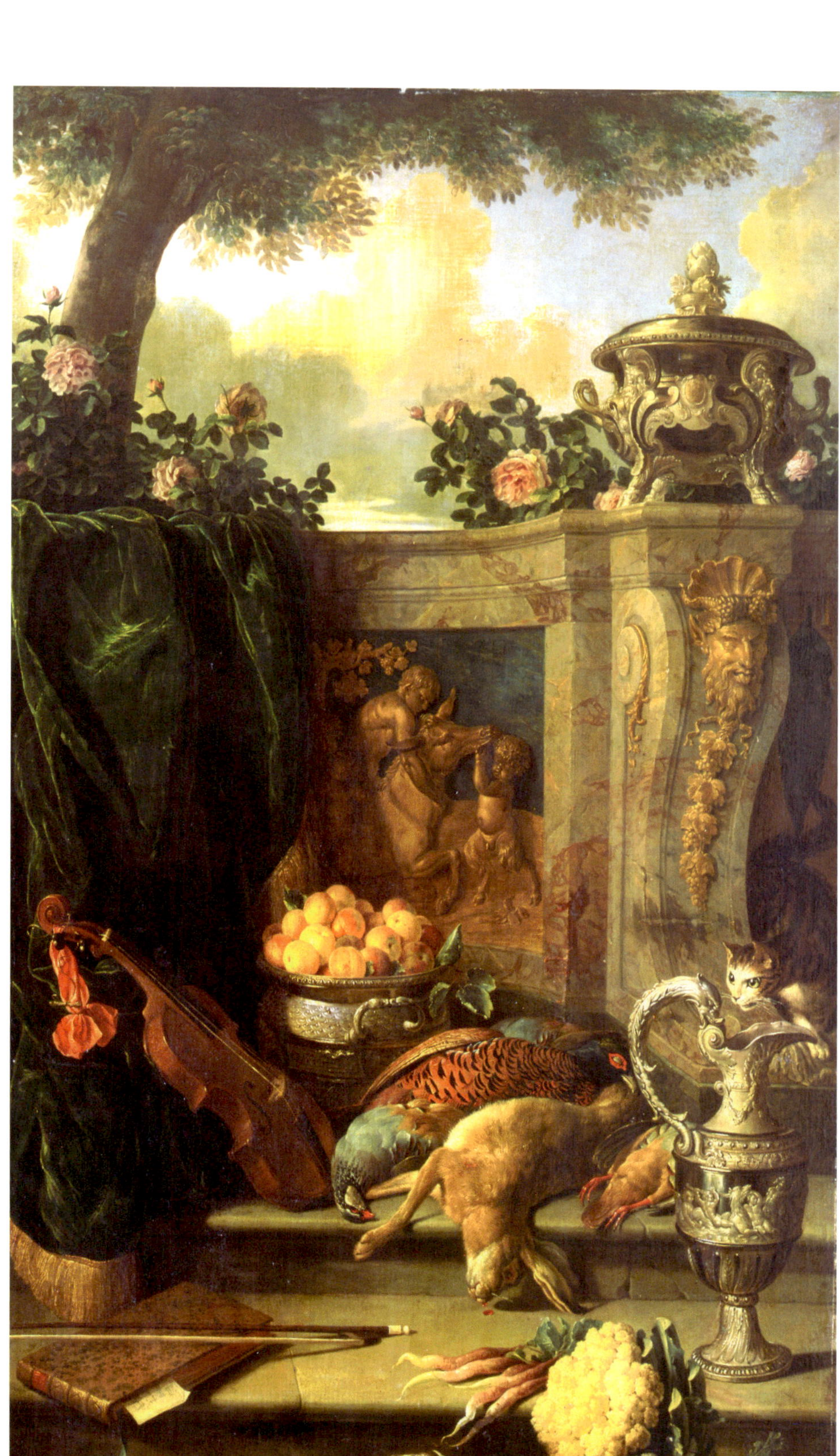

FIG. 7.

Alexandre-François Desportes (French, 1661–1743).

Still Life with Tureen [after Thomas Germain], *Bas-Relief, Ewer, Violin* [and Cauliflower], 1733, oil on canvas, 118 × 94 cm (46½ × 37 in.). Mulhouse, France, Musée des Beaux-Arts de Mulhouse.

housed at the Louvre, the Germain family became particularly close to neighboring sculptor Edme Bouchardon (1698-1762) and animal painters Alexandre-François Desportes (1661-1743) and Jean-Baptiste Oudry (1686-1755), whose canvases sometimes incorporated views of Germain silver (see fig. 7; figs. 8, 9).[15] The painters' hunting subjects influenced, in turn, the silversmiths' sculptural renderings of game and hounds (see figs. 3, 4).[16] A friendly and highly productive two-way rivalry seemingly thrived within this collective ambiance, wherein the qualities and theoretical hierarchy of different media and genres—particularly still life—were visualized and given form.

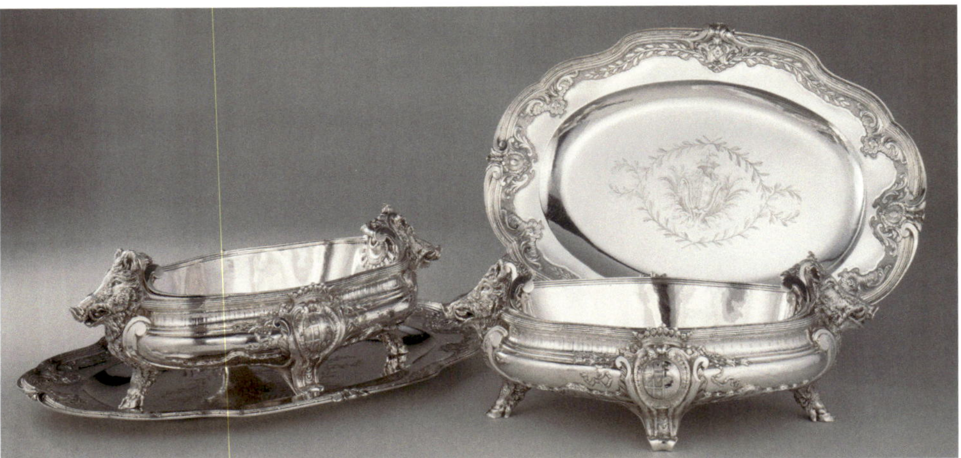

FIG. 8.

Thomas Germain

(French, 1673-1748).

Pair of tureens, liners, and stands, Paris, 1726-29, with arms altered later by François-Thomas Germain (French, 1726-91), 1764, silver, tureen: 17.5 × 47 × 25.4 cm (6⅞ × 18½ × 10 in.), stand 3.7 × 57 × 40.6 cm (1⁷⁄₁₆ × 22⁷⁄₁₆ × 16 in.). Los Angeles, J. Paul Getty Museum.

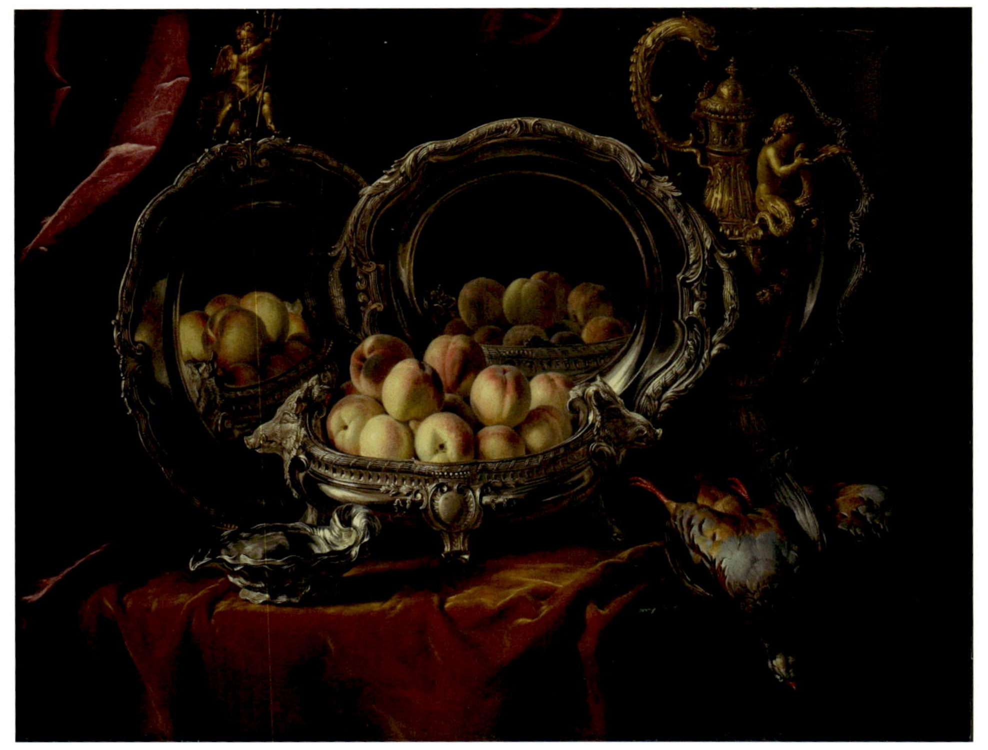

FIG. 9.

Alexandre-François Desportes

(French, 1661-1743).

Still Life of Silver Tureen with Peaches, Paris, not dated but executed by 1739, oil on canvas, 91 × 118 cm (35⅞ × 46½ in.). Stockholm, Nationalmuseum.

Before his death in August 1748, Thomas Germain secured the approval for the transfer of the title *sculpteur-orfèvre du roi* and all its benefits to his son François-Thomas Germain, who was then only twenty-two years old.[17] The son, like his father, also received artistic training beyond what was normal for a silversmith. Prior to apprenticing to his father, he attended drawing classes conducted by the painter Carle van Loo (1705-65).[18] He also learned modeling from the sculptor Jean-Baptiste Lemoyne, the younger (1704-78), at the Académie royale de peinture et de sculpture in Paris, where he was in the company of other young students, including the future sculptors Etienne Maurice Falconet (1716-91), Jean-Jacques Caffieri (1725-92), and Augustin Pajou (1730-1809). Under the sponsorship of his uncle, the silversmith Léonor Lagneau (d. 1750), François-Thomas was admitted as a master in the Parisian guild in 1748.

An inventory taken upon the death of the father reveals he left a library that included designs by the contemporary silversmith Juste Aurèle Meissonnier (1695-1750) and an unspecified number of working models, valued at 1,500 livres, stored in both the lodgings and the workshop (fig. 10).[19] François-Thomas inherited these valuable models and was able to make use of them repeatedly throughout his own

FIG. 10.

Gabriel Huquier (French, 1695-1772), after Juste Aurèle Meissonnier (French, 1695-1750). *Tureen,* ca. 1738-45, etching, 17.9 × 27.5 cm (7 × 10⅞ in.). From Juste Aurèle Meissonnier, *Oeuvre de Juste Aurèle Meissonnier…* (Paris: Huquier, ca. 1742-48), pl. 62. Los Angeles, Getty Research Institute.

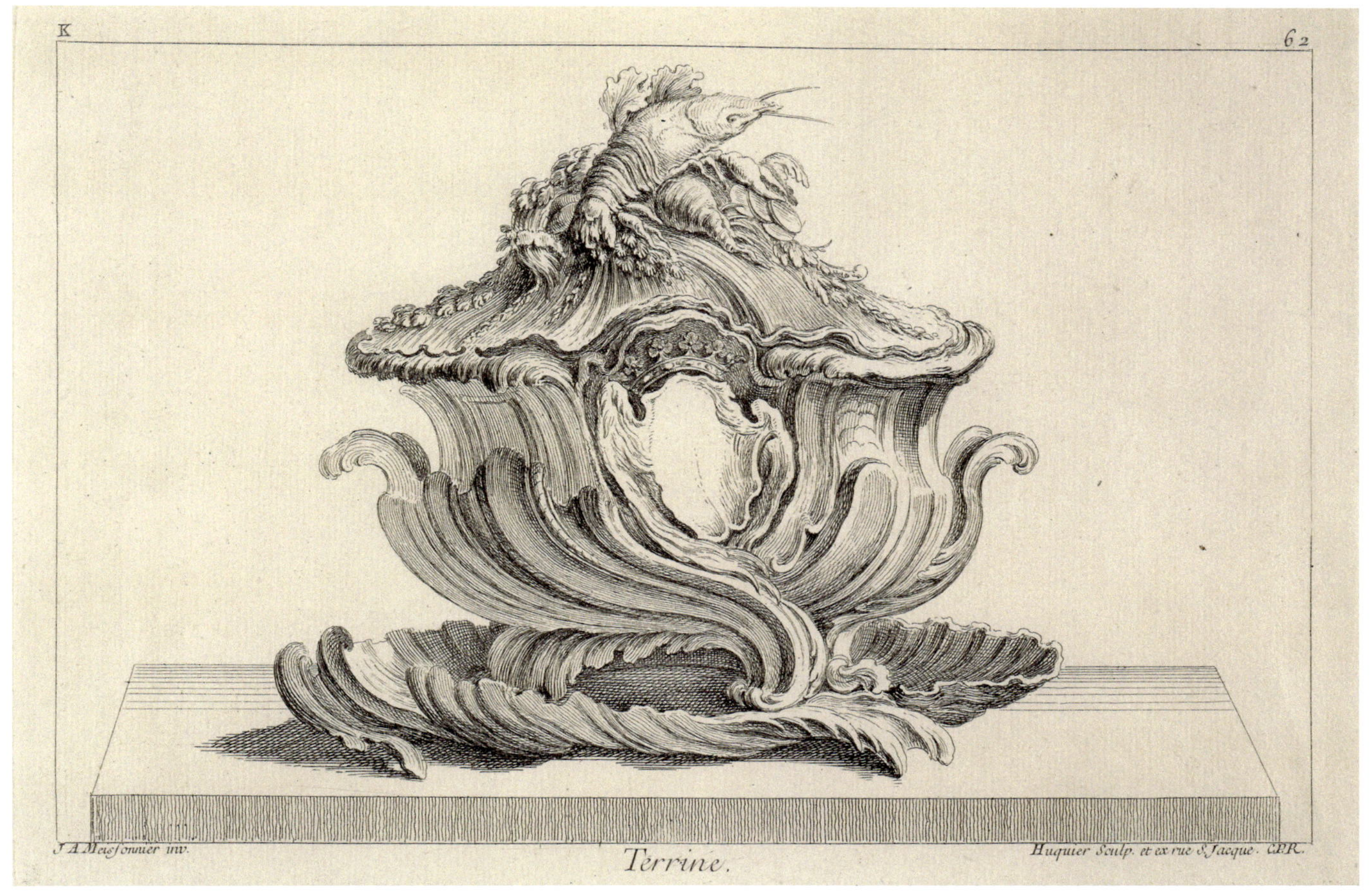

career, which was enormously successful for the first fifteen years or so, until a decline in French commissions brought about by the Seven Years' War and poor fiscal management led to his bankruptcy in 1765.[20] In general, François-Thomas augmented the collection of models, strove to improve the workshop's sand casting and gilding techniques, doubled the number of forges from three to six, and hired an additional twenty highly skilled chasers and engravers by 1752. Subsequent documents dating from the 1765 bankruptcy enumerate the type, quantity, and material of the models in the later Germain atelier, which were valued then at the considerable amount of 50,000 livres.[21]

Surveying the products of the father and son, it is not surprising to observe continuity in overall style, design, and craftsmanship in the output of the uninterrupted activity of the Germain workshop. Indeed, clients neither expected nor wanted anything less, especially in those instances in which the son had to complete unfinished orders begun during his father's lifetime. And while François-Thomas utilized the prized models he inherited from his father's stock for new commissions, he did not just simply and slavishly churn out replicate casts. His own distinguished reputation was established upon the extraordinary quality of his—and, by extension, his workshop's—chasing and finishing techniques. Indeed, the December 1752 issue of the journal *Mercure de France* praised the appearance of the cauliflowers, gherkins, morels, truffles, parsley, and peas that adorned the tureen covers he created for the "Nabab de Golgonde," claiming, "The resemblance of all these vegetables seems to rival the products of nature."[22]

Among the surviving works of silver by both generations, repetitions of the same forms differ more or less in the positioning of the component parts and, moreover, in the chasing and finishing details. Consider, for example, the comparative casts of an ortolan (or bunting, the small game bird regarded, historically, as a culinary delicacy): one cast and chased in the workshop of the elder Germain in 1729-30 for an oval tureen delivered to Louis-Jules Barbon Mancini-Mazarini (1716-98), who succeeded to the title of duc de Nivernais in 1730 (see fig. 3), and the other, almost identical example cast and chased in the workshop of the younger Germain for the centerpiece, known as *La machine d'argent,* delivered to Christian Ludwig II, Duke of Mecklenburg-Schwerin (1683-1756) in 1754 (see fig. 4).[23]

Though dated some twenty-five years apart, the similarity of the two ortolan casts suggests that both could have originated from the same model. From a plaster piece mold formed around the original model, multiple wax casts could have been created. Freed from the piece mold, each wax could have then been manipulated and adapted as required for the specific composition through a process known in French as *marcottage* (layering), in which smaller parts, such as the different beaks or limbs, were removed or grafted onto the main form of the wax body.[24] The surface texture and finish of the resulting casts in silver, each taken from its own modified wax cast, were worked with a variety of chasing tools to achieve subtly different effects. In this comparison, the legs of the birds are quite different: in the earlier version by Thomas Germain, the right leg crosses the left; each foot has three toes; and the treatment of the skin on the legs is rather cursory (fig. 11). In the later version by François-Thomas Germain, the left leg crosses the right; each foot has four toes; and the legs are chased with a more naturalistically accurate scaly surface (fig. 12).[25]

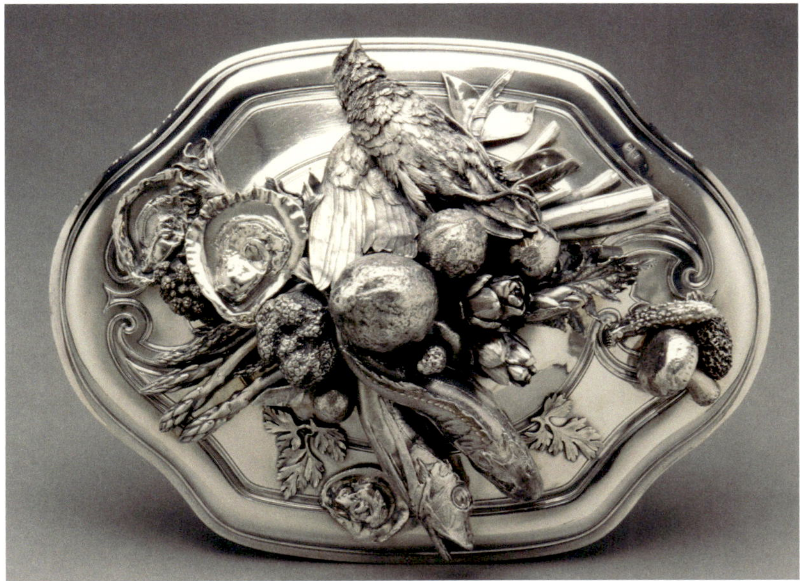

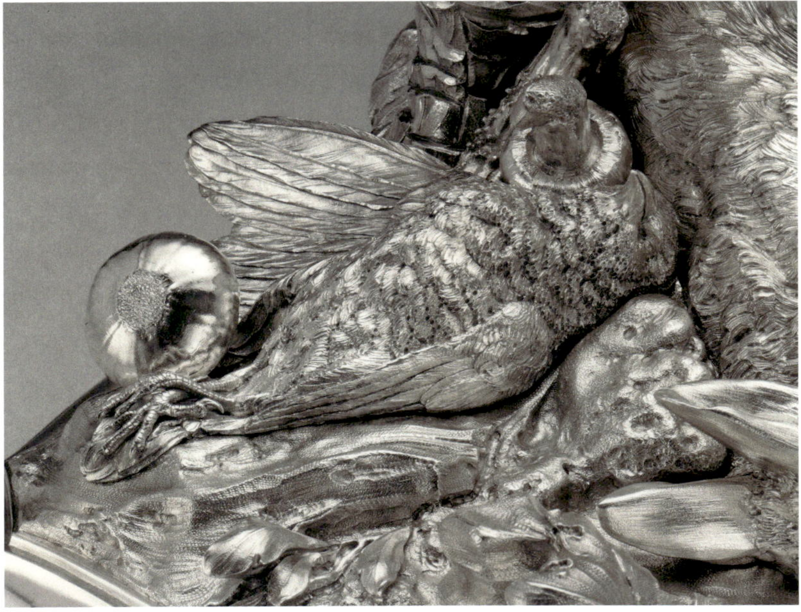

FIG. 11.

Detail of figure 3, p. 126, showing an ortolan.

FIG. 12.

Detail of figure 4, p. 126, showing an ortolan.

In 1765, the Germain workshop possessed lead models of vegetables, herbs, fruit, fish, and game, as well as seven boxes containing, as itemized per box: (1) cauliflower and artichokes; (2) lettuces, chicory, wheat, parsley, chervil, pimpernel; (3) celery, asparagus, scallions, onions, peas; (4) spearmint, grape vines, laurel leaves, pinecones; (5) pomegranates, oranges, lemons; (6) different fish; and (7) diverse game. The same document noted that some models were taken "from nature," meaning actual specimens were used.[26] The workshop also contained lead models of two rabbits, two snipe birds, four ortolan birds, twenty-four different cauliflowers (with five copper models for cauliflower leaves), beans, turnips, truffles, mushrooms, morels, gherkins, and even banana leaves. In summary, there were models for all the ingredients needed "to make a meal, or cover a tureen, or fill out a centerpiece."[27]

Contemporary cookery books attest to the rich and varied culinary culture of seventeenth- and eighteenth-century France, revealing the range of comestibles presented on the dining tables of the period. In the larger, more prosperous households, savory dishes were, generally, richly flavored, a blend of multiple and diverse ingredients combining meat, game, poultry, and/or fish, sauces, meat juices, drippings of fat, vegetables, and seasonings. This was especially the case during the first course of the meal, when soups and stews such as the ragout (a slow-simmered pungent stew usually served in an oval tureen) and the *pot à oille* (a variant of the Spanish *olio,* made from a variety of game or fish and vegetables served in a round tureen) were presented and consumed (fig. 13).

In the poem of 1736 titled "Le Mondain," the poet, author, and epicurean Voltaire (1694–1778) described the sensory pleasure of dining when an excellent cook was in charge of such dishes:

> The cheerful supper next invites
> To luxury's less refined delights.
> How exquisite those sauces flavor!
> Of those ragouts I like the savor,
> The man who can in cookery shine,
> May well be deemed a man divine.

He went on to describe the hospitality, house, interior decoration, and silver plate that accompanied these praiseworthy sauces and ragouts:

> All at this house a welcome find;
> In building it, the architect
> No grace passed over with neglect.

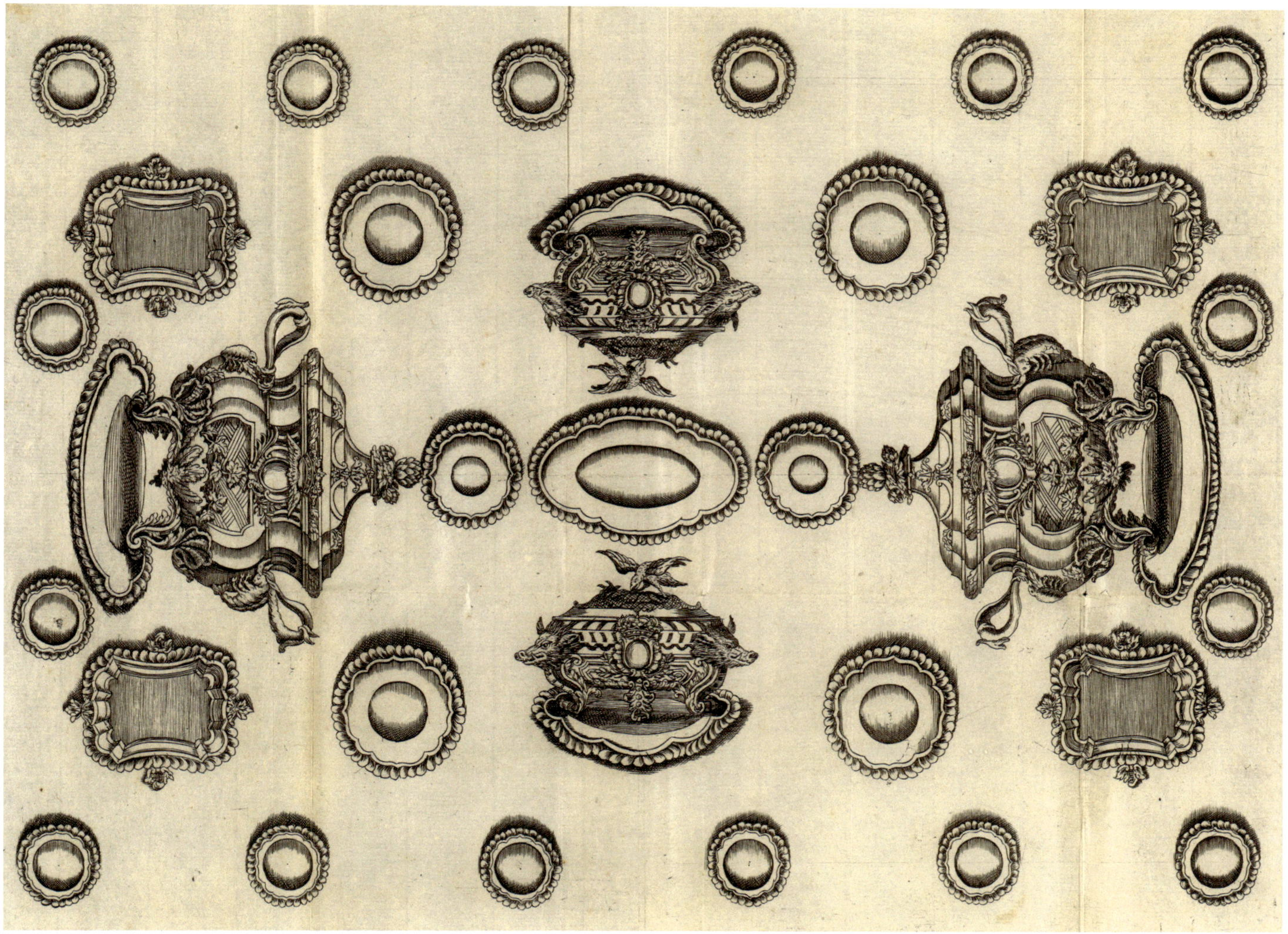

To adorn the rooms, at once combine
Poussin, Correggio the divine,
Their works on every panel placed
Are in rich golden frames incased.
His statues show Bouchardon's skill,
Plate of Germain, his sideboards fill.
The Gobelins tapestry, whose dye
Can with the painter's pencil vie,
With gayest coloring appear
As ornaments on every pier.[28]

Moreover, Voltaire named the specific cook of these delicious delights as "Martialo," now identified as François Massialot (1660–1733), author of the 1691 cookbook

FIG. 13.

Table with fifteen to sixteen settings.

Engraving, 20.3 × 25.3 cm (8 × 9¼ in.).
From Vincent La Chapelle, *Le cuisinier moderne,* vol. 6 (The Hague: L'auteur, 1742), loose plate. Cambridge, Harvard University, Radcliffe Institute, The Schlesinger Library.

titled *Le cuisinier roial et bourgeois* (The royal and bourgeois cook). For Voltaire, Massialot's flavorful sauces and savory ragouts represented the epitome of French haute cuisine, a cookery style in keeping with a household decorated with paintings by Nicolas Poussin (1594–1665) and Correggio (1489–1534), sculptures by the contemporary Edme Bouchardon, sideboards laden with silver trays and tureens by Thomas Germain (see fig. 9), and tapestries woven at the French royal Gobelins manufactory.

This style of cooking originated in the activities of large and wealthy aristocratic and upper bourgeois households that were responsible for feeding not only the master and extended family on a daily basis but also the domestic servants and stable hands.[29] The same kitchen staff was responsible, additionally, for preparing entertainments, banquets, and feasts for large numbers of guests on ceremonial occasions and for smaller parties on informal social gatherings. The kitchens in such households were organized into two principal areas: the larger, hot and steamy kitchen with the open fireplace for roasting and cooking in its coals (fig. 14) and, from around 1750, the waist-high stewing stove called a *potager.*[30] Then there was a smaller, so-called cool kitchen, or *office,* in which cold salads, desserts, and sugary confections were created. The quantity of food prepared and consumed in these large households naturally led to the simultaneous presence of many main ingredients on any given day, comprising several types and cuts of meat, poultry, fish, and a rich variety of seasonal vegetables, herbs, and mushrooms.[31] These kitchens developed practical systems of modular food preparation that delegated specific steps of the process to specialized staff and efficiently utilized every morsel of food, drip of fat, or leftover in another dish or else in the stockpot, called the *pot-au-feu.*[32]

François Massialot had very practical experience as a cook, having worked in some of the most elite, princely French households of his day, including those of Louis XIV's son, Louis, grand dauphin (1661–1711); the king's sister-in-law, Elizabeth Charlotte of Bavaria, princess Palatine (1652–1722); and her son, the king's nephew and future regent, Philippe II d'Orléans (1674–1723). In other words, Massialot served the very class of people who commissioned tablewares from the same caliber of silversmiths as the Germains. His book contained recipes for fundamental basic mixtures, stocks, reduced juices, coulis, and sauces that could be customized in an infinite variety of ways, utilizing whatever was at hand in the kitchen on any given day and sometimes prepared in advance.[33] Massialot knew full well the sequence of dishes that constituted the main meal, *le diner* (dinner), in such households. He wrote for experienced cooks, arranging the recipes according to the sequenced presentation of the dishes on the table. The first course, or *entrée,* comprised soups, bisques, ragouts, and sausages set out in larger vessels; these were surrounded by many smaller platters with lighter fare, called *grands entremets,* made from colored jellies, eggs, organ

FIG. 14.

Antoine Aveline (French, 1691–1743), after Jean Mondon (fl. 1736–60).

Noon, Paris, ca. 1738, engraving, 35.5 × 43 cm (14 × 17 in.). New York, Columbia University, Avery Architectural and Fine Arts Library.

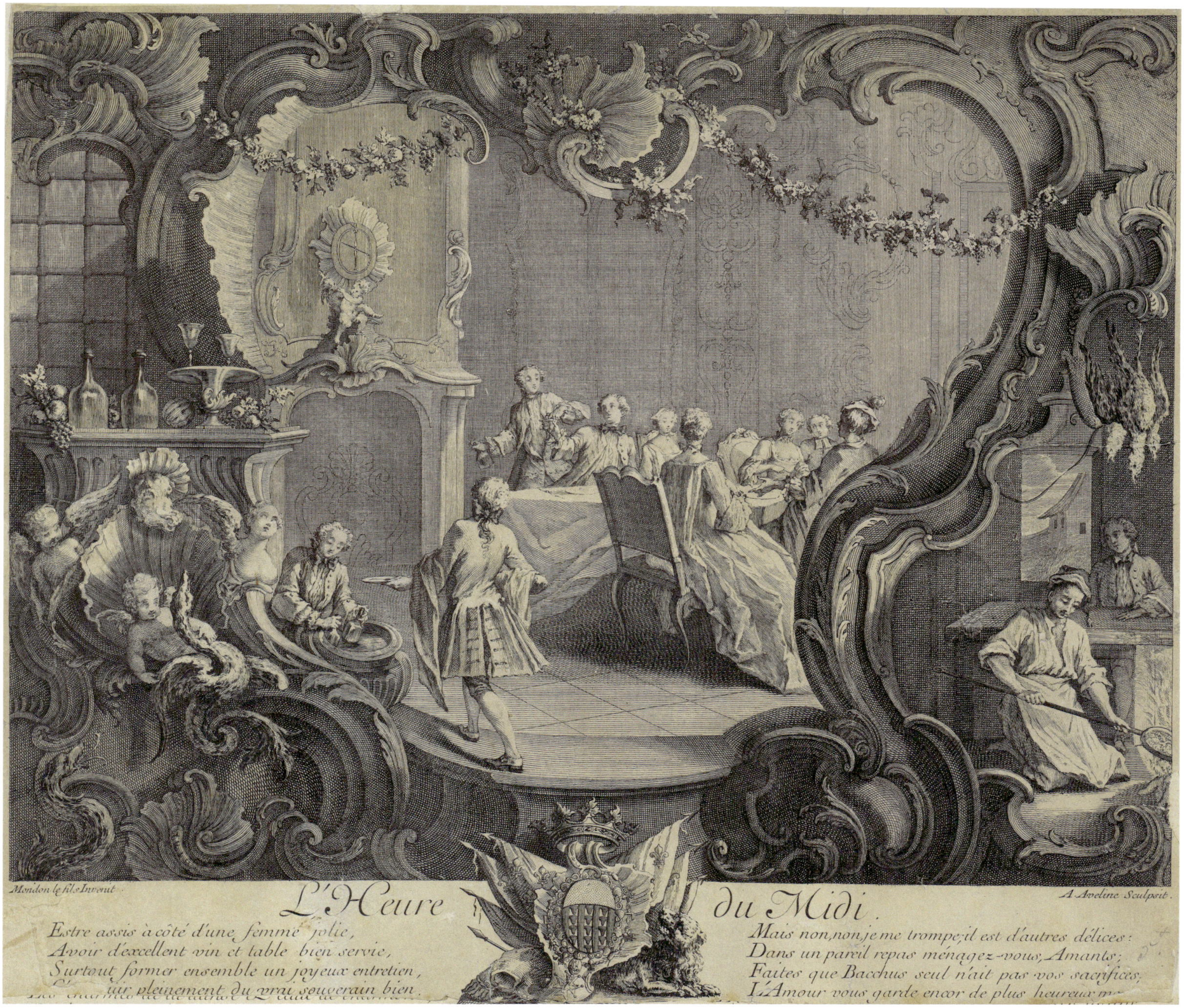

Mondon le fils Invenit
A. Aveline Sculpsit.
L'Heure du Midi.
Estre assis à côté d'une femme jolie,
Avoir d'excellent vin et table bien servie,
Surtout former ensemble un joyeux entretien,
...ir pleinement du vrai souverain bien.
Mais non, non je me trompe, il est d'autres délices:
Dans un pareil repas ménagez-vous, Amants;
Faites que Bacchus seul n'ait pas vos sacrifices,
L'Amour vous garde encor de plus heureux m...

meats, and vegetables. The second course, or *service,* featured roasted game, small birds, and young meat such as suckling pig, baby boar, or wild piglet; it was accompanied by many more auxiliary dishes, called *petits entremets* or *hors d'oeuvres,* which often included delicately flavored vegetables such as cauliflower and peas or mushrooms in sauces.[34] Each course consisted of a variety of different foods brought to the table simultaneously and arranged symmetrically. The guests took servings from vessels of different sizes and shapes; silver or pewter vessels were typically used for the savory courses. This manner of dining was known as *service à la française.*

Menus, however, had to be adapted constantly due to "difficulties of supply and storage, seasonal fluctuations, and the dictates of the church calendar," as culinary historian Barbara Ketcham Wheaton explains.[35] Winter weather and summer heat disrupted the availability of supplies from far and near as spoilage threatened saltwater fish, perishables, and imported goods shipped via riverboat from the seaports and delicate fruit delivered by wagons from the countryside. Other factors affected daily and seasonal menus, too. In winter, for instance, feast was followed by frugality as the festivities of Christmas and Epiphany gave way to the usual reductions in produce. Spring, however, experienced a resurgence of fresh vegetables, but meat and dairy consumption—encompassing milk, butter, cheese, and eggs—was restricted by the fast and abstinence days of Lent.[36] By also offering meatless recipes, *Le cuisinier roial et bourgeois* gained popularity precisely because it catered to religious dietary conventions, and because it countered supply difficulties with helpful suggestions for ingredient substitutions.

Of course, Massialot's renowned cookbook was not the only source available. French cuisine, particularly Parisian, experienced a burst of cookbook production in the long century spanning from about 1650 to the 1770s.[37] And there was an alternative approach to cookery that also offers insights as to why the Germains and other silversmiths of the period chose to represent so precisely the ingredients of a dish. Researcher Marie-France Noël-Waldteufel described this transition as a move from the *goût alimentaire* (alimentary taste) to culinary science.[38] This alternative was based on the premise that ingredients should look and taste like themselves, that they should not be heavily spiced or disguised, and that they should be grown locally and eaten in season. Adherents to this style considered themselves "purists" who stood apart from the "transmutationists" of haute cuisine—those other cooks who transmuted ingredients into something different and unrecognizable by techniques that required special skills or equipment.[39] For the eighteenth-century proponents of the "purist" approach, cooking became a logical, structured science for the creation of healthy and nutritious dishes that were delicate in flavor and agreeable to the palate and the stomach. Seasoning was meant to aid digestion, to enhance but not mask the main ingredients.

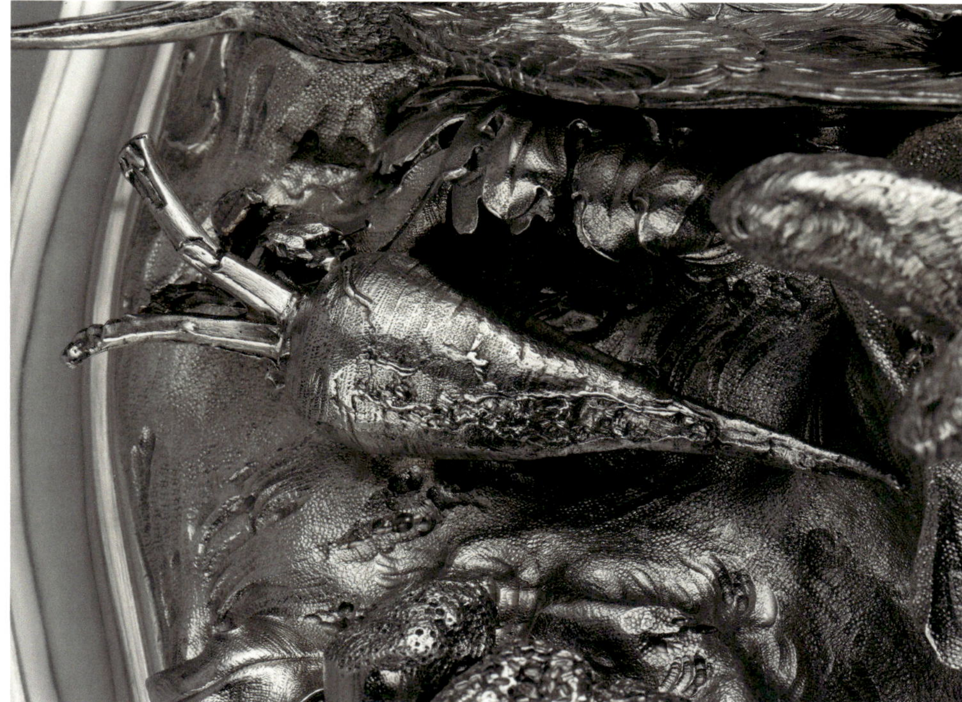

This alternative style began in the garden and ended at the table (fig. 15). The horticulturalist Nicolas de Bonnefons (fl. mid-1600s) was one of its earliest proponents. Combining gardening tips with recipes, he published two influential books: *Le jardinier françois* (The French gardener) in 1651 and *Les délices de la campagne* (The delights of the countryside) in 1654, both with many subsequent editions through the eighteenth century. Bonnefons's writings targeted those more modest households with kitchen gardens, especially the landed gentry and recently ennobled with country residences. In addition to keeping recipes simple and naturally tasty, he carefully considered their basic ingredients and origins, even down to the quality and taste of the water, which he distinguished according to its various sources: rivers, springs, wells, or rain.[40] Furthermore, he instructed novice cooks on how to choose ingredients. This approach brought "the spirit of the garden in to the dining room table."[41] From about this time, a diet of fresh foods began to be considered medically healthier and morally closer to what the creator provided in the Garden of Eden (see Willan, "Behind the Scenes").[42]

Cookery, at its highest execution, however, remained an artfully crafted luxury. It did not follow, necessarily, that a more natural cuisine was any less technically challenging to create, that the science of cooking was simple, that ingredients were always recognizable, or that specialty foods were less expensive or easier to procure.[43] The preface from one book in this new style, *Les dons de Comus; ou, Les délices de la table* (Gifts of Comus; or, The delights of the table), published in 1739 by François Marin

FIG. 15.
Detail of figure 4, p. 126, showing a turnip.

(fl. 1735-45), alluded to these complexities: "Modern cookery is a kind of chemistry. The cook's science consists today of analyzing, digesting, and extracting the quintessence of foods, drawing out the light and nourishing juices, mingling and blending them together, so that nothing dominates and everything is perceived, producing the kind of union which painters give to their colors, and making them homogeneous, so that from their different flavors result only a fine and piquant taste…a harmony of all tastes joined together."[44] At elite tables, both the menu and its presentation continued to manifest the status, identity, and culinary fashionableness of the host, just as the table setting and serving vessels, in form and material, reflected his wealth and aesthetic discernment.

Most assuredly, Thomas Germain was current with these diverse and divergent culinary trends, for he was a member of the Société des arts.[45] This society is little known today, but in mid-eighteenth-century Paris, it was at the forefront of cross-disciplinary dialogue. Its twice-weekly meetings temporarily bridged the growing divide "between the amusements of the literary salons and the learning of academies, by encouraging a polite discourse between scientists, artists, men of letters, and men of taste in order that the secrets of nature exposed by science might serve as models for novelties in art."[46] The 1730 statutes of the society explained its mission as: "Scientists and artists of great ingenuity and taste perfect the fine arts through the help of the sciences" to advance agriculture and economy, medicine and animal husbandry, textile and dye industries, civil and military architecture, naval engineering and navigation, timekeeping and mathematical instruments, and optics and metallurgy. Society members worked toward the collection, classification, dispersal, and application of information, especially scientific knowledge, in order to aid the practical arts, crafts, and industries. Advocates of empirical observation and reason, they supported technical innovations and scientific collections that had the dual purposes of compiling and advancing knowledge, on one hand, and of describing and instructing, on the other. Thomas Germain, then, was right in the milieu of those intellectual elite, including amateur scientist and client Joseph Bonnier de la Mosson (1702-44) and painter and neighbor Jean-Baptiste Oudry, who were passionately interested in the utilitarian applications of the interrelated disciplines of natural history, medicine, agriculture, metallurgy, economics, and the arts.[47]

The Germains' contributions to empirical observation were the very accurate, three-dimensional casts, made directly or indirectly from nature, that adorned their silver creations. Indeed, they brought nature to the table in an explicit and tangible manner. They communicated biological and botanical details, on a one-to-one scale, in a way that no engraved image or scholarly prose could ever do. The Germain crayfish exemplifies this point perfectly (see fig. 2).[48] In French eighteenth-century cuisine, the delicate scent of crayfish was the most sought-after aroma.⁴⁹ Countless recipes were created expressly to bring out its sweet perfume. And many of these recipes called for cooking and serving the creatures in their shell so that they arrived at the table looking very much like themselves. Here, for instance, is a recipe for a "Bush of Crayfish" in François Menon's *Nouveau traité de la cuisine* (1739; New treatise of the kitchen): "Take fifty good crayfish, wash them, put them live in a pot with wine from Champagne, add a bouquet [a tied herbaceous bundle of bay, parsley, tarragon, and thyme], roots, onions, cloves, a touch of garlic, a piece of butter, salt, and pepper. When they are cooked, serve them on a napkin, putting parsley under the crayfish to spice them up, and serve as hot as you can."⁵⁰

For the many other recipes that called for shelled and minced crayfish meat, the Germain model reminded viewers of the creature's natural appearance. The rage for these freshwater crustaceans inspired many fishing expeditions along riverbanks, and, whether for profit or pleasure, the catch always garnished the table so that diners experienced empirical encounters that called upon their senses of sight,

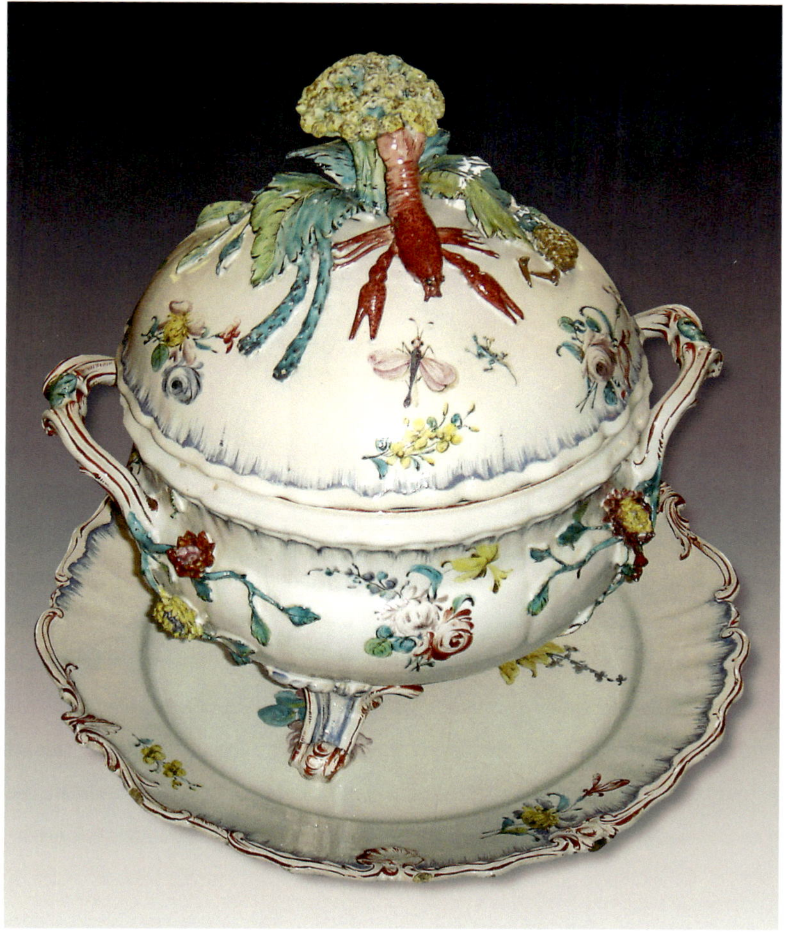

FIG. 16.

Sceaux Porcelain Manufactory of Jacques Chapelle (b. 1721, fl. at Sceaux 1750–63).

Lidded tureen and stand, Sceaux, 1750–60, soft-paste porcelain with polychrome enamel decoration, tureen height: 33 cm (13 in.); stand diameter: approximately 37.6 cm (14¾ in.). Private collection.

touch, smell, and taste. This sensory experience could be complemented intellectu-
ally by trivia relating to the natural world. For instance, guests could be reminded of
the crayfish entry in the *Encyclopédie,* which presents the fact that crayfish have the
ability to regenerate severed limbs, or with common colloquialisms, such as the one
that described a face flushed as "red as a crayfish" (fig. 16).[51] Well-read guests could
quote also the adage "Sages, like crayfish, sometimes move backwards," from Jean de
La Fontaine's fable titled "L'écrevisse et sa fille" (The crayfish and her daughter), and
reminisce upon Oudry's accompanying illustration to the 1759 edition.[52]

The lifelike animal and plant forms on the serving vessels of Thomas and
François-Thomas Germain stimulate one's visual senses and, through anticipation,
one's appetite. Indeed, the visual presentation was deliberately meant first to awaken
one's sense of taste and then to increase one's pleasure of the meal. For as *L'art de
bien traiter* (The art of treating well) explains: "The manner of presentation charms
the eye and as a fore taste of the good things that are to be found there, it seems at
first that one's eyes are about to devour these delicious dishes: the pleasure of seeing
them is greater than that of touching them, and it is an inconceivable satisfaction,
during the entire repast, to have such pleasing objects present which excite the appetite even more in that they are made expressly to waken it."[53]

NOTES

1. The themes of this chapter were first explored during the course of preparing the exhibition
    titled *Paris: Life and Luxury,* held at the J. Paul Getty Museum, Los Angeles, April-August 2011,
    and in the accompanying publication, Charissa Bremer-David, ed., *Paris: Life and Luxury in the
    Eighteenth Century,* exh. cat. (Los Angeles: J. Paul Getty Museum, 2011). They were further
    developed in a lecture titled "Of Cauliflower and Crayfish: The High Art of Dining in
    Eighteenth-Century France," presented by the present author in October 2012 at the Getty
    Center, Los Angeles, in conjunction with the American Friends of Attingham Tracey L. Albainy
    Lecture Series. The author sincerely thanks Mimi Hellman, Skidmore College, Saratoga Springs,
    New York, for intellectually stimulating discussions on the topic and for her comments on this
    essay. For other assistance, additional thanks are due to Jane Bassett, Tonny Beentjes, Meredith
    Chilton, Grace Chuang, Didier Cramoisan, Bernard Dragesco, and Elizabeth A. Williams.

2. Regarding a parallel aspect of human artifice in eighteenth-century French material culture,
    see Mimi Hellman, "The Nature of Artifice: French Porcelain Flowers and the Rhetoric of the
    Garnish," in Alden Cavanagh and Michael E. Yonan, eds., *The Cultural Aesthetics of Eighteenth-
    Century Porcelain* (Farnham, Surrey, England; Burlington, VT: Ashgate, 2010), 39-64.

3. The term *sculpteur-orfèvre* was not a classification within Le corps des marchands orfèvres-
    joyailliers (the Parisian guild of workers in precious metal), which was founded before 1260 and
    whose members practiced the crafts of gold/silversmithing, jewelry making, and enameling.
    Indeed, the hybrid term bridged two distinctly different traditions: sculpting—taught as a fine art
    since 1648 by the Académie royale de peinture et de sculpture and also by the Académie de Saint-
    Luc, which was the school associated with the guild of painters and sculptors—and gold/silver-
    smithing—regulated as an artisanal craft by Le corps des marchands orfèvres-joyailliers but tied
    closely to the royal authorities responsible for controlling purity standards for precious metals,
    the minting of coins, and the collection of taxes. Historically, the hybrid term *sculpteur-orfèvre*

was adopted or applied only rarely, when the individual excelled at designing, modeling, casting, and finishing works in the round. The most celebrated *sculpteur-orfèvre* in France was Benvenuto Cellini (1500–1571), who was both a renowned caster of large works in bronze as well as a carver of marble and a trained goldsmith. He created, for instance, the famed salt cellar of enameled gold for François I (now in the Kunsthistorisches Museum, Vienna). In the first half of the eighteenth century, Thomas Germain and his son, François-Thomas Germain, were exceptionally regarded by the French crown and the public-at-large as *sculpteurs-orfèvres.*

The term *goldsmith* is a literal translation of the French word *orfèvre,* deriving from the French term for gold, *or.* Historically, an *orfèvre* also worked with other precious metals, notably silver, or with processes that combined precious metals, as in gilding silver. English-language authors, however, customarily employ the term *silversmith* when writing about a French *orfèvre* whose products, the focus of their study, are made of silver or of silver-gilt. Accordingly, the term *silversmith* is used throughout this chapter in place of the French word *orfèvre.*

Pierre Le Roy, *Statuts et privileges du Corps des marchands orfèvres-joyailliers de la ville de Paris: An 18th-Century Compendium of the Laws Governing Silversmithing in Paris* (Los Angeles: J. Paul Getty Museum, 2003); and Bill G.B. Pallot, *The Art of the Chair in Eighteenth-Century France* (Paris: ACR-Gismondi, 1989), 32–33. On the relationship between sculptors and silversmiths in the eighteenth century, see Yves Carlier, "Sculpteur et orfèvrerie à Paris au XVIIIe siècle: Jacques et Jacques-Nicolas Roëttiers," *Revue de l'art* 105 (1994): 61–69.

4. Clare Le Corbeiller, "Robert-Joseph Auguste, Silversmith—and Sculptor?," *Metropolitan Museum Journal* 31 (1996): 211–18; and Ole Villumsen Krog, ed., *A King's Feast: The Goldsmith's Art and Royal Banqueting in the 18th Century,* exh. cat. (London: Kensington Palace, 1991), 194–95, no. 81.

5. On broccoli, see Marie-France Noël-Waldteufel, "Manger à la cour: Alimentation et gastronomie au XVIIe et XVIIIe siècles," in *Versailles et les tables royales en Europe,* exh. cat. (Versailles: Musée National des Châteaux de Versailles et de Trianon, 1993), 71, 82n44.

6. Interestingly, the cauliflower heads ornamenting the Germain wares may have originally had a powdery white, soft matte finish, which would have chromatically reinforced their appearance as that vegetable. Such a finish was achieved through a traditional workshop practice called frosting or whitening, which involved first heating (annealing) and then pickling the silver form in order to eliminate the oxides and deplete the copper alloy from the surface, leaving a fragile white external finish. When aesthetically desirable, this finish was carefully retained and set off by contrastingly burnished highlights, as suggested by the whitened artichoke finial on the tureen portrayed in the canvas painted in 1733 by Alexandre-François Desportes, *Still Life with Tureen* [after Thomas Germain], *Bas-Relief, Ewer, Violin* [and Cauliflower]. See note 15 below and figure 7 in this essay. The cauliflower head on the 1754 centerpiece called *La machine d'argent,* made by François-Thomas Germain, was actually cast directly from nature. See note 48 and figure 4 in this essay. Information courtesy of Tonny Beentjes, head of the Metalwork Conservation Program, University of Amsterdam.

7. Jean François Revel, *Culture and Cuisine: A Journey through the History of Food,* trans. Helen R. Lane (Garden City, N.Y.: Doubleday, 1982), 165–66.

8. Olivier de Serres, *Le théâtre d'agriculture et mesnage des champs,* 3rd ed. (Paris: Abr. Saugrain, 1605), bk. 6, chap. 8, 533: http://gallica.bnf.fr/ark. Barbara Ketcham Wheaton, *Savoring the Past: The French Kitchen and Table from 1300 to 1789* (New York: Scribner, 1996), 66, 284n75. Unless otherwise noted, all translations in this essay are the present author's.

9. François Menon includes a description of *brocolis* as well as *choux-fleurs,* though he provides more recipes for the latter in *Nouveau traité de la cuisine,* vol. 1 (Paris: Au Palais, 1739), 219 (*brocolis*); 90, 93, 116, 174, 258–59, 401 (*choux-fleurs*).

10. On the first and second generations of the dynasty, François Germain (d. 1676) and Pierre Germain (1645–84), see Michèle Bimbinet-Privat, *Les orfèvres et l'orfèvrerie de Paris au XVIIe siècle,* vol. 1, *Les hommes* (Paris: Paris Musées, 2002), 347–48.

11.   Germain Bapst, *Études sur l'orfèverie française au XVIIIe siècle: Les Germain, orfèvres-sculpteurs du Roy* (Paris: J. Rouam, 1887); and Ubaldo Vitali, "Meissonnier's Goldsmith Persona: A Sublimation of Forms and Techniques, natura ed invenzione," in *The Thyssen Meissonnier Silver Tureen Made for the 2nd Duke of Kingston,* Sotheby's, New York, 13 May 1998, 75.

12.   In the same year, he married Anne-Denise Gauchelet (d. 1758), the daughter of a silversmith. Madame Germain kept the account books for the workshop, as shown in the 1736 double portrait of husband and wife painted by Nicolas de Largillière (1656-1746), now in the Fondation Calouste Gulbenkian, Lisbon, inv. no. 431.

13.   The title variations of *orfèvre du roi, orfèvre ordinaire et sculpteur du roi,* and *orfèvre-sculpteur du roi* were inconsistently applied to Thomas Germain in the records of the period. The appellation *sculpteur* was meant at the time to distinguish his skill and work from that of the artisanal ranks who produced simpler, less sculptural metal forms such as dishes, trays, and salvers. His contemporaries certainly recognized his talent as a sculptor, as he earned a medal in sculpture from the Académie royale de peinture et de sculpture prior to his departure for Rome in 1688. By January 1723, the duality of his reputation in Paris was proclaimed in the circular *Le Mercure,* "On connoît assez le génie second du sieur Germain, qui traite l'Orfèvrerie en habile sculpteur" (One also knows well the second genius of Sieur Germain, who, in the guise of a sculptor, works silver). For the commission for the main altar at Notre-Dame de Paris around this time, he supplied a bronze cross and six monumental bronze candlesticks (each cast with different saints in bas-relief) after having submitted three successive models in clay, in plaster, and in wood painted the color of bronze. This process was in keeping with the customary approval review for significant sculptural commissions and testified to Thomas Germain's skill in working various modeling materials. From 1723, Louis XV decided that the number of *orfèvres du roi* would be limited to the current three (Nicolas Besnier, d. 1754; Claude Ballin, 1661-1754; and Thomas Germain), who would each take responsibility for commissions from the *maison du roi* on an annual basis. In 1740, some contemporaries bemoaned the slight that prevented Thomas Germain from being accepted as a sculptor into the Académie royale, "Il y a présentement à Paris deux excellent hommes qui mériteroient d'estre de ces Académies [royales], savoir M. Germain, orfèvre du Roy, comme sculpteur" (There are two great men in Paris currently who merit belonging to the [royal] Academies, namely M. Germain, silversmith to the king, as a sculptor). Marianne Roland Michel, *Lajoüe et l'art rocaille* (Neuilly-sur-Seine, France: Arthena, 1982), 143, 377n63. He was also regarded as the architect for the reconstruction of the church Saint-Louis-du-Louvre in Paris. *Mercure de France,* January 1723, 76, reprinted in *Mercure de France,* vol. 4 (January-June 1723) (Geneva: Slatkine Reprints, 1968), 26; and *Mercure de France,* September 1748, 229-31, reprinted in *Mercure de France,* vol. 55 (January-June 1748) (Geneva: Slatkine Reprints, 1970), 174-75. Bapst, *Germain,* xxx-xxxi, 25, 34, 36, 34n2, 38.

14.   Archives Nationales (Paris, France), Série O[1] Maison du Roi—Direction générale des bâtiments, jardins, arts et manufactures royales O[1] 1045—2805 [hereafter AN O[1]]: O[1] 1063 fo 204 as quoted by Bapst, *Germain,* 38. Thomas Germain could not move into the Louvre lodging until the death of the previous occupant on 28 September 1724. The suite of ten rooms was large compared to other apartments there. Christiane Perrin, *François Thomas Germain: Orfèvre des rois* (Saint-Rémy-en-l'Eau, France: Éditions d'Art Monelle Hayot, 1993), 35. Concerning the layout and number of lodgings at the Galeries du Louvre and the significance of a royal appointment within that protected enclave, see Bimbinet-Privat, *Orfèvres,* 93-103.

15.   Notably, the two canvases by Alexandre-François Desportes: (1) *Still Life with Tureen* [after Thomas Germain], *Bas-Relief, Ewer, Violin* [and Cauliflower], 1733, oil on canvas, 118 × 94 cm, Musée des Beaux-Arts, Mulhouse, D.73.1.19 and (2) *Still Life of Silver Tureen with Peaches,* n.d. but executed by 1739, oil on canvas, 91 × 118 cm, Nationalmuseum, Stockholm, MN 800. Georges de Lastic and Pierre Jacky, *Desportes* (Saint-Rémy-en-l'Eau, France: Éditions d'Art Monelle Hayot, 2010), 1:217-18; 2:200, no. P 728; 2:208, no. P 752. Desportes's *Still Life of Silver*

Tureen with Peaches visualizes Wheaton's discussion on the values assigned to the hierarchy of fruits and vegetables that appear in still-life paintings throughout the seventeenth and eighteenth centuries. Produce, such as peaches, that required a substantial investment of the landowner's time, space, equipment, and skilled labor was customarily portrayed by painters in equally valuable silver or porcelain presentation vessels, while less expensive produce, such as root vegetables, was typically portrayed within copper or earthenware kitchenware. See Wheaton, *Savoring the Past,* 126.

16. This was spectacularly exemplified by the *surtout-de-table* (centerpiece), possibly originally ordered in 1729-31 by the financier Samuel-Jacques Bernard (1686-1753), now in the Museu Nacional de Arte Antiga, Lisbon, inv. no. 1827. Leonor d'Orey, *The Silver Service of the Portuguese Crown* (Lisbon: Edições Inapa, S.A., 1991), 68-83, 194, no. 2; and Perrin, *François Thomas Germain,* 84-85, 157.

17. On 13 February 1748, Louis XV signed the warrant granting the succession of the title "orfèvre-sculpteur de…Maison [du roi]" to François-Thomas Germain upon the death of his father. François-Thomas Germain emphasized this distinction throughout his career, often engraving works of both silver and bronze with the inscription "Fait par F.T. Germain Sculp.Orf. Du Roy Aux Galleries Du Louvre AParis" (as found, for example, on the silver stands for a pair of tureens in the Museu Nacional de Arte Antiga, Lisbon, inv. nos. 1831, 1832, 1833, and on the four gilt-bronze wall lights in the J. Paul Getty Museum, Los Angeles, 81.DF.96.1-2). Moreover, François-Thomas Germain hosted a school of drawing and sculpture within his workshop for four years, from 1751 to 1755. AN O[1] 1191, as quoted by Bapst, *Germain,* 108. See also Perrin, *François Thomas Germain,* 18-20, 259n23, 260n33.

18. François-Thomas Germain, *Mémoire a consulter et consultation pour le Sieur François-Thomas Germain, ecuyer, sculpteur-orfevre du Roi* (Paris: Imprimerie de Guillaume Desprez, 1766), 7.

19. Juste Aurèle Meissonnier, *Oeuvre de Juste Aurèle Meissonnier* (Paris: Chez Huquier, ca. 1742-48; reprint, New York: Benjamin Blom, 1969), 35n163; and Henry H. Hawley, "Meissonnier's Silver for the Duke of Kingston," *The Bulletin of the Cleveland Museum of Art* 65, no. 10 (1978): 312-52, 335nn17-18; and Bapst, *Germain,* 88-90.

20. On 26 October 1759, the French controller-general of finances ordered the meltdown of the royal household's gold and silver, including that of the king, and its conversion into bullion in order to offset the costs of the Seven Years' War. Private citizens were expected to follow suit. Michèle Bimbinet-Privat, "The Royal Silver," in Marc Bascou, Michèle Bimbinet-Privat, and Martin Chapman, eds., *Royal Treasures from the Louvre: Louis XIV to Marie-Antoinette,* exh. cat. (San Francisco: Fine Arts Museum of San Francisco, 2012-13), 83, 89n1. For the effect on François-Thomas Germain's activity, see also Perrin, *François Thomas Germain,* 81.

21. The 1765 total value of 50,000 livres included the workshop tools as well as the models. In 1748, the former were valued at 3,454 livres. Perrin, *François Thomas Germain,* 14, 46.

22. The term *Nabab* (or *Nawab*) de Golgonde referred to the Mughal viceroy who controlled Golconda, a fortification near Hyderabad. The unnamed individual honored by this diplomatic gift was most likely Muhyi ad-Din Muzaffar Jang Hidayat, Nizam of Hyderabad (r. 1750-51) or his deputy, who were allies of the French during the Second Carnatic War (1748-54). *Mercure de France,* December 1752, 148-50; reprinted in *Mercure de France,* vol. 63 (July-December 1752) (Geneva: Slatkine Reprints, 1971), 317. H.H. Dodwell, ed., *The Cambridge History of India,* vol. 5, *British India, 1497-1858* (Delhi: S. Chand, 1968), 134-37.

23. The ortolan is a small songbird symbolic of the French countryside; it is usually seen around Bordeaux in late summer when on migration to northern Africa. Due to its diminishing population, there has been a ban since 1999 on snaring the bird in France. Historically, the ortolan was considered a culinary delicacy with a unique and subtle scent that reminded diners of leisurely halcyon days. In the eighteenth century, they were popular game birds and, when in season, were included in many recipes, thus rendering their forms as strikingly suitable ornaments for serving

vessels. Within recent times, diners customarily covered their heads with a draped napkin while eating them, the better to enjoy the aroma. Regarding the tureen now in the Detroit Institute of Arts, see Tracey Albainy, "Eighteenth-Century French Silver in the Elizabeth Parke Firestone Collection," *Bulletin of the Detroit Institute of Arts* 73, issues 1-2 (1999): 8-29. Regarding the centerpiece traditionally known as *La machine d'argent,* now in the J. Paul Getty Museum, see Alexander von Solodkoff, "A Lost 'Machine d'Argent' of 1754 by François-Thomas Germain for the Duke of Mecklenburg," *Studies in the Decorative Arts* 7, no. 2 (2000): 122-35; and Alexander von Solodkoff, "The Rediscovery of a 1754 'Machine d'Argent' by François-Thomas Germain," *Studies in the Decorative Arts* 13, no. 2 (2006): 93-103.

24. Perrin, *François Thomas Germain,* 59-60.

25. The present author thanks conservators Jane Bassett, the J. Paul Getty Museum, and Carole Forsythe, formerly of the Detroit Institute of Arts, for the examination of these comparative casts.

26. Perrin, *François Thomas Germain,* 60, 268n153.

27. Archives Nationales (Paris, France), Le minutier central des notaires de Paris, LXXXIII-511, dated 22 May 1765, as transcribed in the auction catalog *La Machine d'argent,* Sotheby's, New York, 20 May 2004, 40, 42n1.

28. Voltaire (born François-Marie Arouet), "Le Mondain" (1736), in *La Henriade, divers autres poèmes L'édition encadrée des oeuvres de Voltaire,* vol. 12 (Geneva: Cramer et Bardin, 1775), 64-68. For the English translation, "The Worldling," in Tobias Smollett, John Morley, and Oliver Herbrand Gordon Leigh, eds., *The Works of Voltaire: A Contemporary Version,* trans. William F. Fleming, vol. 36 (New York: St. Hubert Guild, ca. 1901), 84-88. This was not the only instance in which Voltaire praised the work of Thomas Germain. Other poems that mention the silversmith include "Des vous et des tu" (1730) and "Le pauvre diable" (1758). Later, in February 1766, the son, François-Thomas, appealed directly to the aged Voltaire, asking for relief in the face of his financial ruin.

29. Linda Civitello, *Cuisine and Culture: A History of Food and People* (Hoboken, N.J.: John Wiley, 2004), 162.

30. Meredith Chilton, "From the Garden to the Table: The Transformation of Gastronomy and Dining in Seventeenth- and Eighteenth-Century France," in Elizabeth A. Williams, ed., *Daily Pleasures: French Ceramics from the MaryLou Boone Collection,* exh. cat. (Los Angeles: Los Angeles County Museum of Art, 2012), 27-28.

31. Noël-Waldteufel, "Manger à la cour," 69-84.

32. Wheaton, *Savoring the Past,* xxi, 95, 114; and Civitello, *Cuisine and Culture,* 162.

33. Chilton, "Garden to Table," 28.

34. Wheaton, *Savoring the Past,* 153. On the origin of the word *entremet,* see Peter Brown and Ivan Day, *Pleasures of the Table: Ritual and Display in the European Dining Room, 1600-1900,* exh. cat. (York: York Civic Trust, 1997), 90n19. On menus and the sequence of courses, see Noël-Waldteufel, "Manger à la cour," 74-76.

35. Wheaton, *Savoring the Past,* 9-12.

36. Civitello, *Cuisine and Culture,* 93.

37. Anne Willan, *The Cookbook Library: Four Centuries of the Cooks, Writers, and Recipes that Made the Modern Cookbook,* ed. Darra Goldstein (Berkeley: University of California Press, 2012), 128-256.

38. Noël-Waldteufel, "Manger à la cour," 69, 74, 80n1.

39. On the long debate between transmutationists and purists, see Wheaton, *Savoring the Past,* 53. Jean-Claude Bonnet, "The Culinary System in the *Encyclopédie,*" in Robert Forster and Orest Ranum, eds., *Food and Drink in History: Selections from the Annales, Économies, Sociétés, Civilisations,* vol. 5, trans. Elborg Forster and Patricia M. Ranum (Baltimore: Johns Hopkins University Press, 1979), 139-65.

40. Nicolas de Bonnefons, *Les délices de la campagne* (Amsterdam: Raphael Smith, 1655), 4 (water), 127 (cauliflower), 341-42 (crayfish), http://gallica.bnf.fr/ark. Wheaton, *Savoring the Past,* 125, 180.

41. Chilton, "Garden to Table," 24-44; and Brown and Day, *Pleasures of the Table,* 25.

42. Bonnet, "Culinary System," 142.

43. Jennifer J. Davis, "Masters of Disguise: French Cooks between Art and Nature, 1651-1793," *Gastronomica: The Journal of Food and Culture* 9, no. 1 (2009): 36-49.

44. Quotation from the later, revised edition of the work: François Marin, *Les dons de Comus; ou, L'art de la cuisine, réduit en pratique, nouvelle edition, revue, corigée et augmentée par l'autuer,* vol. 1 (Paris: Chez Pissot, 1758), xxii-xxiii, http://gallica.bnf.fr/ark., as translated by Wheaton, *Savoring the Past,* 197, 297nn9-10. The book's introduction, from which this quote is taken, is ascribed to two Jesuits named Pierre Brunoy and Guillaume Hyacinthe Bougeant. See also Revel, *Culture and Cuisine,* 187.

45. Thomas Germain, "orphevre cizeleur, au[x] galleries du Louvres," was admitted as a member to this society on 31 October 1728 (probably under the category of "les arts des métaux"), according to a document drawn on 6 February 1735 for the Swedish architect and inventor Carl Johan Cronstedt and now preserved in the Nationalmuseum, Stockholm, CC 3459, http://www.clairaut.com/n16septembre1728p01pf.html. On Thomas Germain's association with the circle of artists, scientists, and technicians that composed the Société des arts and the network this organization provided him, see Roland Michel, *Lajoüe,* 30-33; Jean-Nérée Ronfort, "Science and Luxury: Two Acquisitions by the J. Paul Getty Museum," *The J. Paul Getty Museum Journal* 17 (1989): 46-61; and Vitali, "Meissonnier's Goldsmith Persona," 78-80. Concerning the society in general, see Roger Hahn, "Science and the Arts in France: The Limitations of an Encyclopedic Ideology," *Studies in Eighteenth-Century Culture* 10 (1981): 77-93.

46. Katie Scott, *The Rococo Interior: Decoration and Social Spaces in Early Eighteenth-Century Paris* (New Haven, Conn.: Yale University Press, 1995), 169.

47. Perrin, *François Thomas Germain,* 91. A portion of Joseph Bonnier de la Mosson's natural history cabinet, which was open to the interested public during his lifetime, is now housed in the Muséum national d'Histoire naturelle, Paris. Scott, *The Rococo Interior,* 166-76; Philip Conisbee, *French Paintings of the Fifteenth through the Eighteenth Century* (Washington, D.C.: National Gallery of Art, 2009), 336-42.

48. For an account of the technical challenges involved in casting a crayfish from life, see Pamela H. Smith and Tonny Beentjes, "Nature and Art, Making and Knowing: Reconstructing Sixteenth-Century Life-Casting Techniques," *Renaissance Quarterly* 63, no. 1 (2010): 128-79.

49. Revel, *Culture and Cuisine,* 200.

50. François Menon, "Buisson d'écrevisses," in idem, *Nouveau traité de la cuisine* (Paris: David, 1739), 296. Translation courtesy of Grace Chuang.

51. Mimi Hellman, "Feast for the Eye: Elusive Temptations," *Gastronomica: The Journal of Food and Culture* 11, no. 2 (2011): 7-11. Hellman cites Denis Diderot and Jean Le Rond d'Alembert, eds., *Encyclopédie; ou Dictionnaire raisonné des sciences, des arts et des métiers par une société des gens de lettres,* vol. 5 (Paris: Briasson, 1751-72), 354-56.

52. Jean de La Fontaine, "L'écrevisse et sa fille," in *Fables choisies, mises en vers,* vol. 4, bk. 12 (Paris: Chez Desaint & Saillant, 1759), fable 10, 94.

53. L.S.R., *L'art de bien traiter, divisé en trois parties* (Paris: J. Du Puis, 1674), 372-73, as translated by Revel, *Culture and Cuisine,* 227. Known only by the initials L.S.R., the author of *L'art de bien traiter* remains unidentified.

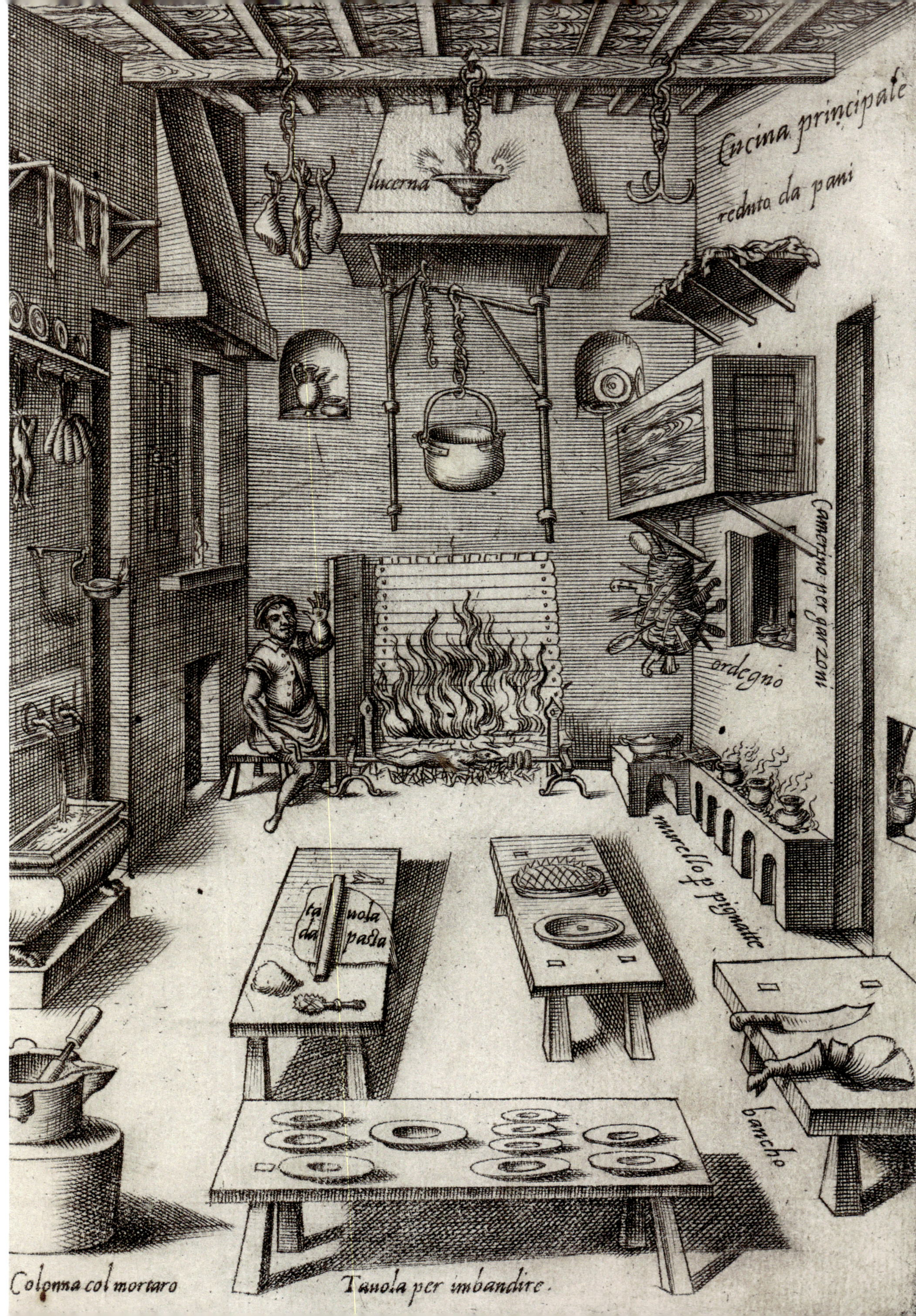
Cucina principale
reduto da pani
lucerna
banchi
Camerino per garzoni
ordegno
murello p pignatte
tauola da pasta
bancho
Colonna col mortaro
Tauola per imbandire.

BEHIND THE SCENES

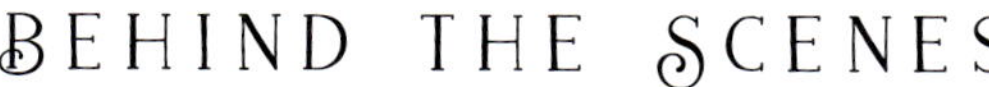

ANNE WILLAN

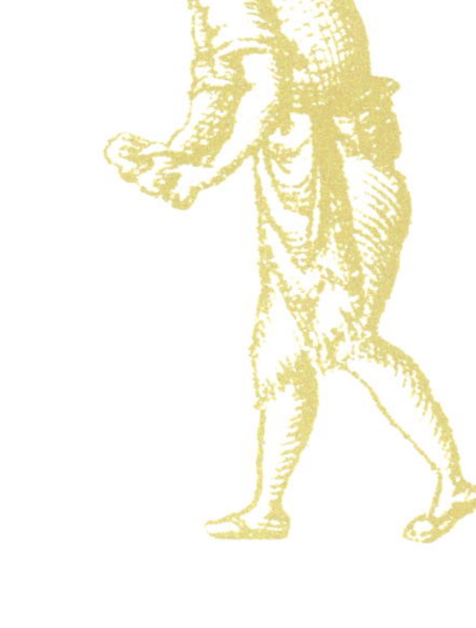

The eye-dazzling splendor of late-seventeenth-century feasts is carefully described in contemporary texts, but remarkably little is said about what food was actually eaten at the table. Accounts tiptoe around menus and what dishes were available at Roman and Bolognese feasts and events offered by Louis XIV in the parks of Versailles. General references are made about the ambitions ("everything to create a magnificent collation"[1]) and foods ("the Delicacy of the Meats, Wines, and other liquors, as well as the Abundance"[2]), but details are scanty. The scribes who chronicled such feasts were educated men more interested in the fashionable decorations, music, guests, ambience, and all the essentials of wealth and power on display. The tough, sweaty work of the kitchen was most probably outside their sphere. In any case, the menu was a movable creation, needing adjustment at the last minute to take advantage of every possible ingredient available, and such details might not have been recorded.

For more information on the food, we must turn to the many cookbooks that are meticulous in advising household stewards and cooks on how to piece together a memorable feast. In the world of food, Italy was the leader well into the seventeenth century, and the feasts of the time are clearly outlined in a handful of cookbooks. In *La singolare dottrina* (1560; The singular doctrine), Domenico Romoli, steward to Pope Julius III, suggests six courses for a June dinner dubbed "alla francese," opening with cold dishes set out on the table and followed by antipasti, *alleso* (a boiled course that must have included roasts), a *fritto* (a fried course of smaller, more frivolous dishes), *torterie* (cakes), and, finally, *fruttarie* (fruits).[3] The Italian influence was further spread throughout Europe by a monumental cookbook, Bartolomeo Scappi's *Opera,* published in 1570 (fig. 1). Catherine de' Medici's personal copy, bound in red velvet with her coat of arms embossed in gold braid on the cover, survives in the Bibliothèque nationale de France. Catherine was a gourmand of renown, so this book is a tribute to Scappi's prowess.[4] Scappi divides his material into six parts that contain information

FIG. 1.

The Main Kitchen.

Engraving, 18.6 × 13 cm

(7½ × 5 in.).

From Bartolomeo Scappi,

Opera…(Venice: Appresso Michele

Tramezzino, 1570), pl. 1.

Los Angeles, Getty Research

Institute.

on meat, fish, and other ingredients; menus for stupendous meals; and more than a thousand impressively detailed recipes. He covers specialties from a dozen Italian regions and mentions some French, Hungarian, and Spanish dishes. Similar international influences can be seen a hundred years later in *Lo scalco alla moderna* (1692–94; The modern steward), by Antonio Latini, steward to the Spanish court of Naples.

By the mid-seventeenth century in France, inspiration for feasting had blossomed in a handful of cookbooks, beginning with *Le cuisinier françois* (1651; The French cook), by François Pierre de la Varenne, cook to Nicolas Chalon du Blé, marquis d'Uxelles; two books on gardening and cooking in 1651 and 1654 by Nicolas de Bonnefons, a member of Louis XIV's household; a cookbook from Pierre de Lune, who enjoyed the court title of *valet de chambre* to the king; and an anonymously authored book called *Le pastissier françois* (1653; The French pastry cook). To round out the art of creating a splendid feast, in 1662 came *L'escole parfaite des officiers de bouche* (The ideal school for household officers), a compendium of advice for the *maître d'hôtel,* the carver, and the sommelier, with recipes for cooks and pastry cooks, including some for preserving foods. All these books are a contrast to the Renaissance elegance of their Italian forerunners. They all look similar: sturdy volumes usually bound in brown leather tooled in gold on the spine and small enough to be carried in a pocket for reference. That so many have survived is a testimony to both their popularity as well as their endurance, because they were undoubtedly used from day to day, not just kept on the shelves of a library.

When planning menus, both Italian and French cooks observed the seasons. In *Le nouveau cuisinier* (1656; The new cook), Pierre de Lune lists the dishes suited to the four seasons of the year and gives recipes for cooking them. As *Le nouveau cuisinier* was published only twelve years before Louis XIV's great outdoor feast at Versailles in mid-July of 1668 for hundreds of members of his court, it is likely his menu would have opened with an array of potages, as recommended by de Lune. These were far more than simple soups; they featured great tureens filled with meats, poultry (fish on fast days), and vegetables served in broth. For summer, contemporary cookbooks propose such potages as baby turkey with cucumber, pheasant with truffles, a melon broth with baby chicken, leg of veal larded and stuffed, shoulder of lamb with turnips, and a dozen more ideas, all with accompanying recipes.

In such feasts, the main course, the entrée, showcased platters of grand meats, such as breast of veal *en ragoût,* chicken or pigeon in white sauce, veal tongue, sautéed lambs' tails with extra-large lamb chops, and marinated chicken in a pastry crust—all demanding the skills of the professional carvers who hovered around the tables, behind the seated guests. Carvers also had reference manuals that illustrated which knives to use, proper cuts, and the correct way to hold forks with roasts aloft (fig. 2). At the Versailles outdoor feast, the center of the table would have been laden with great crusted pies served cold and filled with seasonal ingredients. Rabbit and game birds were favorites at that time; they were enriched with pork fat and laced with spices, though in smaller amounts than the overwhelming seasonings of medieval times. These pies were a boon to the cook, as they could be made a week or more ahead and kept in a cool cellar.

Placed on the table between the *grandes entrées* were *entremets,* smaller tastes to tickle the appetite, such as single-ingredient *tourtes* of pistachios, morel mushrooms, artichokes, apples, pomegranate seeds, or almond frangipane. One or two egg dishes might have been included at the feast, such as *oeufs à la florentine* or an omelet flavored with lemon zest. Only a very few single vegetables are suggested in contemporary books, including cauliflower, creamed fava beans, and the baby green peas that were such a rage that Madame de Maintenon exclaimed, "There is no end to this interest in peas.... Some ladies sup with the King, and sup well at that, only to return home to eat peas before retiring, without any care for their digestion."[5]

L'escole parfaite des officiers de bouche, published in 1662, included pullout

FIG. 2.

Holding a carving knife.

Engraving, 13.2 × 17.4 cm (5¼ × 6¾).

From Mattia Giegher, *Li tre trattati di messer Mattia Giegher, bavaro di Mosbvrc, trinciante dell'ill.ma natione alemanna in Padova* (Padua: Per Paolo Frambotto, 1639), pl. 1. Los Angeles, Getty Research Institute.

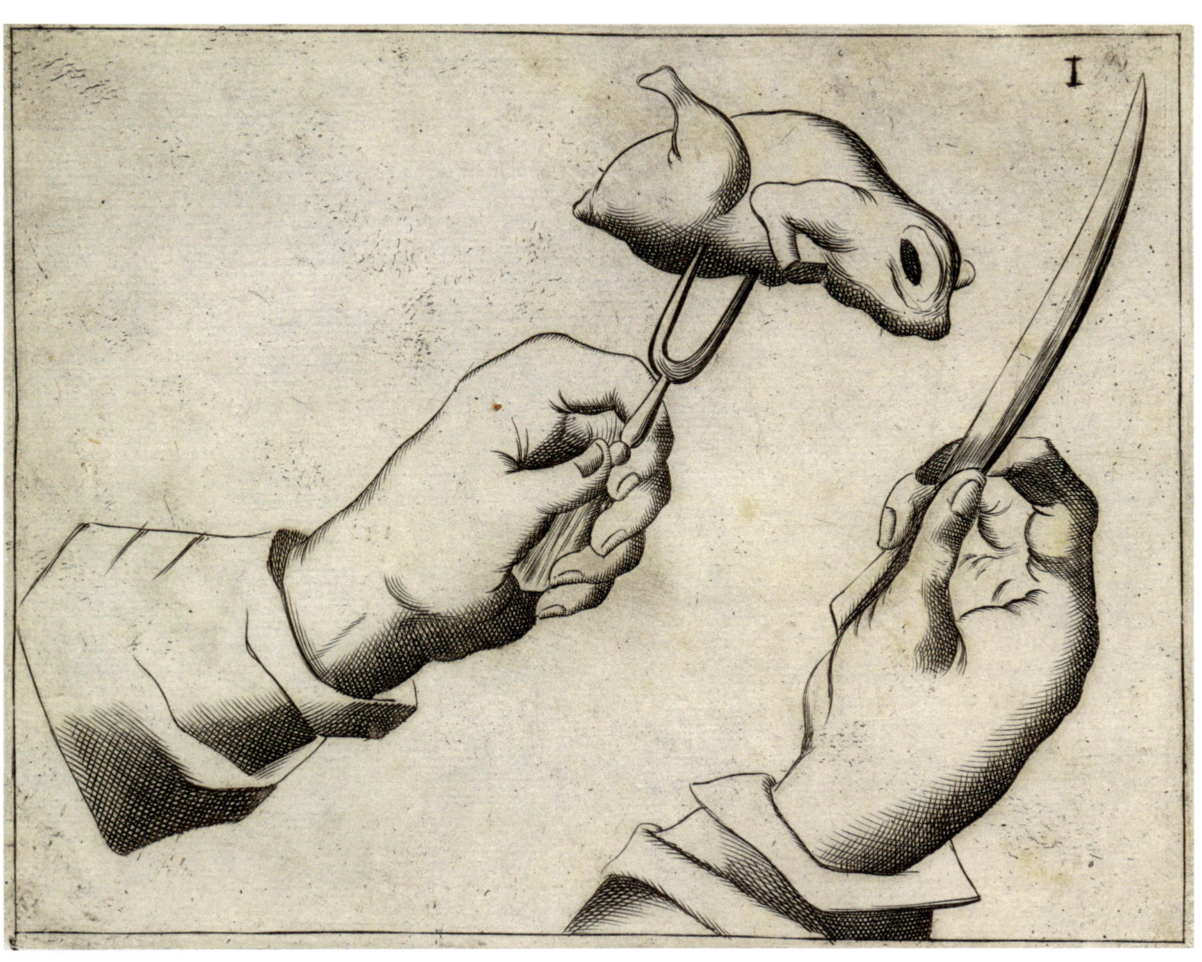

diagrams on how each course should be arranged on the table. Every time the table was cleared (sometimes only partially) and reset with different dishes, it was called a *relevé* (remove) (fig. 3). For the main course, entrées such as a potage and two marinated beef roasts take pride of place in the center of the table; they are surrounded by minor entrées and *entremets,* including savory and sweet *tourtes* (already the French favored pies with a bottom crust as well as a top crust), with side dishes such as plum fritters and melted cheese. One diagram is devoted to "Fruit, as well as Dessert" centered with "a basket filled with fruits or oranges" and "Two other laden baskets of firm preserves or fruit pastes, or other jellies arranged symmetrically, or Biscuits."[6] A feast of similar grandeur in Italy would have had six courses instead of three, but fewer dishes in each one. In both countries, an alternative to service of several

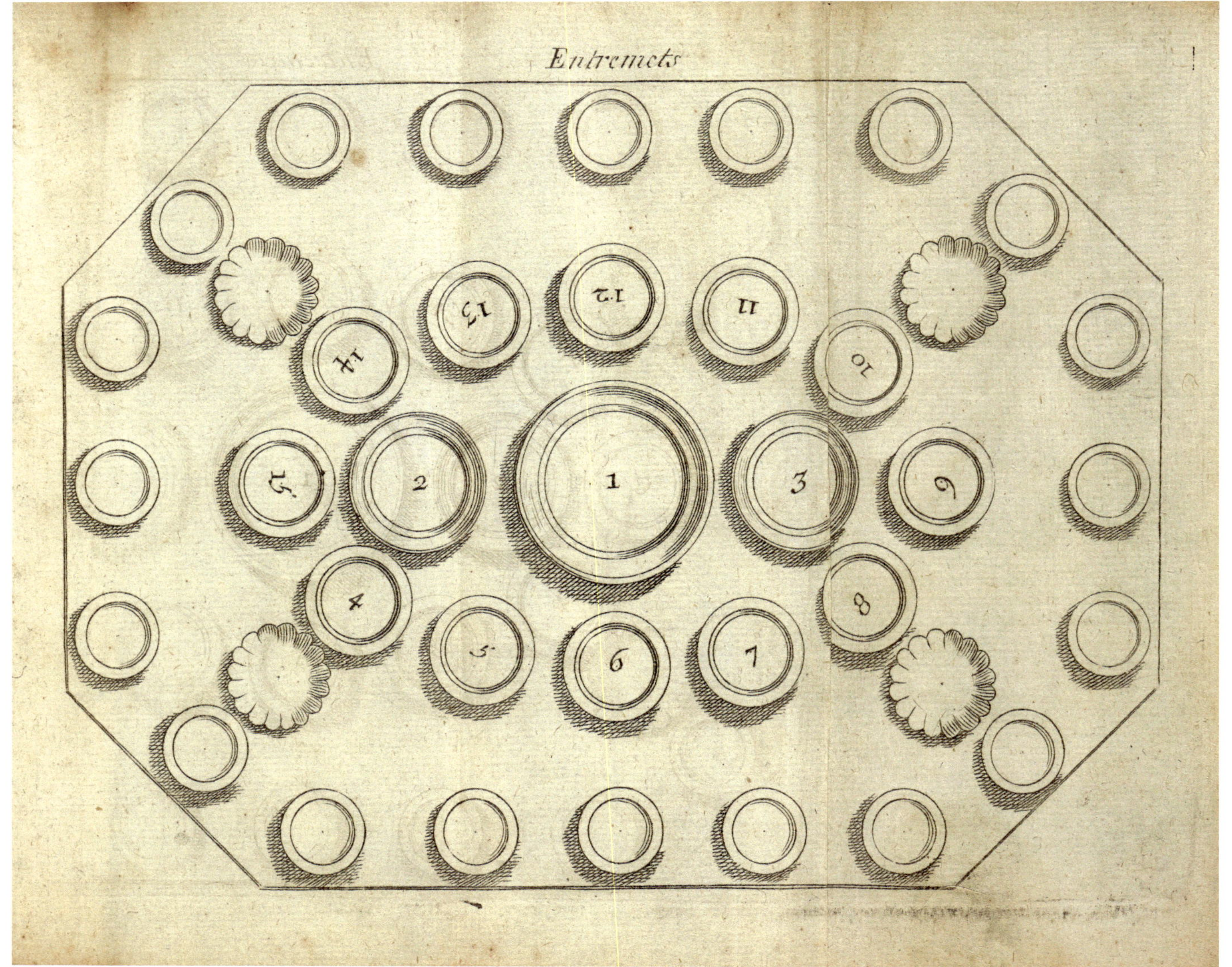

courses was the *ambigu* (fig. 4). Here, all the dishes to be served are spread out on the same table like a hotel buffet. "This service could not be better named," remarks the unknown compiler of *L'escole parfaite,* "because it is composed of Roasts, Entremets, and Dessert."[7] There is perhaps a hint of disapproval, as an *ambigu* is easier to prepare and serve but lacks the finesse of multicourse service.

Although service was simpler, a buffet could be rewarding in its magnificence. For the great Versailles festival in July 1668, the chronicler André Félibien describes the setting of the table itself: "I will say only that the foot of the Rock between the shells and the foam was arrayed with a quantity of pastries, fruit comfits, conserves, pastes and sugared fruits, which seemed to have grown between the stones and be part of them" (see Reed, "Court and Civic Festivals," fig. 11).[8] Stretching upward beside the

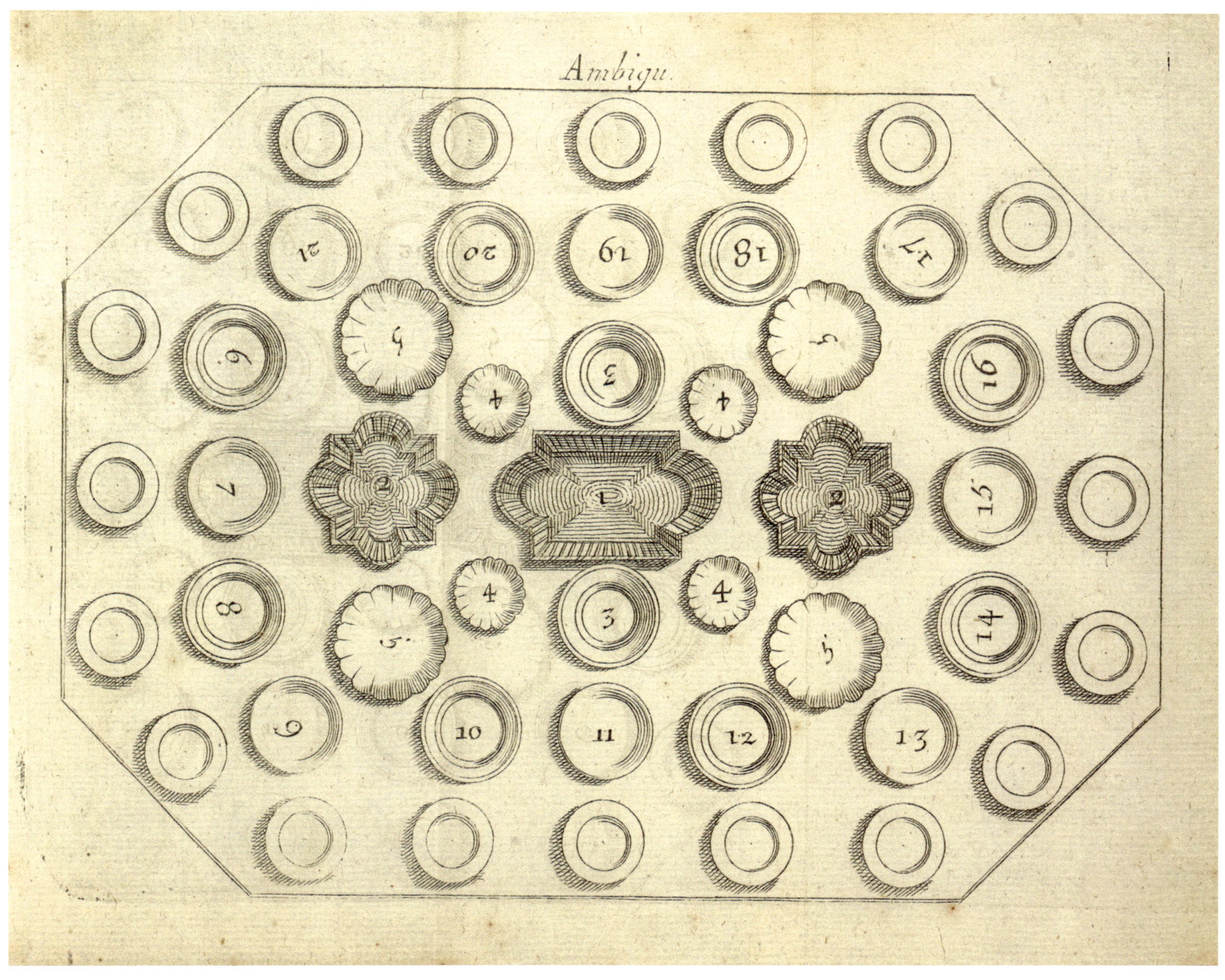

central rock were "eight pyramids of flowers, each of which was composed of thirteen porcelain dishes filled with different foods." Félibien goes on to recount the five courses that were customary at a festive dinner, but the "fifty-six main dishes" served at each course must have been exceptional by any standard, and so were the "dessert platters…laden with sixteen porcelains in pyramids, where all that was most exquisite and rare for the season appeared to the eye."[9]

INTERNATIONAL EATING

In the latter half of the seventeenth century, great feasts were an international attraction. The rich traveled from country to country on grand tours to view the artistic achievements, while less wealthy artisans and traders journeyed on the job. When Roger Palmer, Earl of Castlemaine, was sent on a special embassy for King James II to Pope Innocent XI in 1686, he and his household had plenty of opportunities to absorb French fashions in entertainment. He spent eleven days in Paris on his journey to Rome, and memories of the king's great feasts at Versailles twenty years earlier would still have been bright. The earl must surely have kept a sharp eye on the French manners of his hosts, as the leaders of fashion and culture.

Castlemaine had attended the coronation of his own King James II on 23 April 1685. Francis Sandford chronicled this resolutely English display at length in the festival book published for the occasion (see Reed, "Court and Civic Festivals," fig. 16).[10] The dishes were laid out as a vast buffet, an *ambigu.* The menu lists only the main ingredients, such as in the medieval era, whereas the French and Italian menus in cookbooks of the time detail how ingredients are to be cooked—typical dishes might be *canard en ragoût; roüelle de veau aux huîtres;* or *salsa verde fatta con anisi e erbe odorifere, servita con zuccaro e canella.*[11] The newly crowned king and queen had 145 different dishes at just their end of the table, including a whole lamb larded, a marrow "patie," stags' tongues, sweetbreads, and glasses of lemon jelly, all laid out with a cold whole salmon, lampreys, hot oyster "pyes," and some "sallet and pease."[12] (There are fewer fast days and greater tendencies to mix fish and meat in a Protestant country.) In England, the more honored the guests, the better and more varied the dishes they were served, but in France and Italy, all were treated equally. The English account is unique in naming the head cook, Patrick Lamb. As master cook to the king, Lamb wrote *Royal Cookery; or, The Compleat Court-Cook* (1710), a celebrated early cookbook for professionals.

When Castlemaine reached France, entertainment was different. In Avignon, his delegation was received in style by the papal vice legate and honored with a "magnificent…supper of…four services, each, of nine grand Dishes, and fourteen Intermesses, and to render it yet greater, it wanted not the pride of the Italian Musick."[13]

The *entremets* would have filled in the gaps between the giant platters and tureens of the main dishes. At a couple of stops along Castlemaine's journey, a "regal" (treat or snack) is mentioned, but again no details are given. Such gifts were a courtesy from the donor rather than valuable in themselves, like the comestibles of "All sorts of Fowl, Wines, Sweet-meats, and other Delicacies of that nature"[14] that awaited Lord Castlemaine at his official residence, the Palazzo Pamphilj in Rome, when he returned from his first audience with the pope. The aging pontiff was prostrate with gout in his private apartments, but nonetheless spent what must have been a gratifying hour chatting with his visiting ambassador.

The subsequent feast held by Castlemaine in January 1687 was sumptuous almost beyond imagination—a pageant of gold and silver platters, ornaments, and fabrics, much of which had been brought by sea (see Imorde, "Edible Prestige," figs. 1-3). The account compiled by John Michael Wright, who made the trip with Castlemaine, does not reveal whether French or English fashions were favored, except for the opulent servants' liveries that had been tailored in England. The few foods that are mentioned—"Parmigian" cheese and "lardo"—sound firmly Italian. Perhaps this display inspired the equally magnificent reception given six years later by Senator Francesco Ratta on his retirement from a two-month term as gonfalonier, an honorary position as city elder of Bologna. Ratta probably wanted to impress the more than sixty colleagues who were invited, but the menu must have been cramped by the early arrival of Lenten fasts that year (Catholic Easter was on March 22), so that choices were limited to "very rare fish."[15] No wonder the illustrations indicate an emphasis on sweets as the backbone of the feast.

SWEET DISTRACTIONS

During the seventeenth century, the reduced price of sugar brought to the table a myriad of sweetmeats, including cakes and cookies, candied fruits, preserves, and caramels. Italian confectioners were the masters of the towering sugar sculptures called *trionfi* that were intermingled with the food: "In a smaller scale on the table…[they] appear like civic monuments in an urban square or freestanding sculptures in formal gardens."[16] These table pieces were created in pastillage, a pliable, long-lasting paste based on sugar mixed with moistened gum tragacanth (a natural binding agent). Today, glycerin, gelatin, and liquid glucose are sometimes added as well. By the early seventeenth century, pastillage, as a medium for sculpture, rivaled the more costly marzipan and blown or pulled sugar, which does not last as long; decorations in pastillage can be kept almost indefinitely in a dry place. The paste is colored, rolled, shaped, and then left to dry before assembly into astonishingly fragile creations towering as high as five feet. Once the pastillage is dry, details can be pointed and polished, as in soft stonework.

The sugar itself was important: John Evelyn, writing in *Acetaria: A Discourse of Sallets* (1699), remarked, *"Of sugar* (by some call'd *Indian-Salt*)…it should be of the best refined, white, hard, close, yet light and sweet as the *Madera's:* Nourishing preserving, cleansing, delighting the Taste, and preferrable to *Honey* for most uses."[17] With *Nouvelle instruction pour les confitures, les liqueurs, et les fruits* (1692; New instructions for preserves, liqueurs, and fruits), François Massialot influenced the future course of French confectionery. He wrote with authority that breathed hands-on experience, defining the scope of this new métier in over four hundred pages.

Uncolored, the crisp, white surface of pastillage resembles bisque porcelain. Alternatively, the paste may be painted on the surface and coated with varnish as a further protection (thus often rendering it inedible). Pastillage can be shaped and colored as miniature fruits and vegetables for decoration or packed into boxes as a gift. In the seventeenth century, before the price of true porcelain declined, pastillage would be molded into delicate serving bowls and plates. Two small bowls might be filled with candies and stuck together as an edible surprise, perhaps resembling a walnut. Special wooden tools were devised for sculpting the pastillage; and to create larger shapes or sharp edges, pastillage might be pressed into metal molds.

Working with pastillage was (and still is) a time-consuming specialty, a skill that demands technical and creative abilities (fig. 5). The art of pastillage is summed up in *Le cannameliste français* (1751; The French confectioner) by Sieur Joseph Gilliers, head of the *office* (cold kitchen) of the high-living King Augustus of Poland (who was also the duc de Lorraine, and one who spent a good deal of time at the French court). The curious name of the book comes from *sucre à canne* (cane sugar). To judge from the illustrations in *Le cannameliste* and those in *Castlemaine's Embassy* more than half a century earlier, pastillage sculptures had changed little. Both feature bulbous vases, curvaceous bouquets of flowers, and somewhat tortured miniature trees (nothing could be a straight line in this era of the baroque) (fig. 6). However, Gilliers also takes us behind the scenes to show cooks in the kitchen sifting sugar, cutting and molding the pastillage into shape, and deconstructing a pedestal to illustrate the skeleton beneath the skin of pastillage. Tools, molds, ideas for candelabra and a grotto, and a table landscape for their display are all demonstrated on paper.

Surely these elaborate structures, while edible in theory, were not always pulled apart and eaten on the spot; indeed, some were treasured and stored from one event to the next. Certainly at Louis XIV's festival of L'isle enchantée in 1664, there was a free-for-all when guests finished their supper: "The King abandoned the tables to the pillage of those who followed; and the destruction of such a lovely arrangement again served as an agreeable diversion for the entire Court, through the rushing and confusion of those who demolished these marzipan Castles and these Mountains of

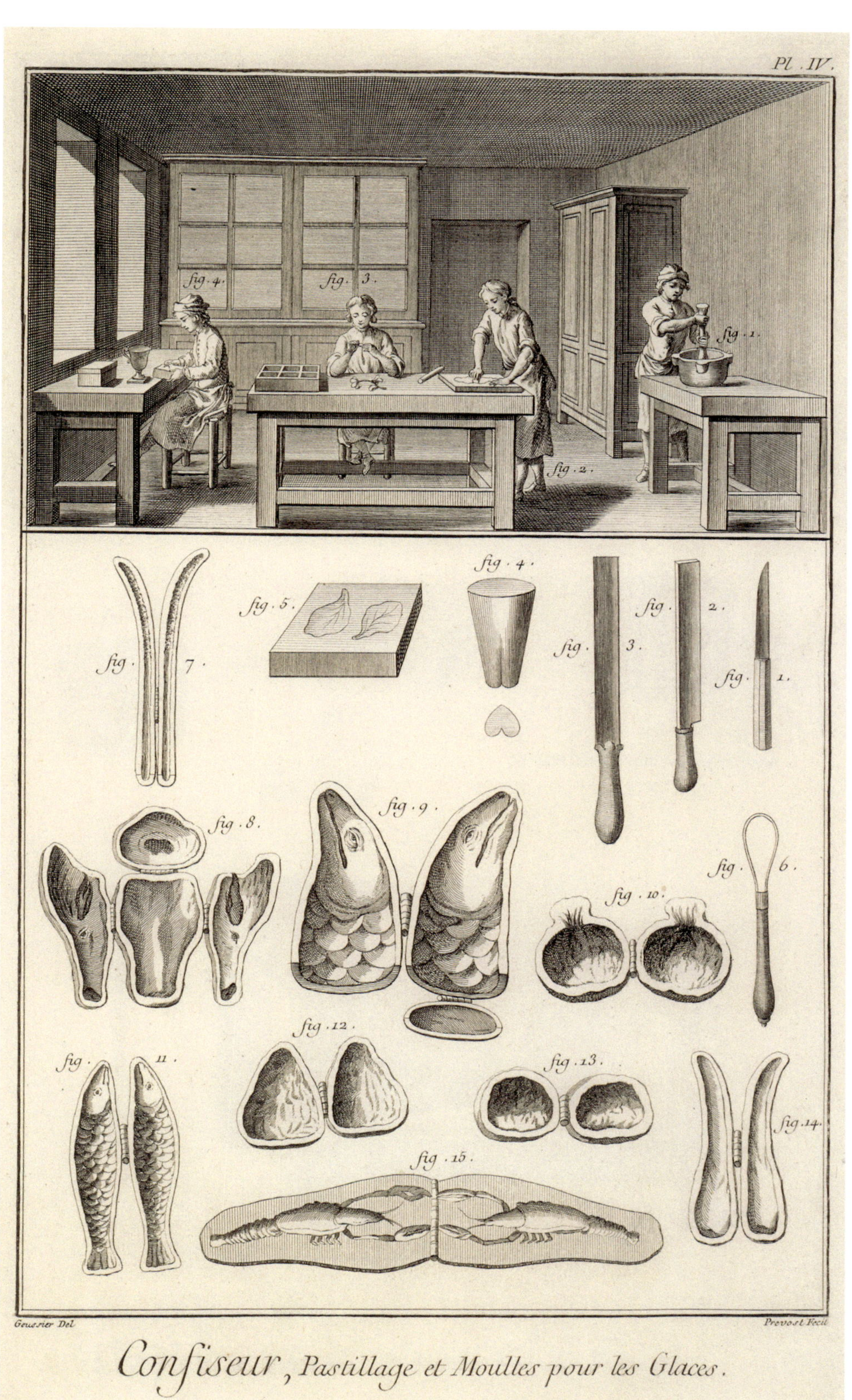

Confiseur, Pastillage et Moulles pour les Glaces.

FIG. 5.

Benoît-Louis Prévost (French, 1747–ca. 1804), after Louis-Jacques Goussier (French, 1722–1799).

Confectionary, Candy Making, and Ice Molds, etching and engraving, 35.3 × 22.5 cm (13⅞ × 8⅞ in.). From Denis Diderot, ed., *Encyclopédie; ou, dictionnaire raisonné: Recueil de planches,* vol. 3 (Paris: Chez Briasson, 1763), pl. 4-1. Los Angeles, Getty Research Institute.

FIG. 6.

Jean-Charles François (French, 1717-69), after Nicolas-Gabriel Dupuis (French, 1698-1771). Surtouts and a geometric table plan.

Etching, 33.8 × 21.8 cm (13⅓ × 8½ in.).

From Sieur Joseph Gilliers, *Le cannameliste français; ou, Nouvelle instruction pour ceux qui desirent d'apprendre l'office…* (Nancy: De l'imprimerie d'Abel-Denis Cusson…, & se vend à Lunéville, chez l'auteur, 1751), pl. 11.

Los Angeles, Getty Research Institute.

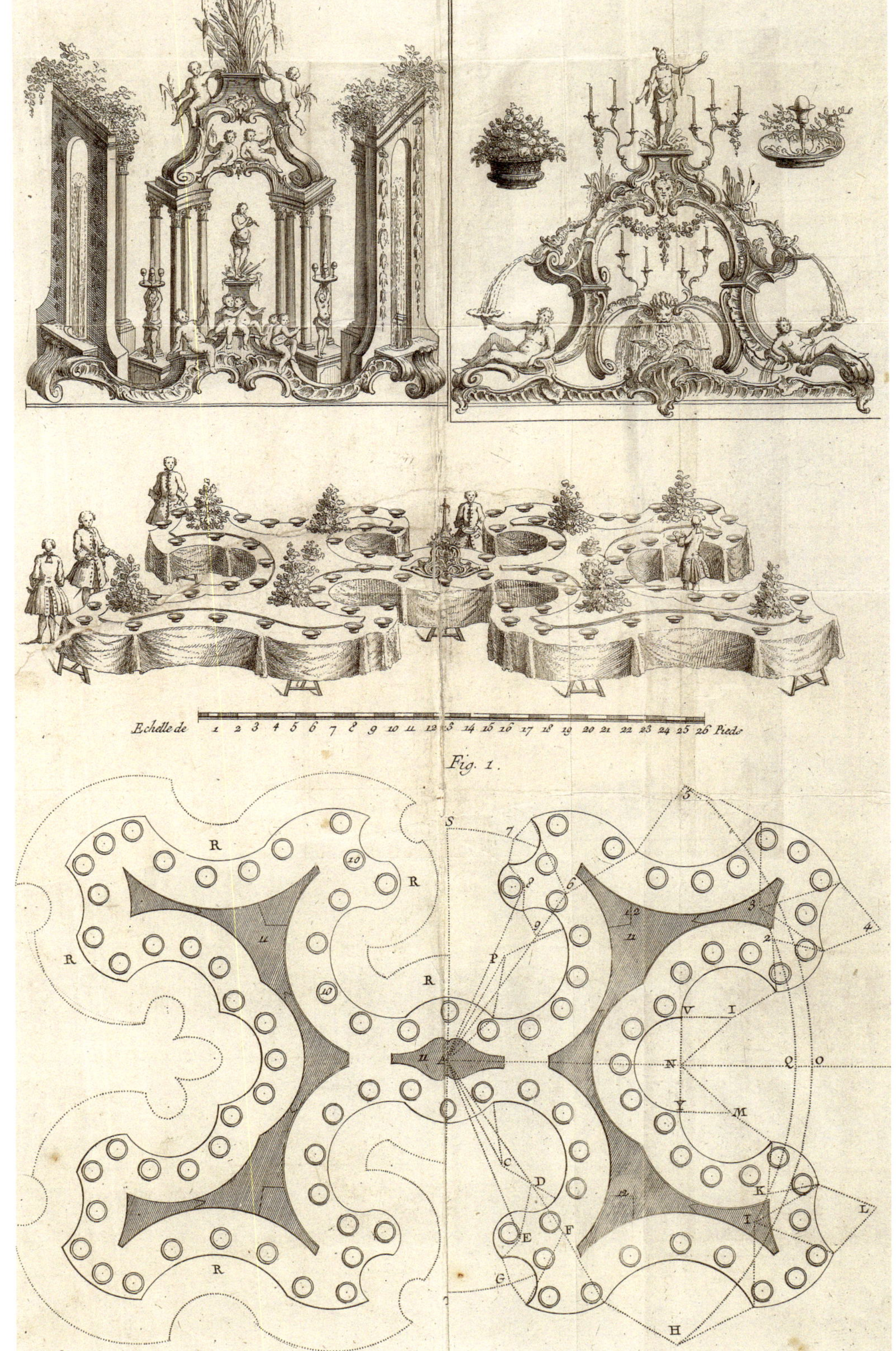

candied fruits."[18] Perhaps that is why, at the Versailles feast of 1668, the king directed that the ladies should be presented with the edible statuary. Lord Castlemaine followed the same custom at his embassy feast in Rome; the *trionfi* were given to the ladies to take home. Local onlookers seem to have been admitted afterward, because "after a little time (as the Liberty or Confidence of the standers by encrease)," the final course of sweetmeats "were all snatch'd and carried away."[19]

COOKS MOVE INTO THE GARDEN

At the height of summer, a course centered wholly on fruit was a popular alternative to a sugary ending to a feast. For Louis XIV's inaugural celebration at Versailles, L'isle enchantée, entire avenues of fruit trees were created: "In the first of these walkways there were only Portugal Oranges [sweet oranges]. The second was all of Bitter Orange and Cherry trees mixed together. The third was lined with Apricot and Peach trees. The fourth, with Currants of Holland. And in the fifth, there were only Pear trees of different types."[20] Some trees were hung with fresh fruits, while on others the fruits were candied. One clearing was surrounded by beds of melons "whose quantity, size, and beauty were surprising for the season [mid July]." Whether in France or Italy, all the summer menus of the time make a great play of fruits, particularly berries, which were used in both sweet and savory dishes.

In winter, matters were very different. A few varieties of late-picked pears and apples might last into Lent, and whole bunches of grapes could be laid on straw and dried in a cool, dry loft to become raisins on the stem. A standby was autumn quince, which was not a table fruit but was wonderful in compote or fruit paste. *Le confiturier de la cour* (1659; The maker of preserves to the court) lists fruit jams, fruit jellies, fruit pastes, confits of whole fruits in sugar syrup, and the dried fruits themselves as favorites on the table. In *L'arte de ben cucinare* (1662; The art of cooking well), Bartolomeo Stefani, the self-styled "Bolognese cook," suggests the alternative approach for winter of a closing course of fruit with a dozen different *bacili* (bowls) of sweetmeats, including pistachios, spiced pears, nougat, spiced citron peel, and pots of fragrant white preserves. *Le pastissier françois,* the first French book on pastry, talks of the new little cookies known as *petits fours,* because they needed to be baked in small ovens. Often based on almonds or other nuts and flavored with orange flower water, jasmine, or citrus, they became a fashionable item.

The nobility led the way into the garden by developing new varieties of fruits and vegetables. From the Loire came the buttery Vigourouse pear and Reine Claude plums (our greengages), named for the wife of King Francis I and developed in his walled garden in the early sixteenth century. As the building at Versailles progressed, "over 1,000 orange trees found their way into royal palaces."[21] The trees were cultivated in tubs and moved in winter into the spacious purpose-built *orangeries* that can still be seen there. At the same time as the explosion of cookbooks in France came a new genre—books on gardening. For his new palace at Versailles, the young King Louis XIV, then in his mid-twenties, commissioned Jean-Baptiste de La Quintinie, the leading gardener of the age, to create a *potager* (vegetable garden), which is described in La Quintinie's *Instruction pour les jardins fruitiers et potagers* (1690; Plan for fruit and vegetable gardens). When Louis XIV entertained, the vast panorama of geometric beds of vegetables and avenues of espaliered fruit trees was all part of the show. In their pleasant formal compositions, the gardens resembled table arrangements.

Meanwhile, his subjects nearby in Paris were encouraged to pass leisure hours in their suburban gardens. Fruits created far more interest than vegetables. It took time for an orchard to grow to maturity, whereas vegetables are the work of one or two seasons' activity. In his *Le jardinier françois* (1651; The French gardener), master gardener Nicolas de Bonnefons urges, "Enter into this garden, whomever you may be, dear reader, I promise that you will find happiness."[22] His *petit volume* (as he called it) was just the right size to slip into a lady's dress pocket. The fact that educated men and women (Bonnefons singles out housewives) were taking an interest in growing their own produce and in its appearance on the table marks a major shift that points to the pleasures of eating, attending to taste. "It must be admitted," he declares in his opening "Letter to the Ladies," "that fruits, left only with the seasoning of Nature…take the prize for satisfying the taste."

France was late coming into the field of gardening. Italian cooks and their masters had long been conscious of the importance of the freshest of vegetables and the new hybrid varieties of fruits. The Dutch, the masters of water management and its use in cultivation, had been exporting their gardening skills overseas since the sixteenth century and the Reformation, particularly to England. An exiled Italian gentleman, Giacomo Castelvetro, who was tutor to King James I and Anne of Denmark, hoped to help the English expand what he regarded as their narrow repertoire of fruits and vegetables. At the turn of the sixteenth century, he wrote his *Brieve racconto di tutte le radici, di tutte l'herbe et di tutti i frutti, che crudi o cotti in Italia si mangiano* (Brief account of all the roots, all the herbs, and all the fruits which Italians eat raw or cooked). Castelvetro talks of delicate Bergamot pears, which "[he did] not recall ever having seen…in England."[23] His little rhyme sums up the Italian attitude to salad:

> Salt the salad quite a lot,
> then generous oil put in the pot,
> and vinegar, but just a jot….
> And if you do not enjoy this, complain to me.[24]

The manuscript provides a graphic picture of the Italian vegetable garden before the spread of New World imports. Imagine a world with no potatoes, tomatoes, corn, peppers, chilies, or most kidney beans—a world dominated by the cabbage family, greens such as cardoons, lots of lettuces, spinach, endive, and chicory. Roots included fennel (a medicinal balance to the melancholic humor of Galen), carrots, salsify, kohlrabi, celery, and onions. Globe artichokes were always intriguing, with their exotic shape and tingle on the tongue. Mushrooms were used far more widely than now as a filling for pies, a garnish for meat, and puréed as a basis for soups or a pungent thickener for sauces. As for the truffle—that mysterious earthy fungus that is blacker than any other ingredient in the kitchen—it was universally prized.

THE NEW WORLD

The ingredients arriving from the New World were an excitement for gardeners and cooks alike in the seventeenth century, though opinions on them varied enormously from country to country. Just a few novelties were quickly welcomed on European tables because they resembled already familiar ingredients. The root artichoke mentioned by Nicolas de Bonnefons in 1666 was one example; it was not unlike the turnip or rutabaga. Turkey took hold at once—the great wild game birds such as the bustard and swan had long been scarce, and cooks seized on this impressive replacement that could rival a big roast of meat on the grand platters of honor. The most controversial of the new ingredients were two members of the notorious deadly nightshade family, potatoes and tomatoes. The English accepted potatoes relatively early, but in France they were shunned until the late eighteenth century. It was a French scientist, Antoine Parmentier, at Louis XVI's invitation, who finally induced the French to try potatoes by planting a field of them right next door to the Potager du Roi at Versailles. Everywhere, tomatoes continued to be unpopular for centuries. The earliest printed tomato recipe for a kind of salsa appeared in 1692 in Antonio Latini's *Lo scalco alla moderna,* so it is conceivable but unlikely that they might have appeared on the table of Senator Francesco Ratta just a year later.

Corn, the staple grain in the New World, was gradually cultivated in certain European regions, including the Po valley in Italy, but not nearly as rapidly as its ubiquity in polenta might suggest. Even today, corn is regarded in some country areas as food for animals and not for humankind. Wheat bread was the mainstay on all European tables in the seventeenth century, its presence so taken for granted that it is hardly mentioned. Bread turns up as toast and croutons, the foundation of puddings, as a thickener for sauces, and would almost certainly have been on the table (or on the side buffet) at the grandest of feasts. Bread came in many shapes and sizes, and for the affluent it was quite white and refined. Most was based on wheat flour, but rye and millet were grown in country districts too. Even in small villages, the baking of bread was a separate trade involving a large, wood-fired oven that was almost constantly hot or warm from one day to the next.

SETTING THE SCENE

The setting and ambience for a successful feast can be just as important as the food on the table. Louis XIV loved to entertain outdoors; and, according to his historian André Félibien, the extensive park at Versailles provided the requisite background, with "delicious copses where the darkness of the trees prevents the sun from being felt…a large number of pleasant walkways form a kind of labyrinth."[25] However, outdoor feasts are by nature seasonal. For much of the year, space had to be found indoors; special chambers were set aside for dining in great houses. At least one antechamber would be decorated to set the scene. At the Earl of Castlemaine's feast, his guests traversed "three large and richly furnished rooms."[26] They had passed a predinner buffet set with "Fruit, Sweetmeats, Parmegian Cheese, and other delicacies belonging to the Desert [*sic*], or last Course," so that they knew what to expect and could "better judge what the whole will be."[27]

In Bologna in the Palazzo Vizzani, Senator Ratta's guests were welcomed in the main hall by a towering mountain "almost seven meters [twenty-three feet] high made of silver and symbolizing the Apennines…veiled in a grateful green…culminating in a silver palm tree…[and] at the base of this fantastic architecture were more than fifty large silver bowls containing preserves and candied fruits, and more than twenty-four filled with citrus" (see Reed, "Court and Civic Festivals," fig. 18).[28] The dining hall itself was agleam with gold and silver, reflected in great mirrors of Venetian glass around the walls. Curious tables in each corner mimicked jagged grottoes, with limestone stalagmites possibly shaped in pastillage or gelatin made from fish bones, thus creating make-believe cellars for the bottles of wines and liqueurs that were stacked on the tables. In a further stretch of reality, windows along one side of the room opened onto a balcony lined with potted orange trees and branches of cedar, hung overhead with vines, all in the depths of winter. Here were more sweet snacks, spread on tables as a further diversion—by this time, dessert was not uncommonly served in a separate room.

THE SHAPE OF THE TABLE

Despite the sumptuous decor, this feast held in the Palazzo Vizzani must necessarily have been a more provincial affair than those held by the Earl of Castlemaine and Louis XIV. The sixty-plus guests—"nobles, elders and senators from Bologna's leading families and neighboring city states"—were seated at a single enormous round table, thus avoiding problems of placement.[29] The U-shaped configuration of tables of medieval times, anchored by the high table to display the most important guests, was long gone. By the end of the seventeenth century, fashionable tables might be round or rectangular, often depending on the shape of the dining room. In *Arte de reposteria* (1747; The art of pastry), Juan de la Mata, a confectioner to the Spanish court, illustrates no fewer than ten different table shapes, including a horseshoe and a wavy oval designed for ninety seated guests.[30] In Rome, Castlemaine was constrained by the long gallery used as a dining room and forced to adopt a lengthy rectangular table eight feet wide, seating over eighty guests, many of them cardinals. Following the English custom, the earl sat at one end of the table surveying two lines of assembled guests, though the continental habit was to center the host, hostess, and important guests at a halfway point (see Imorde, "Edible Prestige," fig. 1).

As for Louis XIV, the outdoor setting in the Versailles park permitted tables of all shapes and sizes. Only the most important guests, in groups of thirty or more, were seated at all, and the king was careful to be placed next to his favorites. "Three hundred of the women present were invited to a seated supper, with Louis' mistress, Louise de la Vallière, next to him [and] another table at which the Marquise de Montespan and Madame Scarron [later the Marquise de Maintenon], her great friend, were keeping in a buzz of laughter. Years later, people remembering the Divertissement said it had contained the past, the present, and the future."[31]

Images that record these dining tables celebrate the centerpieces—the towering sugar-paste sculptures that soared above the center of a round table, or those that stretched along a rectangular arrangement from the central high point, creating a gradual progression of trees, flowers, mythical figures, even portraits of ancestors. In Castlemaine's case, they were half life-size. "Their use at Entertainments, is to gratifie the Eye, as the Meat, Musique, and Perfumes, do the other Senses."[32] The twenty-three-feet-high mountain that opened the Ratta festival must surely have risked collapse under its own weight. The circular dining table itself was laden with twenty-four *trionfi* of sugar paste; six were five feet in height, six of three feet, and twelve of two feet. Subjects varied from garlands of flowers to allegorical figures, and each gilded figurine supported a finely crafted bowl of sugar.

In these illustrations, it can be hard to tell what materials are used—pastillage, silver, faience or Chinese porcelain, vermeil or gold, or even gelatin. Juan de la Mata gives careful instructions on how to extract transparent liquid gelatin from fish bones. He sets it in glittering lakes on deep serving dishes or cuts it in ornamental "shapes such as orchids, flowers, fleur de lis, sprigs, half-moons, grape leaves."[33] He also seems to have used the gelatin to glue together more solid objects "following pictures and ideas and each one [arranged] differently on a base of china plates, or crystal mirrors and columns of different sizes" (fig. 7).

Food at such grand feasts would jostle for place on the dining table. Dishes such as grand roasts would be on display beside the *trionfi,* with the intervening spaces filled with little platters or bowls of less important *entremets* and side dishes such as little birds or veal escalopes. Before the Castlemaine feast, the centerpieces and side dishes of the first cold course were on display "for two whole days, (according to the Roman way) that everyone's curiosity might have some share in the Entertainment."[34] The little dishes spread with "all sorts of rellishing bits, whether salt, sweet, or soure; as Pickles, Butter, slices of delicate Bacon, Bologna-Sauciges, Taratufoli [truffles], Composts, &c." were so tempting they had to be protected by a company of "Swissers," forerunners of today's Swiss Guards.

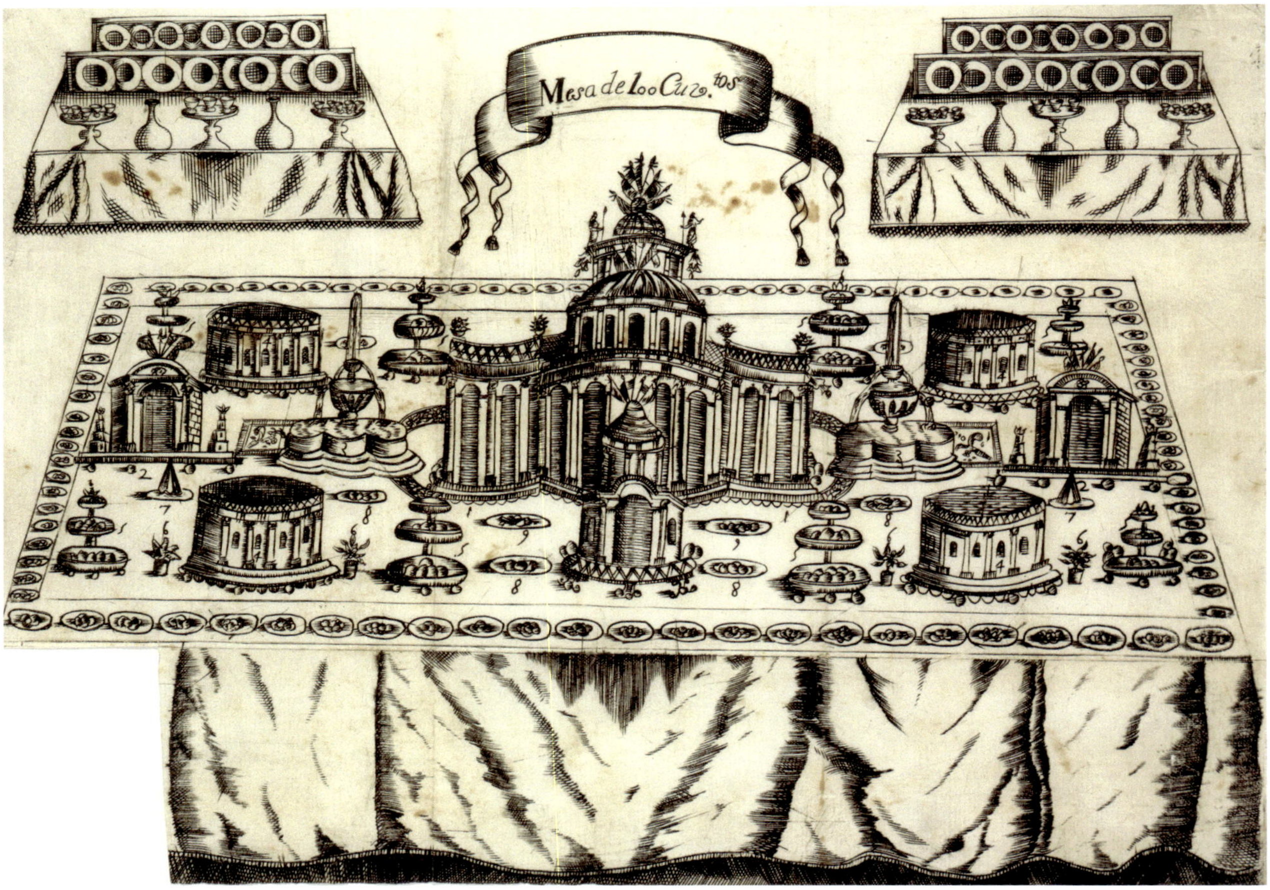

Tables were almost always draped with white damask linen cloths, the better to showcase the display. At the borders of the table came the diners' individual dinner plates, set with flatware and bread. At Ratta's banquet, flatware and bread would have been set on each plate and then covered with a starched napkin intricately folded into shapes such as butterflies, mountain landscapes, eagles, or swans (fig. 8). Furniture included chairs; Castlemaine supplied "eighty fair arm'd Velvet Chairs, which touch'd

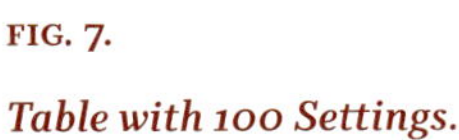

one another, only between every four, there was place left for a Carver, and over against him, for a Sewer [a butler who oversaw a section of the table]."[35] The walls were hung with tapestries (especially in the winter) and portraits of ancestors, the reigning monarch, or local nobility, while great mirrors and candelabra helped illuminate the chamber.

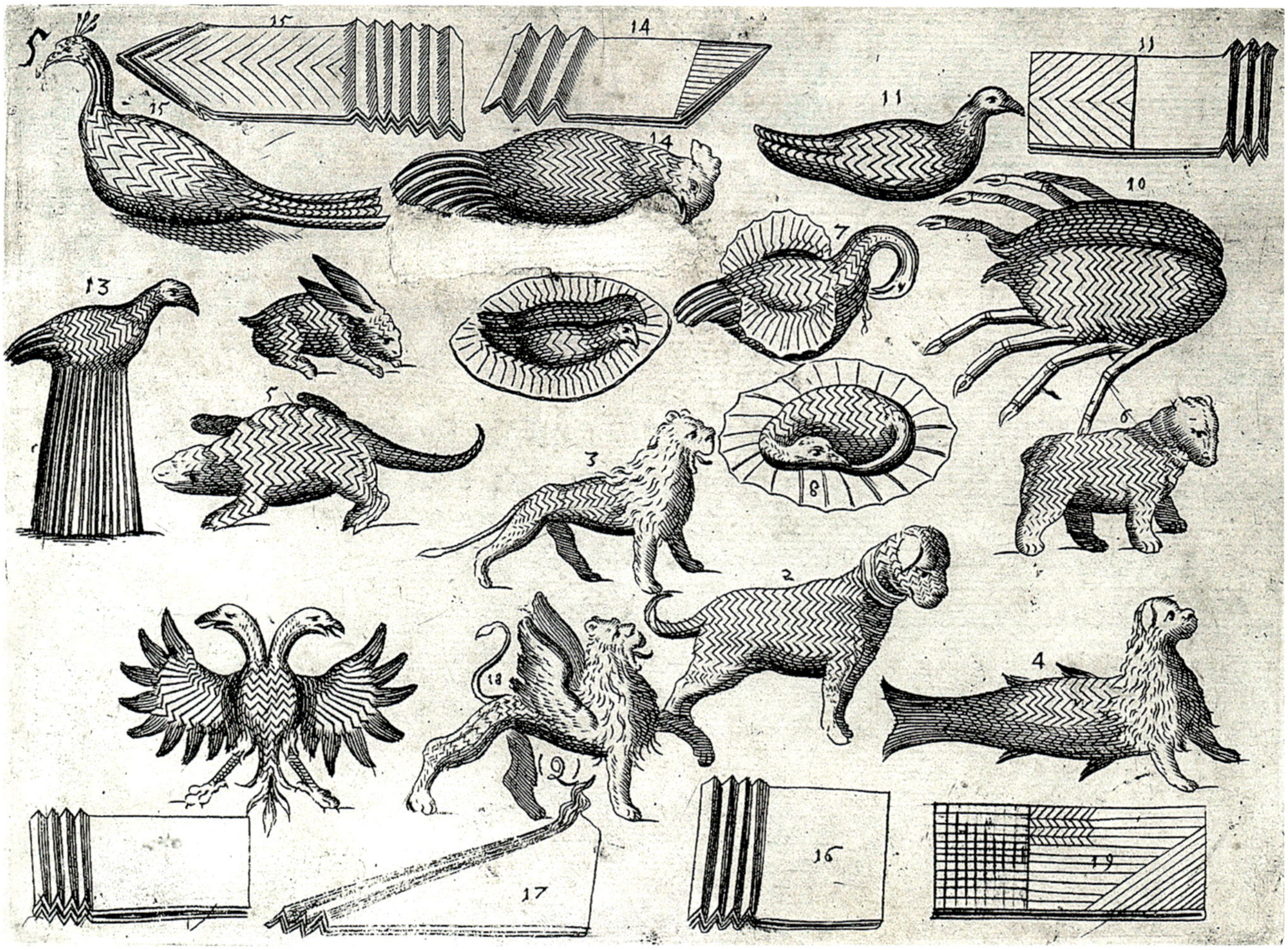

THE CREDENZA CROWNS ALL

All dining rooms were furnished with a large piece of furniture, the *credenza*, to hold cold dishes that might be sweet or savory, depending on the stage of the meal. As its name suggests, the credenza first appeared in Italy. During the Renaissance, it was adopted at formal feasts throughout Europe, by the name of *buffet* in France and *sideboard* in England. The seventeenth-century credenza was a series of tiered shelves ideal for displaying valuable plates; as such, it was a fixture within the dining room. (In the park at Versailles, similar temporary structures for display and edibles were created.) The grander the household, the more expensive the credenza. With tall ceilings in the dining halls, these constructions could be huge. Sometimes the term *cupboard* was used, implying doors that could be locked for safety. This was the display case for the host's valuable silver and gold.

For his feast at the Palazzo Pamphilj, the Earl of Castlemaine might have been granted the standard English ambassadorial spending allowance of 360 pounds of silver and 60 pounds of vermeil (silver plated with gold), including such items as ewers, serving platters, and tureens.[36] These treasures, useful as well as decorative (see Bremer-David, "Of Cauliflower and Crayfish"), were the equivalent of money in the bank and were likely interspersed on the credenza with colorful platters and vases of rare porcelain imported from China.

When the credenza was set up for a feast, the lower levels were laden with cold foods, drinks, and the glasses for serving the drinks. Shelves were crammed with bottles and ewers of wine, liqueurs, flavored drinks, and water. Beneath the lowest shelf were huge silver cisterns of water, with ice when available, stacked with more bottles for chilling. Also displayed on these shelves during a meal were the bowls and platters of cold courses.

AT HOME IN THE HOUSEHOLD

The Earl of Castlemaine traveled to Rome with only a couple of friends and what seems to have been regarded as a modest household. This included his head of household, John Michael Wright, who wrote the official account of the journey and subsequent entertainments in Rome; a gentleman of the horse; an Italian secretary; a butler; two pages; two valets; and "half a dozen others of his Family [his household]."[37] More servants and most of the earl's possessions, including "his Lordships Plate, Furniture, Liverys, and other *Impedimenta* of so long a Journey"[38] had been sent separately by ship to Civitavecchia, the port of Rome. There the household rapidly expanded. By the time Castlemaine moved into his official residence, "his Excellences Family, consist[ed] of above an 100 Persons, 60 of which were in Livery."[39] The chosen livery was scarlet, lined with silk brocade scattered with flowers of gold on a blue ground. Luxuriant in the same colors, eight pages wore doublets and trunks "of the *Roman* fashion" adorned with gold lace and bands of blue, white, and black silk; embroidered gloves; and a white feather here and there.[40]

The first staff member to be hired by the Earl of Castlemaine must have been the *scalco* (chief steward). With all the festivities envisaged, a Roman expert would have been vital, for the *scalco* supervises the other staff. He (always a man) knew local purveyors, as he was in charge of buying the food, wine, and all household supplies. In consultation with the cooks, he chose appropriately seasonal menus and planned how they would be presented. He orchestrated every feast, the decoration of the dining room and any anterooms, the music, and possible other entertainments, such as dancing or fireworks. The opening portrait in *Lo scalco alla moderna* (1692), published in Naples, shows the author, Antonio Latini, *scalco principale* to the court. A pensive, almost intellectual figure, Latini is depicted richly clad in a full wig, lace jabot, and handsome robe, holding his book (fig. 9). *Lo scalco alla moderna* features carving instructions and recipes; pullout engravings show how to carve fruits and how to place plates and platters of food on the table in front of diners (fig. 10). In a third illustration, a grand table is set with at least a dozen *trionfi,* individual plates of

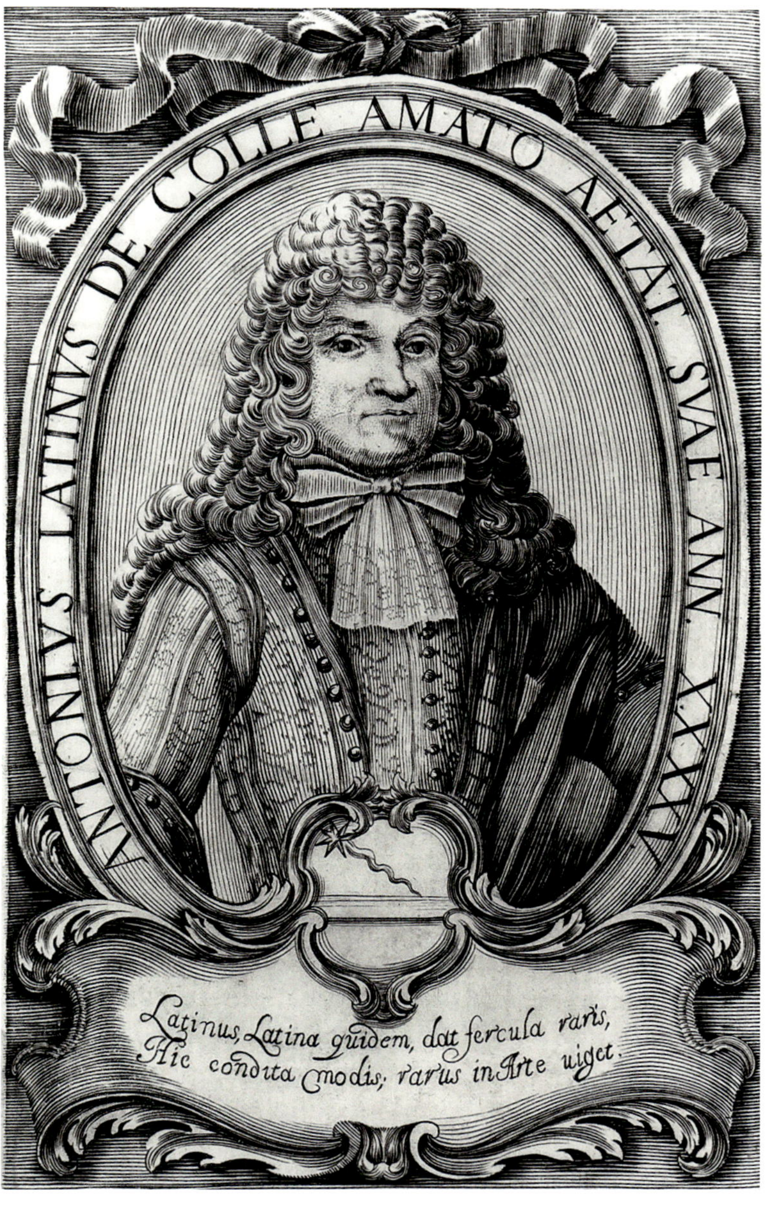

FIG. 9.

Portrait of Antonio Latini.

Engraving. From Antonio Latini, *Lo scalco alla moderna, overo l'arte di ben disporre li conviti, con le regole più scelte di scalcheria, insegnate, e poste in prattica,* à beneficio de' professori (Naples: Dom. Ant. Parrion & Michele Luigi Mutii, 1692), frontispiece.

London, Wellcome Library.

what look like artichokes but are probably intricately folded napkins (another *scalco* sideline), and some dishes of little nibbles that might actually be edible (fig. 11).

The *scalco* would also have overseen the setting of the tables with flatware. Only toward the end of the seventeenth century were matching sets of cutlery provided by the host; guests would bring their personal spoons and knives, joined from the late sixteenth century onward, by the table fork. Bi- and tri-pronged forks had long been in the kitchen, and the Italians were the first Western Europeans to adopt this handy but slightly barbaric metal implement for eating at table. The first "little fork that is not used in any other country" was observed in Italy by the English traveler Thomas Coryat in the early 1600s.[41] Table forks spread gradually north; in England, King Charles II had sets of cutlery made for his children so they could practice eating with them. But as late as the coronation feast of King James II in 1687, a proud diner can be seen brandishing his fork, clearly a rare item (see Reed, "Court and Civic Festivals, fig. 16). Drinking glasses appeared even later on the dinner table and were stocked at the side on the credenza. Until the late seventeenth century, goblets made of vermeil, silver, or more humble pewter were often shared. The luxury of Venetian glasses for

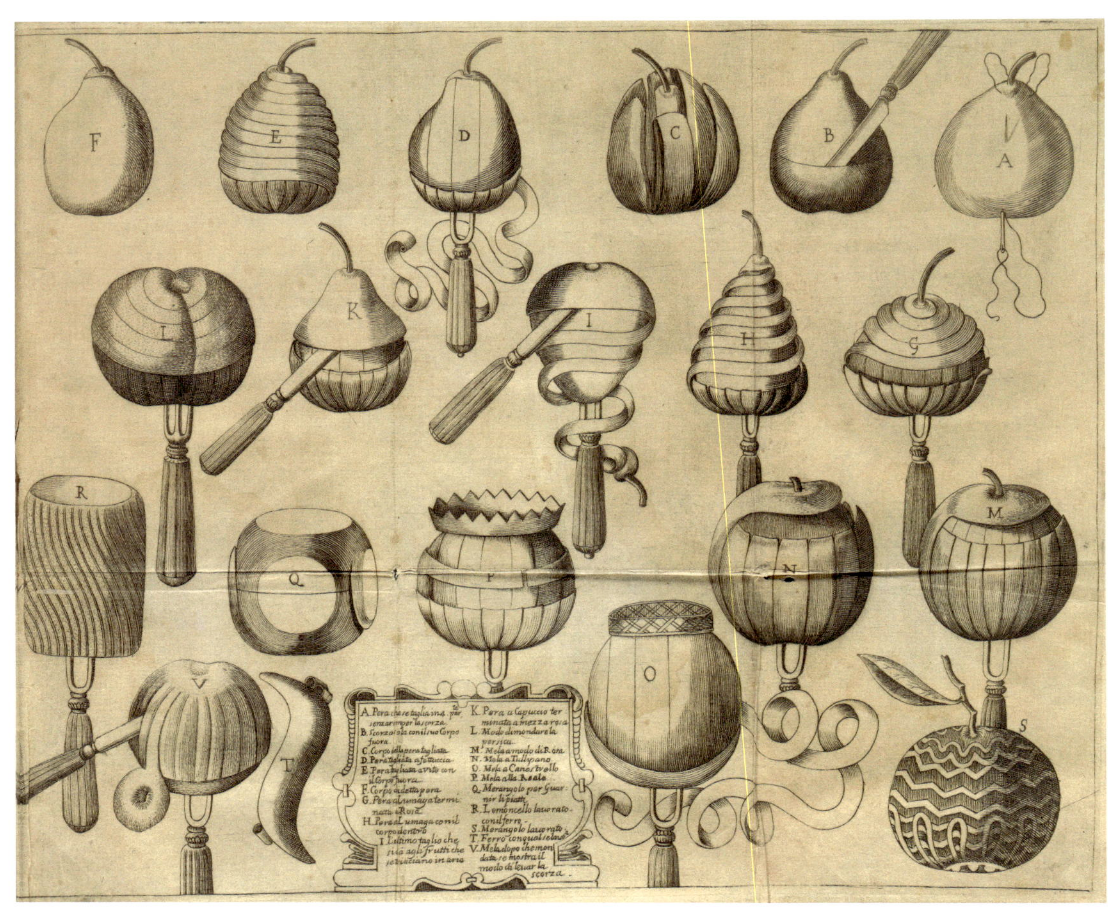

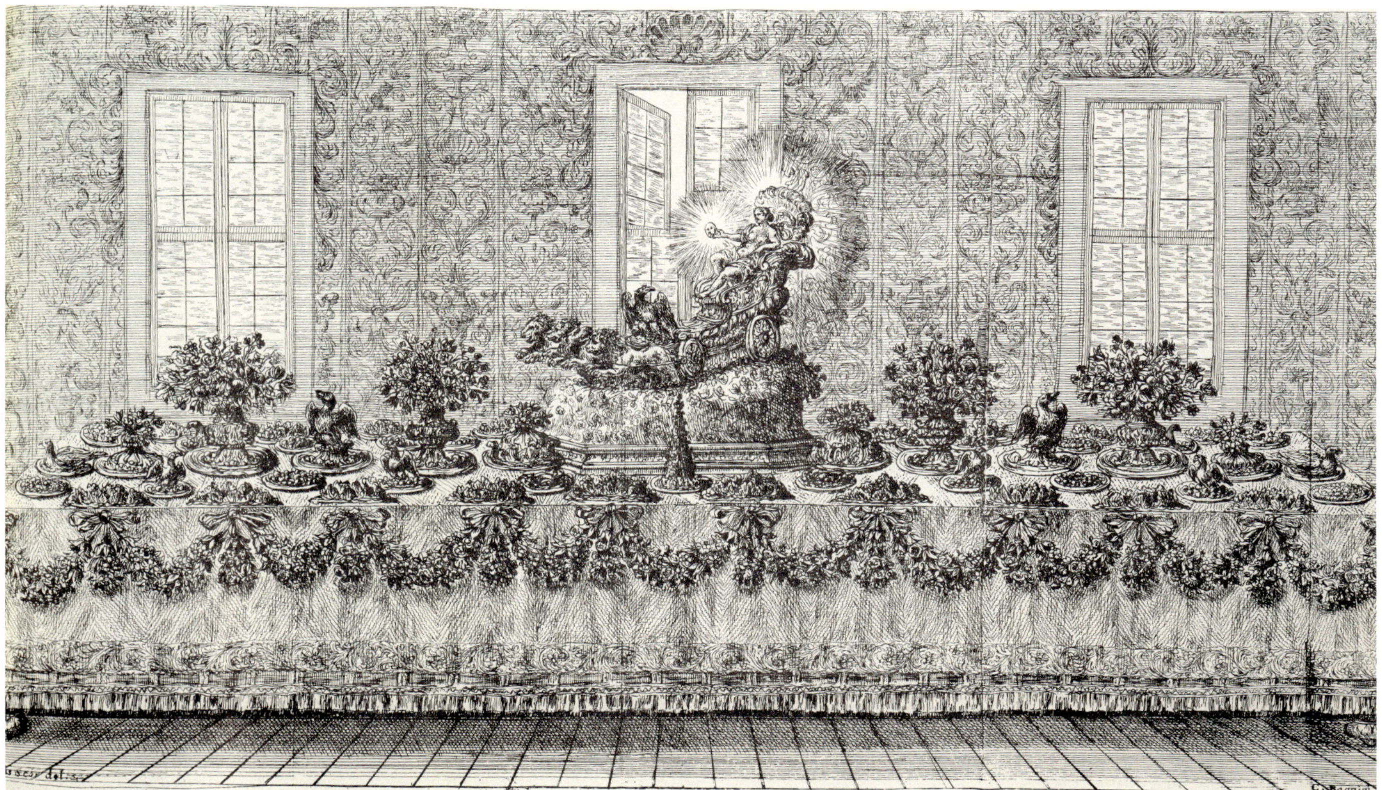

drinking spread first through Italy, and Castlemaine boasts of a special *credenza*
of "glasses, which were of Venice, in great store, and of all sorts."[42]

Men who held the position of *scalco* (called *maître d'hôtel* in France) were educated, even aristocratic people, and were often relatives of the master of the household. Moving down the scale for table service, two experts were key: the carver and
the sewer, or butler, who oversaw the setting of the tables, then the arrival and service
of both food and drink. At the Castlemaine feast, a carver and a head server were on
hand for every eight guests, and each guest seated at the table had a personal servant.
At each course, two "Imperial" dishes (and many smaller ones) were "plac'd by the
Sewers, before the Prospective Carvers, who cutting of every thing, gave it to the Sewers, and they, to each Guest in their District, whether he eat of it, or not."[43] Almost
nothing has been written about the head server, though he is at least as important as
the carver. The careful timing and polished manual skills needed to carry, deliver, and
serve complex, often heavy platters, is considerable. As in any good restaurant today,
the server must be attentive without being obtrusive, directing his underlings and
gauging the progress of each course so the meal is neither hurried nor dilatory.

The carver was a highly trained artist, and Latini illustrates his tools: six pointed
knives in graduated sizes and the same number of two-pronged forks with long

FIG. 11.

Place setting for a grand table.

Engraving. From Antonio Latini,
Lo scalco alla moderna [1692] (Lodi,
Italy: Bibliotheca Culinaria, 1993).
London, Wellcome Library.

stiletto-like points (fig. 12). One fork has three prongs, for foods that tend to crumble. The carver was in charge of dismembering great roasts of game, meat, and poultry, cooked on or off the bone. Whole fish were also his domain, and his imaginative talents could be displayed in carving patterns in the peel of whole fruits. At the very least, he could pare the peel of an apple in one long, continuous strip. Watching the carver at work was all part of the entertainment. The art of carving dates back at least to medieval times, and a handful of beautifully illustrated books from the seventeenth century are devoted to the subject. Outline sketches of meat, fish, and fowl are crisscrossed with lines to show the direction and order in which incisions should be made (fig. 13). The lines in carving books like those by Mattio Molinari and Mattia Giegher are so precise that they can be used in any language; no written instructions are needed.[44]

Castlemaine must have found a good *scalco* to manage his feast, for his guests agreed "that the common fate of feasts…Drinking hot and Eating cold, was here surely changed to the contrary."[45] Nonetheless, the event seems to have gone too

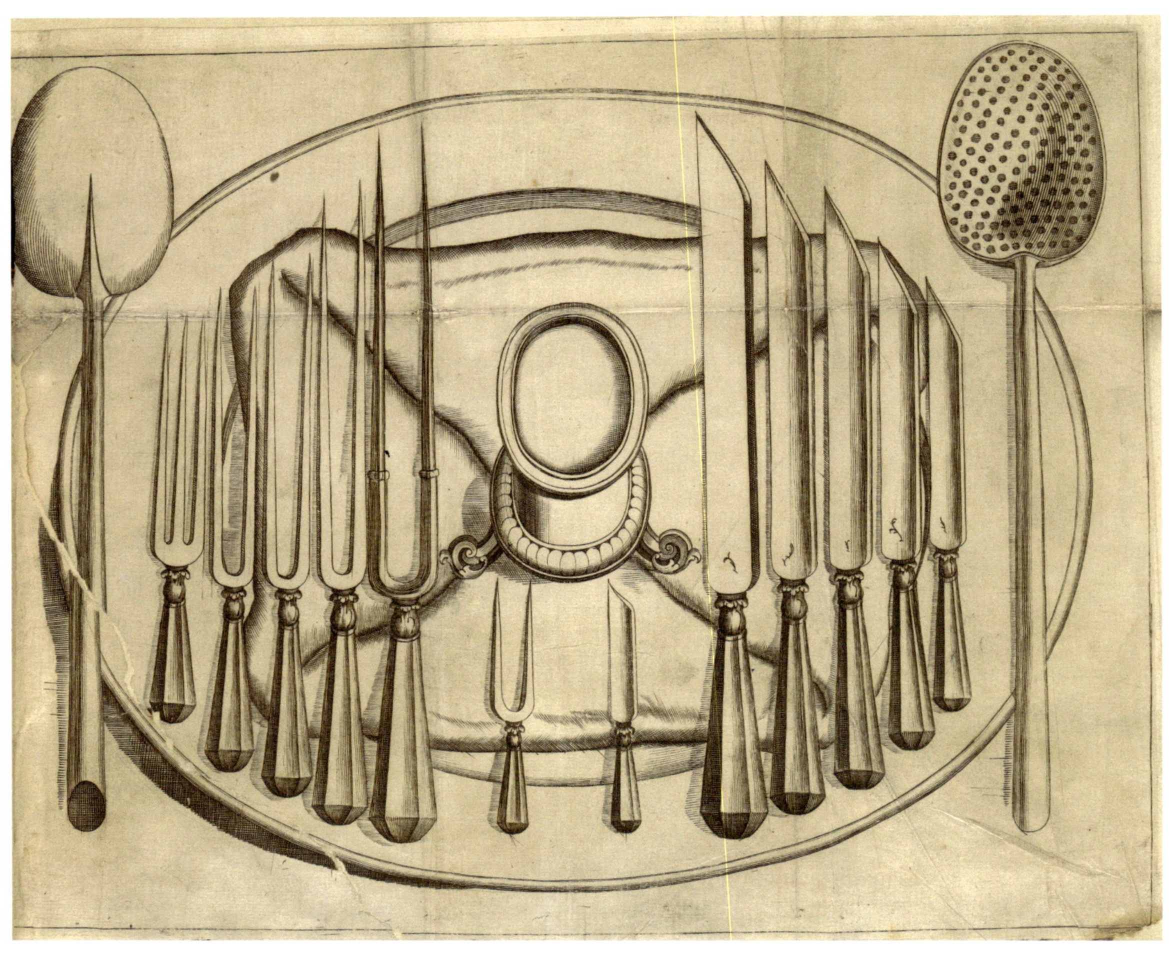

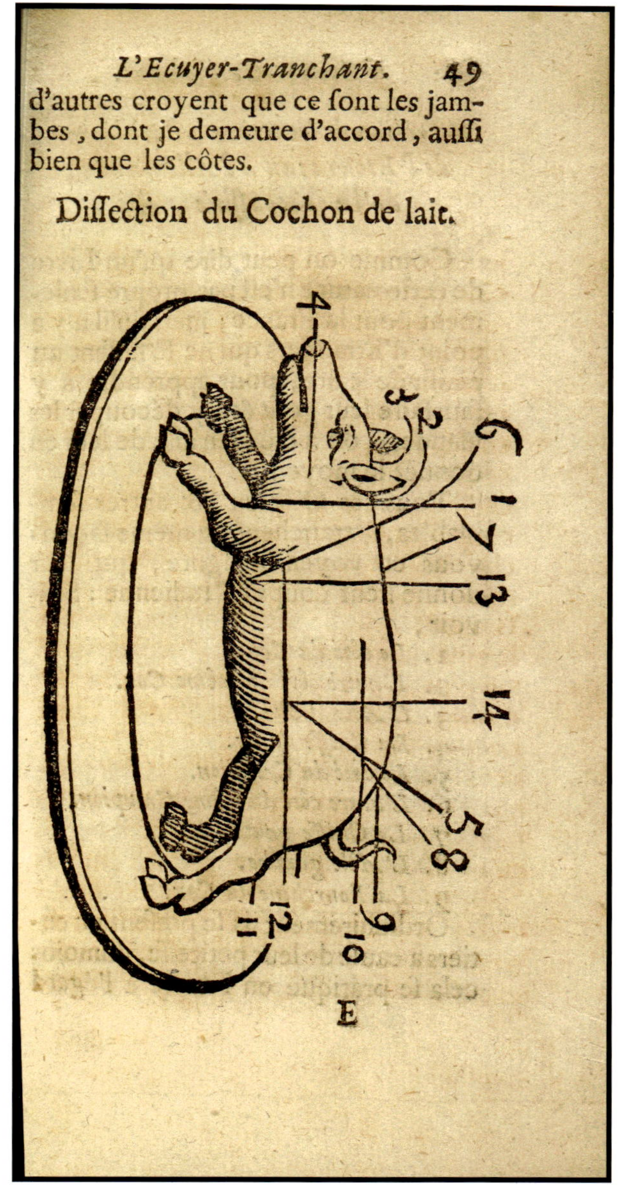

slowly and "the Company (who had abandon'd themselves to mirth) beginning to be satisfied, the aforesaid twelve courses, or changes, were by the Officers (to avoid tediousness) contracted to ten."[46] The head cook must have torn out his hair. Nothing could be worse for a talented cook than to have the last two courses—the climax of his whole endeavor—be abruptly lopped off, a decision presumably taken by the *scalco*. The ambassadorial feast must have flattered the celebrities who attended and, by extension, the ailing Pope Innocent XI, but the immense endeavor was ultimately unsuccessful. Only two years later, King James II was ousted from the throne of England when a male heir was born.

IN THE KITCHEN

Behind the scenes in the kitchen, once again it is Bartolomeo Scappi in Rome, the personal cook to two cardinals and two popes, including Pius IV, who so eloquently sums up the attributes of a master cook: "To be a prudent and satisfactory cook, one must, as far as I can gather from long experience over many years, have good principles, the best habits, optimal results, and always maintain respect for the work…like a great architect who lays out a firm foundation and on it presents to the world a useful and marvelous edifice."[47] Several tables were likely to be in the head cook's charge: that of the master with his family and guests; separate arrangements for the steward and other senior officers; and, for the remaining servants, a big common table with more frugal fare that included leftovers. In a well-run kitchen nothing was ever wasted.

Scappi compares his responsibilities to those of the *scalco* (the French term *chef,* meaning leader, was not coined until the mid-eighteenth century[48]). The head cook oversaw the buying of meats, fish, and produce and their storage; he managed the stocks of spices, sugar, flour, and other dry goods. During the busy summer and early fall seasons, he supervised the preparation of huge quantities of preserves to last through the cold months. On a country property, the cook would be in charge of the poultry, rabbits, and other domestic animals for the table. He would take a keen interest in the dairy, with its milk and cream, butter and cheese, and also in the fish pond (on old properties such as the royal Château de Chantilly in France, fish were raised in the moat). In cities, the master cook for a wealthy household would scour the food markets, often acting in concert with the steward. These activities had to be tracked; by the end of the seventeenth century, the head cook had to be literate enough to follow records kept by a scribe.

All this was background to the activity of cooking. The kitchen was divided into two sections: the main hot kitchen, supervised by the master cook, and the separate cold kitchen (*office*), in the charge of a pastry chef, called in France the *officier de bouche.* The *office* was responsible for sweet desserts and pastries, candies, preserves, fruit syrups and distilled liqueurs, as well as cold hors d'oeuvres and salads for the table. Most importantly during this period, the cold kitchen looked after pastillage and sugar work. For Senator Ratta's feast, no fewer than three sugar sculptors executed "a spectacular choreography inspired by the fantastic set designs of Francesco Bibiena, a fellow Bolognese and at the time the greatest European interpreter of Baroque splendors."[49] Savory pies were prepared in the main kitchen, cakes and sweet pies in the *office,* and all then taken to the wood-fired bread oven for baking (fig. 14). A substantial main kitchen might have a small wood-fired oven beside the fireplace, but, more often, the bread oven was situated away from the main house because of the heat, noise, and danger of fire. Indeed, on a great property, the kitchen might be a

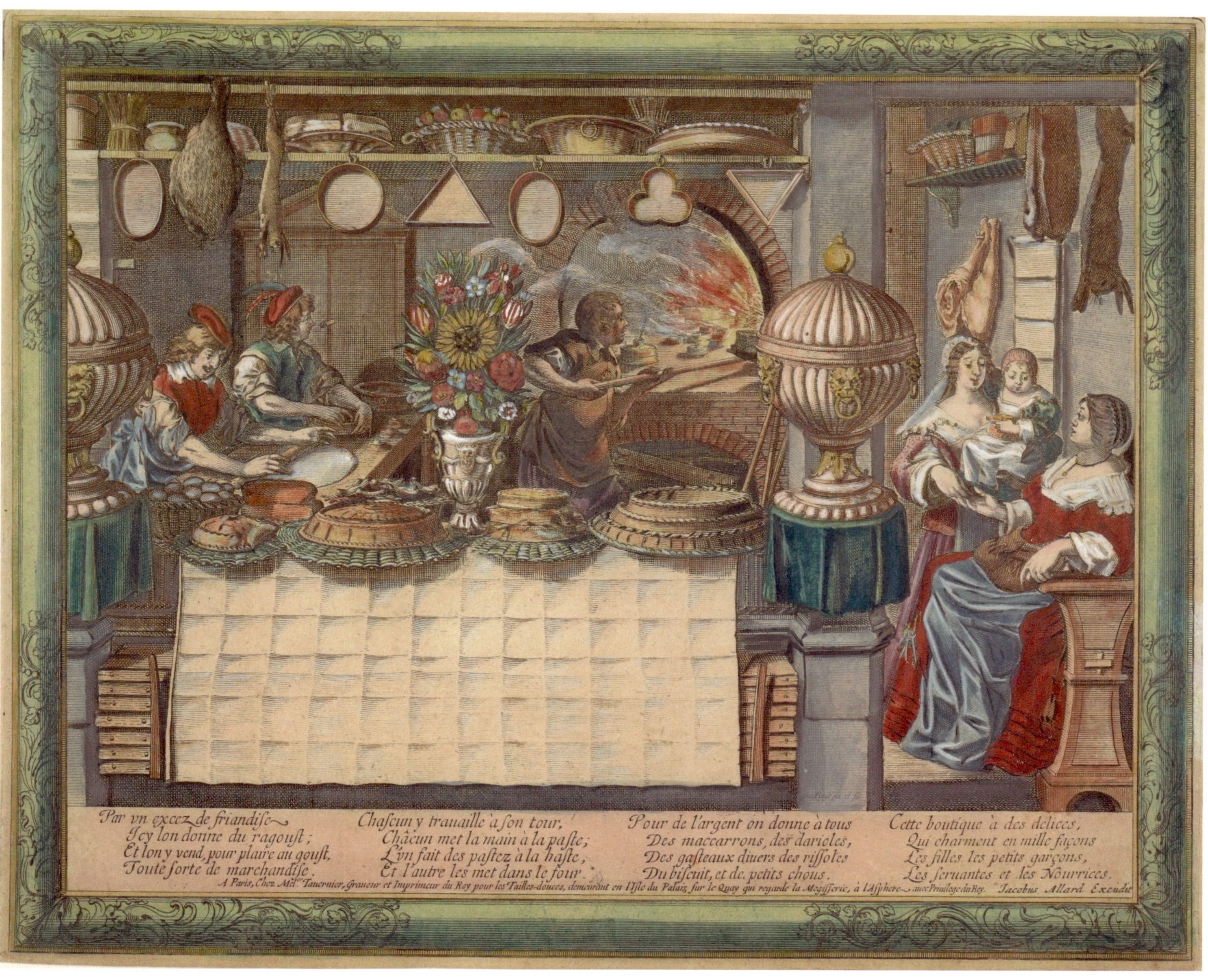
Par vn excez de friandise
Icy lon donne du ragoust;
Et lon y vend, pour plaire au goust,
Toute sorte de marchandise.

Chascun y trauaille à son tour,
Chacun met la main à la paste;
L'vn fait des pastez à la haste,
Et l'autre les met dans le four.

Pour de l'argent on donne à tous
Des maccarrons, des darioles,
Des gasteaux diuers des rissoles
Du biscuit, et de petits chous.

Cette boutique à des delices,
Qui charment en mille façons
Les filles les petits garçons,
Les seruantes et les Nourrices.

A Paris, Chez Mel.er Tauernier, Graueur et Imprimeur du Roy pour les Tailles-douces, demeurant en l'Isle du Palais, sur le Quay qui regarde la Megisserie, à l'Asphere. auec Priuilege du Roy.   Jacobus Allard Excudit

FIG. 14.
Abraham Bosse (French, 1602–76).
Jacobus Allard (Dutch, fl. ca. 1660).
The pastry shop, Netherlands,
17th century, hand-colored etching,
engraving, gouache and gold,
26.5 × 33.5 cm (10.4 × 13.3 in.).
Los Angeles, Getty Research Institute.

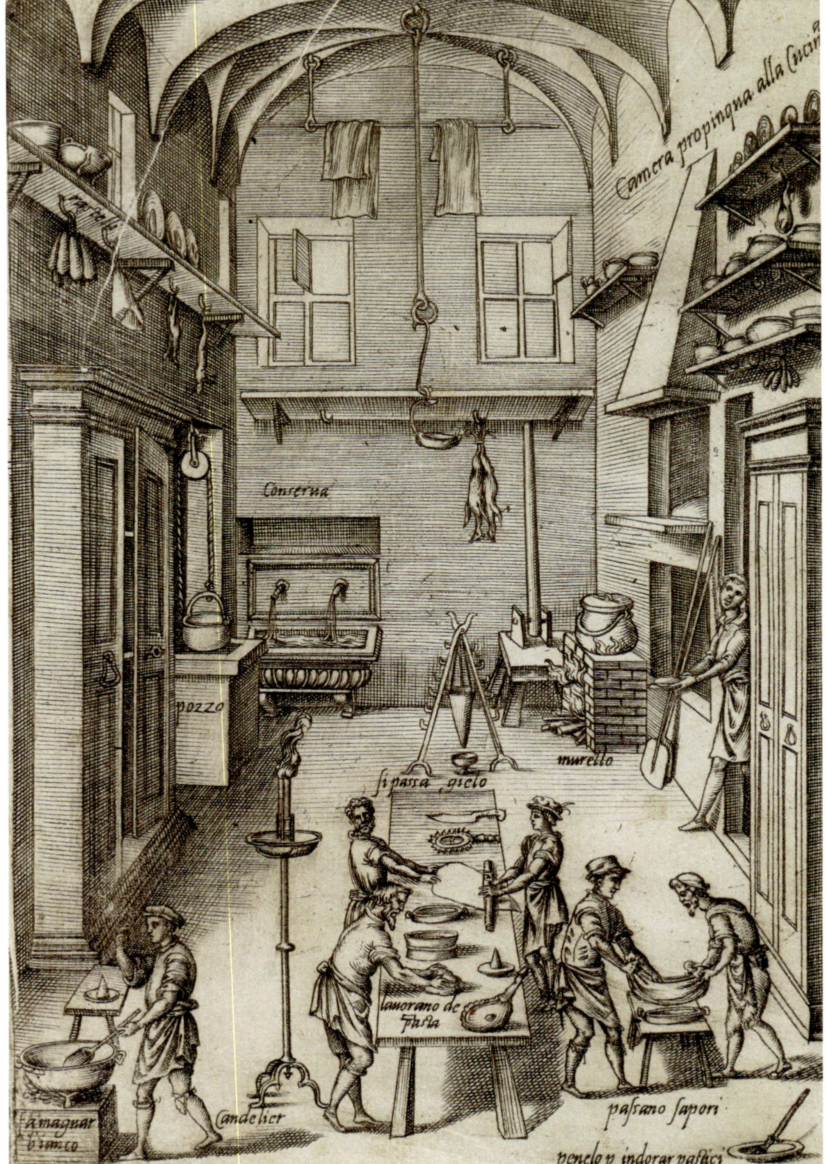

FIG. 15.

Room Next to the Kitchen.

Engraving, 18.5 × 14 cm (7¼ × 5½ in.). From Bartolomeo Scappi, *Opera*…(Venice: Appresso Michele Tramezzino, 1570), pl. 2. Los Angeles, Getty Research Institute.

FIG. 16.

Outdoor workshop.

Engraving, 18.5 × 14 cm (7¼ × 5½ in.). From Bartolomeo Scappi, *Opera*…(Venice: Appresso Michele Tramezzino, 1570), pl. 3. Los Angeles, Getty Research Institute.

hundred yards or more from the mansion, as in the Palais des ducs de Bourgogne in Dijon, where the kitchen had six fireplaces, and also at Versailles, where the kitchens were hidden in outbuildings behind the Aile Colbert.

Once again, Bartolomeo Scappi is the authority. In the twenty-five magnificent plates at the back of his book, he reveals the ideal kitchen of the late sixteenth century, setting the scene for the next two centuries (figs. 15, 16; see fig. 1). Here is the luxury of running water in a stone sink, light and a cross draft coming through open windows and doors, and the turnspit waving his hand to us from the shelter of a screen. Every detail is considered: hams hang from the ceiling in the smoke of the fire, knives are

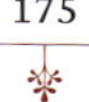

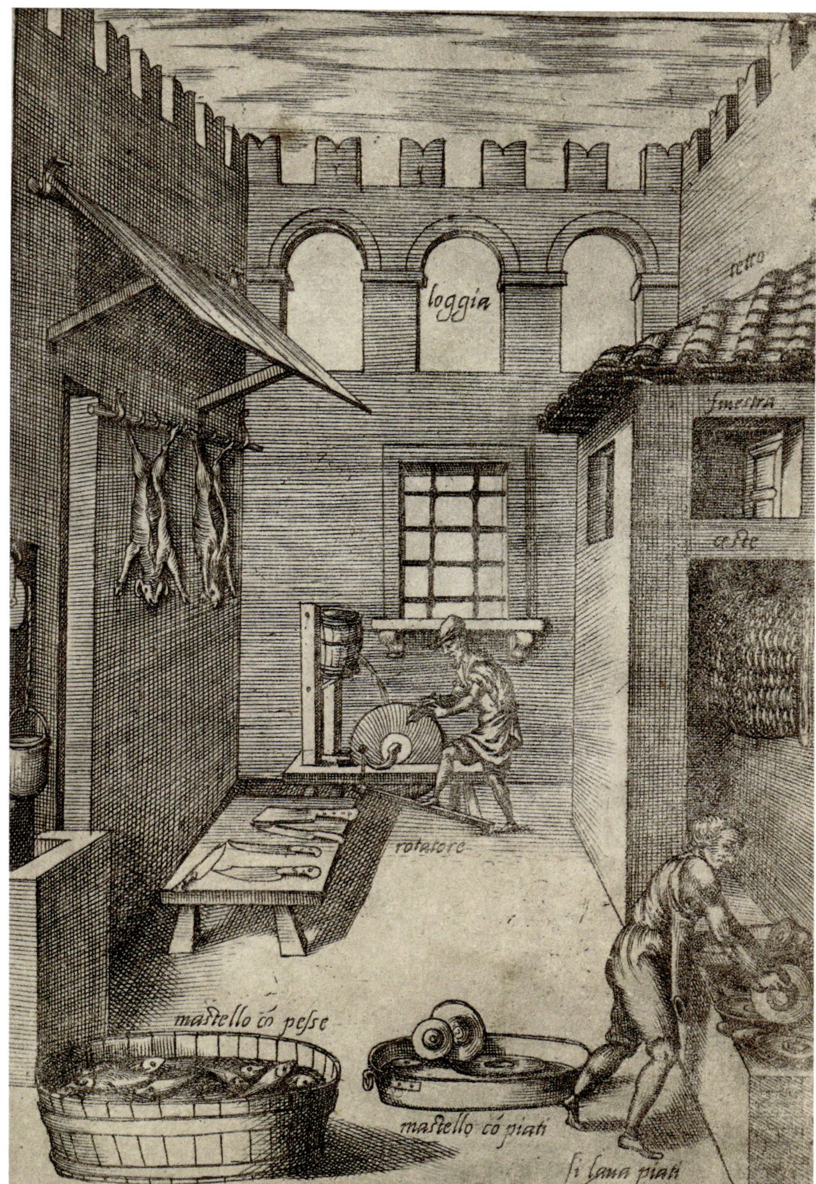

impaled in a bale of straw for safety, and bread is stored on a high shelf away from stray dogs. Pasta is being rolled on the central table, with the fluted ravioli cutter beside it, and the mortar and pestle set on a sturdy stone column has not changed to this day. In the cold kitchen, fish are swimming in a tub of water, a reminder that the master cook must "know every sort of meat and fish, and any other thing that will be delivered daily…and the types most appropriate to roast or boil…which parts are more prone to spoilage and which are the most durable, the most piquant, and the most delicate."[50]

Scappi illustrates a cook's catalog of equipment: pots and knives of all different shapes and sizes, ladles, sieves, a colander, a nutmeg grater, a waffle iron, bellows for

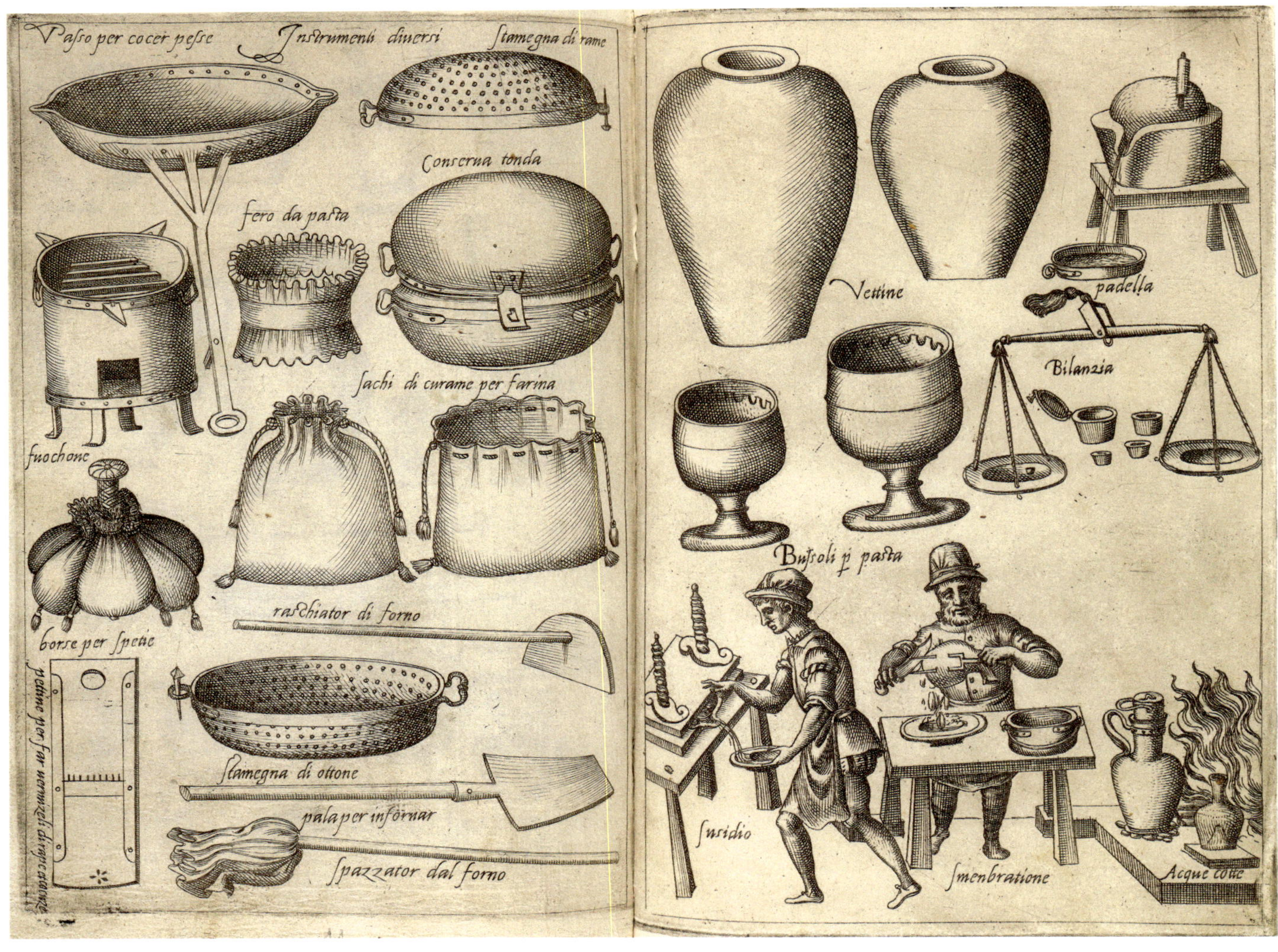

the fire, a hamper for bottles, a duck press, and so on (fig. 17). Among the prints is possibly the first image of a knife, spoon, and fork together as tableware. Only men are shown in action, and the role of women in the seventeenth century professional kitchen is obscure. Minor players, male or female, were not documented and only a very few early images of women cooks survive, all of them toiling beside a simmering cauldron and blazing fire. Not until the late seventeenth century, when educated women started writing their own cookbooks, did their influence emerge, and this was in England, not Italy or France.

One innovation shown by Scappi, the raised stove, would later revolutionize the backbreaking work of cooking over an open fire, and with it the dishes that could be brought to table. One side of Scappi's kitchen is flanked by a bank of brick arches topped by grates holding burning charcoal at just the right height for stirring and whisking the simmering pots on top (see fig. 1). This is an early depiction of the *potager,* the ancestor of the closed ranges of today. With a *potager,* not only could the heat be more easily adjusted for slow-simmered ragouts and sauces, opening the way for more delicate dishes, but a single experienced cook could control a whole bank of cooking pots. The *potager* was slow to spread north into France, but by the mid-seventeenth century, it was undoubtedly available as an adjunct to the open fire in the elite kitchens of Paris and Versailles.

COLD CREEPS IN

Side by side with the sweet frivolities and statuary in the cold kitchen, an innovation was emerging from the Middle East: iced desserts and drinks (the name *sorbet* comes from the Arabic *sharâb*). As early as 1575, after visiting Venice, Catherine de' Medici's son Henry, the future king of France, remarked on the Italian habit of drinking wine chilled (sometimes flavored with ambergris or musk). By the mid-seventeenth century, the anonymous author of *Le confiturier de la cour* (1659) had given recipes for *les eaux d'Italie* (Italian waters) flavored with jasmine, orange flowers, roses, coriander, cherries, cinnamon, anise, and more. *Confiturier* has the first printed recipe for sorbet; called "Sorbec d'Alexandrie," it was a meat-based syrup with sugar and has no instructions for being served chilled. The first sorbets as we know them, frozen concoctions that hold their shape, appear in Latini's *Lo scalco alla moderna* (1692); by the end of the century, ices were being sold in the streets of Naples (snow was available year-round from Mount Vesuvius). Chilled drinks and sorbets would undoubtedly have been a feature at the Ratta and Castlemaine feasts, and just possibly at Versailles. However, richer ice creams that needed a churn freezer did not appear until the following century.

The head of the cold kitchen was in charge of drinks as well as candied fruits and syrups (fig. 18). The list of beverages in François Massialot's *Nouvelle instruction pour les confitures, les liqueurs, et les fruits* (1692) was formidable. It included chilled flower waters, chilled waters of fruits, liqueurs made from fruits and plants, the spiced red and white wines called *ypocras* dating from medieval times, ratafia (a wine-based aperitif), and distilled drinks, including *eau de vie.* Sorbets and specialty drinks had all the elements of fashion and rarity that creators of festivals hoped to emulate. At a feast, all such treats were stocked on the credenza, together with a wide range of glasses for serving them. One duty of the servant behind each guest's chair was to keep his master supplied with drinks to order. Tea, coffee, chocolate, lemonade, and orangeade were mentioned in *Nouvelle instruction,* but neither beer nor water.

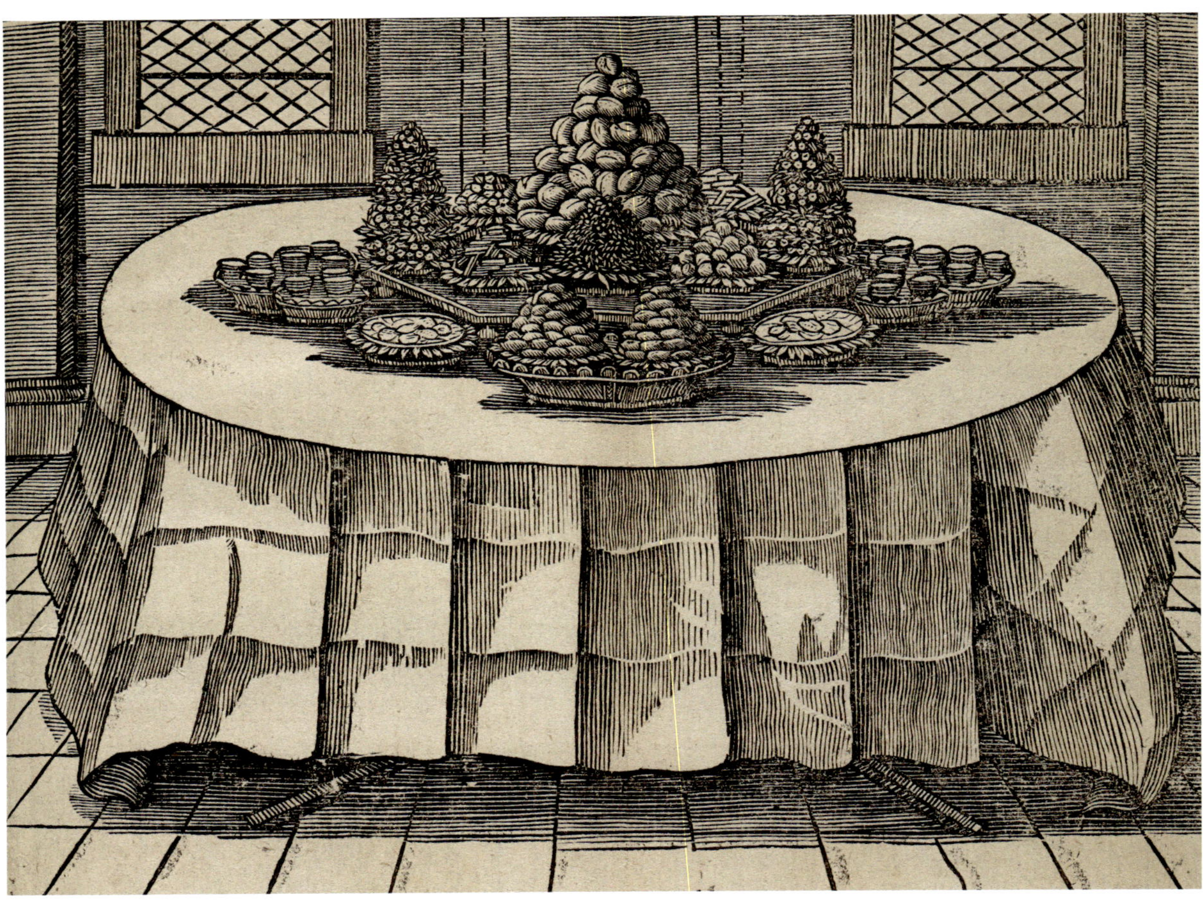

A PERFECT PARTY

The triumphant close to André Félibien's account of the great feast in the park of Versailles sums up the lasting impression that all creators of festivals hope to achieve. The most successful festivities appeal to all the senses—ears should be filled with the sounds of music and the buzz of conversation; eyes should be dazzled by the glitter of fine accoutrements. Fireworks achieve a double effect of sound and sight. The right mix of guests must be chosen, some to impress, others to admire, all to be delighted by the spectacle and the experience. An exultant Félibien sums up the 1668 festival at Versailles:

[It] surpassed all that had gone before…taking into consideration the multiple embellishments and decorations; the number of lights that illuminated them; the quantity of water that had to be brought and the way it was channeled; the sumptuousness of the meals where could be seen an unimaginable quantity of all sorts of meats: and finally all the adjuncts to these magnificent displays and the work of so many different craftsmen, none had ever been so astonishing, nor had evoked such admiration.[51]

NOTES

Unless otherwise noted, all translations in this chapter are mine.

1. André Félibien, *Relation de la feste de Versailles du 18. juillet mil six cens soixante-huit* (Paris: Pierre le Petit, 1668), 7.

2. [John] Michael Wright, *An Account of His Excellence Roger Earl of Castlemaine's Embassy: From His Sacred Majesty James the IId.…to His Holiness Innocent XI* (London: Tho. Snowden for the author, 1688), 69.

3. Domenico Romoli, *La singolare dottrina di M. Domenico Romoli sopranominato Panuto* (Venice: Michele Tramezzino, 1560), 65.

4. Carolin Young, "Catherine de' Medici's Fork" (paper presented at the Oxford Symposium on Food and Cookery, 2005).

5. Jean-Louis Flandrin, "From Dietetics to Gastronomy: The Liberation of the Gourmet," in Jean-Louis Flandrin, Massimo Montanari, and Albert Sonnenfeld, eds., *Food: A Culinary History* (New York: Columbia University Press, 1999), 425.

6. *L'escole parfaite des officiers de bouche, contenant le vray maître-d'hôtel, le grand écuyer-tranchant, le sommelier royal, le confiturier royal, le cuisinier royal, et le patissier royal* (Paris: Jean Ribou, 1662), 499.

7. *L'escole parfaite,* 505.

8. Félibien, *Relation de la feste de Versailles,* 41-42.

9. Félibien, *Relation de la feste de Versailles,* 42.

10. Francis Sandford, *The History of the Coronation of…James II…and of His Royal Consort Queen Mary…with an Exact Account of the Several Preparations in Order Thereunto, Their Majesties Most Splendid Processions, and Their Royal and Magnificent Feast in Westminster-Hall* ([London]: T. Newcomb, 1687).

11. For the recipes, see the following: François Pierre de la Varenne, *Le cuisinier françois* (Paris: Chez Pierre David, 1651), 37; Pierre de Lune, *Le nouveau cuisinier* (1656), 220; and Vittorio Lancellotti, *Lo scalco prattico* (Rome: Francesco Corbelletti, 1627), 245.

12. Sandford, *The History of the Coronation of…James II,* 108-9.

13. Wright, *An Account,* 10.

14. Wright, *An Account,* 19-20.

15. Claudio Benporat, Arnaldo Forni, and Sala Bolognese, eds., *Disegni del convito fatto dall'illustrissimo signor senatore Francesco Ratta…* (Bologna: Arnaldo Forni, 1991; facsimile reproduction of Bologna, 1693), last page of facsimile.

16. Marcia Reed, "The Edible Monument," in Harlan Walker, ed., *Food in the Arts: Proceedings of the Oxford Symposium on Food and Cookery, 1998* (Devon, UK: Prospect, 1999), 143.

17. John Evelyn, *Acetaria: A Discourse of Sallets* (London: Printed for B. Tooke, 1699), 102.

18. Félibien, *Relation de la feste de Versailles,* 11.

19. Wright, *An Account,* 69.

20. Félibien, *Relation de la feste de Versailles,* 9.

21. Nancy Mitford, *The Sun King* (New York: New York Review of Books, 1967), 10.

22. Nicolas de Bonnefons, *Le jardinier françois: Qui enseigne a cultiver les arbres, et herbes potagères; avec la manière de conserver les fruits, et faire toutes sortes de confitures, conserves, et massepains* (Paris: Anthoine Cellier, 1651), xix.

23. Giacomo Castelvetro, *The Fruit, Herbs, and Vegetables of Italy,* trans. Gillian Riley (London: Penguin, 1989), 68.

24. Castelvetro, *The Fruit, Herbs, and Vegetables of Italy,* 68.

25. Félibien, *Relation de la feste de Versailles,* 7.

26. Wright, *An Account,* 53.

27. Wright, *An Account,* 53.

28. Benporat, *Disegni del convito,* last page of facsimile.

29. Benporat, *Disegni del convito,* first introductory page.

30. Juan de la Mata, *Arte de reposteria…* (Madrid: Antonio Marin, 1747).

31. Mitford, *The Sun King,* 15.

32. Wright, *An Account,* 55.

33. La Mata, *Arte de reposteria,* 188.

34. Wright, *An Account,* 67.

35. Wright, *An Account,* 55.

36. Helen Jacobsen, *Luxury and Power: The Material World of the Stuart Diplomat, 1660-1714* (Oxford: Oxford University Press, 2011), 14.

37. Wright, *An Account,* 4.

38. Wright, *An Account,* 53.

39. Wright, *An Account,* 31.

40. Wright, *An Account,* 31.

41. Thomas Coryat, *Coryat's Crudities: Hastily Gobled Up in Five Moneths Travells . . . ; Newly Digested in the Hungry Aire of Odcombe . . . , and Now Dispersed to the Nourishment of the Traveling Members of This Kingdome* (Glasgow: James MacLehose, 1905), vol. 1, 236-7.

42. Wright, *An Account,* 53.

43. Wright, *An Account,* 68.

44. Mattio Molinari, *Il trinciante* (Padua: Liuio Pasquati, 1636). *Mattia Giegher, Li tre trattati di messer Mattia Giegher* (Padua: Paolo Frambotto, 1639).

45. Wright, *An Account,* 69.

46. Wright, *An Account,* 68-69.

47. Bartolomeo Scappi, *Opera de M. Bartolomeo Scappi, cuoco secreto di Papa Pio Quinto …* (Venice: Tramezzino, 1570), opposite p. 2.

48. François Menon, *Les soupers de la cour,* 4 vols. (Paris: Chez Guillyn, 1755).

49. Claudio Benporat, "Commento di Claudio Benporat," in Benporat, *Disegni del convito.*

50. Scappi, *Opera,* opposite p. 2.

51. Félibien, *Relation de la feste de Versailles,* 59.

CONTRIBUTORS

Charissa Bremer-David is curator of sculpture and decorative arts at the J. Paul Getty Museum. Her curatorial work and publications concern artistic, nonedible designs in silver and porcelain, in particular the naturalism of these miniature sculptures and how they reflect broader scientific and philosophical interests as well as the latest culinary developments. She is the author of *French Tapestries and Textiles in the J. Paul Getty Museum* (1997) and editor of *Paris: Life and Luxury in the Eighteenth Century* (2011).

Joseph Imorde is professor of art history at the Universität Siegen. His recent research on baroque art focuses on the concept of sweetness in the work of the Florentine painter Carlo Dolci and on the art and consumption of sugar in early modern Europe. He is the author of *Michelangelo Deutsch!* (2009) and editor of *Die Grand Tour in Moderne und Nachmoderne* (2008) and *Dreckige Laken: Die Kehrseite der "Grand Tour"* (2012).

Marcia Reed is chief curator at the Getty Research Institute. Her research focuses on works on paper, especially the literature of art history, illustrated books, prints, and maps. She has curated many exhibitions, including *China on Paper: European and Chinese Works from the Late Sixteenth to the Early Nineteenth Century* (Getty Research Institute, 2007-8), *The Magnificent Piranesi* (J. Paul Getty Museum, 2007-8), and *The Getty Research Institute: Recent Print Acquisitions* (Getty Research Institute, 2012); she coedited the exhibition catalog for *China on Paper* (2007).

Anne Willan is a preeminent authority on French cooking, founder of the École de Cuisine La Varenne in Paris, and author of more than thirty books. Inducted into the James Beard Cookbook Hall of Fame in 2013 for her body of work, Willan has more than fifty years of experience as a teacher, cookbook author, culinary historian, and food columnist. Her publication *The Cookbook Library: The Cooks, Writers, and Recipes that Made the Modern Cookbook* (2012) draws on her and husband Mark Cherniavsky's extensive collection of rare books and prints.

ILLUSTRATION CREDITS

Photographs of items in the holdings of the Research Library at the Getty Research Institute are courtesy the Research Library. Every effort has been made to identify and contact the copyright holders of images published in this book. Should you discover what you consider to be a photo by a known photographer, please contact the publisher. The following sources have granted additional permission to reproduce illustrations in this book.

Food, Memory, and Taste
Fig. 4. Mauritshuis, The Hague.

Court and Civic Festivals
Figs. 1, 2. J. Paul Getty Museum.
Fig. 13. Bibliothèque nationale de France.
Fig. 22. © Trustees of the British Museum.

Of Cauliflower and Crayfish
Figs. 1, 2. J. Paul Getty Museum, 82.DG.13.1-2.
Figs. 3, 11. Detroit Institute of Arts, 55.183.a-c, Founder's Society Purchase, Elizabeth Parke Firestone Collection of Early French Silver Fund / Bridgeman Images.
Fig. 4, 12, 15. J. Paul Getty Museum, 2005.43.
Fig. 5. New York, The Metropolitan Museum of Art, 1993.334.2. Purchase, Gift of The Hearst Foundation, by exchange; Gift in memory of Frederick P. Victoria; The Metropolitan Museum of Art Volunteer Anniversary Gift; Ralph and Frances DeJur Foundation Gift, 1993. *Metropolitan Museum Journal* 31 (1996), 215, fig. 7.

Fig. 6. Photo: Kit Weiss. *Metropolitan Museum Journal* 31 (1996), 213, fig. 3.
Fig. 7. Musée des Beaux-Arts de Mulhouse. D.73.1.19. © Collection Société Industrielle de Mulhouse.
Fig. 8. J. Paul Getty Museum, 82.DG.12.1-2.
Fig. 9. Nationalmuseum, Stockholm, MN 800.
Fig. 13. Schlesinger Library, Radcliffe Institute, Harvard University.
Fig. 14. From Avery Classics, Avery Architectural and Fine Arts Library, Columbia University.
Fig. 16. Photo: Bernard Dragesco, courtesy of Vincent l'Herrou.

Behind the Scenes
Figs. 9–12. Wellcome Library, London.

INDEX

Books published by the Getty Research Institute

A Kingdom of Images: French Prints in the Age of Louis XIV, 1660–1715
Edited by Peter Fuhring, Louis Marchesano, Rémi Mathis,
and Vanessa Selbach
ISBN 978-1-60606-450-4 (hardcover)

Display of Art in the Roman Palace, 1550–1750
Edited by Gail Feigenbaum
ISBN 978-1-60606-298-2 (hardcover)

The Catholic Rubens: Saints and Martyrs
Willibald Sauerländer
Translation by David Dollenmayer
ISBN 978-1-60606-268-5 (hardcover)

Display & Art History: The Düsseldorf Gallery and Its Catalogue
Thomas W. Gaehtgens and Louis Marchesano
ISBN 978-1-60606-092-6 (paper)

*China on Paper: European and Chinese Works from the Late Sixteenth
to the Early Nineteenth Century*
Edited by Marcia Reed and Paola Demattè
ISBN 978-1-60606-068-1 (paper)

Futures & Ruins: Eighteenth-Century Paris and the Art of Hubert Robert
Nina L. Dubin
ISBN 978-0-89236-023-0 (hardcover)

*Printing the Grand Manner: Charles Le Brun and Monumental Prints
in the Age of Louis XIV*
Louis Marchesano and Christian Michel
ISBN 978-0-89236-980-5 (hardcover)

Devices of Wonder: From the World in a Box to Images on a Screen
Barbara Maria Stafford and Frances Terpak
ISBN 978-0-89236-590-6 (paper)

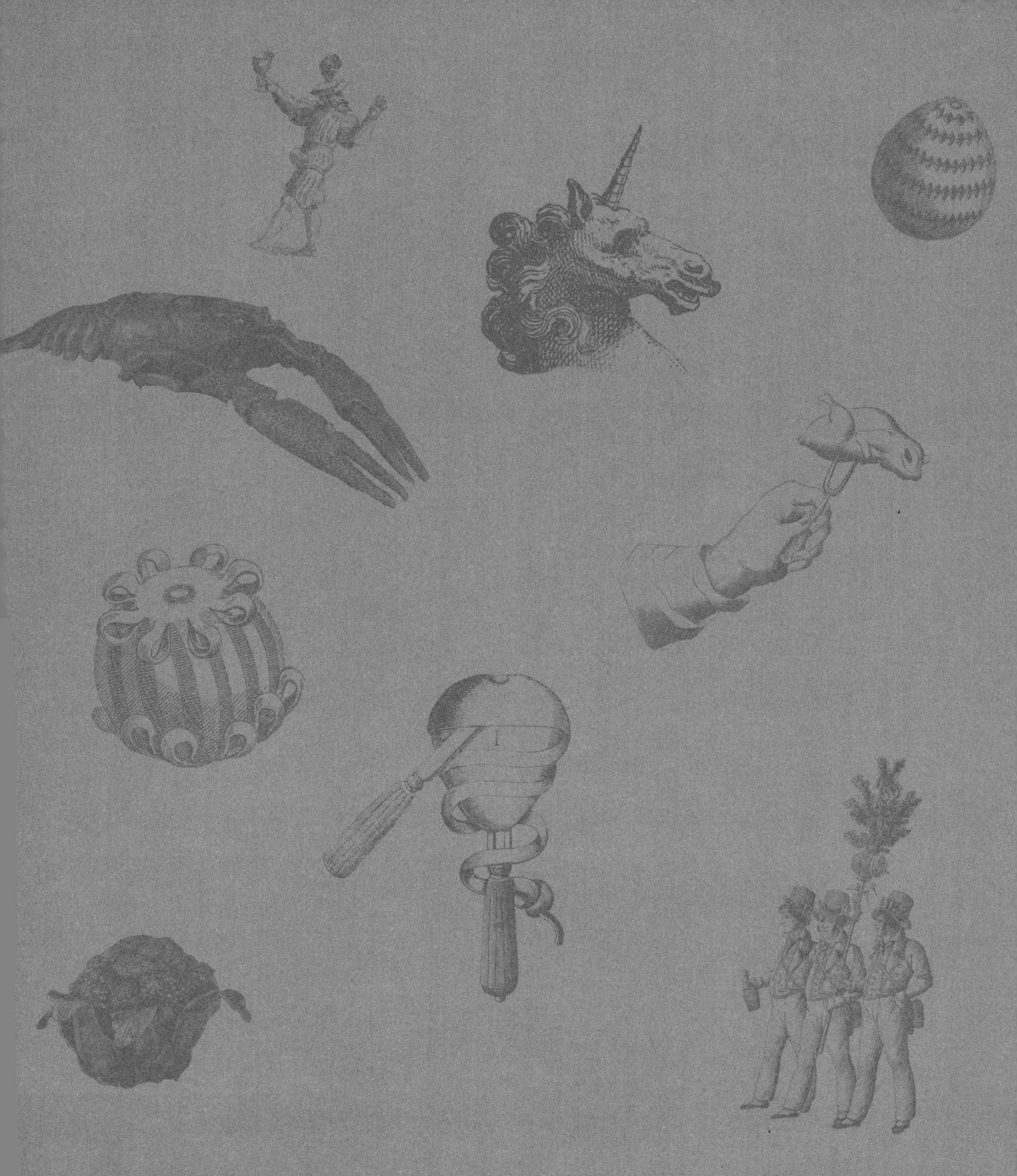

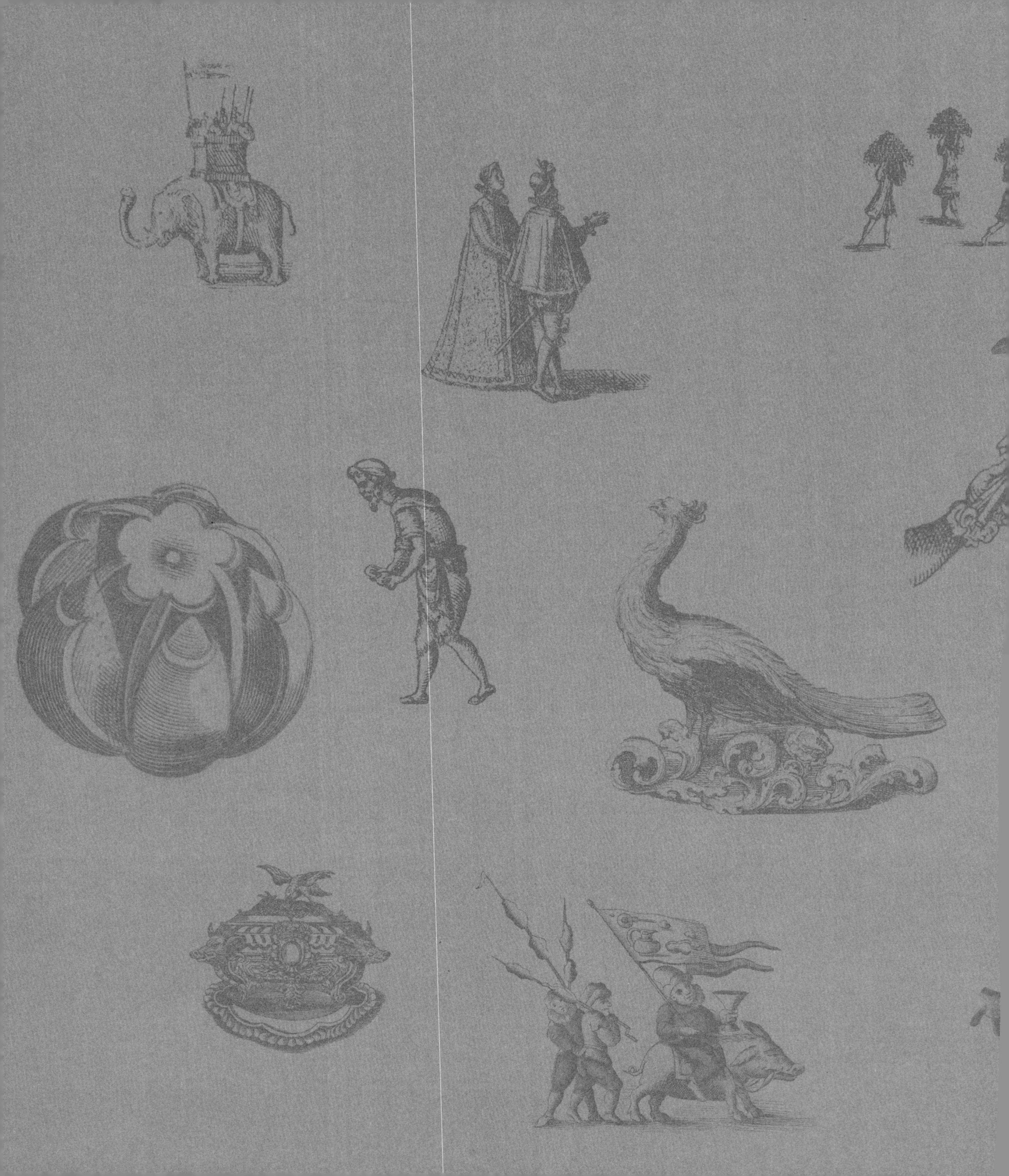